**MARY AND JOHN GRAY LIBRARY
LAMAR UNIVERSITY**

Purchased

with the

Student Library Use Fee

DISCARDED

The Struggle for Control of the Modern Corporation

Organizational Change at General Motors, 1924–1970

The Struggle for Control of the Modern Corporation provides a fascinating historical overview of decision-making and political struggle within one of America's largest and most important corporations. Drawing on primary historical material, Robert F. Freeland examines the changes in General Motors' organization between the years 1924 and 1970. He takes issue with the well-known arguments of business historian Alfred Chandler and economist Oliver Williamson, who contend that GM's multidivisional corporate structure emerged and survived because it was more efficient than alternative forms of organization. This book illustrates that for most of its history, GM intentionally violated the fundamental axioms of efficient organization put forth by these analysts. It did so in order to create cooperation and managerial consent to corporate policies. Moreover, it was the top managers who advocated these changes. The corporate owners vehemently opposed them, touching off a struggle over corporate organization inside GM that lasted for decades. Freeland uses the GM case to reexamine existing theories of corporate governance, arguing that the decentralized organizational structure advocated by efficiency theorists may actually undermine cooperation, and thus foster organizational decline.

Robert F. Freeland is Assistant Professor of Sociology at Stanford University. He has published in the *American Journal of Sociology*, the *Journal of Law and Economics*, and *Business and Economic History* and is the recipient of the 1998 Social Science History Association's President's Book Award for this book.

Structural Analysis in the Social Sciences

Mark Granovetter, editor

Other books in the series:

1. Mark S. Mizruchi and Michael Schwartz, eds., *Intercorporate Relations: The Structural Analysis of Business*
2. Barry Wellman and S. D. Berkowitz, eds., *Social Structures: A Network Approach*
3. Ronald L. Breiger, ed., *Social Mobility and Social Structure*
4. David Knoke, *Political Networks: The Structural Perspective*
5. John L. Campbell, J. Rogers Hollingsworth, and Leon N. Lindberg, eds., *Governance of the American Economy*
6. Kyriakos M. Kontopoulos, *The Logics of Social Structure*
7. Philippa Pattison, *Algebraic Models for Social Networks*
8. Stanley Wasserman and Katherine Faust, *Social Network Analysis: Methods and Applications*
9. Gary Herrigel, *Industrial Constructions: The Sources of German Industrial Power*
10. Philippe Bourgois, *In Search of Respect: Selling Crack in El Barrio*
11. Per Hage and Frank Harary, *Island Networks: Communication, Kinship, and Classification Structures in Oceania*
12. Thomas Schweizer and Douglas R. White, eds., *Kinship, Networks and Exchange*
13. Noah E. Friedkin, *A Structural Theory of Social Influence*
14. David Wank, *Commodifying Communism: Business, Trust, and Politics in a South China City*
15. Rebecca Adams and Graham Allan, *Placing Friendship in Context*
16. Robert L. Nelson and William P. Bridges, *Legalizing Gender Inequality: Courts, Markets, and Unequal Pay for Women in America*

The series *Structural Analysis in the Social Sciences* presents approaches that explain social behavior and institutions by reference to *relations* among such concrete entities as persons and organizations. This contrasts with at least four other popular strategies: (a) reductionist attempts to explain by a focus on individuals alone; (b) explanations stressing the causal primacy of such abstract concepts as ideas, values, mental harmonies, and cognitive maps (thus, "structuralism" on the Continent should be distinguished from structural analysis in the present sense); (c) technological and material determinism; (d) explanations using "variables" as the main analytic concepts (as in the "structural equation" models that dominated much of the sociology of the 1970s), where structure is that connecting variables rather than actual social entities.

The social network approach is an important example of the strategy of structural analysis; the series also draws on social science theory and research that are not framed explicitly in network terms, but stress the importance of relations rather than the atomization of reductionism or the determinism of ideas, technology, or material conditions. The structural perspective has become extremely popular and influential in all the social sciences, and this series brings together such work under a single rubric. By bringing the achievements of structurally oriented scholars to a wider public, the *Structural Analysis* series hopes to encourage the use of this very fruitful approach.

Structural Analysis in the Social Sciences | 17

The Struggle for Control of the Modern Corporation

Organizational Change at General Motors, 1924–1970

Robert F. Freeland
Stanford University

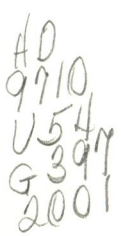
CAMBRIDGE
UNIVERSITY PRESS

PUBLISHED BY THE PRESS SYNDICATE OF THE UNIVERSITY OF CAMBRIDGE
The Pitt Building, Trumpington Street, Cambridge, United Kingdom

CAMBRIDGE UNIVERSITY PRESS
The Edinburgh Building, Cambridge CB2 2RU, UK
40 West 20th Street, New York, NY 10011-4211, USA
10 Stamford Road, Oakleigh, VIC 3166, Australia
Ruiz de Alarcón 13, 28014 Madrid, Spain
Dock House, The Waterfront, Cape Town 8001, South Africa

http://www.cambridge.org

© Cambridge University Press 2001

This book is in copyright. Subject to statutory exception
and to the provisions of relevant collective licensing agreements,
no reproduction of any part may take place without
the written permission of Cambridge University Press.

First published 2001

Printed in the United States of America

Typeface Sabon 10/12 pt.   *System* QuarkXPress®   [BTS]

A catalog record for this book is available from the British Library.

Library of Congress Cataloging in Publication Data
Freeland, Robert F., 1957–
 The struggle for control of the modern corporation: organizational change at
General Motors, 1924–1970 / Robert F. Freeland.
  p. cm. – (Structural analysis in the social sciences; 17)
 Includes bibliographical references and index.
 ISBN 0-521-63034-7
 1. General Motors Corporation – Management. 2. Organizational change.
3. Industrial management. I. Title. II. Series.
HD9710.U54 G397 2000
338.7'6292'0973 – dc21
                                                                          00-036302

ISBN 0 521 63034 7 hardback

For my parents

and to the memory of Carol Hatch

... we must shake off the sadness and take her and place her before us, though she may be faded, a figure from days long past, and we must have the confidence to be amazed that she ever did exist.

Contents

List of Figures and Tables		page x
Acknowledgments		xiii
1	The Modern Corporation and the Problem of Order	1
2	Creating Corporate Order: Conflicting Versions of Decentralization at GM, 1921–1933	43
3	Administrative Centralization of the M-form, 1934–1941	81
4	Participative Decentralization Redefined: Mobilizing for War Production, 1941–1945	127
5	The Split between Finance and Operations: Postwar Problems and Organization Structure, 1945–1948	175
6	Consent as an Organizational Weapon: Coalition Politics and the Destruction of Cooperation, 1948–1958	223
7	Consent Destroyed: The Decline and Fall of General Motors, 1958–1980	271
8	Conclusion	295
	Appendix: General Motors' Financial Performance, 1921–1987	324
	References	340
	Index	355

Figures and Tables

Figures

1.1	The multidivisional form	page 10
3.1	General Motors' top governing committees, 1937	105
3.2	Return on invested capital and related performance indicators, GM and Chrysler, 1934–1941	124
5.1	General Motors' top governing committees, 1946	195
6.1	General Motors' top governing committees, 1958	266

Tables

3.1	Responsibilities and powers of General Motors' top governing committees, 1933 versus 1937	102
3.2	Membership of Policy Committee and Administration Committee, May 1937	106
3.3	General Motors' Policy Group membership, November 1937	108
4.1	General Motors Corporation: turnover broken down into constituent elements, 1937–1941 versus 1942–1945	140
4.2	General Motors Corporation: return on invested gross and net capital, 1937–1941 versus 1942–1945	141
4.3	Membership of Administration Committee, 1941, and membership of War Administration Committee, 1942	146

Figures and Tables

4.4	General Motors Policy Group membership, February 1943	155
4.5	Membership of War Administration Committee, 1944, and membership of Administration Committee, 1945	170
5.1	Responsibilities and powers of GM's top governing committees, 1946	196
5.2	Membership of Financial Policy, Operations Policy, and Administration Committees, June 1946	197
6.1	Turnover of real estate and plant, working-capital turnover, and return on investment, 1942–1945 versus 1950–1953	238
6.2	Membership of Operations Policy Committee and Administration Committee, January 1955	242
6.3	Turnover of real estate and plant, working-capital turnover, and return on investment, 1948–1956	247
A.1	Financial data, GM 1921–1987	327
A.2	Period averages for selected data	339

Acknowledgments

This book has been a long time in the making. Without the intellectual and personal encouragement of my closest friends and colleagues it would have taken longer still, for it is only through my relationships with them that this endeavor in sociology has taken on and sustained meaning. Their friendship and intellectual engagement have sustained me; without them, this book could not have been written. Theirs is a gift I scarcely know how to acknowledge, much less repay. Fortunately, none of them are highly calculative exchange theorists, so they are not awaiting repayment with balance sheet in hand, ready to figure the sum due. That is why I treasure them so highly, and it is undoubtedly why I have learned so much from them.

I have been very fortunate to have had two teachers whose commitments to scholarship and to their students have been without parallel. It would be difficult to overstate the influence that Mark Gould has had on my intellectual development in general, and on this work in particular. During my years as an undergraduate at Haverford College, Mark introduced me to social theory and taught me how to do social science. Any ability that I have to construct a logically coherent theoretical argument comes largely from the courses that I took with him and the continuing exchanges that we have carried on for more than two decades. During the period in which I researched and wrote this book he has patiently provided me with invaluable feedback, guidance, and encouragement. In the process he has become not only the most important intellectual influence on my work but also one of my closest and most valued friends, one who has had an enormous impact on my life.

Michael Burawoy became my mentor and advisor while I was a graduate student at Berkeley, and there is no way I would have finished this book without him. Michael was crucial in helping me to link general theoretical concepts to concrete evidence, and I still marvel at his ability to extract a compelling sociological analysis from data in which I see only a jumble of details and contradictions. More than anybody else, Michael also had the unenviable task of combining coercion and consent to motivate me to finish the dissertation from which this book is drawn. That was no easy task, but Michael managed it with his usual charm and aplomb, proving – much to his horror, I'm sure – that he's pretty good at manufacturing consent. Over the years, Michael has also given much of himself – taking me out to meals, introducing me to the intricacies of academe, helping me through difficult times, delivering delightfully inebriated readings from works such as *The Art of Massage*, and even buying me a Lexus. Perhaps the major drawback to leaving graduate school is that I have had much less opportunity to enjoy his company.

Another important teacher was the late Carol Hatch, to whose memory this book is dedicated. Carol did not have a teaching position at Berkeley, but she nonetheless had a significant intellectual influence on generations of graduate students there. Over the course of countless conversations Carol forced me to examine many assumptions that I took for granted, pointed out contradictions in my theoretical arguments, and exploded many of my pretenses and intellectual rigidities with her humor. More than anybody I have known, she drew me out and enabled me not just to talk about my ideas, but to play with them in order to see what, for better or worse, they might have the potential to become. Even as she did this, drinking endless cups of coffee and chain-smoking cigarettes, Carol would always be carrying on at least four other conversations with me – plotting over department politics, discussing current events, comparing personal histories, excoriating the nefarious, and looking through the mountains of paper on her desk for some memo that she had to finish immediately. And of course, even when she was relentlessly critical, Carol was also fiercely loyal; she never lost faith in me. At those times when I found it difficult to keep working on this book for myself, I vowed to complete it as a gift for her. All things considered, I'm sure she would have preferred some expensive jewelry. But I'm equally certain that were she still here, Carol would be delighted to accept this book, criticize it, and help make it a much better work.

Marc Schneiberg has been one of my best friends and most important intellectual collaborators since we met as undergraduates. Because he too is an organizational and economic sociologist, our almost weekly conversations have been crucial in helping me to shape the conceptual framework and the arguments contained within this book, and he has been a never-ending source of ideas for me to steal and claim as my own. Marc's friendship, generosity, and emotional support have also helped me to endure manifold disasters – deaths, divorce, deflagration, and graduate school, to name but a few. More important, having Marc around just makes life a lot more meaningful and a lot more fun. I look forward to collaborating with him for many more decades to come.

Acknowledgments

Two other people have had especially important positive influences on this book. Neil Fligstein played a key role in helping me to situate this project in the wider context of the sociological literature on organizations, and he repeatedly urged me not to lose track of the political dimensions of social order. Beyond that, his optimism and enthusiasm for my project had an impact even on my usually dyspeptic nature, helping me to see beyond whatever substantive difficulties I faced at the moment. It would be difficult to imagine a better colleague than Mark Granovetter. Mark has provided crucial feedback that has helped me to sharpen and refine the analytical arguments contained in this book, and he has demonstrated considerable patience and good humor during the revision process. As a colleague, Mark has pushed me to broaden my intellectual horizons, while also helping me to keep the academic process in proper perspective.

Because this book has been a long time in the making, numerous other people have had opportunities to comment on various portions of the manuscript. At Berkeley, Suava Salameh provided particularly insightful criticism, while her friendship and support helped make life much more enjoyable. I also received considerable feedback from the "Smith group," which included at various times – in addition to Suava and the secretive and anonymous Mr. Smith – Patrick Heller, Mary Kelsey, Hyun Ok Park, Chris Rhomberg, Brian Rich, Anders Schneiderman, Gay Seidman, Rob Wrenn, and Mona Younis. Nancy Chodorow and Jerry Karabel also provided helpful input at various junctures. At Columbia, Richard Nelson, Harrison White, Patrick Heller, Yasuo Watanabe, and David Gibson were sources of useful feedback on various aspects of this work. And at Stanford, John Meyer and Dick Scott provided written and verbal comments that have been more important than they probably realize in helping me to rethink various aspects of the argument contained in this book. Finally, Charles Perrow provided detailed critical commentary of the entire manuscript, which was of enormous help during the revision process. The initial research for this project was supported by a grant from the Hagley Museum and Library's Center for the History of Business, Technology, and Society. At Hagley, Patrick Nolan, Michael Nash, Marjorie McNinch, and Gail Pietrzyk were particularly helpful.

There are many others on whom I have relied for intellectual and moral support. Though most of them don't give a damn about organizational sociology, they have been no less fundamental in helping me to complete this project. Karla Hackstaff has long been one of my closest friends, and there is no way I can adequately express how important she has been to me. Her intellectual influence has taken a number of forms, including reading and commenting on early chapter drafts of this book and providing comments on job talks. Most important, however, is that Karla has always been there for me when I have needed her, whether helping me through personal tragedies, commemorating triumphs, or simply sharing her life with me. Jennifer Pierce was my best friend for years, and later my wife, during which time she helped sustain me intellectually and personally. Over time I have come to realize that much of what she gave to me during those years remains with me, even though our relationship does not. As a fellow traveler from Haverford, Ward Bell has always challenged me to deliver when I have made glib and dismissive theoretical pronunciations. He also continues to indulge my vanity by assuring me that, despite our pointed lack of success in the academic world, we are still smarter than the rest of our erstwhile colleagues. Throughout my years at Berkeley, and beyond, Vicki Smith and Steve McMahon have been constant sources of intellectual engagement and friendship. In addition to helping me keep academe in its proper perspective and providing transcontinental intelligence reports, Mary Waters has offered support and advice at various junctures. Karla, Jennifer, Ward, Vicki, Steve, Mary, Michael Burawoy, Carol Hatch, Mark Gould, Marc Schneiberg, Suava Salameh, Judy Auerbach, Karen Chin, John Diliberto, Kimberly Haas, Maureen Katz, Kwok Kian Woon, Tom Long, Zena Ratner, Terry Strathman, and Chris Williams have all been important in a variety of less (and sometimes more) tangible ways as well, providing intellectual stimulation, camaraderie, fine and not-so-fine dining, music, gossip, flirtation and debauchery, friendship, transference and countertransference, network diagrams explaining a great deal of what goes on in academe, and much more – I leave it to them to figure out who provided what. Little of this is evident in the book that follows, but the book would never have been written without it. I owe them all an enormous debt of gratitude.

Finally, it is no coincidence that the bulk of this book was written only after I met Jodi Lerner. Jodi has been my companion, partner, and closest friend for more than seven years. Throughout this time she has supported me wholeheartedly in my endeavors, and she has never lost faith that I would surmount whatever difficulties I encountered. More importantly, she has accepted me as I am, something all too rare in my life. Knowing that she will be there at the end of the day makes facing blank pieces of paper (or computer screens) much easier. By sharing her love, she has reawakened joy in my life. Through Jodi I have also come to know the Honorable Winston K. Lerner. Although he is not an academic, and although he retains an unfortunate theoretical and practical bias in favor of fiat, Winston is certainly the intellectual equal of many social scientists. He has used his acumen repeatedly to remind me that even the most sophisticated theoretical arguments are useful only insofar as they have practical applications. In addition, his curmudgeonly good nature and his playful sparring have been sources of great warmth, affection, and companionship. I am grateful that he and Jodi have seen fit to make me part of their family.

1

The Modern Corporation and the Problem of Order

Analysts of the modern industrial corporation tell a remarkable story. In it, the invisible hand of the market has become cramped and atrophied, perhaps broken beyond repair. The damage has been inflicted by none other than the modern corporation, its visible hand clenched into a fist, pounding away at the fetters of the market, struggling to bring about a "managerial revolution in American business."[1] This story is told not by critics of modern capitalism, nor by those advocating a return to unencumbered free markets, but by analysts who see this managerial revolution as inevitable and desirable. Only with its success has capitalism come into its own, attaining previously unimagined levels of productivity and profit. In their account, the modern corporation emerges triumphant precisely because the visible hand of management is more efficient than market allocation. At the heart of this efficiency are new forms of organization that lower the cost of governing the business enterprise. The triumph of managerial capitalism has led to the dominance of a new type of business organization: the decentralized or multidivisional form (M-form) characterized by a number of distinct operating divisions and overseen by a hierarchy of professional managers.[2] Described as the "most significant organizational innovation of the twentieth century," the M-form has been perhaps the most important single factor underlying the success of the managerial revolution.[3]

The ascendance of the modern corporation is not the end of the story, for many of the enterprises that led the managerial revolution now face serious difficulties. They have been challenged by foreign competition and declining profit rates, while critics have asserted that they are plagued by wasteful and inefficient production, inept decision-making, and the practice of placing short-term profits ahead of the firm's

---

1 Chandler (1977).
2 The term "M-form" (for "multidivisional form") originated with Williamson (1975). I use the terms "M-form," "multidivisional structure," "decentralization," and "decentralized structure" interchangeably.
3 Williamson (1985, p. 279).

long-run interests. The efficiency of the M-form itself has been called into question by charges that it is ossified and bloated by bureaucracy, plagued by information-flow deficiencies, and too large and unwieldy to govern effectively. The situation has become so critical in some cases that long-dormant shareholders have intervened to take control of governing committees or replace top management, events that were nearly unthinkable in earlier decades. At least in some industries, the victory of the managerial revolution and the efficacy of the decentralized form appear to be in doubt.

Perhaps the foremost example of the modern corporation's triumph, as well as its decline, is General Motors. GM created and perfected one of the earliest multidivisional structures, during the 1920s, under the leadership of Alfred P. Sloan, Jr., and Pierre S. du Pont. Following the seminal work of Alfred Chandler, GM's organization, along with that of its largest shareholder, E. I. du Pont de Nemours, has been regarded as one of the paradigmatic examples of increased efficiency through decentralization.[4] After implementing the M-form, GM quickly became one of the most successful corporations in history, a position it held for nearly half a century. Surpassing Ford in the late 1920s to become the leader in the automobile industry, GM amassed a record of profitability that stretched unbroken into the 1970s; in some years, its share of automobile sales was over 50 percent of the North American market. The corporation became one of the most important institutions in the U.S. economy, single-handedly capable of having a serious impact on the country's economic well-being. By 1956, one government study concluded that "there is probably no company in the United States that affects the lives of the citizens of the country as much as General Motors."[5] Analysts inside and outside of GM attributed the corporation's incredible success in large part to the decentralized structure that it put into place in the 1920s. GM's organization was taken as a model of efficiency, and Alfred Sloan, who served as the corporation's president or chairman of the board for over thirty years, continues to be hailed as "an organizational genius" who was "relentlessly given to profit maximization."[6]

By the 1960s, GM's long record of success was beginning to show cracks. As early as the mid-1950s, GM began to lose market share to foreign competitors such as Volkswagen in the small market for economy cars. Because this market accounted for only a tiny fraction of GM's profits, the corporation was slow to react to the developing trend toward

---

4 Chandler (1962); Chandler and Salsbury (1971).
5 U.S. Senate, as quoted in Cray (1980, p. 10).
6 Williamson (1991b, p. 79, fn. 8).

smaller, more fuel efficient autos. When it finally decided to develop such a car, the result was the ill-fated Corvair. The car that Ralph Nader dubbed "unsafe at any speed" led to millions of dollars in lawsuits against GM and increased government regulation of the automobile industry. Perhaps more important, from GM's point of view, the corporation's reputation as a forward-looking producer of high-quality autos was called into question. But GM's problems ran even deeper than considerations of quality, safety, and customer relations. Between 1964 and 1969, the return on investment for the Chevrolet division, long the mainstay of GM's profit base, reportedly plummeted from 55.4 percent to 10.3 percent.[7] Following the 1973 oil embargo, GM's overall sales and profits fell dramatically, and its long dominance of the U.S. auto industry was shattered. The corporation that once had been hailed as the paradigm of efficiency was now charged with wasteful and inefficient production, failure to plan for the future, and inability to recognize emerging trends. Yet on paper, at least, GM's organization looked very much like the M-form that had been erected in the 1920s.

Why did the decentralized structure that served Alfred Sloan and his successors so well prove to be so ineffective later in GM's life? To address this question, I set out to examine the changes in GM's organization over time. Initially, I expected that my research would focus primarily on the latter stages of GM's history, for the period prior to 1960 seemed well documented. Chandler's pathbreaking work focused extensively on the period from 1920 to 1925, when the M-form was created. Arthur Kuhn's comparison of GM and Ford extended the analysis through 1938, one year after the corporation's first formal reorganization.[8] Decades before these works were published, Peter Drucker had written about his experiences in GM during the 1940s, providing a less systematic description of the decentralized structure that nonetheless seemed consistent with Chandler's analysis.[9] Finally, Alfred Sloan's best-selling autobiography provided a firsthand account of the development of GM's organization over the years.[10] Sloan's account emphasized that the GM structure had changed little between 1925 and 1960, and, like Chandler, he attributed the corporation's success to that organization.[11] While a few reviewers noted inconsistencies in Sloan's story, there appeared to be no reason to doubt that the M-form had changed only minimally prior to 1960.[12] Nonetheless, I set out to examine the primary historical documents that were available – internal memos and reports disgorged by the

---

[7] Wright (1979, p. 100). [8] Kuhn (1986). [9] Drucker (1972).
[10] Sloan (1964). [11] Chandler served as a research assistant for Sloan's book.
[12] See Wolff (1964).

U.S. government's 1949 antitrust suit against GM and E. I. du Pont de Nemours, and the business papers of various Du Pont and GM executives, many of which had been unavailable to earlier researchers.[13]

These historical documents told a surprising story. According to prevailing views of the modern corporation – accounts that had been constructed using GM as a key source of evidence – the most important factor behind the M-form's ability to lower costs was the fact that it created a firm separation between long-range planning and daily operations. The M-form decomposed the corporation into operating divisions (like Buick and Chevrolet) and a general office or corporate headquarters.[14] Executives at headquarters were responsible for making long-term policy and entrepreneurial decisions that affected "the allocation . . . of resources for the enterprise as a whole."[15] This reduced the possibility that operating men would attempt to divert resources to their own units by promulgating and pursuing self-interested policies. Division management was responsible for making daily operating decisions utilizing resources allocated by the general office. This ensured that operating decisions would be carried out by the men closest to the facts, rather than being made by top executives who lacked detailed information and knowledge about operating issues. The division of labor between strategic planning and daily operations was thus seen as a fundamental prerequisite for the success of the M-form; an organization that failed to separate these functions would be inefficient.[16] Yet at GM, the textbook M-form described in the literature had existed for only a brief time. Soon after its inception, top executives deliberately introduced changes that conflated strategic and tactical planning. During its decades of phenomenal success, GM had thus been governed by an organization that, according to organization theory, violated the fundamental principles of efficient decentralization.

Nor was that the end of the story, for historical documents revealed a number of other surprises. First, the changes in GM's organization had by no means been uncontested. Owners favored an M-form like that described in organization theory, and representatives of E. I. du Pont de Nemours, which owned about 25 percent of GM's voting stock during most of the period under study, sought constantly to impose such a

13 Throughout this book, the name "Du Pont," with initial capital letters, refers to E. I. du Pont de Nemours, which owned about 25 percent of GM's voting stock during the period under study. The use of "du Pont," with initial lowercase *d*, refers to individual members of the du Pont family, several of whom played key roles in GM's history.
14 The terms "general office," "headquarters," and "corporate headquarters" are used interchangeably throughout this book.
15 Chandler (1962, p. 11).
16 Williamson (1975, pp. 148–154; 1983, pp. 352–356).

structure on GM.[17] Top GM executives, led by Alfred Sloan, resisted Du Pont's version of the M-form and sought to introduce variations that, according to both owners and organization theory, were inefficient. Owners and managers struggled over the issue of organizational form for decades, creating intense debate and frequent organizational change. A second surprise was that although Alfred Sloan and his colleagues fought passionately to preserve "corrupted" versions of the M-form, their public pronouncements belied this fact. In his autobiography, for instance, Sloan explicitly endorsed the idea that operating executives should be kept off of governing committees responsible for planning and resource allocation, and he insisted that any departures from this principle at GM had been "exceptions" to the rule of good organization.[18] But internal memos revealed a very different Sloan. In 1945, for instance, he described GM's Administration Committee, which at that time was responsible for approving policy, authorizing appropriations, and reviewing divisional performance:

> Every division ... is represented directly or indirectly on the Administration Committee. The five car divisions – the biggest part of the corporation – are represented directly. Frankly, I can not conceive how any ... organization could[,] in a more scientific way, bring to bear on an important problem the concerted ability of the organization as a whole.[19]

---

17 Throughout this book, I use the term "owners" to refer to the coalition of E. I. du Pont de Nemours and J. P. Morgan, who together controlled more than 25 percent of GM's voting stock and a significant number of the positions on GM's board. I use this term more out of convenience than analytic specificity. These shareholders dominated GM's board in a way that others could not. Nonetheless, it is important to remember that Du Pont and Morgan remained minority owners; we should not confuse their preferences or actions with those of all shareholders.
  It is also important to note that a number of top management executives at GM, including Alfred Sloan, were large individual shareholders. In 1940, for instance, Sloan owned some 3.8 million shares of GM common – less than one percent of corporation stock outstanding, but still sufficient to constitute a considerable financial incentive. To speak of such executives as managers rather than owners may therefore seem odd. As the empirical evidence will clearly show, however, the interests of these men were driven first and foremost by their structural positions as managers. Differences between outside owners like the du Ponts and management men like Sloan broke down along remarkably consistent lines. Moreover, as I show later, when Sloan and others withdrew from management but continued to serve on GM's board and its subcommittees, they suddenly found themselves agreeing with outside owners on policy issues, even to the point of repudiating positions they had taken when they were managers. Positions within the governance structure do matter, it seems, in shaping one's interests and point of view on a variety of issues. On Sloan's holdings of GM common, see United States Congress (1956, pp. 3567–3575).
18 Sloan (1964, p. 113).
19 Alfred P. Sloan, Jr., to Walter S. Carpenter, Jr., June 14, 1945, Accession 542, Box 837.

The inclusion of division managers hardly sounded like an exception to the rule here. Indeed, for most of his tenure as GM's chief executive, Sloan fought passionately for an organization that incorporated division managers into the planning and resource allocation process. Either Sloan's thinking on the M-form had changed over the years, or there was a serious discrepancy between the ideology and practice of decentralization at General Motors.

The biggest surprise, however, was that GM's long decline began only after it reintroduced a textbook M-form in 1958, following the most profitable and successful decade in its history. For most of its corporate life, GM was governed by an M-form that violated the principles of efficient organization and, according to prevailing theories, should have failed miserably. Yet during those periods, GM succeeded magnificently, becoming one of the largest, most profitable corporations in the world. In 1958, following decades of struggle between owners and managers, GM finally implemented an M-form that established a firm distinction between strategic planning and daily operations. The new organization kept division managers out of planning by putting executives at headquarters firmly in control of top committees responsible for strategy formulation. But the new structure created internal dissension and contestation that played a key role in GM's eventual economic decline. Not only had GM's success defied the prescriptions of organization theory, so too did its failure. Faced with these unexpected and puzzling findings, I set out to understand and explain the changes that had occurred in GM's organization over time.

The main thesis of this book is that the variations in GM's organizational form are easily accounted for when corporate governance is understood as a social and political process rather than a simply economic one. The primary imperative facing governance mechanisms is to establish and maintain social order within the firm by creating cooperation between different levels of the firm and by motivating subordinates to carry out corporate goals. Drawing on economic models, existing theories of the firm contend that order and cooperation are effected through incentive alignment that rewards compliance to organizational goals and punishes malfeasance, thereby aligning the interests of individual actors with that of the firm. Within this context, top executives govern through fiat and authority, issuing orders that subordinates obey out of self-interest. I argue that this Hobbesian view of order is untenable, particularly given the conditions of complex interdependence and imperfect information that characterize the modern corporation. Order within complex organizations cannot be maintained by fiat and sanctions because it always entails an element of consent or voluntary acceptance on the part of those who are governed. Yet the creation of consent often requires a departure from principles of efficiency. Indeed, I argue that the same factors that give rise to technical efficiency in the modern corporation have unintended social consequences that disrupt consent, creating constant tension between efficiency and internal order. For this reason, a strict adherence to the textbook M-form often undermines consent, leading not to effective governance, but to organizational decline.

This thesis may seem unremarkable. Anybody who has spent time inside large firms knows that political machinations are common and that managers do not govern merely by issuing orders. Yet these simple facts, when understood through the proper conceptual lens, have profound consequences for existing theories of the firm and for our understanding of corporate governance. To understand why this so, and to grasp the revolutionary implications of the GM case for organization theory, it is helpful to have a deeper understanding of prevailing accounts of the modern corporation.

Efficiency Views of the Modern Corporation

The story of organizational form at General Motors is a story of corporate governance. Governance centers on the question of how cooperation and order are created and maintained within the firm. As Oliver Williamson puts it, governance involves the creation of "good order and workable arrangements."[20] Efficiency views of the firm contend that new types of organization like the multidivisional form arise and persist because they are more efficient than alternative methods of organizing the firm, and such views hold that their efficiency derives primarily from their governance attributes. New forms of organization succeed, that is, because they help establish "good order and workable arrangements" within the firm, thereby lowering the cost of running the enterprise. In this view, the creation of order reduces the cost of running the firm, market mechanisms favor lower-cost forms of organization, and firms with superior governance arrangements are therefore more likely to survive and prosper.[21] Efficiency analyses of the M-form focus primarily on relations between top executives and lower-level management in the

20 Williamson (1996, p. 11), quoting Fuller.
21 Strictly speaking, successful firms are those that lower the sum total of production and governance costs. Efficiency theories of the firm tend to assume that the action is on the governance side of the equation; production costs are seen as largely independent of organization. *Ceteris paribus*, the firm with the lower governance costs prevails.

firm, and they ask how cooperation and coordination are achieved between these levels. They also consider a second level of governance, the division of labor between owners and managers that has come to be known as the separation of ownership and control. Here, the question is how owners can ensure that the firm will continue to be run in shareholders' interests once they delegate significant decision-making power to professional managers. The M-form literature suggests that these two aspects of corporate governance are interrelated and that problems at both levels are alleviated through internal reorganization. In this section, I outline both of these arguments in more detail, with an eye to showing why the GM case proves problematic for each.

The claim that the multidivisional form emerges and succeeds because it is more efficient than existing alternatives arises in the historical work of Alfred Chandler, who shows that the growth of the modern corporation took place in two stages.[22] In the first, firms expanded to serve national and international markets, entering and sometimes creating new markets for mass-produced goods. As they grew, these firms internalized previously independent steps in the production process, taking over functions formerly carried out by independent suppliers and distributors. This resulted in the creation of large, vertically integrated firms with enormous investments in plant and equipment. Growth through vertical integration led to increased profits in the short run, for it created enormous economies of scale and scope that reduced production and distribution costs. But over the longer run, the new firms repeatedly found that growth through integration eventually led to internal chaos, causing initial profits to turn suddenly into huge losses. These difficulties occurred because the increased size and complexity of integrated firms overwhelmed the governance capabilities of traditional, centralized enterprises organized along functional lines. As firms grew and internalized diverse activities across different markets, there was a rapid increase in complexity and in the types of decisions that needed to be made. Eventually, the costs of governing and coordinating activities within the firm increased so substantially that they outweighed the economies created by integration. Intelligent decision-making in the face of complexity hinged on a second stage of development – structural reorganization of the firm. In the long run, growth without reorganization of the governance process led "only to economic inefficiency."[23] The success of the modern corporation was achieved only with the creation of the decentralized or multidivisional form.

22 See Chandler (1962; 1977; 1979; 1990); Chandler and Salsbury (1971); Chandler and Daems (1980).
23 Chandler (1962, p. 16).

The M-form is characterized by two features, *both* of which must be present for decentralization proper to exist.[24] The first is divisionalization, or the decomposition of the firm into a number of distinct operating units dedicated to specific product markets and functioning as independent profit centers.[25] Each division administers a specific product line and is responsible for generating its own profits. Divisional management is responsible for making decisions regarding a single product line and for administering day-to-day operations. The second defining feature of the M-form is the creation of a general office or corporate headquarters to oversee the corporation. Rather than focusing on a specific division or product line, headquarters executives are responsible for monitoring, evaluating, and coordinating the activities of the various divisions and for carrying out long-range planning for the corporation as a whole. To assist them in these functions, the general office relies on financial and technical staffs that oversee and audit divisional activities, making corporate headquarters "less the captive of its operating organizations."[26] The result is an administrative hierarchy in which the general office oversees long-range strategic planning, while the divisions take charge of making operating decisions for specific product lines. The task of making operating decisions is thus decentralized, while that of long-range planning and coordination is centralized (Figure 1.1). This organization improves efficiency by rationalizing information flows, creating clearer lines of authority, and removing "the executives responsible for the destiny of the entire enterprise from the more routine operational activities," giving them "the time, information, and even psychological commitment for long-term planning and appraisal."[27]

The efficiency view of the M-form is formalized in the transaction cost economics (TCE) of Oliver Williamson.[28] TCE brings governance to

---

24 Some analysts imply that divisionalization alone is sufficient to achieve effective decentralization (e.g., Stinchcombe 1990, pp. 150–151). Chandler (1962; 1991a) clearly argues that divisionalization must be accompanied by coordinated control through a general office before we can speak of a decentralized structure. This is apparent in his treatment of GM, for GM created divisions early on in its history. Yet Chandler argues that GM achieved efficient governance only when divisionalization was accompanied by the creation of a general office and its attendant control mechanisms. A company that is divisionalized yet has no general office (or a very weak general office) constitutes a holding company. As we will see later, Williamson is even more explicit on this point.
25 In Chandler's analysis, divisions can also arise to serve geographical regions rather than product markets proper. This formulation has been the source of some controversy (Stinchcombe 1990). Because GM's (and Du Pont's) divisions are organized along product lines, I stick to the narrower definition.
26 Chandler (1962, p. 310).
27 Chandler (1962, p. 309).
28 See Williamson (1975; 1985; 1996). There are many scholars who adopt a general focus on transaction cost analysis. Williamson's work is the best-known version

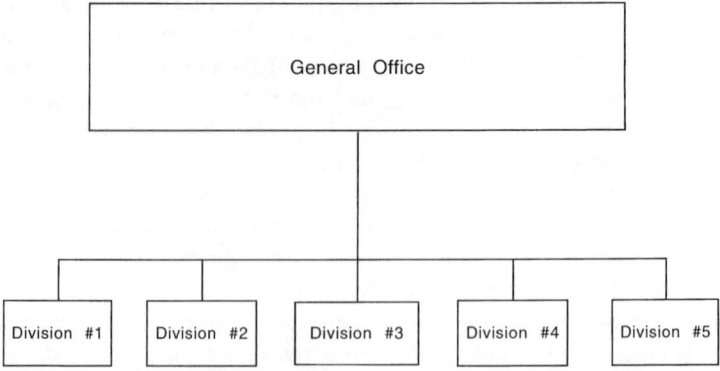

Figure 1.1. The multidivisional form. (Adapted from Alfred D. Chandler, Jr., *Strategy and Structure: Chapters in the History of the American Industrial Enterprise*. Cambridge, MA: MIT Press, 1962, p. 10.)

center stage in organizational analysis by focusing on transaction costs – the costs involved in devising, monitoring, and carrying out transactions within and between firms. Traditional economic accounts treat the firm as a frictionless production function in which actors possess perfect information about the world around them and subordinates follow orders from above without resistance. TCE, on the other hand, assumes that economic actors are characterized by bounded rationality and opportunism. The former refers to the fact that while these actors are intendedly rational, they possess incomplete information and have cognitive constraints that often prevent them from reaching optimal solutions to complex problems.[29] Opportunism denotes "self-interest seeking with guile," reflecting the fact that actors may pursue their own goals at the expense of the larger organization, and may use deception in doing so.[30] Once assumptions of perfect information and unquestioned compliance are replaced with those of bounded rationality and opportunism, transactions are no longer costless. The process of identifying and controlling opportunism and bounded rationality takes time and money, and the primary imperative facing economic organizations is to "devise... governance structures that have the purpose and effect of economizing

---

among organizational analysts, and it has been by far the most concerned with issues of internal organization.
29 Simon (1976). I use the terms "bounded rationality" and "imperfect information" interchangeably.
30 Williamson (1975, p. 26).

on bounded rationality while simultaneously safeguarding transactions against the hazards of opportunism."[31]

The more developed aspects of Williamson's framework attempt to explain why some transactions move out of the market and into the firm.[32] The basic idea is that under certain conditions transactions between independent firms become susceptible to opportunism and bounded rationality, making them costly to monitor. As a consequence, they are internalized within a single firm, where the incentives for opportunism are transformed and transaction costs reduced. This is especially likely to occur when a transaction requires an independent firm to make investments in highly specialized assets that cannot be used for other purposes without significant financial loss. Once such transaction-specific investments have been made, neither buyer nor seller can turn to the market as a credible alternative if problems develop between the two parties. The supplier who has made transaction-specific investments cannot sell her specialized wares to other purchasers, while the buyer who has encouraged this investment will lack other sources of supply. In this situation, both parties have an incentive to behave opportunistically: knowing that the other party lacks alternatives, each can try to extract surplus from the other, and costly disputes may occur. Such problems are particularly likely when unforeseen contingencies arise or when parties have asymmetrical access to information. Under these conditions, the costs of monitoring, opportunism, and haggling can be attenuated by moving the transaction out of the market and into the firm.[33]

TCE also argues that the failure of the traditional, centralized form of organization and the success of the M-form spring from issues of opportunism and bounded rationality. The failure of the centralized or "unitary" form of organization (U-form, in TCE's jargon) is attributed to problems of bounded rationality created by vertical integration.[34] In

---

31 Williamson (1985, p. xiii).
32 See especially Williamson (1985, Chapters 4–5). Unlike Chandler, Williamson does not believe that vertical integration is inefficient unless it is accompanied by decentralization. Rather, he argues that the two processes provide independent sources of cost reduction.
33 In a well-known article, Klein, Crawford, and Alchian (1978; Klein 1988; 1992) argue that General Motors' 1926 purchase of Fisher Body was motivated by such opportunism. After the two companies entered into a long-term contract specifying that Fisher would supply all of GM's car bodies, market conditions shifted, and closed bodies replaced open bodies on most cars. Knowing that GM lacked alternative sources of supply, Fisher attempted to "hold up" GM by effectively charging more for closed bodies. GM responded by purchasing Fisher and ordering it to lower prices. For a discussion of the empirical and theoretical errors in this rendition, see Coase (in press) and Freeland (in press).
34 The term "U-form" originates in the work of Williamson (1975, p. 133). The U-form is organized along functional lines, meaning that the "principal operating units" within the corporation are functional units such as sales, finance, and manufacturing.

the U-form, both long-term planning and daily operating decisions are made by a handful of top managers and owner-entrepreneurs. Entry into multiple markets leads to exponential growth in the number and types of decisions that must be made by these men, causing them to become overloaded. As their cognitive limits are reached, top executives narrow their focus to the exigencies of the moment, focusing on operating issues and neglecting long-range planning. Increased complexity also leads to "impacted" information, as communications between different parts of the corporation break down, and subunits fail to convey critical information to top management (and vice versa). Bounded rationality and impacted information, in turn, exacerbate problems of opportunism, since inadequate information at the top makes it more difficult for executives to detect malfeasance at lower levels of the organization. Lacking adequate oversight, operating managers attempt to divert resources to their own units and to pursue self-interested goals over corporate interests as a whole. Bounded rationality thus leads top managers to become overloaded and to neglect long-range planning, and it allows subordinates to engage in opportunistic pursuit of subordinate goals (subgoals). As these processes are elaborated, inefficiency grows, and profits turn to losses. The breakdown of governance and good order thus begets economic crisis.

The M-form alleviates problems of bounded rationality and opportunism by combining the "divisionalization concept with an internal control and strategic decision-making capability."[35] The creation of divisions addresses problems of bounded rationality. It rationalizes information flows and relieves the communication overload on top executives by decomposing the organization into separate units, each responsible for gathering information from and making operating decisions for a specific market. Divisionalization also reduces the number of operating managers reporting directly to the chief executive officer (CEO), replacing central authority with a more finely graded managerial hierarchy. These steps reduce overload at the top by clarifying lines of authority and communication. Yet, as Williamson emphasizes repeatedly, divisionalization alone is not sufficient to create efficiency. To quell problems of opportunism, it is also necessary to create a general office with the capacity to monitor and evaluate divisional performance and to carry out strategic planning. Through monitoring and evaluating the activities in the divisions, headquarters carries out the task of loss prevention, ensuring that corporate goals and profit targets are being met, and intervening to remedy problems or to discipline management.[36] Through the task of strategic planning, headquarters carries out the entrepreneurial

---

35 Williamson (1985, p. 284).   36 Chandler (1991b).

task of value creation, defining "the basic long-term goals and objectives of the enterprise," and specifying the "courses of action and the allocation of resources necessary for carrying out these goals."[37] Value creation thus involves decisions to move into new markets, expand volume in existing ones, create new productive facilities, and allocate investment funds to different units within the corporation.[38]

There are two key developments underlying headquarters' ability to engage successfully in value creation and loss prevention. The first is the creation of financial and statistical controls that help to transmit information from divisions to headquarters. Most important here are financial systems that measure return on investment and establish an internal capital market. Such mechanisms enable general office staff to monitor divisional activities and engage in loss prevention more effectively. By setting up divisions as profit centers, headquarters can measure and evaluate divisional performance and profitability. Information about divisional performance allows headquarters to align incentives in a way that encourages adherence to corporate goals and discourages opportunism. Using this information, top executives can construct incentive mechanisms – bonus awards, stock incentives, promotion ladders – that reward divisional managers whose units perform well and punish or remove those whose operations do not meet expectations. Information about return on investment also serves as a key component of strategic planning. By assessing which markets (divisions) achieve high returns and combining this knowledge with information on projected demand, the general office can expand in profitable areas, while divesting itself of less lucrative operations. In this way, financial controls are used to create an internal capital market that is a fundamental source of the M-form's efficiency.[39] Financial control systems and incentive mechanisms are thus central to headquarters' ability to carry out strategic planning and loss prevention, allowing top executives to exercise the authority or fiat that – according to Williamson – distinguishes hierarchy from market.

The creation of financial and statistical controls is a necessary but not sufficient condition for effective general office oversight. The efficacy of such controls rests on a second development – the maintenance of a clear separation between strategic planning and daily operations. Value creation and loss prevention are carried out by committees rather than individuals. Williamson emphasizes that while financial controls provide better information to these committees, they cannot ensure that executives who compose these bodies will take heed of this information,

---

37 Chandler (1962, p. 13). 38 Chandler (1991b); Williamson (1985, p. 284).
39 Williamson (1975, pp. 143–148).

particularly when self-interested motives are at work. Division managers, for instance, have partisan interests in specific operations, making them less likely to be objective when asked to engage in loss prevention or value creation. They will tend to promote policies that benefit their own units rather than the corporation as a whole, especially when decisions involve the allocation of investment funds and other resources; similarly, they will be less objective in evaluating the performances of their own units. A planning committee that includes divisional representatives is thus likely to engage in subgoal pursuit rather than a consideration of overall corporate interests. General office executives are less inclined to have particularistic interests in specific divisions and are thus more likely to be concerned with the corporation as a whole. Although division managers may be called on to recommend strategic plans for their own units, only general executives free of operating responsibilities can appropriately serve on the committees responsible for approving plans and allocating capital. For this reason, it is essential to minimize partisan (divisional) participation in the planning process; failure to do so will almost certainly lead to opportunism. Moreover, although financial controls provide better information to top executives, this information is not so detailed as to allow these men to make informed operating decisions. It is thus necessary to ensure that executives in headquarters do not become overly involved in operating matters. Here, too, the continued separation between strategic and tactical planning is essential. The efficiency of the M-form is not simply a function of making better information available at the top; it is also a matter of ensuring that the appropriate actors are in charge of utilizing that information. The maintenance of a firm distinction between strategic planning and daily operations is thus a necessary precondition for the M-form's efficacy.[40]

Finally, Williamson argues that the creation of the M-form and its related financial controls mitigates the corporate control dilemma identified by Adolf Berle and Gardiner Means, thereby helping owners to retain effective control over management. Writing in the 1930s, Berle and Means showed that the growth of the modern corporation forced

---

40 Chandler (1991b; 1992; see also Goold and Campbell 1987) acknowledges in recent work that the relationship between general office and divisions is likely to change over time. Yet he argues that increased divisional involvement in planning is accompanied by tighter reliance on financial controls in order to avoid divisional opportunism. Moreover, even when strategic plans are formulated entirely by the divisions, capital allocation decisions remain in the hands of general executives. The separation between strategic and tactical planning thus remains intact, for as divisions become involved in planning, the general office exercises tighter financial control and audit. The applied strategic planning literature reports similar findings (e.g., Bower 1970; Lorange and Vancil 1977; Lorange 1980; Burgelman 1986). Such studies appear to have had little or no impact on TCE's characterization of the M-form.

shareholders to delegate many strategic and operating decisions to professional managers. They argue that this trend creates a separation of ownership and control, wherein owners retain little command over the firm, while managers have little incentive to increase shareholder value.[41] Williamson concurs that the separation of ownership and control leads to problems of managerial indiscretion, but he contends that the M-form mitigates these problems by creating internal controls that substitute for less effective market sanctions.[42] The M-form's financial control mechanisms provide owners with more detailed information about corporate performance than would be available through the stock market, allowing owners to better assess internal performance. Moreover, through their representation on the board and its subcommittees, owners can use this information to discipline management and veto proposed capital expenditures, thereby allowing shareholders to constrain managerial indiscretion.[43] The M-form thus alleviates problems associated with the separation of ownership and control in two ways. First, it provides owners with more accurate information about internal performance than would be available from the stock market; second, it ensures that owners are represented on the committees charged with utilizing such information. For this reason, Williamson argues, "the fundamental analytic reasons for decomposing complex systems along M-form lines are reinforced if residual risk bearing and management are separated."[44] The earliest multidivisional organizations were thus implemented by strong owners who sought to alleviate the consequences of the ongoing separation of ownership and control.

With this background, it is easy to see why the GM case proves problematic for efficiency theories of the firm. Because TCE sees the separa-

---

[41] Berle and Means (1965). The managerial-discretion hypothesis is predicated on the assumption of imperfect competition. Berle and Means explicitly assume that large corporations are immune to the discipline of competition in product markets, leaving little chance that the invisible hand of the market will constrain managerial malfeasance. They implicitly assume that there are also imperfections in capital markets that prevent owners from detecting or effectively constraining managerial malfeasance. See Williamson (1975, pp. 135–136; 1983; 1985, pp. 318–322).

[42] Williamson (1975, p. 135). In acknowledging that a managerial-discretion problem exists, Williamson distinguishes his position from that of agency-theory, which contends that the development of a market for corporate control (stock market) and a market for managers (managerial labor market) largely resolves the problems associated with the separation of ownership and control. Williamson's point, with which I concur, is that agency-theory arguments rely on the assumption that market signals adequately reflect the value of firms and managers. Such an assumption is quite dubious in a world of pervasive imperfect information. Agency theory has been extensively concerned with the corporate control dilemma. For an overview, see Alchian and Demsetz (1972); Jensen and Meckling (1976); Fama (1980); Fama and Jensen (1983); Demsetz (1988).

[43] Williamson (1985, Chapter 12). [44] Williamson (1983, p. 357).

tion between strategic and tactical planning as a necessary precondition for effective governance, it explicitly identifies two corruptions of the M-form that lead to inefficiency, even when both financial controls and divisionalization remain intact. The first, which I term "participative decentralization," occurs when divisions gain representation on the committees responsible for strategic planning and resource allocation. This destroys the most basic safeguards against opportunism, for "the concentration of strategic decisions and controls in the general office is precisely what the M-form ... is designed to accomplish," and if the divisions become involved in these decisions, "partisan political input [is] reintroduced" and "the organizational integrity of the M-form [is] fundamentally compromised."[45] A second type of corruption, which I call "administrative centralization," occurs when the general office becomes extensively involved in operations. This leads top executives to forsake long-range planning and develop partisan interests in operations. As a result, accountability "is seriously compromised," executives pursue pet projects at the expense of profits, and the M-form becomes "thoroughly corrupted."[46] In each case, the conflation between strategic planning and daily administration destroys the fundamental design principles that lead to the M-form's success; in TCE's view, a corrupted M-form can only lead to inefficiency.

TCE's theoretical assessment of the corrupted M-form is belied by organizational practice at General Motors. As I show later, for most of GM's history, top executives struggled to introduce participative decentralization by including division managers on top planning committees. During the 1930s they went to the opposite extreme, giving headquarters control of strategic planning and daily operations. Despite being characterized by TCE as corruptions of the M-form, these changes led to continued success rather than economic decline. Moreover, GM's struggles over organizational form challenge the claim that decentralization helped to remedy problems associated with the separation of ownership and control. GM's majority shareholders vehemently opposed the changes that would create participative decentralization and administration centralization. Like transaction cost theorists, owners argued that such modifications would lead to opportunism and inefficiency. Despite their financial veto power and their control of key subcommittees of the board, however, owners at GM remained unable or unwilling to impose the textbook M-form that they preferred. No matter which level of corporate governance we examine – relations between owners and general office or relations between headquarters and operating management – the GM case flatly contradicts efficiency theory's empiri-

---

45 Williamson (1983, pp. 355–356). 46 Williamson (1975, p. 148).

cal predictions concerning organizational form. In doing so, it raises serious doubts about the explanatory framework underlying those predictions. In the following section, I examine the theoretical logic underlying efficiency theory more closely, with an eye to showing why its conceptual understanding of governance proves problematic in the empirical world.

Governance and the Problem of Order

A focus on governance revives what sociologists term the problem of order.[47] Once the view that actors inside the firm cooperate spontaneously and follow rules unproblematically is replaced with the assumption that information may be incomplete and actors opportunistic, governance is no longer a "solved political problem."[48] Instead, the corporation becomes a Hobbesian world in which actors pursue their own ends by any means available, and in "the absence of any restraining control [these] means are found in the last analysis to be force and fraud."[49] In this world, actors inside the firm must be induced to carry out organizational ends cooperatively, and they must be prevented from pursuing their own interests at the expense of organizational goals. Moreover, their performance must be consummate rather than perfunctory: in implementing corporate goals, subordinates must go beyond "minimally acceptable" efforts and "include the use of judgment, filling gaps, and taking initiative."[50] It is in this context that governance comes to the fore. The firm is a mechanism designed to overcome the problem of order and to motivate cooperation and consummate performance.

The image of corporate order provided by efficiency theory is similar to the notion of social order outlined by Thomas Hobbes. Williamson and other efficiency analysts depict the firm as a Hobbesian sovereign that uses its authority to constrain force and fraud, thereby effecting cooperation.[51] In this model, top executives achieve order by appealing to subordinates' self-interest. Cooperation and consummate performance are created by rewarding compliance to corporate goals and punishing disobedience, thereby making "the cost of malfeasance prohibitively high."[52] The primary mechanisms behind the efficacy of authority in the M-form are the financial systems that measure divisional performance

---

47 Parsons (1968); Durkheim (1984); Granovetter (1985; 1992); Gould (1990; 1991).
48 Lerner (1972), as quoted in Bowles and Gintis (1989, p. 146).
49 Parsons (1968, p. 90).
50 Williamson (1975, p. 69; 1985, p. 262).
51 Bowles (1985); Granovetter (1985; 1992); Gould (1990).
52 Granovetter (1992, p. 38).

and serve as an internal capital market. These systems provide those at the top with more accurate information about internal performance than is available within a centralized organization. With this knowledge, decision-makers can better align individual incentives with the goals of the firm, denying bonuses or investment funds to subordinates and units who do not perform well, rewarding divisions and managers who achieve a high return on investment, and disciplining or removing managers who fail to perform at expected levels. Once such reward and punishment mechanisms are in place, top executives govern "by appeal to fiat," issuing orders that individuals obey out of self-interest.[53] Subordinates strive to implement top management's orders in consummate fashion, both to maximize positive payoffs and to minimize negative sanctions. Order is thus achieved by aligning individual interests with those of the firm.[54]

Although efficiency theory makes the problem of order central to organizational analysis, the resolution that it offers is fraught with difficulties. Even under the best of circumstances, fiat and sanctions tend to constitute "inadequate tools for control" of the organization.[55] I argue that under conditions of complex interdependence like those characteristic of the M-form, such mechanisms prove particularly problematic as a means of maintaining order. One reason for this inadequacy is well known and easily understood. It boils down to the fact that no incen-

---

53 Williamson (1975, p. 30).
54 Some readers may object that TCE's view of authority cannot be reduced to issues of incentive alignment. In his debates with agency theorists, Williamson (1975; 1985; 1996) has long insisted that "authority matters" and that the firm is more than simply a nexus of contracts. In making this claim, he is arguing in part that governance entails more than incentive alignment through the use of the price mechanism. Yet these claims arise in the debate over why transactions move out of the market and into the firm. Here, he is contending (correctly, in my view) that firms can do things (invoke authority) that markets cannot. In this argument, authority is based in the fact that "the implicit contract law of internal organization is that of forbearance" (Williamson 1996, p. 98). That is, while courts will become involved in disputes between independent contractors, they are much less likely to intervene in such disputes when they take place within the firm. Absent outside intervention, disputes must be resolved internally, and those with authority in the firm will generally prevail. This may explain why firms have recourse to modes of governance that markets lack, but it can hardly be the source of the M-form's advantage over the U-form. There is no difference on this dimension when comparing different forms of internal organization; the courts will refuse to become involved in internal disputes regardless of whether they take place inside a U-form or an M-form. The superiority of the M-form rests solely on its information-processing and incentive-alignment attributes – on the fact that the M-form's more accurate information about internal performance allows managers to better align incentives so as to encourage cooperation and discourage malfeasance. TCE's efforts to break with the incentive-based view of governance are thus incomplete; when comparing different types of internal organization, it consistently reverts back to the incentive-alignment model.
55 Selznick (1948, p. 26).

tive system is perfect. There will always be areas of behavior that cannot be accurately observed or measured and that therefore cannot be easily shaped through rewards and punishments. If our starting point is to assume that imperfect information and opportunism are always present to some degree, then we must admit that even the most comprehensive sanctions will suffer informational deficiencies that leave them susceptible to distortion and manipulation by opportunistic actors.[56] TCE readily acknowledges this point, but insists that it is of little concern. Rather, the argument is comparative: the M-form and its control mechanisms do a better job of providing information and aligning incentives than can the centralized form or holding companies, making the decentralized structure relatively more efficient. In taking this position, however, TCE elides two key issues. First, the question of whether the M-form's more extensive information and more comprehensive sanctions are "good enough" never comes up. TCE simply assumes that these mechanisms are sufficient for creating and maintaining order. It never considers the possibility that the M-form's control mechanisms, though better than those found in the centralized structure, might still remain inadequate. Second, although TCE acknowledges that there are gaps in the M-form's control mechanisms, it does not investigate the ways in which these deficiencies limit the efficacy of authority inside the M-form.[57] Instead, it assumes that headquarters' control over information and sanctions will, on average, be strong enough to render such issues nonproblematic, at least in comparison to the centralized or holding company forms of organization. In this way, TCE replaces the image of the firm as a frictionless production function with the image of the firm as a (relatively) frictionless governance structure.

I wish to problematize this view by emphasizing the extent to which order based in fiat and sanctions is necessarily incomplete. To do this, I conceptualize the M-form as a three-way division of labor among owners, general executives, and division managers. As we have seen, in the traditional business firm, the functions of these three actors are fused in a single individual or in a small group of owner-managers. But as traditional firms grow and enter multiple markets, a division of labor occurs wherein each of these actors takes on specialized roles; each comes to

---

56 This phenomenon is well known. For an overview of the problems that incentive systems encounter in organizations, see Meyer (1994).
57 Williamson (1975, Chapter 7; 1985, Chapter 6) has devoted significant attention to the limits of internal organization in general, but much less attention to the limits of the M-form specifically. Moreover, as Perrow (1981) and Freeland (1996) both point out, TCE has been less successful in integrating its arguments about the efficiency of internal organization with its arguments concerning the limits of bureaucracy. Insofar as it recognizes the problems of bureaucracy, its explanations are generally *ex post* in nature.

carry out a distinct function, and each addresses a specific type of environmental uncertainty.[58] Each division, for instance, specializes in serving a specific market, assessing how changes in demand affect the trade-offs among engineering, manufacturing, and marketing decisions within that market.[59] Similarly, owners also take on an increasingly specialized role, focusing less on management and more on "risk-bearing" and obtaining outside investment funds for use in the business.[60] This division of labor occurs primarily to facilitate and enhance technical efficiency; what was once a unified governance task is decomposed into its constituent elements so that each task can be carried out more efficiently by a specialized actor within the corporation. But this division of labor is hardly a source of social order. To the contrary, although decomposition and specialization may increase technical efficiency, they are also significant causes of social *disorder*. The M-form's tripartite division of labor creates complex interdependence in which owners, executives, and managers all control distinct information and resources. A division that specializes in producing for a specific market, for instance, develops access to detailed information about that market and about the ways that changes in market demand affect engineering and production processes within the division.[61] Much of this information constitutes embedded or "personal knowledge" that cannot be easily communicated to other sectors of the corporation via statistical and financial controls.[62] Specialization is thus a source of information asymmetry within the firm. By creating an organization in which owners, executives, and managers all carry out specialized aspects of governance, the M-form ensures that each of these actors will gain privileged access to and control over distinct types of information, making it "generally impossible" for top executives "to create incentives that completely realign individual self-interest and organizational efficiency."[63]

The recognition that the M-form's division of labor institutionalizes information asymmetry problematizes the image of order based in fiat and sanctions. TCE correctly emphasizes that those atop the organiza-

---

58   The notion that organizations develop specialized units to address distinct types and sources of uncertainty has been prevalent in organization theory (Scott 1998). My thinking on this issue has been largely shaped by the work of Stinchcombe (1990, especially Chapter 4), who explicitly applies this idea to the M-form.
59   Stinchcombe (1990).
60   Jensen and Meckling (1976); Fama and Jensen (1983).
61   Stinchcombe (1990, Chapter 4).
62   See Polanyi (1962).
63   Miller (1992, p. 136). The quote is somewhat out of context. Miller's point is that it is impossible to align incentives completely in *any* hierarchy; the image of order through incentive alignment self-destructs on logical grounds. My point is that such misalignments are likely to be especially pronounced within the M-form, which institutionalizes information asymmetry through its division of labor.

tion respond to this situation by attempting to create control mechanisms that provide better information. In addition, and less explicitly emphasized in the efficiency literature, top executives attempt to establish control over key resources as a means of regulating the actions of subordinates.[64] As we will see in Chapter 2, for example, GM headquarters extended its control over the divisions by wresting power over cash flows and earnings away from them. Only after it did so could an internal capital market be established that would allocate capital to the divisions based on their performance. My point is simply that such attempts to reestablish control are always partial and incomplete. To paraphrase W. Richard Scott, the creation of financial controls does not resolve the problem of order so much as it constitutes a structural recognition of that problem.[65] The division of labor among owners, executives, and divisions creates a situation of complex interdependence in which no single actor controls all of the resources and information necessary for maintaining order in the firm. Insofar as this is the case, there will always be some room for subordinates to manipulate or evade reward and punishment mechanisms in order to pursue their own agendas, and those at the top of the hierarchy will always find themselves at least partially dependent on subordinates to provide information that goes beyond the abstract data provided by financial controls.[66] Insofar as this is the case, fiat and sanctions will not be sufficient for maintaining order in the firm over the long run. Rather, they will be "inadequate tools for control" that must be supplemented or replaced by other means of governance.

The shortcomings of fiat and sanctions are apparent when we examine the relationship between owners and managers in the M-form. We have seen that the M-form incorporates safeguards designed to help owners retain control over managers: through representation on subcommittees of the board, major shareholders are given financial veto power over policy proposals. General office executives formulate strategic plans for the business, but owners can approve or deny headquarters' requests for funds by exercising control over the critical resource of externally generated capital. Owners also control the remuneration of top executives and can fire those who do not perform well.[67] Yet these safeguards fail

---

64 Pfeffer and Salancik (1978); Pfeffer (1980).
65 Scott (1998, p. 48) makes this point with reference to the creation of staff functions, not with reference to the creation of financial controls. The creation of staff is itself an acknowledgment of information asymmetry.
66 Williamson (1975, Chapter 7; 1985, Chapter 6) sometimes recognizes this fact, but he remains unable to outline the limits of fiat and bureaucracy with adequate specificity. See also the exchange between Shanley (1996) and Freeland (1996).
67 Formally this right usually belongs to the board of directors as a whole, but in practice it often resides with a smaller subcommittee of the board.

to rectify problems of managerial discretion. Despite their control of situational sanctions and the information provided by financial controls, owners remain dependent on management's more detailed knowledge of the business. Sanctions provide shareholders with "only a negative or veto power on the government of their enterprise and on the allocation of its resources. They [have] neither the information nor the awareness of the company's situation to propose realistic alternative courses of action," and they thus remain "captives of the professional entrepreneurs."[68] Even the ability to fire managers simply means trading dependence on one set of executives for dependence on another. The point is that not even control over resources (investment funds) nor control over sanctions (ability to hire and fire management) nor access to better information (abstract knowledge provided by the M-form's financial controls) can enable owners to remedy problems of managerial discretion. Headquarters' control over more detailed information means that owners' financial veto power remains partial and limited.[69]

Similar problems arise in the relationships between general office and divisions. Once we recognize that the M-form institutionalizes information asymmetry, it becomes apparent that decomposition into headquarters and divisions does not resolve the problem of order so much as it re-creates it at a new level. To paraphrase Williamson, insofar as imperfect information exists between headquarters and divisions, a divisional discretion problem plainly exists.[70] The same control problems that plague relations between owners and headquarters also emerge when the general office attempts to oversee the divisions. These problems can be traced to information asymmetries that are part and parcel of the M-form; the divisions' privileged access to information about the markets that they serve and the technical processes that they oversee provides them with detailed knowledge that headquarters cannot dislodge through either financial controls or control of resources like investment capital. These information asymmetries allow the divisions to exploit lacunae in financial control mechanisms in a strategic fashion. If division managers are evaluated primarily on indicators like return on investment and market share, for instance, they may maximize their achievement on these measures by deliberately sacrificing performance on other dimensions (e.g., product quality) that are not easily evaluated by headquarters. Divisional control of information is particularly important in the

---

68 Chandler (1962, p. 313).
69 In addition, as Bolton and Scharfstein (1998) point out, headquarters executives may have very different priorities when bargaining with division managers than owners would. There is a wealth of information presented in the following chapters that supports this contention.
70 Williamson (1975, p. 135).

strategic planning process, where the abstract information provided by financial controls must be supplemented by more detailed knowledge of operations before a future course of action can be plotted. General office executives here remain partially dependent on the divisions for information and its interpretation, just as owners remain dependent on headquarters in assessing strategic plans. This gives the divisions additional bargaining power and leverage, and, just as in the case of owners, the general office finds that the knowledge provided by financial controls is not sufficient to allow control through fiat.

Once we acknowledge that information asymmetry is institutionalized as part and parcel of the M-form, we must temper TCE's image of order. There will always be information asymmetries in the M-form that will leave headquarters partially dependent on divisions, and owners partially dependent on headquarters. Insofar as this is the case, it is quite likely that fiat and sanctions will need to be supplemented by other means of creating order. But this is far from the only factor limiting the efficacy of fiat based in sanctions. An even more fundamental problem is the need for what I term "consent," or the voluntary acceptance of authority on the part of actors in the firm. It is to this issue that I now turn.

Consent and the Problem of Order

Governance cannot be reduced to a matter of sanctions or force, because it always entails an element of voluntary acceptance or consent on the part of those who are governed. Even though top executives may utilize coercion, subordinates' willingness to accept orders and work toward organizational goals ultimately rests on at least some degree of voluntary compliance.[71] In this section, I make two related arguments. First, I

71 Barnard (1975). A wide range of social theorists have endorsed the view that compliance ultimately rests on voluntary submission to authority. The classic formulations can be found in Weber (1964) and Simmel (1950). Within organization theory, this view has been most strongly propounded by Barnard (1975) and Selznick (1948; 1949; 1969). More recently, it has been taken up in the Marxist writings of Burawoy (1979; 1985) and in the game-theoretic approach of Miller (1992). For a more skeptical account, see Perrow (1986, pp. 71–75). I am sympathetic to Perrow's admonition that we should be careful not to use the concept of consent to obscure overt domination. But two caveats are in order. First, the work of Burawoy and others shows that even in cases of extreme coercion, some degree of consent persists. Second, and more important in the present context, Perrow focuses on relations between management and relatively low level workers. This book examines interaction between managers at the very top of the organizational hierarchy. While some degrees of subordination and coercion certainly exist in these relations, division managers retain enormous amounts of power and discretion; they are hardly as powerless as shop-floor workers. For this reason alone, it is crucial that top management secure their consent, for their resistance can have devastating consequences.

contend that consent cannot be secured through appeals to self-interest and the manipulation of reward and punishment mechanisms. Indeed, as many of the early classics in organizational sociology recognized, over-reliance on fiat and sanctions more often undermines consent, producing resistance and opposition rather than cooperation and consummate performance.[72] As a consequence, governance based in fiat is bound to be deficient, and executives who attempt to create order primarily through the manipulation of situational sanctions will imperil internal stability. Second, I argue that the division of labor characteristic of the M-form transforms the nature of authority within the firm, making consent more rather than less important as a means of establishing order in the modern corporation. In doing so, it creates tension and contradiction between the logics of efficiency and order. It is thus in the modern corporation that the need for consent and the dangers of overreliance on fiat are most pronounced, making it necessary for those in charge of the M-form to find other means of maintaining cooperation and order within the firm.

Whereas efficiency theories of the firm understand governance in terms of self-interest and incentive alignment, the idea of consent derives from the view that the task of governance "is not so much to shape the self-interested behavior of subordinates as to inspire them to transcend self-interest."[73] Consent encourages actors to pursue organizational goals even when doing so is antithetical to their own interest. It is able to do so because it creates order in a different way than do the mechanisms of governance described by efficiency theory. Fiat and sanctions create order by altering the *situation* in which action takes place. That is, reward and punishment mechanisms shape action by changing the situational constraints and payoffs that actors face, thereby appealing to the self-interest of those actors. Consent, on the other hand, creates order by changing actors' *intentions* in a way that is independent of situational constraints.[74] It shapes behavior by inculcating the belief that acting in a specific way is desirable or correct, regardless of the rewards or punishments that will accrue to an individual for behaving in that manner. Insofar as an actor voluntarily accepts authority, she will strive to implement corporate goals even when sanctions are absent or imperfect. For this reason, consent is particularly important when "positive contribution, not mere passive conformity, is sought."[75] Governance systems that motivate by appealing to self-interest encourage rational actors to do the

---

72 See, for example, Gouldner (1954); Blau (1955); Crozier (1964); Blau and Meyer (1971, Chapter 4).
73 Miller (1992, p. 2).   74 See Parsons (1969); Etzioni (1961).
75 Selznick (1969, p. 101).

minimum necessary to collect rewards and avoid punishments. Consummate performance, however, "is much more a matter of taking initiative to advance organizational objectives" in a way that goes beyond minimal effort based in self-interested calculation.[76] Consent and consummate performance are thus rooted in the "non-rational dimensions of organizational behavior" that are "at once indispensable to the continued existence of [an organization] and at the same time the source of friction."[77]

Insofar as sociologists discuss the voluntary acceptance of authority, they most often do so by invoking Max Weber's concept of legitimacy.[78] Weber argues that changes in actors' intentions are the outcome of value commitments that are internalized as moral imperatives. In this approach, actors voluntarily accept authority when they believe it to be legitimate or legal, and governance regimes are accepted insofar as their practices are consistent with cultural values.[79] When organizational practices violate cultural values, subordinates view the governance regime in question as unjust or illegitimate. Consequently, they do not regard its expectations as morally binding, and they will fail to carry out orders from above in consummate fashion. Although the concept of legitimacy is often invoked in organizational studies, it proves problematic when attempting to explain order within the firm, for at least two reasons. First, such approaches tend to treat legitimacy as an outcome of preexisting beliefs that actors bring to the workplace from the outside world. Organizations can do little to create feelings of moral commitment, for such sentiments are "fundamentally maintained within a society generally"; they can generate order only by ensuring that their practices are consistent with existing social values and laws.[80] Second, the cultural values seen as the source of legitimacy are extremely broad, making them capable of subsuming a huge range of practices. Legitimacy theories are poorly equipped to explain how organizations choose among the wide range of available alternatives, and they offer no explanation of why modes of authority that are accepted in some organizations prove inef-

---

76 Simon (1991, p. 32); see also Selznick (1969, p. 97). Efficiency theory tends to read Barnard's (1975, Chapter 11) discussion of the "economy of incentives" as an argument that cooperation can be constructed through an appeal to self-interest (e.g., Williamson 1995, Chapter 8). And indeed, Barnard's discussions show deep ambivalence over this issue, as he struggles to outline the ways in which rational and non-rational dimensions of behavior come together to create or hinder cooperation. Ultimately, however, he concludes that cooperation within the firm depends on a "sense of responsibility which makes the sacrifices involved a matter of course" – a distinctly nonrational explanation (Barnard 1975, p. 282).
77 Selznick (1948, p. 25).   78 Weber (1964).
79 See, for example, Halaby (1986); Edelman (1990).
80 Ouchi (1980, p. 138).

fective or subject to challenge in others. The classic legitimacy approach thus outlines the general parameters that constrain all governance regimes, but it is less successful in accounting for variation within these very broad constraints.[81]

I use the term "consent" to refer to voluntary acceptance of authority that is produced within the organization itself, rather than being imported from the world outside the firm. As Ian Macneil notes, the act of moving transactions from the market to the firm transforms the way in which they are regulated. Transactions that take place inside the firm lose the anonymous character of market exchange and take on the properties of "a minisociety with a vast array of norms beyond the norms centered on exchange and its immediate processes."[82] More generally, internal transactions are no longer evaluated simply in terms of efficiency, but are subject to a wider range of normative assessments regarding their appropriateness within a hierarchical context and within the firm itself. Insofar as organizational analysts have recognized this transformation, they have tended to view it primarily as a source of inefficiency. The well-known norm of reciprocity that frequently emerges within organizations, for instance, is commonly seen as a source of friction that impedes efficiency.[83] It is my contention, however, that while such norms may lead to inefficiency in some situations, they are also at the heart of consent and of subordinates' willingness to carry out corporate goals in consummate rather than perfunctory fashion. When managerial orders and expectations are consonant with an organization's formal and informal norms, subordinates will consent to managerial authority and will strive to implement corporate goals, even when those goals conflict with their

81 Perhaps for this reason, the new institutionalism in sociology focuses extensively on organizational isomorphism, arguing that organizations tend to "look alike" because they all respond to and adopt similar legitimated models. In these arguments, legitimacy is based less in moral imperatives than in cognitive scripts, mimetic behavior, and "rational myths," but it nonetheless continues to be imported from the world outside the organization. For an overview, see Meyer and Rowan (1977); Meyer and Scott (1983); Powell and DiMaggio (1991); Scott and Meyer (1994). For an important exception to the focus on isomorphism, see Dobbin (1994).
82 Macneil (1978, p. 901). As Granovetter (1985) points out, this should not be taken to imply that normative criteria are absent in market transactions, only that they are usually less pronounced. A wide range of literature suggests that as competitive market contracting gives way to "market failure" and bilateral exchange, trust and other norms become more salient.
83 Williamson (1975, pp. 119, 126), for instance, notes that transactions inside the firm "easily" become subject to norms of reciprocity and "internal justice" that "impair incentives" and lead to inefficient behavior. While he concedes that such norms might theoretically support efficient exchange, Williamson goes on to conclude (p. 120) that "Distinguishing logrolling distortions from 'constructive cooperation' between internal parties is . . . made difficult by the various and subtle forms that internal reciprocity can take." On the norm of reciprocity more generally, see Gouldner (1961) and Blau (1964).

own self-interest. When orders from above violate such norms, however, subordinates will resist, often by engaging in perfunctory performance rather than outright rebellion. This is the source of the fundamental dilemma noted by Selznick: the very practices that generate the initiative and identification necessary for efficiency and consummate performance are, under other circumstances, sources of friction and inefficiency. There is thus no one best way to organize. Rather, there are trade-offs between efficiency and order, and managers must constantly choose which they will pursue.

Existing studies usually argue that the norms underlying consent are anchored in the informal aspects of organization.[84] The most common approach sees consent as the outcome of informal norms that arise spontaneously from social relations in the workplace and from the fact that transactions within the firm become embedded in personal and group relationships. Many studies of life on the shop floor, for instance, contend that workers' effort is governed by informal norms that encourage productivity up to a certain level, but discourage output beyond that level.[85] Workers voluntarily accept and strive to implement managerial directives when they are consonant with the range of acceptable effort defined by norms created spontaneously within the work group, but resistance occurs when management attempts to increase effort levels above this range. A closely related view holds that the informal norms underlying cooperation are anchored in a firm's unique history and management style. Here, consent is still seen as the outcome of compliance to norms, but these norms are grounded less in spontaneous social interaction than in historical precedent and leadership style. The gypsum miners in Gouldner's classic study, for instance, rebel when a new supervisor attempts to replace the mine's lax style of management with close supervision and strict adherence to bureaucratic rules.[86] Their resistance is based primarily in the fact that the new regime violates implicit and long-standing expectations that workers will be granted wide discretionary latitude in exchange for hard work. In each case, the norms underlying consent derive from the fact that economic transactions become embedded in more general social relations, causing purely calculative norms of exchange to be supplemented and tempered by norms of reciprocity and fairness.[87] Moreover, in both of these understandings, the norms that arise out of social embeddedness and historical contingency are the sources of *both* consummate performance and inefficiency. Both the

---

84 See Scott (1998, Chapter 3) for an overview of such "natural systems" approaches.
85 See, for example, Roethlisberger and Dickson (1939); Blau (1955); Burawoy (1979).
86 Gouldner (1954).
87 On the more general concept of embeddedness, see Granovetter (1985).

promises and the perils of hierarchy are rooted in these nonrational dimensions of organizational behavior.

I focus on a less investigated source of the normative expectations underlying consent. Following Barnard, it is my contention that a firm's formal structure and its division of labor themselves give rise to informal norms and expectations that are central to issues of consent. As we have just seen, the classic studies in industrial sociology emphasize the spontaneous and natural character of informal organization, arguing that it is either the outcome of personalities and social relations unique to the firm or the path-dependent result of an organization's distinctive history. Perhaps because they focus extensively on these spontaneous and historically arbitrary elements of the firms they examine, such studies have relatively little to say about formal organization. Indeed, they often seem to see the formal aspects of organization as largely irrelevant to social order in the firm. Yet, as Chester Barnard notes, informal organization is deeply and systematically shaped by formal organization.[88] That is, a firm's formal structure and its division of labor shape informal organization in crucial ways. Formal elements of organizational structure thus play a key role in engendering informal expectations and norms about how the firm should operate. It is my contention that the norms underlying consent are systematically shaped by the firm's formal structure, though often in quite unexpected ways. An important case in point concerns the tension between authority and expertise identified by Max Weber. I will argue that the division of labor characteristic of the modern corporation gives rise to implicit normative expectations that are at the heart of the tension between authority and expertise. I further contend that these normative expectations are central to issues of consent in the multidivisional form.[89]

In his seminal analysis of bureaucracy, Weber notes that increasing specialization creates strain and disjuncture between expertise and authority.[90] As actors and subunits in the firm become more specialized, each develops a recognized sphere of competence. This, in turn, is the source of recurring tension. On the one hand, specialized subunits are presumed to be closest to the facts and most technically qualified to make decisions in their area. On the other hand, higher-level executives are responsible for making policy decisions that routinely turn on technical issues and

---

88 Barnard (1975, Chapter 9).
89 The normative expectations created by the division of labor may be magnified or diminished by conditions specific to the firm in question. Thus, I will show that General Motors' long history of divisional autonomy intensified the need for consent there. Nonetheless, the need for consent is fundamentally anchored in the division of labor within the firm.
90 Weber (1978). This observation has engendered considerable discussion. For seminal discussions and extensions of Weber's observations, see Parsons (1947, pp. 58–60); Gouldner (1954); Selznick (1969, pp. 93–95).

The Corporation and the Problem of Order

that often impinge on subunits' ability to carry out their tasks. This creates a constant tension between presumed competence (which rests with lower-level units) and actual authority (which rests with higher-level units). Executives with the formal authority and responsibility for overseeing specialized units or actors often have only a limited grasp of the technical issues at stake, and they may lack the competence to make intelligent technical decisions regarding those units.[91] Such an executive often finds him or herself "confronted by a group ... of people who are nominally his subordinates, but whose special expertness allows them to dispute his judgment."[92] Existing accounts emphasize that as a result of this situation, higher-level managers must find ways of incorporating expertise into the decision-making process in order to ensure that outcomes are technically competent. As Selznick notes, ensuring technically competent decisions requires that "new forms of organization" be found that "give the expert greater weight in the determination of policy."[93] What is less recognized, however, is that the tension between authority and expertise persists even when managers are competent to oversee the units beneath them and even when they have adequate information with which to make decisions regarding those units. The sources of this continuing tension are the subjective or normative expectations engendered by specialization itself.

How does specialization create normative expectations within the firm? The economist Herbert Simon notes that specialization narrows subordinates' zone of indifference. That is, actors who are specialists in a particular area are less likely simply to carry out superiors' decisions without question.[94] They are likely to use their expertise to examine and evaluate orders originating at higher levels in the hierarchy, especially when those directives impinge on an expert's sphere of presumed competence. It is my contention that this narrowing of the zone of indifference occurs because specialization creates normative expectations about how decisions in the firm "ought" to be made. The creation of specialized subunits or actors with defined spheres of competence produces expectations that the expertise of these units will be incorporated into the decision-making process. When policy decisions turn on questions involving knowledge of a particular area, actors or units with expertise in that area will often feel entitled to input into such decisions.[95] Indeed, such expectations often involve a sense that subordinates have a "right" to be heard or represented in the decision-making process. Such beliefs may be partly political and strategic in nature, involving attempts by sub-

---

[91] Scott (1998, pp. 47–48).   [92] Blau and Meyer (1971, p. 73).
[93] Selznick (1969, p. 94).
[94] See Simon (1976, p. 131). The term "zone of indifference" is from Barnard (1975).
[95] See Selznick (1969, p. 83); Parsons (1969, pp. 417–418); Blau and Meyer (1971, Chapter 4).

ordinates to defend their turf from executive encroachment. But they run much deeper than simple politics. A planning process that fails to solicit expert advice will be viewed as irrational because it violates the very logic of specialization within the firm. From the subordinate's point of view, it makes no sense to create specialized subunits and then to ignore their expertise and knowledge when making decisions. A planning process that does so transgresses implicit norms regarding the correct or rational procedures for making effective decisions.[96] Research suggests that subordinates will resist the outcomes of such an "irrational" planning process, even when those outcomes are technically correct. If upper management makes decisions unilaterally and forces them on lower-level actors, subordinates with high levels of expertise are likely to conclude that the decisions are not "consistent with the facts of the situations."[97] This reaction is impervious to the substance of the decision; what is important is the procedure by which it is reached and the extent to which subordinates perceive that they have influence in the decision-making process. This is an important source of the frequently expressed complaint, parodied in today's Dilbert comic strip, that those at the top of the organizational hierarchy are bumbling incompetents who do not know what they are talking about.

The belief that expertise should be incorporated into the decision-making process is central to issues of consent. When planning processes incorporate expert opinion, subordinates will accept outcomes as justified and will work harder toward their implementation. This acceptance springs from a belief that decisions made in this fashion are "more rational" because they are consistent with the firm's division of labor. When top management makes decisions in a way that appears to eschew expert opinion, subordinates are likely to view the resulting decisions as unjustified and either will put forth less than consummate effort in carrying them out or will engage in outright resistance to their implementation. Again, these reactions have relatively little to do with the content of the decision itself. Consent arises not simply because a decision is substantively correct, but because it is justifiable within the context of the firm's division of labor. The tension between expertise and authority thus puts continual pressure on higher-level executives to justify their decisions to

---

[96] This suggests that rationality itself has a strongly endogenous component. To be sure, specialization is legitimized via broad societal values that privilege rational-legal forms of authority, as both Weber (1964) and the new institutionalism in sociology (Meyer and Rowan 1977; Meyer and Scott 1983; Powell and DiMaggio 1991; Scott and Meyer 1994) have emphasized. But the specific content of what constitutes rational action within the firm is anchored in and deeply shaped by the firm's division of labor. Even the "world-level" image of rationality identified by Meyer (Scott and Meyer 1994, Chapters 1–2) thus has strongly endogenous components.

[97] Lawrence and Lorsch (1967, p. 66).

lower-level actors. Even if top executives have access to "perfect" information and consistently produce rational and efficient policies, subordinates in positions of expertise are likely to consent to those policies only insofar as the planning process is congruent with expectations generated by the firm's social structure. This results in a paradox. Although a complex division of labor may be technically efficient, it creates social disorder. This disorder is not simply a result of the fact that specialized units possess different subgoals that must be aligned.[98] Rather, the creation of specialized subunits gives rise to normative expectations about how decisions ought to be made, and these expectations are at odds with the formal distribution of authority in the firm. As a result, the more extensive the firm's division of labor, the more problematic it is to secure consent from subordinates. Increasingly, top executives must justify their decisions in order to secure the consent of subordinates who possess high levels of expertise. Authority based in simple fiat must thus give way to different means of governance, lest the exercise of hierarchical authority undermine order within the firm.

The simplest way to incorporate expertise into planning in a way that generates consent to organizational goals is to allow subordinates to exercise voice in planning and policy formulation, even if they are not formally responsible for doing so. Selznick notes, for instance, that consent "is furthered by respectful and considerate treatment, including some forms of communication and consultation" with subordinates, and he argues that the need for consent creates an emphasis on consultation rather than fiat.[99] This view is supported by a wide range of research showing that when subordinates participate in or have influence over planning, they are more likely to accept the resulting decisions as their own and exercise initiative in their implementation.[100] Such participation in planning can take a number of forms, including informal consultation and the use of staff or other mediators to create understanding and agreement among parties.[101] Perhaps the most direct method of creating

---

98 The classic statement of this view is March and Simon (1993).
99 Selznick (1969, pp. 101, 83).
100 See, for example, Salancik (1977a; 1977b); Pfeffer (1980, pp. 173–177); Lind and Tyler (1988, Chapter 8).
101 Lawrence and Lorsch (1967). Some confusion arises in the traditional claim that it is the staff that possesses high levels of expertise. In fact, the staff arises in large part to help justify executive decisions to lower-level units (thus its "advisory" role) and to assist top executives in breaking divisional monopolies over knowledge and expertise through surveillance and monitoring. As Scott (1998, p. 48) points out, however, the genesis of the staff does not so much resolve the tension between authority and expertise as it constitutes a structural recognition of that problem (Dalton 1950; 1959). It is widely recognized, for instance, that the "advisory" role of the staff is often a fiction; staff advice is really a veiled form of executive order. Precisely for this reason, however, it is likely to elicit resistance or perfunctory compliance rather

consent is to let subordinates with high levels of expertise participate directly in the planning process, giving them formal representation on committees responsible for making decisions or formulating policies. Direct participation ensures that experts will have an opportunity to voice their judgments. Moreover, unlike methods that rely on informal consultation, formal representation makes it difficult for superiors to solicit and then ignore advice, especially when subordinates' representation is accompanied by the right to vote on decisions. In the latter instance, subordinates will be able to exercise at least minimal influence over planning.

Even formal participation on the part of subordinates should not be equated with a simple image of democratic governance, however. By incorporating subordinates into the decision-making process, top executives may well be attempting to engage in co-optation – that is, to gain the consent of subordinates without actually sharing substantive power in any meaningful way.[102] Toward this end, higher-level executives will continue to use their formal and informal authority in attempts to control decision premises, set agendas, and limit the scope of policy decisions.[103] Through such efforts, they attempt to ensure that the participation of subordinates is more symbolic than substantive; subordinates cast a vote in the decision-making process, but they have little real control over the options presented to them. Such efforts can never be completely successful, however. Because co-optation ultimately involves "trading sovereignty for support," it "always comes at a price" of allowing subordinates to exercise influence over decisions, sometimes in ways that contravene the preferences of top executives.[104] Once subordinates are formally incorporated into the planning process, there is always the risk that they will manage to use their representation in a way that will subvert or modify leadership's goals.[105] When this occurs, leaders cannot

---

than consummate performance from operating management. Staff actions, too, are limited by the need to manufacture consent.
102 Selznick (1949).
103 March and Simon (1993); Pfeffer (1980).
104 Scott (1998, pp. 201, 77).
105 Selznick (1948, p. 35) is quite clear that co-optation constrained both subordinates and leaders, creating public commitment to and responsibility for policy decisions on the part of subordinates and "constrain[ing] the field of choice available to the organization or leadership" and sometimes subverting the goals of leadership. Yet subsequent analyses have tended to focus on the former phenomenon while neglecting the latter. This leads to the view that "commitment is too easy" (Salancik 1977b). Through being symbolically incorporated into the decision-making process, subordinates are co-opted and become committed to carrying policies through, while their actual power over the decision-making process remains slight to nonexistent. The GM case suggests that when participation remains merely symbolic, it is likely to lead to cynicism and disaffection rather than cooperation and commitment. (See Adams 1996 for a popular parody of the cynicism resulting from such attempts at

simply react by invoking force, for if they do, subordinates will withdraw support, and stability will be threatened. When efforts at co-optation fail, therefore, leaders must be prepared either to allow subordinates to have their way or to forge some sort of compromise between the parties involved.

A focus on consent and the limits of fiat leads to an understanding of governance different from that put forward by efficiency theory. In this view, the primary imperative facing governance mechanisms is to establish and maintain social order within the firm. This notion is similar to TCE's insight that governance concerns good order and workable arrangements. But here, the task of maintaining order cannot be understood primarily as an exercise in economizing, for the same arrangements that lead to technical efficiency also disrupt social order in the firm. In this world there are real trade-offs between order and efficiency that create a constant tension between the goal of economizing and that of sustaining cooperation and consummate performance. If the primary imperative facing governance mechanisms is to maintain order, executives will sometimes be willing to forgo efficiency for the sake of sustaining cooperation. In doing so, they may agree to decisions, policies, or even long-term organizational arrangements that they know to be suboptimal from an economic point of view. Here, governance is not a simple matter of using the best information available to arrive at policy decisions that are then enforced via fiat and sanctions. Rather, it is an inherently political process in which top executives must be willing to forge a compromise between actors in the firm in order to preserve cooperation and promote consummate performance. In the following section, I seek to outline how this ongoing political compromise influenced the mechanisms of governance at General Motors, showing how issues of resource dependence, asymmetric information, and the need for consent came together to influence organizational form.

Organizational Change at General Motors

In the chapters that follow, I show that the changes in GM's organization were the result of conflict and compromise between owners and

> symbolic co-optation.) Moreover, it is important to remember that Selznick's notion of co-optation focused on attempts to incorporate external actors into the decision-making process. Such actors possessed neither formal line authority in the organization nor detailed information about the issues being considered. The situation is quite different when we consider the co-optation of high-level managers inside the corporation. These actors have considerable power and control significant resources and information. This makes it all the less likely that their consent will be secured through symbolic incorporation alone.

managers. Each of these actors pursued distinct versions of the M-form, with varying degrees of success over time. Owners favored a decentralized structure like that described by efficiency theory. They sought to create a clear distinction between strategic planning and daily operations that kept the divisions out of the planning process and utilized fiat and incentives as the primary mechanisms for motivating divisional management. This version of decentralization gave the general office the principal responsibility for maintaining order through formulating long-range policies and ensuring that the divisions carried those policies out. Yet headquarters' capacity to discharge these responsibilities was constrained both by the need to elicit divisional consent from below and by owner control from above. These constraints put the general office in a bind. To create consent, top executives sought to deploy the familiar strategy of trading sovereignty for support: they endeavored to create participative decentralization by bringing division managers directly into the strategic planning and resource allocation process. But owners would have none of it. Intent on maximizing profitability, owners insisted that the M-form was "not . . . set up to secure cooperation, but . . . to *rule* the business of the corporation," and they vetoed headquarters' plans to include the divisions in the governance process.[106] Over the short run, this led to informal participative decentralization, in which headquarters informally included division managers in the planning process as a means of creating consent. Over the longer run, it touched off a prolonged struggle. Intent on modifying GM's organization, and prevented from doing so by owner oversight, general office executives sought to weaken owner control from above. Equally adamant that participative decentralization should be avoided and owners' capacity to oversee headquarters should be preserved, owners fought to preserve the textbook M-form. What emerged was a constantly shifting political compromise, shaped on one side by the need for divisional consent, and on the other by owners' ability to constrain the general office.

GM's original multidivisional structure, described in detail by Chandler, was the version favored by owners.[107] There were two key features to this organization. First, as outlined earlier, it created a firm distinction between strategic planning and daily administration. Strategic planning and resource allocation would be carried out by an Executive Committee consisting of general office executives and a few shareholder representatives; divisional men would not be allowed to sit on this committee, but would be left in charge of making operating decisions for

---

106 Lammot du Pont to Alfred P. Sloan, Jr., August 8, 1945, Accession 542, Box 837. Emphasis in original.
107 Chandler (1962); Chandler and Salsbury (1971); see also Chapter 2 herein.

their divisions.[108] Second, and less emphasized in the existing literature, owners' version of decentralization was designed to preserve owner control of the corporation.[109] Owners believed that "there is just one central motive in industrial management,... the permanent welfare of the owners of the business," and they devised the M-form as a means of ensuring that this central motive would be realized.[110] Thus, while the M-form delegated formal responsibility for value creation and loss prevention to professional managers in headquarters, it also created safeguards that gave large shareholders substantial veto power over these executives' decisions. There were two sources of this veto power. The first derived from owners' control over the scarce resource of investment capital. Although owners delegated the task of formulating policies to the general office, all proposed policies involving significant expenditures had to be approved by an owner-controlled Finance Committee, where representatives from Du Pont and J. P. Morgan far outnumbered management. Through this committee, owners could veto management proposals by refusing to provide the funds necessary to implement them. In addition, owners retained the ability to hire, fire, and sanction top management, giving them considerable leverage over general office executives. Together, these safeguards allowed owners to steer the policy process, discipline management, and veto proposed changes to the M-form itself. Owners thus remained confident that the M-form would allow them to exercise ultimate authority over any significant decisions at GM.

Owners' image of the M-form was strongly influenced by their experience as owner-managers at Du Pont, as well as by their initial experiences at GM. Their preference for an owner-controlled Finance Committee is easily understood. Domination of the Finance Committee helped owners to curb managerial discretion, despite owning only about 25 percent of the corporation's voting stock. The du Ponts had used this arrangement at E. I. du Pont de Nemours, where they found that an owner-dominated Finance Committee allowed them to retain control over the corporation, even as non–family members took over an increasing number of management positions. Owners favored a firm distinction between strategic planning and daily administration for several reasons. First, like efficiency theorists, they believed that divisional representation

---

108   As we will see in Chapter 2, this formulation of owner preferences came only after owners' initial version of the M-form – one in which owners made both strategic and operating decisions – failed.
109   The literature has tended to overlook the extent to which the M-form was originally created as a means of retaining owner control over increasingly complex organizations.
110   Brown (1927, p. 5); reprinted in Chandler (1979).

in planning would promote opportunistic behavior. Division managers were not sufficiently objective to evaluate their own operations and allocate resources to them, they argued; such decisions should be made by executives who did not have a direct interest in those units. Second, owners held divisional management directly responsible for the financial crisis that almost led to GM's bankruptcy in 1921. This experience convinced owners that operating management at GM was irresponsible and in need of control. Perhaps most important, owners favored a textbook M-form because it mirrored the organization that was already in place at Du Pont.[111] There, long-range planning and resource allocation were carried out by an Executive Committee composed of heads of the various staff functions like manufacturing, sales, and engineering. These men were not attached to specific divisions, and they held no line authority over the operating side of the organization. This arrangement had worked well at Du Pont, and owners believed that it should be carried over to GM. Their enthusiasm for the textbook M-form was thus based not only in abstract reasoning but also in their own experience as managers at Du Pont.[112]

Top executives in GM headquarters had a different view of decentralization. They rejected the idea of a firm distinction between strategic planning and daily administration, seeking instead to include division managers in the planning and resource allocation process.[113] In doing so, they repeatedly argued that such modifications were necessary to create divisional consent and initiative. Although divisional inclusion in planning took different forms over the years, GM's top management favored a type of participative decentralization that put managers from GM's largest and most important divisions directly on the committees in charge of policy approval and resource allocation. The only exception to this rule prior to 1958 occurred from 1934 to 1942, when headquarters pursued a policy of deliberate administrative centralization that not only removed divisional men from the planning process but also put general office executives in charge of most operating decisions. Initially the question of who would be included in the planning process constituted the only major difference in owners' and managers' conceptualizations of the M-form. But when owners prevented general office executives

111 See Chandler (1962, Chapter 2).
112 This raises the question of why the textbook M-form worked at Du Pont but did not seem effective at GM. I address this issue in Chapter 8.
113 Under Alfred Sloan, GM's headquarters also strove to include owner representatives in the planning and resource allocation process. Sloan explicitly identified this as a means of working out a compromise among owners, general office, and divisions. His efforts to include owners were eventually stymied by institutional factors, and his successors at headquarters did not think it important to include owners in planning and resource allocation.

from implementing participative decentralization, a second difference emerged: headquarters began to resist the split between finance and operations that gave owners financial veto power over proposed policies. Complaining that owners' control of finances amounted to a "dictatorship," top executives argued that it was not "logical to set up an organization around the stockholders," because shareholder concerns were too narrowly financial.[114] Informed decisions about prospective policies could not be made from such a narrow financial point of view, they argued, but required an in-depth understanding of both the operating and financial implications of those policies. Headquarters argued that the Finance Committee should be replaced by a body composed primarily of executive management, with only a handful of owner representatives. Moreover, they maintained, this committee's scope should not be limited to financial issues, but should consider the long-range competitive implications of proposed policies. Chafing at owner control from above and determined to modify GM's organization, top executives thus initiated struggle on a second front, seeking to weaken owners' financial veto power.

The ability of owners and managers to implement the specific forms of organization that they favored varied as a result of institutional and technical constraints. This is seen most clearly in the case of owners' ability to insist on a textbook M-form. It might seem surprising that their ability to implement such an organization was ever in question. As shareholder of between one-quarter and one-third of GM's voting stock, E. I. du Pont de Nemours was seemingly in a position to decree any type of organization that it desired. Yet owners' ability to control organizational form varied as a result of two factors. The first is easily understood. Owners' willingness and ability to control organizational form at GM varied as functions of state regulation and other forms of legal intervention (e.g., minority-shareholder suits) that challenged the legitimacy of owner intervention in management affairs. When state regulation challenged owners' right to intervene, owners became less willing to exercise direct control over GM's internal affairs. Sometimes state intervention was diffuse and indirect – more a matter of the climate of the times than any specific action directed at Du Pont or other shareholders. In the 1930s, for instance, Du Pont executives believed that New Deal antitrust and securities regulations were beginning to distinguish between shareholders who owned stock as a matter of investment and those who attempted to exercise control over a company by becoming involved in

---

114 The first quote is from Alfred P. Sloan, Jr., to Walter S. Carpenter, April 11, 1942a, Accession 542, Box 837. The second is from Alfred P. Sloan, Jr., to Donaldson Brown, February 2, 1945, Accession 1334, Box 1.

management decisions. They reacted by removing themselves from GM's Executive Committee and other bodies involved in making operating decisions, and they became more circumspect about exercising financial veto over general office initiatives. During other periods, government intervention was much more direct. In the late 1940s, for instance, the U.S. Justice Department launched an antitrust suit against Du Pont and GM, charging them with restraint of trade. Many aspects of the suit revolved around the question of whether Du Pont had controlled operating decisions at GM, and during the ten-year period that the suit ground through the courts, Du Pont executives were reluctant to intervene in management decisions, insisting that their stake in GM was for investment purposes only.

The second factor limiting owners' ability to control organizational form at GM was the extent to which capital funds constituted a scarce resource. Owners' version of decentralization was implicitly predicated on the assumption that capital was a scarce resource and that money was not available to finance every worthwhile initiative proposed by management while still paying dividends to shareholders. Through their control of the Finance Committee, owners would determine which management proposals to sponsor and which to reject. Yet GM's enormous earning power wreaked havoc with this image of owner control by creating continuing and extensive capital surplus. As earnings filled GM's coffers, capital became a slack resource rather than a scarce one, and owners' ability to exercise financial veto declined.[115] Owners were no longer able to veto management proposals simply by claiming that adequate funds were not available. As Alfred Sloan would later recall, once GM's enormous earnings created surplus, "we all knew that we had the money ... to do anything we wanted."[116] Slack capital resources led to a subtle shift in how proposed projects were evaluated. Rather than focusing on whether funds were available and at what cost, such assessments turned increasingly on the trade-offs between various long-term consequences of a particular proposal, including not only financial returns but also questions of strategic benefit, competitive advantage, market share, and organizational fit. Here owners were at a decided disadvantage, for they lacked the knowledge to make informed judgments about such issues. The abstract information provided by financial controls was rarely sufficient to make such assessments, and owners lacked the detailed personal knowledge of the business that would allow them quickly to grasp the relevant issues. Even when owners opposed man-

---

115 Resource dependence theorists have long argued that slack resources may undercut an actor's basis of power within the firm. See Pfeffer and Salancik (1978).
116 Alfred P. Sloan, Jr., to Donaldson Brown, February 2, 1945, Accession 1334, Box 1.

agement initiatives, they found it difficult to justify their position in anything other than financial terms. Although they continued to voice their opposition to management plans, owners reluctantly reacted to these conditions by relinquishing much of their financial veto power, giving general office executives greater control over policy, financial decision-making, and organizational form.

Owners' ability to control organizational form was crucial in determining how corporate headquarters went about organizing divisional consent. When capital was scarce and state intervention minimal, owners did not hesitate to insist on a textbook M-form characterized by both a strong separation between strategic and tactical planning and owner control over financial decision-making. This prevented the general office from implementing formal participative decentralization, in which the divisions would have participated directly on the committees responsible for strategic planning and resource allocation. Headquarters' response was to use informal means of creating consent, having division managers take part in meetings of top committees, but precluding them from exercising a direct vote in this process. This period of GM's history was relatively short-lived, for the corporation's tremendous earnings quickly led to continuing slack capital resources. When this occurred, owners found themselves less able to constrain management and exercise control over GM's organizational form, especially when slack resources were accompanied by direct or indirect government intervention that challenged owners' ability to intervene in management affairs. During these periods, two developments took place. First, the general office was able to wrest control of the Finance Committee away from owners, diluting owners' ability to control the corporation. Second, and as a result, during most periods of extensive slack capital resources, the general office established formal participative decentralization in which managers from the car and truck divisions participated directly in the planning and resource allocation process. Owners consistently opposed these developments, but remained unable or unwilling to dissuade headquarters from going ahead with them.

The second factor shaping organizational form at General Motors was the need for consent itself. For most of the period studied in this book, GM's top executives sought to include division managers in planning and resource allocation as a means of creating consent. Such participative decentralization arose neither out of a commitment to industrial democracy nor out of a desire to empower the divisions. Rather, it was a recognition of political reality. Top executives understood that the divisions were likely to resist policy initiatives handed down by headquarters and enforced via fiat, and they knew that the divisions' superior knowledge and control over productive resources meant that this resistance would come at a cost to the corporation. They thus engaged in the strategy of trading sovereignty for support, incorporating divisions into the policy-making process in hopes of co-opting resistance. But they did so only grudgingly. General office executives did not want to share their power with the divisions if they could help it. This influenced organizational form in two ways. First, although they included the divisions in the planning process, top executives attempted to ensure that headquarters would retain the upper hand. They created subtle and sometimes convoluted mechanisms designed to allow the general office to steer and perhaps control the strategic planning process. These mechanisms sought to allow the general office to shape the premises and broad parameters of decision-making and to ensure that headquarters would retain ultimate veto power over divisional initiatives.[117] When these mechanisms failed and the divisions pursued their own agendas, however, top executives only rarely reacted by invoking fiat. Indeed, in the few instances that headquarters used these devices to exercise outright fiat over the divisions, protracted political struggle ensued. When their attempts to retain dominance over the divisions met with resistance, therefore, top executives were more likely either to acquiesce to divisional wishes or to forge a political compromise that all sides could support.

The need for consent influenced organizational form in a second way as well. When the general office believed that it was less constrained by the need to manufacture divisional consent, the form of organization that it preferred shifted dramatically. This was the case during the 1930s, when top executives decided that divisional consent was less important than simple economizing. The reasons for this shift were rooted in market changes wrought by the Great Depression. The depression made it essential to cut costs, forcing top executives to choose economizing over consent. This in itself underscores the extent to which these two goals involved trade-offs. Yet the depression also made divisional consent less essential, creating an environment in which perfunctory compliance on the part of the divisions would suffice. Economic contraction meant that the vast majority of consumers could afford to purchase only basic, low-cost transportation; few were able to spend extra money for technologically advanced bells and whistles (or horns and transmissions). The depression thus changed the nature of competition, making technical innovation less important as a means of achieving competitive advantage. As a result, the pace of innovation slowed, and the task of the divisions became much more routine. They concentrated on producing simple, low-cost cars that changed little from year to year. As divisional

---

117 See the discussion of the Policy Committee and the policy groups in Chapters 3 and 4.

activities became more routine and predictable, the need for divisional initiative declined. Top executives at GM recognized what organization theorists would grasp some thirty years later: routine activities did not require consummate performance on the part of subordinates and could thus be more easily managed via a more centralized structure.[118] During this period, the general office not only removed the divisions from planning but also gave headquarters extensive control over operating decisions. This administrative centralization was born of extremely unusual circumstances, and it enjoyed only limited success (see Chapter 3). Nonetheless, it shows that top executives' commitment to participative decentralization was not simply an unswerving philosophy. Rather, when changes in the market reduced the need for divisional consent, headquarters wasted no time in reclaiming its sovereignty by remaking organizational form.

The changes in GM's M-form were not simply corruptions of a textbook M-form. Rather, they were driven by top executives' attempts to create and maintain order given the three-way division of labor characteristic of the modern corporation. On one side, organizational form was shaped by the need for divisional consent. When divisions were highly differentiated units serving distinct markets (which they were for most of GM's history), headquarters sought to include division managers in the planning and resource allocation process as a means of creating consent. When changes in the external environment made divisional consent less essential, participative decentralization quickly gave way to administrative centralization, in which headquarters became deeply involved in making detailed operating decisions. Organizational form was also shaped by owner control from above. When capital was scarce and government intervention minimal, owners prevented top executives from including the divisions in strategic planning and resource allocation. Top executives responded by trying to find informal means for producing consent and involving the divisions in strategic planning. As owner control weakened, these informal mechanisms gave way to formal reorganization that put the division managers directly on top planning committees. Similarly, administrative centralization reached its peak only after owner control over organizational form was substantially weakened. In each case, organizational form varied as top executives attempted to satisfice between the logics of efficiency and consent by creating a political compromise among owners, general office, and divisions.

The following chapters present a historical analysis of organizational change at General Motors from 1921, when the M-form was first

---

118 Burns and Stalker (1961).

created, to 1958, when the long debate between owners and managers finally drew to an end. In these chapters, I show that variations in organizational form were functions of headquarters' attempts to create divisional consent, on one side, and owners' ability to implement a textbook M-form, on the other. Both of these factors were shaped by the changing technical and institutional environments in which GM operated, for environmental changes produced variations both in the amount of divisional consent that was necessary and in owners' ability to control organizational form. Chapters 2–6 investigate five periods of GM's history in depth, each corresponding to formal or informal reorganization within GM. Chapter 7 examines the period from 1958 through the mid-1970s, in order to assess the consequences of the structural changes made in 1958.[119] In Chapter 8, I return to a discussion of the theoretical issues involved, assessing the implications of the GM case for our understanding of corporate governance and for existing theories of the firm.

119 It is important to note that most of the information for the post-1958 period comes mainly from secondary rather than primary sources. It is thus suggestive at best. It is clear that political factionalism ran rampant inside GM in the 1960s and 1970s. Without access to primary documents, it is much more difficult to assess the linkages between that factionalism and organizational form.

2

Creating Corporate Order: Conflicting Versions of Decentralization at GM, 1921–1933

Analyses of General Motors' organizational history have focused primarily on the period from 1921 to 1925, when the corporation created and perfected the M-form. The basic contours of this structure are well known, having been described extensively both by the men who built it and by analysts of the modern corporation.[1] Yet the textbook M-form outlined in those writings existed only briefly at GM; it quickly gave way to "corrupted" versions of decentralization that involved division managers in strategic planning. Because existing analyses have not examined the changes made in GM's organization over time, they have missed or misinterpreted these developments. In this chapter, I show that top executives sought to introduce participative decentralization as a means of creating divisional consent to organizational policies. Yet owners opposed such divisional participation in planning, and their control of scarce investment funds and key committees during the 1920s enabled them to block management's efforts to modify GM's formal structure. General office executives responded by attempting to create participative decentralization through informal practices, touching off a debate over organizational form that would last for decades.

The chapter begins with an overview of the historical conditions that led to decentralization. GM's M-form arose in response to the three-way problem of order created by the ongoing division of labor among owners, general executives, and division managers. Within this context, two different images of decentralization emerged. Focusing on the separation between owners and managers, owners sought to reestablish shareholder control over a corporation in crisis. Their primary aim was to stem financial losses by reining in the extremely autonomous operating divisions.

---

[1] For scholarly analyses, see Chandler (1962); Chandler and Salsbury (1971); Sloan (1964); Kuhn (1986). For contemporary descriptions from the men who built GM's organization, see Bradley (1926a; 1926b; 1926c; 1926d; 1927); Brown (1924; 1927; 1929a; 1929b); Fordham and Tingley (1924); Mooney (1924); Raskob (1928). Many of these essays, along with other contemporary accounts, are reprinted in Chandler (1979) and Johnson (1980).

To achieve this goal, they implemented a version of decentralization that relied on fiat. Led by Alfred Sloan, the nascent general office had a different vision of decentralization. Their concern was with extracting consent from the divisions in order to achieve a workable political truce between different levels of management. Drawing on primary historical documents, I show that top executives sought to create consent by allowing the divisions to participate in the strategic planning and allocation process.

The owner version of the M-form was the first to be put into place at General Motors. Owners believed that if they established control of investment funds, incentive mechanisms, and decision-making committees, they would possess the ability to govern by fiat. They thus set out to solidify their control of capital and to create sanctions that would allow them to shape incentives and evaluate divisional performance. Initially their strategy relied almost exclusively on the ability to control capital and exercise veto over investment decisions arising from the operating side of the organization. When this strategy led to crisis, owners attempted to centralize further. They took over GM's top decision-making committees and made themselves directly responsible for formulating both financial and operating strategy, with only limited input from general office executives and virtually no input from the divisions. Yet this attempt to wrest control of the corporation away from managers also failed. Using their knowledge and control of engineering and manufacturing processes, the divisions successfully resisted owner directives from above. After failing to implement direct owner control, Pierre du Pont resigned from GM's presidency in 1923, turning it over to Alfred Sloan.

Under Sloan's leadership, GM's headquarters set out to create divisional consent within the constraints imposed by owners. Virtually every analysis of GM under Sloan stresses that during his rule, the M-form was perfected through the creation of a general office that articulated long-range policies free from divisional participation and that administered a set of statistical and financial controls ensuring compliance to those policies. Yet evidence shows that Sloan did not set out to build such a planning body. He understood that under conditions of complex interdependence, governance through fiat was bound to fail. Sloan's version of decentralization focused on creating divisional consent to operating policies. Contrary to existing accounts, including those presented in his own autobiography, primary documents show that Sloan deliberately sought to ensure that divisional managers were represented in policy formulation and evaluation. This strategy was driven by the desire to motivate subordinates, for Sloan believed that if division managers were allowed to take part in creating policy, they would be more committed to carrying it out. Yet because owners frowned on divisional participation in planning, Sloan's efforts met with resistance from above. His attempts to create consent during this period thus came to focus on informal practices rather than formal reorganization.

Two Different Views of Decentralization

General Motors' M-form was born of crisis. The corporation developed the structure in the early 1920s, following a severe financial emergency that led to the departure of founder William C. Durant. After Durant's exit in December 1920, E. I. du Pont de Nemours, the giant chemical concern, became the largest shareholder in GM, controlling some 35.8 percent of the corporation's voting stock.[2] Du Pont representatives moved quickly to reorganize the corporation, adopting a modified version of a plan that was largely the work of Alfred P. Sloan, Jr., then a vice-president within GM. In creating the decentralized structure, both the du Ponts and Sloan were reacting to problems that had arisen during Durant's reign. Yet from the outset, owners and managers favored different forms of decentralization. In this section, I briefly outline the events that led to Durant's departure in order to highlight the issues that led to the creation of the M-form. I then show that owners and managers favored different versions of decentralization – differences that would shape the struggle over organizational form in the decades ahead.

Under Durant, GM was essentially a holding company characterized by "decentralization with a vengeance."[3] The divisions were highly autonomous and acted with little oversight. They made their own purchasing, production, design, marketing, and pricing decisions, and they competed with one another for market share. Most important, divisions controlled their own cash flows and were responsible for their own profit

---

2   "History of the du Pont Company's Investment in the General Motors Corporation," August 17, 1921, *United States v. E. I. du Pont de Nemours, General Motors, et al.* Civil Action 49C-1071, decided in 126 F. Supp. 235, 1954 (hereinafter cited as *U.S. v. Du Pont*), GE #166, p. 9. Unless otherwise noted, all exhibits, depositions, and testimony cited are from this suit, the initial U.S. antitrust suit against Du Pont and General Motors, charging them with violation of the Clayton Act. In 126 F. Supp. 235, the U.S. district court judge decided in favor of the defendants, averring that they had not violated the Clayton Act. This decision was reversed by the Supreme Court in 353 U.S. 586, 1957, which includes many (but not all) of the primary documents from the district court case. Details concerning the disposition of Du Pont's stock holdings in GM were further appealed and were decided in 366 U.S. 316, 1961, which gave the final order for Du Pont to divest itself of GM holdings.
3   The phrase is from Sloan (1964, p. 30).

and loss accounting. Proceeds from sales went directly to the divisions, where managers decided how to use the money. Investment planning was carried out informally between Durant and division managers, and the divisions could borrow funds from banks on their own accounts, with little or no central oversight. Indeed, when Durant wanted money for acquisition of new properties, he sometimes had to bargain with division managers to get the money. Because uniform accounting standards did not exist within the corporation, top executives like Durant often had little idea how much money was in divisional coffers.[4]

Even before these practices led to financial crisis in 1920, Du Pont representatives sought to strengthen their control over the divisions and Durant. From the outset, they attempted to do so primarily through control of capital. E. I. du Pont de Nemours' initial investment in General Motors was predicated on an agreement that Durant would institute a dual committee structure like that in effect at Du Pont: a Finance Committee would have the authority to oversee decisions concerning investment, appropriations, dividends, and working-capital allocations, while operating policy would be formulated by an Executive Committee responsible for formulating strategic plans for the corporation as a whole. The Finance Committee would be dominated by Du Pont representatives, allowing "the Du Pont Company to run the finances of General Motors"; the Executive Committee would be composed of Durant and the various division managers.[5] Because the Finance Committee would have the power to deny funds to any Executive Committee proposal involving large expenditures, the du Ponts believed that they would be able to effectively control Durant and the divisions. On February 21, 1918, a six-man Finance Committee was thus put into place, with Durant the sole non–du Pont representative.[6]

Despite control of the Finance Committee, owners proved unable to avoid crisis in the period prior to 1921. Both owners and managers sought rapid growth during this period, and when it became necessary to reduce expenditures, they could not agree where to make cuts.[7] Following World War I, GM embarked on a huge expansion program to

---

4 See Chandler (1962, pp. 122–130); Chandler and Salsbury (1971, pp. 443–482); Sloan (1964, p. 122); Weisberger (1979).
5 Chandler and Salsbury (1971, p. 451). The following sentence draws on the same source, pp. 449–452.
6 "General Motors Finance Committee," December 10, 1951, document prepared by Du Pont counsel for U.S. antitrust trial. Longwood, 438 (30), p. 5108. General Motors Corporation, *Annual Report*, Detroit, MI: General Motors Corporation, 1918. The 1918 Finance Committee was chaired by E. I. du Pont de Nemours' John J. Raskob; other members were Pierre S. du Pont, Irénée du Pont, Henry F. du Pont, J. A. Haskell, and William C. Durant.
7 Sloan (1964, p. 38).

increase capacity and market share. Encouraged both by Du Pont representatives on the Finance Committee and by Durant and the operating men on the Executive Committee, this growth created an enormous need for additional investment capital, as fixed assets grew from $40,932,209 in 1917 to $345,471,290 at the end of 1920.[8] At the same time, divisions rapidly increased working capital by stockpiling inventory and parts to avoid material shortages.[9] Expansion of fixed and working capital was carried out during a period of increasing postwar inflation, making it ever more costly to sustain growth. When financial conditions worsened late in 1919, Durant and the divisions urged that fixed-capital outlays be reduced.[10] While the Executive Committee acknowledged that inventories and working capital were also ballooning, and even appointed a special Appropriations Committee to look into the matter, it continued to approve enormous overruns on a regular basis.[11] Operating executives wanted to reduce spending, but only through cutting outlays for fixed capital. The Finance Committee, on the other hand, retained an "aggressive expansive posture" and continued the investment program at full force.[12] When it finally decided to rein in spending in late 1919, it focused on the need to cut working capital and inventory. Because divisions controlled their own cash flows, however, Finance Committee directives had little impact.

The financial strain created by rapid growth of both fixed and working capital led to crisis in the latter half of 1920.[13] The earliest difficulties were created by increasing expenditures for working capital. As inflation rose early in 1920, prices for labor and supplies climbed, while division managers continued to increase inventories to avoid future price increases. As a consequence, working-capital appropriations skyrocketed. On May 13, 1920, the Finance Committee and Executive Committee tried to remedy this situation by cutting production schedules, setting limits on inventories, and creating an Inventory Allotment Committee to allocate working capital to the divisions. Like the Appropriations Committee that had been set up earlier, this new group had little impact. Top executives lacked the information needed to evaluate appropriations requests from below, while division managers controlled their

---

8 These figures are from General Motors Corporation, *Annual Report*, 1917, 1920. See also Chandler and Salsbury (1971, p. 480).
9 Chandler (1962, pp. 128–129). Chandler and Salsbury (1971, Chapter 18).
10 Gustin (1973, p. 207). William C. Durant to John J. Raskob, October 31, 1919, as quoted in Weisberger (1979, p. 244).
11 Sloan (1964, pp. 27–30). Chandler and Salsbury (1971, p. 480).
12 Scharchburg, as quoted in Gustin (1973, p. 207).
13 This paragraph draws heavily on information in Chandler and Salsbury (1971, pp. 480–482); Chandler (1962, pp. 128–130); General Motors Corporation, *Annual Report*, 1922.

own funds, had their own lines of credit, and carried out their own purchasing. As a result, the edicts of the various committees did little to limit divisional spending; managers continued to stockpile supplies, and inventories exceeded the $200 million mark. When a recession hit in September 1920, the demand for automobiles dropped dramatically, and sales as well as profits plummeted. By late October, inventories were some $60 million over the limits set in May, and the cash needed to keep the business running was scarce. Many divisions met payrolls and paid suppliers by taking out short-term loans, thereby increasing indebtedness.

Against this backdrop of financial crisis within the firm, Durant continued to speculate on the stock market, buying shares of GM common in an attempt to increase his holdings while maintaining the value of the company's stock.[14] In carrying out these transactions, he used his existing GM stock as collateral. When the recession that had already created fiscal crisis within GM led to a sharp decline in stock values, Durant found himself in a predicament. The value of the GM stock he was using as collateral had fallen precipitously, and he needed over $30 million in cash to cover his losses. If he could not come up with the money, Durant's 300,000 shares of GM would be liquidated on the market, causing the company's stock value to plummet and very likely forcing bankruptcy. Through a series of complicated transactions, E. I. du Pont de Nemours, aided by J. P. Morgan, paid off Durant's stock-market debts in return for ownership of his GM common. Du Pont insisted on Durant's resignation from GM as part of the deal, and E. I. du Pont de Nemours emerged as by far the single largest shareholder of GM. Pierre du Pont continued as GM's chairman of the board, and he took over from Durant as president. Having acquired control of the company, GM's new owners turned to the task of building a new governance structure.

The events of 1920 helped shape owners' conviction that they needed to solidify their control over the organization by subjecting both operating and financial aspects of the business to stricter control. After Durant's departure on December 1, 1920, Pierre S. du Pont began the process of corporate reorganization, adopting a modified version of a plan that was largely the work of Alfred P. Sloan, Jr., then a vice-president within the corporation.[15] From the outset, Sloan and the du Ponts had different views of decentralization. Sloan was concerned primarily with creating a political truce between actors by devising a scheme of organization that all sides would support. Because he had initially entered the corporation when his Hyatt Roller Bearing Company became

---

14 For a more detailed recounting of these events, see Chandler and Salsbury (1971, Chapter 18).
15 Chandler and Salsbury (1971, p. 491).

Corporate Order: Decentralization at GM

a division of GM, Sloan was sensitive to GM's long tradition of divisional autonomy. In outlining a plan for decentralization, he focused primarily on relations between top management and divisions, and he was especially concerned with creating cooperation between these two levels of management. The du Ponts, on the other hand, sought to ensure owner control over both top management and the divisions. Deeply concerned over the events of 1920, they wanted to eviscerate divisional autonomy and put all major decision-making in the hands of owners. In adopting Sloan's plan, they therefore made changes that replaced his focus on consent with an emphasis on fiat from above.

Sloan's version of decentralization sought to establish central control over GM while simultaneously reconciling this control with GM's strong history of divisional autonomy. From the outset, he focused on the question of how to create divisional cooperation and consent to corporate policies. Sloan's plan originated in a study of organization that he carried out in December 1919, one of three reports he authored around this time containing recommendations for reorganization directed to then-president Durant.[16] By his own admission, Sloan placed a strong emphasis on decentralization as a way of attempting to convince Durant and the division managers to accept the proposed reorganization. Aware that these men would resist attempts to curtail their power, Sloan devised a plan that he "thought would be acceptable to all interests rather than what would form an ideal organisation."[17] He thus emphasized that the first principle underlying his proposal was that "the responsibility attached to the chief executive of each operation [i.e., division manager] shall in no way be limited"; yet as he later noted, the second principle of the study contradicted the first by asserting that "certain central organization functions are absolutely essential to the logical development and proper control of the Corporation's activities."[18] Even in his earliest writings, Sloan saw the "contradiction" between establishing central control and maintaining divisional consent to that control as "the crux of the matter" when it came to issues of organization.[19]

Sloan's primary means for reconciling the contradiction between control and consent was to allow interested parties to participate in the strategic planning process. The organization study stressed that central control would be exercised by the Finance Committee and Executive Committee established by Du Pont in 1917. The Finance Committee

---

16 Sloan (1964, p. 45, fn. 2). Alfred P. Sloan, Jr., "Organization Study." *U.S. v. Du Pont.* DTE #GM 1. Chandler and Salsbury (1971, p. 473).
17 Alfred P. Sloan to Pierre S. du Pont, September 1920, as quoted in Sloan (1964, p. 52).
18 Alfred P. Sloan, Jr., "Organization Study." *U.S. v. Du Pont.* DTE #GM 1.
19 Sloan (1964, p. 53).

would be responsible for the "entire financial policy of the Corporation," including accounting, dividends, and approval of appropriations.[20] The operating side of the business would be overseen by the Executive Committee, which would determine the corporation's operating policies and approve appropriation requests from the divisions before sending them on to the Finance Committee for consideration. Sloan's plan stressed that any issue affecting only a single division would be outside the Executive Committee's purview and would be "entirely determined by the General Manager of that division . . . subject only to the executive control of the President."[21] Issues affecting more than one unit would be decided by the Executive Committee, but here each of the divisions would be represented directly, as they had been under Durant. Sloan's rationale for including division managers in strategic planning and resource allocation was that these men "constitute[d] experts . . . in the detailed management of the Corporation's operations," but as would later become clear, he also thought this arrangement would elicit greater cooperation and consent from the divisions.[22] The president of the corporation would be responsible for interpreting and implementing policies decided on by the Executive Committee.

The organization study also called for the creation of a general office staff, but here, too, GM's tradition of divisional autonomy shaped Sloan's thinking. His recommendation that the staff's authority be strictly advisory in nature was an attempt to elicit cooperation from the historically independent divisions. For instance, the study called for reorganizing the divisions into four operating groups that would be overseen by "group executives" from the general office.[23] Group executives would be "absolutely responsible to the President for the operation" of divisions within the group, yet they would lack line authority to give orders to division managers.[24] Instead, they would serve only in an advisory capacity to the divisions, making recommendations and offering interpretation of corporate policy, but lacking the authority to issue orders. Sloan emphasized that group executives would not challenge divisional autonomy: operating decisions would remain "absolutely" in the hands of the division managers. Indeed, Sloan initially recommended that only the Accessories Group, where he would serve as group executive, should have a group executive. Divisions in the Motor Car Group, Parts Group,

---

20 Sloan, "Organization Study." *U.S. v. Du Pont.* DTE #GM 1.
21 Sloan, "Organization Study." *U.S. v. Du Pont.* DTE #GM 1.
22 Sloan, "Organization Study." *U.S. v. Du Pont.* DTE #GM 1.
23 Sloan, "Organization Study." *U.S. v. Du Pont.* DTE #GM 1. See also the summaries in Chandler (1962, pp. 133–140); Chandler and Salsbury (1971, pp. 493–497). The miscellaneous group was dropped by du Pont in implementing Sloan's plan.
24 Sloan, "Organization Study." *U.S. v. Du Pont.* DTE #GM 1.

and Miscellaneous Group – the bulk of the corporation – would continue to report directly to the president. Only after Durant's ouster did Sloan explicitly recommend that the same plan be used for other divisions as well.[25] The organization study also called for the creation of a general office staff to assist top executives and division managers. Like group executives, the staff was to be purely advisory in nature, with no line authority over the divisions. The proposed financial and accounting staff, for instance, would oversee "all financial and accounting functions that pertain to the Corporation as a whole," but under Sloan's plan, each division would have "complete control" of its own finances and accounting.[26] Autonomy would be so great that divisions could continue to use whatever accounting standards and practices they desired, with no uniform methods imposed from above. Similarly, Sloan proposed to create a general advisory staff to advise division managers on broad technical issues, but he again emphasized that each division could "accept or reject the advice of the Advisory Staff as its judgment may dictate, subject to the general supervision of the President."[27] Here, too, Sloan emphasized the advisory nature of the staff in an attempt to elicit cooperation from the divisions.

Although the structure proposed by Sloan looked like the textbook M-form on paper, many features which later analysts would see as essential to decentralization were absent. Most importantly, there was not a strong separation between strategic and tactical planning. Financial policies would be controlled by owners via the Finance Committee, while operating policies would be determined by an Executive Committee where division managers dominated. Strategic planning would thus be in the hands of men with partisan interests in particular operations. Nor did Sloan's study say anything about establishing situational sanctions and financial controls. Although another study authored by Sloan did advocate instituting a system that would allow each division's return on investment to be calculated, these recommendations were not included in the organization study. Instead, the latter recommended leaving even basic accounting methodology totally in the hands of the divisions. Sloan did enunciate the principles of grouping divisions together, appointing group executives, and creating advisory staffs. Yet in many ways these concepts were themselves shaped by the need to create a general office whose authority division managers would accept voluntarily. Sloan showed himself to be extremely sensitive to the historical context of

---

25 Alfred Sloan to Pierre du Pont, September 1920, as quoted in Sloan (1964, pp. 49–50).
26 Sloan, "Organization Study." *U.S. v. Du Pont.* DTE #GM 1.
27 Chandler (1962, pp. 138–140) provides a good summary of the advisory staff's functions.

decentralization and its role in limiting the extent to which fiat could be deployed successfully. As he would later in his career, Sloan proposed to generate cooperation by allowing division managers to participate directly in the formulation of strategic planning.

In adopting Sloan's plan, Pierre du Pont made what Chandler characterizes as "minor modifications."[28] And indeed, the M-form that he put into effect looked much like the one Sloan had outlined at the level of the formal organization chart. Yet Pierre's changes created a version of decentralization that differed from Sloan's in crucial respects. The Du Pont M-form sought to establish owner control over virtually every aspect of corporate governance in order to overcome the "decentralization with a vengeance" that had allowed the divisions to bring the corporation to the brink of disaster in 1920. In part these changes reflected owners' desire to strengthen their control over the financial side of the business. Aware that their attempt to govern operations via the Finance Committee had failed in large part because the divisions continued to control cash surplus and inventory commitments, Pierre turned discretion concerning these matters over to the finance staff, which reported directly to the Finance Committee, now a ten-man group composed of seven Du Pont representatives and three men from the banking industry.[29] Yet Pierre's modifications did more than extend owner power over finance; they also ensured that owners would have direct authority over operating policy. Here, modifications focused less on redefining the formal duties of governing committees than on changing their membership.

The most important step in extending owner control over operations was to transform the Executive Committee from a large group made up primarily of division managers into a four-man body composed of three owner representatives and Sloan. This owner-dominated Executive Committee was given "all the powers of the Board ... in the management and direction of all the business and affairs of the Company," except those assigned to the Finance Committee.[30] Two of its members were now the most powerful men in General Motors: Pierre was president, chairman of the board, and chairman of the Executive Committee, while

---

28 Chandler (1962, p. 140). The organization put into place by Pierre is depicted in Chandler and Salsbury (1971, Chart VI, overleaf to p. 500).
29 The Du Pont members of the new Finance Committee were as follows: John J. Raskob, chair; F. Donaldson Brown; Pierre S. du Pont; Irénée du Pont; Henry F. du Pont; Lammot du Pont; and J. A. Haskell. The other members were: J. P. Morgan's Edward R. Stettinius; Seward Prosser, chairman of the board of Banker's Trust Company and a close friend of Pierre; and George F. Baker of New York's First National Bank. See General Motors Corporation, *Annual Report*, 1921. On the ties between these men and Pierre, see Chandler and Salsbury (1971).
30 General Motors Corporation, *By-laws*, as amended to January 13, 1921.

Du Pont's John Raskob chaired the Finance Committee. Another Du Pont executive, J. A. Haskell, served as vice-president in charge of operations, while Sloan, the only member of the Executive Committee who was not also on the Finance Committee, was named vice-president in charge of the advisory staff.[31] These men had complete authority over strategic planning, and over time they became increasingly involved in daily operations. In theory this arrangement still left many operating issues in the hands of the divisions. For instance, Haskell and Sloan would each head new committees, overseeing operating and staff activities, respectively. The Operations Committee headed by Haskell contained all the division managers previously on the Executive Committee, and in principle it had "many of the same functions" as the old Executive Committee; under Pierre's leadership the Operations Committee "was not regularly active," however, and the Executive Committee made the important decisions pertaining to operations.[32] Similarly, Sloan's advisory staff had no line authority over the divisions, which could theoretically ignore staff advice. But in fact, if irresolvable disagreements arose between the divisions and Sloan's staff, the Executive Committee as a whole would settle the matter.[33]

The changes made by du Pont indicate the different view of decentralization held by owners. While Sloan's plan advocated a committee composed of general executives and division managers to oversee strategic planning and operations, du Pont gave owners direct authority over these functions. Determined to avoid repeating the events of 1920, Pierre made certain that owners controlled the operating as well as the financial side of the business, a move that Sloan would later condemn as a "jury rig."[34] The changes to GM's top governing committees were made in January 1921, but the problem of inducing division managers to carry out policies remained. Here, too, Pierre relied heavily on force and fiat rather than on Sloan's spirit of political compromise. During the remainder of 1921, owners made a number of additional changes that further increased their reliance on and ability to use fiat: they dismissed Durant allies, placed former Du Pont men in key positions, and developed finan-

---

31 Within six months of its implementation, this plan was changed to put Sloan in charge of operations and Haskell in charge of staff activities, probably because Sloan was the only Executive Committee member with any operating experience. Yet even he had little direct experience in the production of automobiles, having come up through the parts and accessories end of the business. See Sloan (1964, p. 56). Chandler and Salsbury (1971, p. 497).
32 The first quote is from Chandler and Salsbury (1971, p. 497). The second is from Sloan (1964, p. 113).
33 Pierre S. du Pont, "Memo to Officers, Directors and Heads of Department," December 29, 1920. U.S. v. Du Pont. DE #303.
34 Deposition of Alfred P. Sloan, Jr. U.S. v. Du Pont, p. 271 (220).

cial controls that would serve as situational sanctions. Owners believed that together these moves would solidify their control over the operating side of the business.

To help extract compliance from the divisions, Pierre dismissed or replaced the division managers who had come to power under Durant. At three of the divisions – Cadillac, Oakland, and Oldsmobile – he summarily fired the managers because they had paid themselves out of divisional accounts without receiving proper authorization.[35] In doing so, they were following practices established and tolerated during Durant's presidency. At Oakland and Cadillac, managers Fred Warner and Richard Collins had incentive-based contracts that paid them a percentage of divisional profit. While payment was supposed to occur only after an audit had been conducted, both men drew money before financial statements were approved. Oldsmobile's Edward Ver Linden did the same, even though he did not have a profit-sharing contract. Although all three men complied with Pierre's request that funds be returned by May 1921, all were dismissed. Pierre also replaced Chevrolet's A. B. C. Hardy, whom he moved to the advisory staff early in 1921. Even Harry Bassett, manager of the highly successful Buick division, was not safe. Late in 1921, "someone" – probably Pierre – proposed making changes in Buick's management, a plan that was dropped when Sloan warned that "it is far better that the rest of General Motors be scrapped than any chances taken with Buick's earning power."[36] Pierre's actions made it "much easier" for owners to establish control over the divisions, for the new managers were unlikely openly to resist owners' orders after such a show of force.[37]

Du Pont also placed trusted allies in key positions at GM in order to solidify owner control over the nascent corporate staff. The most important appointments were those of Donaldson Brown and John Pratt. As treasurer of E. I. du Pont de Nemours, Brown had developed financial control mechanisms that evaluated return on invested capital at the divi-

---

35 Chandler and Salsbury (1971, p. 499). This paragraph draws heavily on the account presented there.
36 Alfred Sloan to Pierre du Pont, December 24, 1921, as quoted in Sloan (1964, p. 61); see also Chandler and Salsbury (1971, p. 525). The fact that Sloan addressed his objections to Pierre suggests that it was probably Pierre who sought to remove Bassett.
37 Chandler (1962, p. 141). Chandler argues that this result was "quite unintentional," but primary documents suggest that Pierre deliberately sought to remove Durant's men in order to strengthen owner control over the divisions. In the case of Cadillac, for instance, Chandler contends that division manager Collins "left the company satisfied with the arrangements" that he and Pierre had reached. Yet documents show that Pierre forced Collins out, agreeing to meet with the division manager out of court to settle differences only if Collins resigned from his position. See Chandler and Salsbury (1971, p. 689, fn. 17); Pierre S. du Pont to John J. Raskob, July 1, 1921, Accession 473, Box 897.

sional level. Following Durant's departure, Du Pont's John Raskob requested that Brown be transferred to General Motors, where he became vice-president of finance on January 1, 1921.[38] Pratt had been transferred to GM from Du Pont's engineering department even before Durant's resignation, and when Du Pont took control of GM, Pierre appointed Pratt to serve as group executive in charge of the Accessories Group.[39] Pratt's friend and former Du Pont co-worker, E. F. Johnson, was brought in as group executive in charge of the Parts Group.[40] After serving for 32 years at Du Pont, Frank Turner was made GM's comptroller in the summer of 1919, a position he retained after Durant's departure. Another Du Pont executive, E. A. Bergland, became a staff vice-president in charge of power and construction projects at GM.[41] With proven allies in key positions, owners were more confident that their orders would be carried out; these allies also provided owners improved access to information from and influence over the fledgling general office.

More important than these personnel changes were attempts to ensure owners' authority through the development of financial and statistical controls.[42] Virtually all of these systems were promulgated by Pierre du Pont and his appointees, though Sloan also supported them. These sanctions rested on the assumption that control of capital would allow owners to steer the governance process and shape the incentives facing divisional management, thereby curbing divisional discretion. Financial controls implemented after 1921 were more successful than their predecessors because they established more extensive owner control over capital. Of crucial importance was the fact that owners wrested profit streams away from the divisions, depriving division managers of one of their most valuable resources and increasing owner authority over surplus. In addition, the new financial controls took virtually every decision involving major expenditures out of management's hands, putting all such decisions under the control of owners. Not only did owners determine operating policy through the Executive Committee, but because most important operating decisions involved issues of "financial policy," they also had to be approved by the owner-controlled Finance Committee. Moreover, the new financial controls were devised and

---

38 Sloan (1964, p. 118).   39 Chandler (1962, p. 141).
40 Chandler and Salsbury (1971, p. 498).
41 General Motors Corporation. Organization Chart, May 31, 1921, in Chandler and Salsbury (1971, overleaf following p. 500). On Bergland's background at Du Pont as one of Pierre's "ablest assistants," see p. 468 of the same source.
42 The development of these controls is reviewed in detail in a number of sources. See the essays reprinted in Chandler (1979). In addition, see Brown (1977); Chandler and Salsbury (1971, pp. 500–505, 549–554); Chandler (1962, pp. 145–153); Sloan (1964, Chapter 8).

administered by the general office finance staff, which was overseen by former Du Pont treasurer Donaldson Brown.

The most significant financial controls fell into one of four categories. *Cash controls* administered by the finance staff established maximum cash balances for each of the corporation's accounts. Excess funds were transferred to reserve accounts, and cash surplus was invested in short-term securities, rather than being left with the divisions. By 1922, all cash receipts were deposited into accounts administered by GM's financial staff; the divisions had no power to draw on the accounts and no direct claims on their own receipts.[43] *Inventory and production controls* set limits on the value of supplies that the divisions could purchase and the number of cars that they could produce. After the Du Pont takeover, inventory commitments were made on the basis of divisional forecasts. Money to purchase labor and supplies was dispensed to the divisions only after the general office reviewed and approved forecasts. Moreover, because inventory commitments constituted working-capital expenditures, the owner-controlled Finance Committee retained ultimate authority over the approval of divisional forecasts.[44] In 1924, inventory controls were tightened by tying production and purchasing forecasts to actual new-car registrations.[45] *Capital controls* implemented similar restrictions on requests for fixed capital. Divisions requesting fixed capital were required to include detailed projections of funds needed and the uses to which they would be put.[46] Requests for new fixed capital were reviewed by the comptroller's office, headed by a Du Pont appointee, then by the owner-dominated Executive Committee and, if over specified limits, by the Finance Committee.[47] Nonetheless, such long-range capital requests relied on information and forecasts submitted and developed by the divisions, and the ability of owners to check this information remained limited.

The most important financial controls were those that measured divisional *return on invested capital*, thus allowing for comparison of divisional performance. Donaldson Brown devised a system that broke return on investment down into "the ratio of sales to profits [profit

---

43 Swayne (1924), reprinted in Chandler (1979).
44 See Donaldson Brown to Finance Committee, April 21, 1921, as quoted in Sloan (1964, p. 126).
45 On the development of inventory and production controls, see Chandler and Salsbury (1971, pp. 502–504); Sloan (1964, pp. 124–139).
46 Chandler (1962, p. 146). In addition, the four-month projections of inventory needs were expanded to include figures reflecting divisional investment in fixed and working capital at the end of each month, allowing headquarters to keep track of divisional investment in these areas. See Brown (1924, p. 196), reprinted in Chandler (1979).
47 Chandler and Salsbury (1971, p. 502).

Corporate Order: Decentralization at GM

margin] and the ratio of sales to investment [capital turnover]."[48] He then disaggregated profit margin and capital turnover into their constituent elements in order to show how various factors were affecting a division's return. Every month, division managers were required to fill out a report that recorded each element of return on investment.[49] These reports allowed divisions to operate as independent profit centers: by comparing the reports of the different divisions, the finance staff could evaluate the performance of each. In addition, the reports allowed the finance staff to determine more precisely which factors accounted for changes in divisional performance over time. Once this yardstick for measuring divisional performance was in place, two additional steps could be taken. First, bonus and incentive systems were created that tied divisional management's remuneration to the performance of their units. Second, Brown developed a "standard volume" method of accounting that allowed headquarters to evaluate performance and determine automobile prices without "the distortion of costs and inventory values" created by fluctuating volume. Together, these elements formed the heart of the incentives and sanctions supporting owner fiat over divisions and headquarters.[50]

The creation of situational sanctions and reliance on owner control from above significantly changed the nature of decentralization. The Du Pont M-form replaced Sloan's emphasis on political truce and consent with a notion of owner control through fiat. Through their control of the Finance Committee and Executive Committee, owners defined financial and operating policy virtually uncontested, putting them clearly in charge of the "value creation" aspect of strategic planning. By creating and administering financial control mechanisms, owners extended their control over capital within the firm and gained access to better information on corporate performance. Armed with improved information and increased control over key resources, they believed that these financial mechanisms would also allow them to ensure divisional compliance

---

48 Chandler (1962, p. 148). Mathematically, the rate of return on invested capital (R) is equal to the profit margin (P) multiplied by capital turnover (T), where profit margin is defined as net profit divided by net sales, and capital turnover is defined as net sales divided by total net investment. See Brown (1924; 1927).

49 Sloan (1964, p. 142). Sloan notes that the use of these forms was dependent on uniform accounting standards across divisions, which were implemented by Brown's finance staff in 1921 and formally approved by the Executive Committee and Finance Committee in April 1922. See also Chandler and Salsbury (1971, pp. 501–502).

50 Return-on-investment reports were not used to formulate "standard-volume" targets and accounting methods until around 1924. Sloan puts the date at 1925, but Brown clearly states that standard-volume accounting was in effect by 1924. See Sloan (1964, pp. 143–148); Brown (1924). Management compensation based on divisional performance was instituted in November 1923, under Sloan's presidency. See Sloan (1964, pp. 410–415).

to policies, thus ensuring loss prevention. Such control would be aided by the fact that owners had replaced the most important and independent division managers and had placed trusted allies in key positions within the general office. The head of GM's Finance Committee, Du Pont's John Raskob, expressed the owners' confidence when he reported to E. I. du Pont de Nemours' board of directors that "we are now in control of the company and are completely responsible for its politics and management."[51] His optimism would prove unwarranted. Despite building sophisticated mechanisms for owner control, governance through fiat would fail.

The Failure of Governance by Fiat

The period of direct owner control that began with Pierre du Pont's ascension to the presidency in December 1920 was by all accounts a failure. Although owners controlled decision-making, cash flows, investment decisions, and situational sanctions, they remained unable to extract divisional compliance to corporate policies. The clearest example of this came when Pierre launched a new competitive strategy designed to take on the industry leader, Ford, by producing a new type of "air-cooled" car. Through their control over manufacturing and engineering facilities and information, division managers resisted this strategy, delaying its implementation for years and demonstrating that owners could not extract cooperation through fiat alone. General office executives, led by Sloan, also opposed the new plan, albeit in a more limited way. They attempted to define Pierre's plan as an issue of operational administration that should be left up to the divisions, rather than a matter of strategic planning to be decided by owners in the Executive Committee. In doing so, they demonstrated that drawing the line between strategic and tactical planning was not simply an economic decision resting on technical grounds: what was policy and what was administration was a matter of intense political negotiation.

The struggle between owners and divisions began less than a month after Du Pont took control of GM. When Pierre took office as president, three of the five car-producing divisions – Chevrolet, Oakland, and Oldsmobile – were losing money.[52] Moreover, GM lacked a viable

51 John J. Raskob to Directors, E. I. du Pont de Nemours and Company, August 19, 1921. Longwood, 435 (27), v. 6, First Series, pp. 1639–1651. This is the cover memo to the "History of the du Pont Company's Investment in the General Motors Corporation," August 17, 1921. *U.S. v. Du Pont*, GTE #166.
52 Sloan (1964, p. 61). In addition to Chapter 5 of Sloan's autobiography, the best sources of information on the events surrounding the air-cooled car are Chandler and Salsbury (1971, Chapters 20–21); Leslie (1983).

Corporate Order: Decentralization at GM

product to compete with Ford, whose Model T accounted for more than 50 percent of automobiles sold in the United States. Pierre decided that the best way to compete with Ford was through the manufacture of a radically new air-cooled engine being developed by Charles Kettering, head of GM's research staff. With fewer parts and more efficient operation than conventional water-cooled engines, the new design (later known as the copper-cooled) promised lower production costs and better performance, a combination that could give GM the edge over Ford.[53] In January 1921 the Executive Committee began studying the viability of using the air-cooled design in Chevrolets; by early February the committee had decided that the engine would be developed for use in a low-priced Chevrolet designed to compete with the Model T. The decision to produce the air-cooled Chevrolet was "virtually an order," and by mid-month the Executive Committee had expanded the program to include cars produced in the Oakland division.[54] On February 23 the committee passed a directive that made the air-cooled engine the center of GM's competitive strategy in the low-priced field.

Sloan opposed attempts to put the new engine into production before it was tested and accepted by the divisions, and when he was unable to convince owners that caution was justified, Sloan attempted to define the program as a matter of operational administration outside the Executive Committee's purview. In April 1921 the Executive Committee appointed a special committee to work out the specifics of GM's competitive strategy. Headed by Sloan and composed of general office and divisional men, the group was instructed that the air-cooled engine would be the technology used to compete, and they were further advised that no changes were to be made at Buick and Cadillac, the two divisions producing a profit. Yet Sloan and his colleagues used this charge as an opportunity to oppose the air-cooled engine. Working together, they devised GM's "pricing pyramid," wherein each of GM's car divisions produced cars in a specific price class, from low-priced Chevrolets to high-priced Cadillacs.[55] The lowest-priced models would strive for the highest sales volume, while higher-priced cars would sell in lower volume but at greater profit per unit. Within each price class, GM's strategy would be to offer a higher-quality car than the competition at a somewhat higher price, hopefully luring buyers to GM. Sloan and his colleagues explicitly advised that the pricing pyramid made the air-cooled engine unnecessary: "the policy ... was valid if our cars were at least equal in design to the best of our competitors in a grade, so that it was not *necessary* to lead

53 Chandler (1962, p. 154). Chandler and Salsbury (1971, p. 518). Leslie (1983, p. 128).
54 Sloan (1964, p. 74). The information in the following paragraphs draws heavily on Sloan's account.
55 Sloan (1964, Chapter 4).

in design or run the risk of untried experiments."[56] The new policy also worked against the air-cooled program by restricting divisions to a single price class. Now, only Chevrolet would compete directly with Ford, making the air-cooled program unnecessary in the other divisions. Moreover, if the air-cooled program affected only one division, it was no longer an issue of policy as defined by Sloan's organization study. Instead, it was an issue of operational administration under the jurisdiction of the division manager rather than the Executive Committee. Sloan and his allies in management thus used the pricing pyramid as a tool in a political battle, attempting to redefine the air-cooled program as a matter of administration rather than policy.

The divisions resisted the air-cooled program even more overtly. Because the air-cooled design had been developed by GM's research labs in Dayton, rather than within the divisions, division managers regarded it as experimental and untested. They argued that it was not yet ready for mass production and would not perform well in the field, and they worried that the new design would disrupt production and prevent them from using up their "huge stock of materials and supplies for existing models."[57] Division managers used their control of manufacturing and engineering to resist the new program, for conversion to mass production and final testing rested with the divisions. At Chevrolet, general manager Karl Zimmerschied and his divisional engineers argued that modifications were necessary to bring the air-cooled engine to mass production. Fearing that the divisions were attempting to sabotage the car, Kettering and his staff in Dayton insisted that the engine design be left intact. Division engineers responded by making changes in ancillary components such as chassis and frames, thereby adding weight to the car and causing the engine to overheat and perform poorly.[58] An exasperated Kettering effectively gave up on Chevrolet and concentrated his efforts on Oakland's air-cooled program. But here, too, management derailed the air-cooled program within a matter of months. In November 1921 Oakland general manager George Hannum told Pierre that the car had failed its road test at the division. It would take at least six months before the engine could be successfully mass-produced, he claimed, for the copper fins designed to dissipate heat could not be reliably welded to the engine, as Dayton's plan proposed. Even more shocking, Hannum unilaterally decided to bring out a new line of water-cooled cars in place of the delayed air-cooled.[59] In one fell swoop, Oakland delayed the air-cooled project indefinitely, showing that even direct orders from the

56 Sloan (1964, pp. 65–66; emphasis in the original).
57 Chandler and Salsbury (1971, p. 516).   58 Leslie (1983, pp. 135–143).
59 Hannum's letter is reprinted in part in Sloan (1964, p. 78). On the manufacturing difficulties, see Cray (1980, p. 209).

Executive Committee and GM's president and chairman of the board were not enough to produce results.

Struggles over the air-cooled car produced a downward spiral of fiat and resistance. When divisional opposition failed to convince owners to abandon the air-cooled program, Sloan's general office began to oppose the program more openly. Early in 1922, for instance, Sloan convened a meeting between general office and divisional men. In violation of Executive Committee directives, they decided to reinstate research and development into conventional water-cooled engines at Chevrolet, creating dual air- and water-cooled programs in that division. In addition, the group decided that the air-cooled program should be abandoned at Oakland for the foreseeable future. Arguing that GM's research staff was busy with the air-cooled design, Sloan hired an outside consulting firm to oversee work on water-cooled development, probably so Pierre and the Executive Committee would not be able to exercise direct authority over these programs.[60] Owners responded with even greater use of fiat. In March 1922, Pierre du Pont appointed himself general manager of Chevrolet, putting former Ford production expert William Knudsen in charge of the air-cooled program there.[61] Together they vowed to put the air-cooled car into production as quickly as possible. Dismayed by this even more blatant use of force, Sloan and the general office began to "act as ... spokesman" for the divisions.[62] The issue came to a head in the Executive Committee on November 8, 1922. Sloan warned that the owners' plan to commit three divisions to the new engine was unwise; a furious du Pont countered "that the decision had been made by the Executive Committee some months ago."[63] A compromise was finally reached in which Oakland's air-cooled program was suspended; Oldsmobile was ordered to give up conventional water-cooled designs and begin production of air-cooled cars by August 1923, and Chevrolet was allowed to keep dual programs, though it would produce water-cooled designs until mass production of the new technology was fully worked out.

Despite this compromise, the combined resistance of divisions and headquarters killed the air-cooled program. Chevrolet produced several hundred air-cooled cars late in 1922, and in January 1923 the air-cooled was "the sensation of the show" at the annual automobile exhibit in New York.[64] Nonetheless, production of the new cars remained woefully

---

60 See Sloan (1964, pp. 81–83).
61 Sloan (1964, p. 83); Chandler and Salsbury (1971, p. 529). Cray (1980, p. 209) contends that former Chevy manager Zimmerschied left after suffering a "physical breakdown" and being hospitalized, purportedly due to stress resulting from the battle over the air-cooled car.
62 The quote is from Chandler and Salsbury (1971, p. 532).
63 Sloan (1964, p. 84).   64 Sloan (1964, p. 85).

behind schedule, and many of the cars that were sold experienced mechanical problems. Significantly, these difficulties did not relate simply to the air-cooled design, but also involved ancillary components and systems, the design and manufacture of which had been left in the hands of the divisions.[65] At the same time as these problems were being experienced, the demand for new automobiles shot to unprecedented heights. Sloan argued that the "only Chevrolet we had to sell was the old... water-cooled model"; trying to get the air-cooled to market under these conditions would simply mean the loss of profit and market share.[66] He thus urged that the air-cooled program be delayed. Pierre continued to support the air-cooled program, but he now advocated delaying the introduction of the air-cooled in order to take advantage of burgeoning demand. Sloan responded by turning up the political heat on Pierre. He discussed Chevrolet's proposed $18 million expansion plans with several GM board members and Finance Committee representatives, suggesting that expenditures should go to facilities for producing the proven water-cooled models. He reported the directors' worries about funding the air-cooled program back to Pierre, and he insisted that it was time for a final decision: Chevrolet could no longer afford to maintain a dual program.[67] Faced with the prospect of abandoning his pet project or spending millions on facilities for a car he knew was not ready for mass production, Pierre abdicated. On May 10, 1923, he resigned his position as president and chair of the Executive Committee, recommending that Sloan take his place in both positions. Ownership rule from above had failed.[68]

The story of the air-cooled engine demonstrates the difficulties of governing through fiat under conditions of complex interdependence. Existing analyses argue that du Pont's failure resulted from conflation between strategic planning and daily administration. They contend that by trying to set "both the policy and the program... on the most significant question that can come before a division, namely its engine and car design," the Executive Committee became involved in operating matters that it

---

[65] Sloan acknowledged that the problems did not relate to "the engine particularly" but to "the whole car." As quoted in Sloan (1964, p. 90). See also Chandler and Salsbury (1971, p. 695, n. 81). Note, however, that the engineering report conducted on the engine after Sloan became president – an evaluation carried out by division engineers – directly indicted the engine design itself. See Sloan (1964, p. 87).
[66] Sloan (1964, p. 86).   [67] Chandler and Salsbury (1971, pp. 533–534).
[68] Although Sloan quickly killed the air-cooled program from a practical standpoint, it continued to exist in a developmental form until 1925, when it finally reached the point that it was judged to be a viable product. But with Chevrolet poised to take away Ford's leadership in sales, there was no interest in pursuing the air-cooled, and the program was abandoned. See Chandler and Salsbury (1971, pp. 543–546, 557–558).

Corporate Order: Decentralization at GM

lacked sufficient knowledge to judge.[69] Yet this very conflation belies the fact that the distinction between policy and administration cannot be made simply on technical grounds. The air-cooled program met the definition of policy spelled out in Sloan's organization study of 1919: it addressed the long-range competitive strategy of the organization as a whole, it involved more than a single division, and it concerned the relations of the various divisions to one another and to the market. The problem, as Sloan would later acknowledge, was that "what would be policy and what would be administration ... could not be decided by a process of logic."[70] The definitions of planning and administration were themselves the outcomes of a political process of bargaining and negotiation.

Even more important, the air-cooled case shows that under conditions of complex interdependence, sanctions and fiat could not create acceptance of policies and consummate performance. Despite financial controls, domination of policy, and the ability to replace managers, governance by fiat failed because Pierre was unable to extract cooperation from the divisions. Indeed, he could not elicit compliance even by making himself general manager of Chevrolet. The failure of fiat occurred for two reasons. First, situational sanctions were necessarily incomplete, leaving divisions enough autonomy to resist the air-cooled program. Indeed, even when owners knew that resistance was occurring, they seemed powerless to combat it. Here, information was subordinate to consent: only by eliciting divisional cooperation could top executives also gain access to the personal knowledge that continued to escape the grasp of situational sanctions and financial control mechanisms, and only by generating consent could they hope to see policies implemented consummately. Second, as a result of their expertise and their areas of responsibility, divisional men believed that they should have a right to decide on the issue of the air-cooled engine. Division men "felt that 'idea men' in Dayton were too cavalier and too unconcerned about the basic engineering problems that had to be solved if the car was to be mass produced."[71] As Sloan would later argue, the issue was not simply a technical question of whether the air-cooled program was technically feasible; it was a question of "how to get [such a program] carried out where it had to be carried out, namely, in the divisions.... We have tried ... forcing the issue ... and we have failed. We have got to go at it in a different manner."[72]

69 Sloan (1964, p. 75).   70 Sloan (1964, p. 55).
71 Chandler and Salsbury (1971, p. 546). See also Alfred P. Sloan, Jr., to Charles Kettering, July 2, 1923, as quoted in Sloan (1964, pp. 89–91).
72 The first passage is from Sloan (1964, pp. 75–76); the second is from Alfred P. Sloan, Jr., to Charles Kettering, July 2, 1923, as quoted in Sloan (1964, pp. 90–91).

Transforming Corporate Authority

The experience of the air-cooled car reinforced Sloan's belief that corporate order could not be achieved through the use of situational sanctions and the exercise of fiat, but required consent. Issuing orders from above created resistance below, he believed, even if the orders were rational and efficient ones. Upon assuming the position of president in 1923, Sloan wasted no time in implementing a new version of decentralization aimed at creating consent between actors. Sloan took two related steps to implement his plan. First, he replaced fiat based on hierarchical position with a more consultative style of management involving persuasion, coercion, and bargaining between superiors and subordinates. Second, he pushed for changes in GM's top committee structure that would create divisional representation at the highest levels of strategic planning. This section focuses on the first step, arguing that the new management style instituted by Sloan constituted a transformation of authority that changed the way decisions were justified within the corporation. It is crucial to keep in mind, however, that by itself this new form of authority had only limited impact on relations between the general office and divisions. Only when combined with changes in GM's top committee structure did it generate consent. The following section thus focuses on such structural changes, examining how this new form of authority was institutionalized at the highest levels of GM's decision-making apparatus.

The transformation of authority that occurred under Sloan involved a shift away from the use of fiat based on formal authority that had characterized Pierre du Pont's regime. In its place, Sloan instituted a much more consultative style of top management in which authority became more firmly tied to technical expertise. This change marked a shift in the bases of order within the firm: authority would no longer be grounded in personal loyalty, as it had during Durant's regime,[73] but neither would it rely primarily on the exercise of fiat, as it had under du Pont. Instead, it would be based in a form of rational persuasion or influence; rather than issuing orders in an effort to extract compliance from subordinates, top executives under Sloan would go to great lengths to spell out the *reasons* for their directives and to convince subordinates via "factual" arguments that proposed policies would prove to be efficacious. An explicit tenet of this new leadership style was that rather than blindly

---

[73] Chandler and Salsbury emphasize that the shift away from personal loyalty as the dominant source of authority and influence began with du Pont. This should not be taken to mean that the du Pont and Sloan regimes were unconcerned with questions of loyalty, only that there was a relative shift in the bases of authority.

accepting orders from above, subordinates could draw on their knowledge and experience to contest decisions. This transformation of authority would play a key role in shaping the methods that Sloan used in attempting to generate consent within GM.

At the heart of this transformation was a mode of persuasion that Sloan and his colleagues referred to as "selling."[74] The basic idea behind selling was that actors' influence in the decision-making process would be grounded primarily in knowledge and expertise rather than in formal authority *per se*. In attempting to gain support for prospective policies and decisions, actors were expected to use both actual knowledge and judgment based on expertise as the means of convincing others to accept proposed policies. In the version of selling promulgated by Sloan in the 1920s, the general office was required to sell the divisions on proposed changes. Cognizant of GM's history of divisional autonomy, Sloan emphasized repeatedly that the role of the general office staff was advisory in nature: neither the emerging technical staff nor the new group executives would hold any line authority over division managers. At least in theory, if these executives wished to implement new policies or practices that affected the divisions, they had to convince operating management to accept such changes through a process of persuasion. Indeed, because Sloan believed that issuing orders to subordinates would only provoke resistance from below, he argued that even executives who held line authority should utilize persuasion, rather than relying on fiat. In this context, subordinates could in principle gain input into decisions and contest policies by defending their positions via factual arguments.

Insofar as existing accounts have examined that selling, they have tended to dismiss it as a form of ideology designed to co-opt divisional interests. Organization theory has long maintained that the advisory role of staff executives is often a convenient fiction in practice, while "suggestions" from top executives who possess line authority may be tantamount to orders, even though they are presented in the form of advice.[75] Similarly, in examining GM's arrangements, Kuhn argues that Sloan "had designed a decision-making atmosphere where only a fool would not know what the chief wanted and what he would reward," and he contends that "division managers [would] want to heed the 'advice' of ... important corporate executives before it became an order."[76] He con-

---

74 See Sloan (1964, pp. 433–434). Note, however, that the discussion of "selling" found there describes the situation in the 1960s, not the 1920s; the relative balance of power between the divisions and the general office had shifted significantly between the two periods, as will be discussed in subsequent chapters.
75 See the discussions in Simon (1976, pp. 126–130).
76 Kuhn (1986, especially Chapter 6). Kuhn's conclusion is influenced by the fact that

cludes that selling was little more than an ideology used to mask increasing centralization by the general office. And indeed, attempts to influence subordinates through rational persuasion were often accompanied by coercion. The emergence of selling neither eliminated reliance on hierarchical authority nor led to a form of democratic governance in which participants met as equals, deciding issues strictly on the basis of available information and expertise.[77] Yet even though selling did not eliminate coercion, neither was it merely an ideology manipulated at will by general office executives in order to co-opt subordinates. Rather, it transformed the nature of corporate authority in a way that provided the divisions with at least limited room for resistance.

At the most general level, selling involved the institutionalization of a new language or new "rules of the game" for justifying decisions. These implicit rules required subordinates and top executives alike to "make a good case for what they propose[d]" by defending their positions "against well-informed and sympathetic criticism."[78] In doing so, actors were expected to utilize particular types of information and appeal to specific forms of expertise; those who did not rely on these forms of justification had little hope of generating support for their proposals. This emphasis on an appeal to the facts placed implicit limits on the use of overt fiat by creating the normative expectation that policies could and would be defended rationally. Top executives who simply issued orders openly violated the norm of justification explicit in selling, and thereby risked disrupting order within the firm. The necessity of adhering to at least the form of rational decision-making meant that fiat based on orders gave way to less direct forms of pressure that combined coercion and persuasion. Within this context, the creation of financial controls and the control of investment funds gave the general office significant leverage over the divisions. Yet the abstract information provided by financial controls was rarely sufficient to create uncontested general office domination, for much of the data used by these controls originated in the divisions, and operating management often had a considerably

---

his study terminated with the reorganization of 1937, perhaps the most centralized period in GM's history. Moreover, Kuhn often recognizes that Sloan's leadership was characterized by a form of *realpolitik* in which "Sloan accepted only the amount of decentralization that was forced on him" (p. 114). Had his study combined this insight with an analysis of the changes that occurred after 1940, he might have altered his conclusions. It is important to note, however, that Kuhn's argument focuses on issues of information processing, and pays little attention to processes of consent.

77 Indeed, to the modern reader the association of the term "selling" with the practice of advertising may well suggest using information in a selective and distorted way, a meaning that was not absent in the GM context, especially in later years, as will be discussed later.

78 Sloan (1964, p. 433).

more detailed understanding of the issues at hand than did their counterparts at headquarters. Moreover, the norm of selling limited headquarters' ability to rely on simple fiat too extensively. Selling therefore resulted in a form of authority that rested less on the formal right to issue orders and more on rational justification. This does not mean that fiat disappeared; rather, it was a tool of last resort, to be used only in extreme cases.

The limits on fiat created by the norm of selling became apparent early in Sloan's tenure as president. In early 1924, general office executives argued that the divisions needed to reduce their inventory levels because of poor sales. Division managers resisted these efforts, challenging general office statistics and arguing that inventories were needed because business would improve in the near future. Headquarters did not respond by issuing orders, even though GM's financial staff had for months possessed independent information indicating that divisional forecasts for sales were "unreasonably high."[79] Instead, Sloan's general office reacted to divisional resistance by pressuring managers to confront the inconsistencies in their claims. Acknowledging that some division managers had challenged headquarters' data concerning the number of cars produced by the divisions and the number of cars still unsold, Sloan noted that both sets of figures originated in "the final ... reports you send in to my office. ... If these figures are wrong then the error must be within your Division because we simply used the figures as you sent them to us."[80] He went on to note that "if there are errors it will be important to develop [why they occurred] so that we can do better next time," in effect putting the divisions on notice that their claims had to be consistent with the facts they presented.[81] Only when continuing divisional resistance led to the brink of crisis in May 1924 did Sloan issue "one of the few flat orders I ever gave to the division managers," commanding them to cut production immediately.[82] When headquarters implemented new methods for determining inventory levels in July 1924, it did so only after general executives and divisional managers reached agreement on the methods to be used.[83] Even then, division managers continued to par-

---

79 Donaldson Brown to Alfred P. Sloan, Jr., December 20, 1923, as quoted in Hayford (1955, p. 24).
80 Alfred P. Sloan, Jr., to H. H. Bassett, A. B. C. Hardy, George Hannum, W. S. Knudsen, and H. H. Rice, March 17, 1924. Reproduced in full in Hayford (1955, pp. 16a–16b).
81 Alfred P. Sloan, Jr., to H. H. Bassett, A. B. C. Hardy, George Hannum, W. S. Knudsen, and H. H. Rice, March 17, 1924. Reproduced in full in Hayford (1955, pp. 16a–16b).
82 Sloan (1964, p. 131).
83 See Hayford (1955, pp. 20, 28–31); Alfred P. Sloan, Jr., to Operations Committee, April 24, 1924, quoted in Hayford (1955, p. 27); Alfred P. Sloan, Jr., to Operations Committee, November 28, 1924, reproduced in full in Hayford (1955, p. 20a); Sloan (1964, pp. 131–136).

ticipate in approving inventory levels, and the general office remained hesitant to overturn divisional estimates. In late September 1924, for instance, almost three months after the new methods had been implemented, Sloan continued to complain that it was "not at all unusual for us to receive information from Divisions in this office which is so glaringly wrong there is no use . . . accepting it."[84] In one case, for instance, a division's car deliveries to customers were found to be only 50 percent of the figure reported by the division. Nonetheless, headquarters responded only with admonitions to do better in the future.

The style of authority implemented by selling was very different from the version of fiat practiced by Du Pont and advocated by TCE. Nonetheless, selling probably would have remained relatively unimportant if it had remained simply a generalized language for justifying decisions and mediating relations between staff and line. But the emphasis on selling was accompanied by structural changes in the constitution of GM's top governing committees, a fact that has remained largely unrecognized in the literature. More specifically, Sloan made structural changes to the M-form that created divisional representation and participation on these committees. It was this combination of structural change and the institutionalization of selling at the highest levels that played a crucial role in completing the transformation of authority within the firm. As long as selling remained at the level of general staff–line relations, top executives could exert pressure on division managers by isolating them and using reward and the threat of punishment. Within top committees charged with planning for the corporation as a whole, however, such coercion was more difficult. Here, the emphasis on appeal to the facts encouraged by selling gave divisions a means of resistance. Because each of the car divisions served a distinct market, each could claim to have access to unique knowledge and information that needed to be taken into account when considering proposed policies. Moreover, insofar as they participated formally in the planning process, division managers were able to vote directly on proposed policies, making general office domination more difficult. In the next section, I turn to the structural modifications introduced by Sloan after he assumed GM's presidency.

The Struggle for Participative Decentralization

Alfred Sloan's ascendance to the position of president is generally regarded as the beginning of GM's long record of spectacular perfor-

---

84 Alfred P. Sloan, Jr., to Bassett, Hannum, Hardy, Knudsen, Rice, Stoll (division managers), September 23, 1924, reprinted in full in Hayford (1955, p. 19a).

mance. The primary source of this success is said to be the fact that under Sloan's leadership the corporation finally erected a clear distinction between strategic and tactical planning, thus creating the necessary basis for successful decentralization. In this section I argue that the notion of general office rule via the textbook M-form is a myth. Alfred Sloan did not set out to make policy the exclusive province of top executives, but sought instead to incorporate interested parties, including the divisions, in the strategic planning and resource allocation process. He did so in the belief that such participation would help to create consent. Yet this strategy was not simply a return to the radical decentralization that had prevailed under Durant, for it was predicated on both the financial controls implemented by Du Pont and the institutionalization of selling, which constrained headquarters and changed the nature of divisional participation in the planning process. Sloan's version of participative decentralization was not a system in which the divisions had unencumbered control over strategic planning, but one in which interested parties attempted to hammer out a political compromise acceptable to all.

Sloan's efforts to create consent were hindered by owners, who adamantly opposed the idea of including divisions directly in the planning process. Distrustful of operating managers who had come up under Durant, and convinced that the divisions had played a large role in both the crisis of 1921 and the failure of the air-cooled car, owners continued to believe that planning should be carried out by general executives free from divisional allegiances and that these plans should remain subject to owner veto from above. Believing that divisional participation in planning would lead only to self-serving opportunism on the part of managers, owners used their control of key committees and their power over financial resources, situational sanctions, and personnel decisions as means of preventing significant changes in either formal organizational structure or the membership of top decision-making committees. Stymied in his efforts to include division managers on the committees formally and legally responsible for policy formulation, Sloan attempted to create such participative decentralization through informal practices that he hoped would achieve the same effect. Because his efforts remained at the informal level, participative decentralization was less successful during this period than it would be later in GM's history. Nonetheless, the period from 1923 to 1933 shows clearly Sloan's reasons for pursuing participative decentralization, and it demonstrates how owners' and managers' divergent philosophies of governance led to a struggle over GM's organizational form that would continue for more than thirty years.

The driving force behind participative decentralization was Sloan's belief that divisional participation in planning and decision-making would create the consent necessary for consummate performance. Throughout his long career, Sloan argued repeatedly that if the divisions were to work voluntarily toward the implementation of policies, they had to accept those policies as their own. The key to generating binding policies, he believed, was not to create a firm separation between strategic and tactical planning, but to allow the divisions to take part in the policy formulation process.

> Even if one man could formulate correct decisions for an organization like ours, he could not get them received sympathetically or acted upon immediately with the necessary understanding and zeal. [Policies] must come from the men who are in daily contact with the problems. . . .
> Everything possible in the organization starts from the bottom. That is where it must and will be carried out, and it is carried out better and sooner if it starts there.[85]

In this context, issues of information were subordinate to and outweighed by issues of consent and consummate performance. If top executives formulated policies and ordered operating management to implement them, divisional management was likely to resist these policies or implement them in perfunctory fashion. When Sloan took over in May 1923 as president of GM and chairman of the Executive Committee, he thus set out to create consent by including divisional management in the formulation of long-range planning and resource allocation.

Sloan's earliest efforts at building consent focused on the creation of interdivisional relations committees in functional areas such as purchasing and engineering.[86] These groups brought together divisional personnel and general office executives to discuss plans and problems within each functional area. Sloan and at least one other member of the Executive Committee served on each of the committees, which were usually chaired by a general office representative.[87] Created in direct response to the experience of the air-cooled car, the interdivisional committees were intended to engender cooperation and communication between staff and line. Committee meetings provided a forum for exchanging information and ironing out differences of opinion on technical matters. Members could discuss the issues raised by decisions made in top governing com-

---

85 Sloan (1924, pp. 194, 140–141).
86 By 1924 there were five interdivisional committees in the areas of purchasing, sales, technical, works managers, and power and maintenance. See Chandler (1962, pp. 155–157); Chandler and Salsbury (1971, pp. 546–549); Sloan (1964, pp. 103–114); Kuhn (1986, pp. 182–185).
87 Chandler (1962, p. 156).

mittees, and they could offer suggestions that might be forwarded to the Executive Committee as proposals. But most of the committees held no authority to implement policy or to issue orders to the divisions. Contrasting this setup to Du Pont's style of governance through fiat, Sloan emphasized that the committees would promote cooperation between staff and line and commented that "we are going to be fully repaid for the way we have handled it as compared with a more military style which I do not think would ever put us anywhere."[88] Despite his enthusiasm for the new arrangement, however, Sloan realized that it did not give division managers the chance to participate as equals in the policy formulation process, making it of only limited use in producing consent.

Sloan turned to a second, more direct strategy for creating consent in mid-1924, when he put key division managers directly on the Executive Committee. As early as the end of 1921, well before he became president, Sloan had attempted to convince Pierre to expand the Executive Committee to include both division managers and general office executives. Pierre had added two new men to the committee in December 1922, nearly a year after Sloan made his recommendations, but neither was a division manager.[89] In mid-1924, Sloan added five more men to the Executive Committee, two of whom were or soon would be division managers.[90] With these additions the committee was transformed from a small, owner-run group into a committee of ten with representatives from ownership, general office, and divisions. Sloan later dismissed the appointments of the two division men as exceptions to organization theory, but such "exceptions" persisted for decades and followed a clear pattern: managers of the largest and most profitable operations were placed directly on the committee in charge of strategic planning.[91] Later analysts have agreed that these moves were compatible with a traditional

---

88 Sloan (1964, p. 111).
89 The two members added by du Pont were Charles Mott, head of the advisory staff and group executive of the car and truck group, and Fred Fisher, president of the partially owned Fisher Body subsidiary. See Chandler and Salsbury (1971, pp. 525–526). Sloan (1964, pp. 100–101).
90 Sloan's additions were as follows: Harry Bassett, general manager of Buick; Lawrence Fisher, who would later become head of Cadillac; Charles Fisher of Fisher Body; Donaldson Brown of the GM finance staff; and John Pratt, group executive over the Accessories Group. All were appointed on September 25, 1924. Du Pont's J. A. Haskell retired from the Executive Committee in September 1923. After Sloan's changes, the committee thus consisted of the following: Sloan; Pierre du Pont; Raskob; Bassett; Brown; Fred, Charles, and Lawrence Fisher; Mott; and Pratt. See General Motors Corporation, "General Motors Corporation Executive Committee," February 12, 1952. Longwood, 441 (33), First Series, v. 32. General Motors Corporation, *Annual Report*, 1923, 1924.
91 Sloan (1964, p. 113).

M-form, since the divisional men on the Executive Committee were too few in number to pursue their own particularistic agendas with any success. Thus, the Executive Committee "clearly made the significant entrepreneurial and strategic decisions" at GM, and within this group "general officers rather than division managers" dominated.[92]

Sloan's original intent was not to put one or two division managers on the Executive Committee, however, but to create participative decentralization by appointing *all* of the general managers from the car and truck divisions to that group. When he became president in 1923, Sloan revived the Operations Committee that Pierre had allowed to atrophy. Officially the Operations Committee was depicted as one of the interdivisional relations committees, designed to bring together division managers with Executive Committee members to engender "a common understanding" of policy through discussion and debate.[93] Yet Sloan's intention was to convert this group of division managers and general executives into the Executive Committee, replacing the general office–dominated Executive Committee with one in which all of the car and truck divsions would be represented directly.[94] Available evidence suggests that owners ultimately thwarted this plan. Because the Executive Committee was legally a subcommittee of the board, all Executive Committee members had to be directors of the corporation. The Operations Committee, on the other hand, was not a legal subcommittee of the board, and its members therefore did not have to be directors. If the Operations Committee was to be given any legal authority to make decisions, or if it was to be merged with the Executive Committee as Sloan proposed, all members would have to be placed on the board. Owners steadfastly refused to appoint more division managers either to the Executive Committee or to the board during this period, effectively preventing Sloan from implementing formal participative decentralization.

When he could not create participative decentralization by placing all the division managers directly on the Executive Committee, Sloan began informally to cede much of the strategic planning function to the Operations Committee. Following the inventory crisis of 1924, for example, Sloan decided that the Operations Committee rather than individual division managers would approve the index volume that served as an estimate of production and sales for the next year.[95] Although decisions made by the Operations Committee had to be approved by the Executive Committee, over time the latter body seems to have become more

---

92 Chandler (1962, pp. 157–158). 93 Sloan (1964, p. 113).
94 Alfred P. Sloan to Lammot du Pont, April 15, 1931. Longwood, 430 (22), First Series, v. 15, pp. 4546–4547.
95 Sloan (1964, pp. 134–135).

of a formality, rubber-stamping decisions made by the former. Systematic data on the substance of decisions made by the Operations Committee and Executive Committee are not available, but the information that is suggests that the group came to control policy more directly as time went on. It recommended GM's venture into the tire and rubber industry, was involved in the decision of whether GM should enter the locomotive business, and recommended to the Finance Committee that GM venture into the airplane industry.[96] In 1932 it "adopted a radical revision" of the corporation's pricing pyramid, indicating that by that time the Operations Committee was deeply involved in shaping the most fundamental matters of corporate policy.[97] Sloan later acknowledged that although the Executive Committee was legally in charge of formulating policy, "it met jointly with the Operations Committee, and because decisions were made with the participation of both policy and operating people, the line between policy and administration was not sharply enough drawn," giving the Operations Committee enormous informal influence.[98] In unpublished documents he went further, referring to the later dissolution of the Operations Committee as a move that "restored" the Executive Committee to its position as the "top group."[99]

Although there are limited data concerning the extent of the Operations Committee's power in decision-making, there is considerably more evidence that Sloan's intention was to incorporate division managers into the strategic planning and allocation process as a means of creating consent. This became particularly clear after May 1929, when Lammot du Pont took over from his brother Pierre as GM's chairman of the board. The transfer of the chairmanship itself may have created bad feelings between owners and general office. Pierre's resignation occurred after Sloan forced Finance Committee chairman John Raskob out of office. Raskob was appointed chairman of the national Democratic party in the summer of 1928. Insisting that it would be improper for a top corporate executive to be involved in partisan politics, Sloan demanded Raskob's resignation as Finance Committee chairman. Banking on his immense power, Pierre threatened to resign as chairman of the board if

---

[96] On the tire venture, see General Motors Corporation, "Minutes from Joint Meeting of Operations and Executive Committees, July 17, 1930." *U.S. v. Du Pont*, DTE #GM286. "Minutes of Operations Committee, October 9, 1930." *U.S. v. Du Pont*, GTE #1091. On airplane acquisitions, see General Motors Corporation, "Operations Committee Minutes, October 29, 1931." Longwood, 430 (22), First Series, v. 24, pp. 4696–4697. "Finance Committee Minutes, November 2, 1931." Longwood, 430 (22), First Series, v. 24, pp. 4698–4699. The committee's role in the decision on the locomotive business is described in John Pratt to Operations and Finance Committees, October 21, 1929, Accession 542, Box 849.
[97] Sloan (1964, p. 177).   [98] Sloan (1964, p. 178).
[99] Sloan (ca. 1962, Chapter 10, p. 25).

Raskob was forced out. But to his surprise, Sloan brought the matter before the Executive Committee where – supported largely by the Fisher brothers who, like Sloan, were staunch Republicans – a split vote favoring Raskob's resignation resulted. The matter then went before the board, which, again in a split decision, voted to accept Raskob's offer of resignation but refused to accept Pierre's, granting him a leave of absence until after the election. Although Pierre and Raskob remained on GM's board and returned to the Finance Committee after the election, both gave up active participation in GM's affairs. Raskob resigned as chair of the Finance Committee on August 9, 1928, to be replaced by Donaldson Brown. Pierre's resignation as chairman of the board came on February 7, 1929, the same day that Lammot took over that position.[100]

Troubled by Sloan's brand of participative decentralization, and probably upset at the role Sloan played in Pierre's resignation, Lammot pushed for changes in GM's organization. In September 1929, the Operations Committee began meeting only in joint session with the Executive Committee, probably to forestall any potential legal objections to its involvement in policy matters.[101] Together representatives from the two bodies discussed and decided on corporate policies. The Operations Committee made decisions and then presented them as "recommendations" to the Executive Committee, which ratified them via a formal vote. This arrangement at least made it clear that formal authority rested with the Executive Committee. More important, divisional representatives on the Operations Committee were replaced by members of the general office staff. Concomitant with Lammot's assumption of the chairmanship, four division managers were removed from the Operations Committee, along with three general office executives.[102] At the same time,

100 The story of Raskob and Pierre's resignations is told in Chandler and Salsbury (1971, pp. 564–587); Cray (1980, pp. 260–262); Burk (1990, pp. 54–55). Chandler and Salsbury report that Pierre resigned as chairman of the board in summer of 1928, when he was granted a leave of absence, but materials drawn up by GM counsel indicate that he remained in office until February 1929. See General Motors Corporation, "Members of Board of Directors and Principal Executive Offices Held and Officers Who Were Not Directors, 1917–1948." Longwood, 438 (30), First Series, v. 32, p. 9593.

101 General Motors Corporation, "General Motors Corporation Operations Committee," document prepared by GM legal staff, December 17, 1951. Longwood, 441 (33), First Series, v. 32. Legal objections would arise if the Operating Committee, which was not a legal entity holding board powers, was seen as formulating or approving GM policy. See Alfred P. Sloan to Lammot du Pont, April 15, 1931. Longwood, 430 (22), First Series, v. 15, pp. 4546–4547.

102 Those removed were Alfred Glancy, Gordon Lefebvre, Irving Reuter, and Edward Strong, general managers of Oakland, GM Canada, Olds, and Buick, respectively; Charles Mott, vice-president of the advisory staff and group executive of the car and truck group; E. F. Johnson, assistant group executive over parts and accessories; and

five men from headquarters were placed on the Operations Committee, four of whom were simultaneously promoted to positions as corporate vice-presidents.[103] The only divisional men who remained on the Operations Committee were Chevrolet's William Knudsen and Lawrence Fisher of Cadillac, both of whom sat on the Executive Committee. These changes transformed the Operations Committee from an arena of discussion and consent between divisions and general office to a committee composed almost exclusively of general office representatives, depriving Sloan of his primary mechanism for incorporating division managers into the strategic planning process.

Having transformed the membership of the Operations Committee, Lammot sought to merge it with the Executive Committee to create a single group legally in charge of policy formulation.[104] By merging the committees, he hoped to allow owners to clearly identify those responsible for policy formulation and resource allocation decisions. Moreover, Lammot probably believed that merger would put an end to the legal difficulties created by the split between the two bodies, for even though there were no longer divisional representatives on the Operations Committee, it was still the case that not all Operations Committee members were on GM's board. Specifically, the new staff vice-presidents – Bradley, Grant, Hunt, and Wilson – were not yet directors. If the Operations Committee was to be merged with the Executive Committee, the four men would have to become board members, a move that Lammot now favored. Undoubtedly aware that Sloan wished to reinstate division managers to the Operations Committee at a future date in order to restore participative decentralization, however, Lammot was careful to note that his recommendation to merge the committees and place the staff men on the board was contingent on the Operations Committee remaining a body composed of general office rather than divisional men. Writing to Sloan, he noted that if the Operations Committee and Executive Committee were merged, "all of the Vice-Presidents will be members of the Board, except [division managers] Glancy, Reuter and Strong, but I see no particular reason for adding any of them to the Board."[105] Like Pierre

> Alfred Swayne, chairman of GMAC. See "General Motors Corporation Operations Committee," and compare to the 1927 organization chart. Note, too, that all three of the general office men removed held line authority over operating groups. Owners would later argue that group executives like these men should be precluded from the Executive Committee because of their lack of time and their interests in specific operations. See Chapters 4–7 herein.

103 The new general office men on the Operating Committee were as follows: John T. Smith, vice-president in charge of New York's legal staff; Albert Bradley, Richard Grant, Ormond Hunt, and Charles Wilson, who were named vice-presidents of finance, sales, engineering, and manufacturing, respectively.
104 Lammot du Pont to Alfred Sloan, April 22, 1930. *U.S. v. Du Pont*, GTE #190.
105 Lammot du Pont to Alfred Sloan, April 22, 1930. *U.S. v. Du Pont*, GTE #190.

before him, Lammot thus moved to make strategic planning the exclusive province of general office executives.

Sloan also favored merging the Operations Committee and Executive Committee, but only if in doing so he could place division managers back on the Executive Committee in order to reincorporate them into the strategic planning process. Still convinced that direct divisional participation in planning was the best way to create consent, Sloan argued that Lammot's plan would create psychological and motivational problems in the divisions. He maintained that if the Operations Committee was to be eliminated, the new Executive Committee should be expanded to include the three divisional managers not already on that body. Without divisional participation in strategic planning, consent would be impaired and policies resisted. Sloan agreed with Lammot that it was not necessary for division managers to be on the Executive Committee from a practical point of view; general executives were sufficiently informed to carry out planning and resource allocation. But, he went on to argue, "from the psychological standpoint" the inclusion of division managers was "very essential," for without it morale and motivation would be "jeopardized."[106] Arguing that the continuing omission of division managers from the Executive Committee was "already a source of embarrassment," Sloan contended that adding staff men to the Executive Committee while continuing to omit division managers would only make matters worse.[107] He thus preferred to keep the Operations Committee and Executive Committee separate, to avoid giving the impression that staff men were being elevated to the Executive Committee while division managers were being omitted. Such a move would destroy morale and create resistance in the operating end of the organization. An irritated Lammot responded by reminding Sloan that it was the prerogative of owners to choose representatives to GM's top governing committees. There was "no indication that any of the stockholders want [division managers] Reuter, Strong and Eddins to represent them," Lammot wrote, though "some influential [stockholders] want Bradley, Wilson, Hunt and Grant to represent them because [they] took the initiative in putting them on what amounts to an Executive Committee."[108] Despite his obvious irritation, however, Lammot did not force the

106 Alfred P. Sloan, Jr., to Lammot du Pont, April 12, 1931. Longwood, 430 (22), First Series, v. 15, pp. 4548–4550.
107 Alfred P. Sloan, Jr., to Lammot du Pont, April 12, 1931. Longwood, 430 (22), First Series, v. 15, pp. 4548–4550.
108 Lammot du Pont to Alfred P. Sloan, Jr., April 18, 1931. Longwood, 430 (22), First Series, v. 15, p. 4544. Dan Eddins was Glancy's replacement following a shuffling of division managers. Lammot's admission that the Operating Committee "amounts to" an Executive Committee was an admission that owners also understood just how much authority the Operating Committee had assumed in the planning process.

changes on Sloan, and the disagreement continued for nearly three years, from late 1929 to early 1932.

Sloan's desire to reincorporate division managers in strategic planning was particularly acute because of another change implemented by owners that has gone unnoticed in the literature. Between 1929 and 1931, owners sought to strengthen control over the divisions by redefining the role of group executives. Sloan's original plan called for group executives to serve in a strictly advisory capacity to the divisions, thus preserving divisional autonomy. Still seeking to rein in the divisions and govern via fiat, however, Lammot and his colleagues decided that group executives should have line authority over the divisions.[109] Like the decision to replace division managers on the Operations Committee, this development promised to limit divisional discretion. Sloan worried that this change would exacerbate tensions by creating the impression that advisory staff were being given authority over the historically autonomous divisions. Again, Sloan acknowledged that the owners' decision made sense "from the strictly theoretical standpoint," but he went on to question whether owners understood the consequences that this action would have "on the morale and attitude" of the divisions.[110]

The depth of Sloan's commitment to reinstating participative decentralization became clear during the Great Depression, which began only months after Lammot's changes to the Operations Committee. Severe economic contraction required cutting costs to the bone. Sloan agreed with owners that the best way to reduce costs was to centralize productive facilities.[111] Unlike owners, however, Sloan worried that attempts to increase centralization would provoke further divisional resistance to the growing strength of general office staff. Division managers and group executives already complained that there was an "alarming tendency towards centralization" in the staff-dominated Operations Committee.[112] If the general office was going to centralize operations, it had to avoid

---

109 Alfred P. Sloan, Jr., to Lammot du Pont, April 21, 1931. Longwood, 430 (22), First Series, v. 15, pp. 4549–4550. The letter indicates that the decision to grant group executives line authority was made by Lammot, Donaldson Brown, and "John." The latter probably refers to group executive John Pratt, a former Du Pont executive, but it could refer to Raskob or John Smith.

110 Alfred P. Sloan, Jr., to Lammot du Pont, April 21, 1931. Longwood, 430 (22), First Series, v. 15, pp. 4549–4550. Over the long run, the decision to give group executives line authority also made those men partisan parties in the planning and allocation process. With authority over and responsibility for specific operations, group executives, as much as division managers, sought to further their own interests in the planning and allocation process. See the preceding note 102 and Williamson (1975, pp. 153–154, n. 20).

111 Sloan (1964, pp. 170–178).

112 Group executive John Pratt, as quoted in Sloan (1964, p. 175). Not surprisingly, staff executives believed that the depression called for increased centralization.

exacerbating divisional resistance. Sloan thus argued that centralization should be accompanied by renewed divisional representation on the Executive Committee. Such a move would make it clear that centralization was an emergency response to economic conditions and not a move to increase staff power over the divisions. Owners balked at this suggestion, and the disagreement dragged on for nearly three years, as GM's profits sank precipitously. In 1932, during the depth of the depression, Sloan finally got his way. Early in 1932, Lammot proposed emergency measures of extreme centralization: the five car divisions would be consolidated into two or three larger units, thereby drastically reducing costs.[113] Du Pont also recommended that the Executive Committee be reduced in size by eliminating both division managers and group executives. Finally, he hinted that he would soon cede his position as chairman of the board to Sloan, making it necessary to consider who would take over as president. Lammot suggested Lawrence Fisher of Cadillac or William Knudsen of Chevrolet as possible candidates, especially if they were each to head one of the combined car divisions.

Most of Lammot's suggestions were instituted in March 1932, when manufacturing operations of Pontiac (formerly Oakland) and Chevrolet were combined under William Knudsen's management, making him the heir apparent to GM's presidency.[114] Buick and Oldsmobile were combined in similar fashion, with Irving Reuter in charge. Cadillac, under the leadership of Lawrence Fisher, was the only unit producing a single line of automobiles. Centralization also occurred in sales: Buick, Oldsmobile, and Pontiac sales were consolidated into a new BOP sales company, while Chevrolet and Cadillac maintained separate sales organizations. GM was thus "reduced from five to three car divisions" for almost two years.[115] Yet on the issue of divisional participation in planning, a compromise was struck. Knudsen and Lawrence Fisher, division managers of Chevrolet and Cadillac, would remain on the Executive Committee. In addition, Irving Reuter and William Fisher, general managers of Buick-Olds and Fisher Body, were added to the Operations Committee in April 1932.[116] Because Lammot refused to acquiesce and make Reuter and Fisher directors, the split between Executive Committee and Operations Committee remained, with the latter doing most of the work

---

113 Lammot du Pont to Alfred P. Sloan, February 12, 1932. Longwood, 430 (22), First Series, v. 16, pp. 4800–4801.
114 In October 1933 Knudsen was given the title of executive vice-president, giving him authority over all of the car divisions. See General Motors Corporation, *Annual Report*, 1933, p. 12.
115 Sloan (1964, p. 177).
116 General Motors Corporation, "General Motors Corporation Operations Committee." The reorganization of divisions led to the retirement of Buick's Strong and Oldsmobile's Eddins.

in formulating policy. Despite Lammot's explicit recommendations to the contrary, then, consolidation of operations was accompanied by more rather than less divisional participation in strategic planning. Although the depression did result in the centralization of productive facilities and increasing staff intervention into what had once been divisional prerogatives, Sloan was careful to ensure that this change was effected not through fiat, but through increased divisional participation in the planning process.

Summary

From the outset, owners and managers adhered to somewhat different versions of decentralization. Owners favored an M-form that gave them firm control over both the Finance Committee and the Executive Committee and that allowed them to govern via fiat. Yet during the period from 1921 to 1923, owners' efforts to govern through fiat failed. Acceptance of Pierre's policies could not be secured through force and situational sanctions. By usurping divisional prerogatives, owners virtually assured resistance from below, as divisions used their knowledge and control of manufacturing and engineering to delay and sabotage the air-cooled engine. Despite their control of investment funds and situational sanctions, owners remained unable to quell this resistance. Indeed, even Pierre's efforts to move the air-cooled car forward by assuming control of Chevrolet were unsuccessful. Alfred Sloan, on the other hand, instinctively understood that the maintenance of internal order required voluntary compliance from all sectors of the corporation, and he knew that GM's history of divisional autonomy made the consent of operating management particularly crucial. He thus sought to create an M-form that relied more on persuasion and coercion rather than outright force. Moreover, contrary to existing accounts, he did not set out to create corporate order by erecting a rigid distinction between strategic and tactical planning. To the contrary, he realized that doing so would lead to continued failure. Between 1923 and 1933, Sloan attempted to generate voluntary acceptance of policies by blurring the boundaries between strategic and tactical planning. He believed that the divisions should be actively and directly involved in long-range planning, for if they helped to formulate policies, they would accept them more readily and enact them more consummately. Sloan believed that the transformation of attitudes rested not on force, but on voluntary compliance; it sprang from a shift in intentions, not from the manipulation of situational sanctions. He thus attempted to institute participative decentralization as a means of creating consent.

Sloan's efforts to create participative decentralization were limited by owners, who opposed efforts to include the divisions in strategic planning and who used their power to prevent division managers from being eligible to serve on the Executive Committee. Unable to place all the division managers directly on the top planning committee, Sloan used the Operations Committee as an informal governing body. When owners objected to this arrangement, Sloan fought to retain it. His commitment to even this partial form of participative decentralization was based more in the desire to create divisional consent than in an effort to garner better information from operating personnel. He repeatedly emphasized the psychological and motivational aspects of incorporating divisional management into strategic planning over the more rational informational issues. Despite his later writings on the subject, Sloan preferred even a compromised version of participative decentralization to a textbook M-form. Subject to constraints imposed by owners from above, Sloan's general office struggled to manufacture divisional consent through this informal arrangement.

3

Administrative Centralization of the M-form, 1934–1941

In the aftermath of the Great Depression, General Motors and Alfred Sloan suddenly abandoned their commitment to participative decentralization. We saw in Chapter 2 that through 1933, Sloan and his top assistants fought to have divisional representatives included in long-range planning and policy creation as a means of manufacturing divisional consent. Between September 1933 and January 1934, however, Sloan and his allies changed course completely, eliminating direct divisional participation in the planning process and taking the first steps toward disbanding the interdivisional relations committees that gave the divisions less formal input into strategic planning. The new governance structure looked very much like a textbook M-form that put headquarters in command of strategic planning while leaving daily operations in the hands of the divisions. Yet it quickly led to administrative centralization in which the general office not only took charge of formulating policy but also usurped administrative decision-making concerning daily operations. This "corruption" of the M-form was quite intentional. It was carried out in the name of cost reduction, as Sloan pursued his belief that centralization created "efficiencies and economies" in operation.[1] In this chapter, I examine the factors that led to centralization and the extent to which it was successful.

The trend toward administrative centralization unfolded in two steps. In the first, the general office took command of resources and decisions once controlled by the divisions. Between 1933 and 1937, general office staff took the place of division managers in formulating policy and began to encroach into operating decisions. Headquarters' new power rested in part on changes associated with the depression. The decline in demand and purchasing power brought on by the depression slowed the introduction of technical change, leading to greater stability in manufacturing and engineering. This effectively reduced informational uncertainty at the top, for in this more stable environment, general executives could

---

1 Sloan (1964, p. 429).

gain a more comprehensive grasp of the technical issues facing the business. Yet better information at the top by itself was not sufficient to put an end to participative decentralization. The market changes associated with the depression also allowed top management to introduce a reorganization that reduced the need for divisional consent. In response to reduced demand differentiation, Sloan implemented a new product policy that helped to reshape the firm's social structure by undermining the bases of divisional autonomy and thus allowing the general office to extend the scope of its authority. Centralization was completed in a second stage, when top management was able to reduce owner oversight significantly by extending management's control over capital surplus and weakening owners' ability to exercise financial veto power. Through the formal reorganization of 1937, Sloan eliminated the owner-controlled Finance Committee that had overseen GM's finances for fifteen years. In its place he created a new Policy Committee dominated by general office executives and legally empowered to carry out all phases of both running and overseeing the business. Firmly in control of both corporate purse strings and operations, Sloan's new organization centralized GM to an extraordinary degree, becoming involved in every aspect of financial, strategic, and operational decision-making.

Administrative centralization enjoyed only mixed success. GM continued to dominate the North American automobile market during the 1930s, pushing its share to over 47 percent by 1940, its highest level ever.[2] Moreover, as the depression dissipated, profits continued to grow. Yet centralization also created problems. On the operating side of the organization, it undermined consent, leading the divisions to resist at least some of the policy directives handed down from above. Under Sloan's leadership, this resistance did not result in outright rebellion, as it would in the 1960s, but it did have an impact on the bottom line. In terms of return on investment – headquarters' own preferred yardstick – GM was outperformed by rival Chrysler in every year from 1935 to 1940. Sometimes the gap was embarrassingly large: in 1936, for instance, Chrysler's return on net investment was nearly twice GM's (see Figure 3.2). Moreover, although the changes that occurred during this period loosened owner oversight, they also exacerbated tensions between owners and managers. Many of the disputes that would wrack GM in the postwar period had their origins in the 1937 reorganization and in the questions it raised about the proper relationship between the financial and operating aspects of the business. Indeed, in many ways the changes made on the financial side of the business during this period would prove more consequential and long-lasting than those made on

2 Wolf (1962, p. 479).

the operating side. Although the period of administrative centralization in the 1930s was relatively short-lived, its effects continued to be felt for decades.

Centralization of Operations

Administrative centralization began with a series of organizational and personnel changes that took place late in 1933. In September, the Operations Committee was dissolved, eliminating the primary institutional mechanism for producing divisional consent, and leaving the Executive Committee as the sole body in charge of formulating and approving operating policy.[3] At about the same time, the two division managers serving on the Executive Committee were promoted to general office positions, leaving that committee free from divisional representation. Concomitant with Sloan's new belief that the Executive Committee should be "in a position to deal frankly and aggressively with any division, or [with] the relationship of one division [to] another," no new division managers were appointed to that body.[4] By November Sloan had explicitly repudiated participative decentralization, arguing that the depression had shown centralization to be more cost-effective. Yet he also acknowledged that if GM was to remain centralized, it would be necessary for corporate headquarters to gain access to information held within the divisions so that Executive Committee members could exercise "intelligent independent judgment" on technical issues central to strategic decision-making.[5]

Headquarters' ability to make informed judgments rested partly on changes in the automobile market created by the depression. The post-depression market was characterized by reduced technical uncertainty and technical innovation coupled with a return to styling competition.

[3] General Motors Corporation, "General Motors Corporation Operations Committee." Document prepared by GM legal staff for U.S. antitrust trial, December 17, 1951. Longwood, 441 (33), First Series, v. 32. Archival records contain no discussion of why the Operations Committee was finally dissolved or whether this move engendered further conflict.

[4] The quote is from Sloan (1964, p. 178). The two divisional men promoted to the general office who remained on the Executive Committee were former Chevrolet manager William Knudsen, who was appointed to the newly created title of executive vice-president in charge of operations on October 16, 1933. Lawrence Fisher, who had been manager of Cadillac, was transferred to a position in corporate headquarters at some time between September 1933 and January 1934. See General Motors Corporation, "Members of Board of Directors and Principal Executive Offices Held and Officers Who Were Not Directors, 1917–1948." Document prepared for U.S. antitrust trial. Longwood, 438 (30), First Series, v. 32, pp. 1948–1949. General Motors Corporation, *Annual Report*, 1933, p. 3; General Motors Corporation, *Annual Report*, 1934, p. 3.

[5] Cf. Sloan (1964, p. 178).

Economic contraction had driven many smaller automobile manufacturers out of business, significantly increasing market concentration.[6] The remaining producers had caught up with Ford and GM in terms of quality and production cost, and by 1933 Sloan had concluded that technical innovation "would not in the future result in effective differences from a selling point of view."[7] Competition would thus rest less on technical change, making divisional expertise in engineering and manufacturing less crucial to organizational success. Decreased technical innovation was accompanied by a renewed emphasis on appearance. In the early 1930s GM had delayed and then abandoned annual model changes in order to save money, but as consumer demand began to increase after 1933, regular model changes returned. As a result, competition in the post-depression era came to center on routinized styling changes coupled with decreased technical innovation. The depression also reduced product variability by destroying market segmentation. Prior to the depression, GM had devised the strategy of a pricing pyramid in which each division produced cars for a specific price range, and in which pricing was inversely related to sales volume. Each car division thus served a unique market segment, with low-priced Chevrolet producing in high volume, and high-priced Cadillac in low volume. The depression led to a decline in consumer purchasing power that caused a collapse of demand differentiation, leading to the destruction of this pricing pyramid. Between 1926 and 1933, the low-priced field expanded from 52 to 73 percent of the industry's unit sales. Had GM maintained five car divisions producing for separate price classes, it would have had "four lines in 27 percent of the market and one line in 73 percent of the market."[8] In response, GM temporarily reduced the number of car divisions from five to three (see Chapter 2), thereby reducing organizational differentiation to match the less differentiated environment.

Reduced technical uncertainty and declining market differentiation were important prerequisites for increased centralization. Facing an environment in which there was little need for rapid technical change, top executives were better able to make knowledgeable decisions about policy and operations. GM's experience during this period is thus consistent with TCE's observation that the degree of general office intervention varies with the extent to which top executives possess the information and cognitive capacities for making such decisions. Yet better information at the top was not sufficient to end participative decentralization, for there was still GM's history of divisional autonomy and the expectation on the part of division managers that they would be involved in various aspects of decision-making. Indeed, as we saw in

6 Cray (1980, pp. 266–267).   7 Sloan (1964, p. 179).   8 Sloan (1964, p. 179).

Administrative Centralization of the M-form 85

Chapter 2, the 1932 decision to combine divisions in order to cut costs was accompanied by increased divisional participation in planning. The elimination of such participation depended on social as well as technical factors. If Sloan's general office wanted to centralize, it would have to reshape divisional expectations and reduce the need for divisional consent. The role of the divisions would have to be redefined so that division managers would no longer expect to participate directly in policy formulation.

Efforts to remake divisional expectations relied, to a limited extent, on direct coercion. By late 1933, an entirely new group of managers took over at the car divisions, as older division managers retired or were promoted.[9] The new managers were given less status in the organization than their predecessors: none were appointed to GM's board of directors nor given the title of vice-president, and because the Operations Committee had been dissolved, none participated directly in policy discussions. Moreover, for the first time in GM's history, the car divisions did not report directly to GM's president, but rather to William Knudsen, who took over in the newly created post of executive vice-president in charge of operations. As former head of Chevrolet, Knudsen had an intimate understanding of daily operations, and his new position gave him line authority over the car divisions. Together these changes undoubtedly made it easier for headquarters to pressure or challenge the divisions when disagreements arose.

Even more important in remaking divisional expectations, however, was a radical revision of GM's product policy that occurred early in 1934. At that time, GM expanded back to five car divisions and eliminated the old pricing pyramid in which each division served a specific market segment. Beginning with the 1934 model year, Chevy, Buick, Olds, and Pontiac would compete with one another in the low-priced field, while simultaneously maintaining production of more expensive models as well. The change in product policy was advocated by Sloan, who presented it as a response to the market conditions outlined earlier. He argued that in a technologically stable industry where competition was based largely on styling, it was important to maximize the combinations of stylistic and technical features available to consumers. Moreover, he maintained that such product diversity would be enhanced if similar cars were sold under different nameplates by separate dealer organizations. In the post-depression market, it was feasible to use the same production line "to make two cars not at a great difference in price and weight, but considerably different in appearance and, to some

---

9 The new division managers were M. E. Coyle at Chevrolet, Buick's Harlow Curtice, Nicholas Dreystadt of Cadillac, Pontiac's Harry Klingler, and Sherrod Skinner at Oldsmobile.

extent, different in technical features" as a means of stimulating sales while keeping costs down.[10] In this way, Sloan argued, the higher cost of maintaining five divisions could be offset by increased sales volume.

Sloan's insistence that the new policy was a rational, technical response to changed conditions did not withstand scrutiny. Indeed, financial executives from the general office as well as owner representatives from Du Pont disagreed with Sloan's analysis.[11] Although overall demand was beginning to increase by the end of 1933, it was still well below 1929 levels. More important, low-priced cars still accounted for the overwhelming majority of sales. Owners and finance staff argued that there was not sufficient demand differentiation to support five divisions producing in different price classes, and they concluded that it would be more cost-effective to continue with only three divisions. Like later organizational theorists, they insisted that divisionalization was warranted only when each operating unit was dedicated to a specific market segment.[12] Moreover, GM was already putting different nameplates on cars that were very similar beneath the hood. The whole point of the reduction to three divisions was to decrease technical variability while maintaining at least the appearance of separate lines. If Sloan wanted to stimulate demand by putting different nameplates on cars that were essentially identical, there was no need to reestablish five manufacturing divisions. All he had to do was continue the practices that had been put into effect in 1932.

Sloan's enthusiasm for the product policy of 1934 was rooted less in its technical merits than in its social and political consequences. The new policy legitimized increased general office intervention in decisionmaking by redefining the role of the divisions in a way that undermined the social and technical bases of their autonomy. The basis of divisionalization was the decomposition of the firm into distinct operating units serving unique markets. This decomposition had both technical and social dimensions. At the technical level, divisions were free to make largely autonomous operating decisions in the areas of engineering, styling, and manufacturing. Theoretically, at least, the divisions were constrained primarily through final product price; each had to restrict its

10 Sloan (1964, p. 180). Sloan's more general discussion of the 1934 product policy can be found on pp. 178–181.
11 See Walter S. Carpenter, Jr., to Alfred P. Sloan, Jr., February 2, 1934, Accession 542, Box 821. Walter S. Carpenter, Jr., to Alfred P. Sloan, Jr., February 12, 1934, Accession 542, Box 821. Alfred P. Sloan, Jr., to Walter S. Carpenter, January 31, 1934, Accession 542, Box 821. Sloan (1964, p. 179).
12 See Stinchcombe (1990); Lawrence and Lorsch (1967). Alfred D. Chandler, Jr., in a personal communication, points out that such difficulty in defining markets is a source of constant stress within the M-form for product-related firms like GM. I will return to this point in Chapter 8. See also Greenwood (1974).

output to a single price range. Insofar as they did so, different divisions were not required to take great notice of one another. At the social level, the decomposition into separate operating units serving distinct markets formed the basis of divisional claims to expertise. Each division manager inhabited a structurally unique position within the corporation in the sense that he was responsible for a distinct market with its own set of uncertainties and trade-offs. This dedication to a specific market segment formed the basis of managers' claims of access to specialized competence, and it was centrally implicated in their expectation that they would be included in planning. As long as each division served a distinct market segment, each division manager could claim that his position in the firm (and thus his knowledge of a particular market) was unique. Through serving a particular market segment, division managers gained a social structural claim to special knowledge and competence, and they used this claim to justify their inclusion in strategic planning.

The product policy of 1934 destroyed the notion of expertise rooted in a division of labor, in two ways. First, it reduced divisional autonomy by creating forced interdependence between divisions. Cars produced by the different divisions would be designed together to share tooling, chassis, frames, and other parts in order to cut costs. Forced interdependence actually increased internal uncertainty by complicating manufacture and distribution; previously autonomous decisions now had to be coordinated. But as Sloan explained, the need for coordination legitimized general office intervention, for "when two or more divisions use common components, the independence of each division is limited to the extent that there must be a common program between them."[13] In effect, the new program redrew the line between policy and operations by ensuring that virtually every engineering and design decision would affect more than one division. As a consequence, actions previously defined as operating decisions to be made in the divisions were now classified as policy decisions to be handled by headquarters. While forced interdependence destroyed the technical bases of divisional autonomy, the decision to expand back to five divisions undermined the social bases of that autonomy. Under the new policy, divisions would no longer serve unique markets, but would compete with one another in the low-priced market segment. As a consequence, they were unable to claim specialized knowledge about a specific market. Lacking claims to specialized knowledge, division managers could justify their inclusion in planning neither by claiming unique expertise nor by arguing that they represented a distinct operating interest. The new policy thus made division managers structurally and functionally equivalent actors: instead of overseeing unique

13 Sloan (1964, p. 181).

markets, they possessed redundant knowledge about a single market in which all competed. Under these conditions, divisional input into policy could virtually be eliminated. The divisions would be pitted against one another in competition, while general office staff took over as the experts.

Sloan tacitly acknowledged that the diminution of divisional autonomy sprang neither from better information at the center nor from the technical interdependence engendered by the product policy of 1934.[14] Only when these factors were combined with the destruction of the pricing pyramid engendered by the return to five operating divisions did central oversight become both essential and possible. Together these factors created increased capacity for central intervention (better information), a technical rationale for such control (forced interdependence that redefined operating problems as policy issues), and a social structural transformation of divisional claims to expertise (the elimination of the pricing pyramid that turned division managers into structurally and functionally equivalent actors). Acknowledging that the restoration of five car divisions would create new operating problems, Sloan's recommendation to the Finance Committee "stated quite emphatically" that the new product policy would require "a very definite managerial policy" of increased control from the top.[15]

Although both owners and key financial executives continued to oppose the new product policy, it was adopted by GM's Executive Committee in January 1934. Ratification was itself a source of controversy, for there was considerable opposition to the policy within the committee. Three committee members – Lammot du Pont, GM's head of finance and former Du Pont executive Donaldson Brown, and group executive John Pratt, another former Du Pont executive – opposed the plan, preferring that GM maintain three divisions. But supported by Sloan and the remaining general office executives on the committee, the policy was ratified, marking the first time since Durant's ouster that a policy "of real importance" was determined by a majority vote rather than by unanimous agreement of the Executive Committee.[16] Indeed, after Du Pont's Walter Carpenter requested more information on the decision, Sloan

14 See Sloan (1964, p. 178).
15 Alfred P. Sloan, Jr., to Walter S. Carpenter, Jr., January 31, 1934, Accession 542, Box 821.
16 Alfred P. Sloan, Jr., to Walter S. Carpenter, Jr., January 31, 1934, Accession 542, Box 821. The members of the Executive Committee at the time of the vote on the policy were as follows: Lammot du Pont; Alfred P. Sloan, Jr.; Donaldson Brown; John Pratt; Fred, Charles, and Lawrence Fisher; William Knudsen; and John T. Smith. Du Pont and Fred Fisher stepped down from the committee in February 1934. See General Motors Corporation, "Executive Committee, 1918–1937," February 12, 1952. Document prepared for U.S. antitrust trial. Longwood, 441 (33), First Series, v. 32. The information is abstracted in U.S. v. Du Pont, GTE #177.

seemed to fear that the owner-controlled Finance Committee might attempt to overturn the new policy. Protesting that the Executive Committee's approval of the new product policy was all that was needed to put the plan into effect, he argued that the Finance Committee should not have any jurisdiction in the matter.[17] To Sloan's relief, Carpenter did not pursue the matter further, and the new product policy was implemented.

The new policy led the general office to take command of both strategic planning and an increasing number of what had once been operating decisions. Under the plan, "a divisional product program, instead of being integral in itself [was] deeply involved with the product programs of many of the other divisions [and had to] be developed from the corporate point of view."[18] The coordination pursued by Sloan turned an increasing number of engineering and manufacturing decisions over to Detroit's technical staff. With the advent of annual model changes in 1935, most styling decisions were transferred to the general office staff as well. The various GM makes competing in the low-priced field were ordered to share chassis, frames, body designs, some engines, and other components, and the "interdivisional borrowing was so extensive that the same assembly lines turned out Buicks, Oldsmobiles, and Pontiacs."[19]

The divisions tried to resist this encroachment into their areas of jurisdiction, but they were unsuccessful. In 1934, for instance, the general office styling staff began an effort to remake all of GM's automobile lines by lowering and lengthening car bodies in order to create a more appealing appearance to consumers. Achieving this goal required significant engineering changes in frames, engine placement, wheelbase length, and even passenger-compartment placing. Divisional engineers "objected that lengthening the body added weight, and shifting the position of the motor changed the standard weight distribution, all of which created new and difficult problems" that would disrupt production.[20] Their concerns went unheeded; determined to go ahead with the program, the general office staff took over responsibility for engineering and implementing changes. Similarly, many divisional engineers were "dead set against" the technical staff's plan to introduce one-piece steel roofs for GM's 1935 models. Recalling older all-steel designs, they argued that the new roofs would be noisy, thus damaging sales. This led to "heated" dis-

17 Alfred P. Sloan, Jr., to Walter S. Carpenter, Jr., January 31, 1934, Accession 542, Box 821.
18 Sloan (1964, p. 184).
19 Cray (1980, p. 295). See also Sloan (1964, pp. 240–247). "General Motors, Part I of a Study in Bigness." *Fortune* 18:40ff. (December 1938), p. 152.
20 Sloan (1964, p. 275).

agreements between divisions and general office staff: "When a division chief engineer would condemn the design for noise-making characteristics, another executive would claim that the trouble was caused not by the design but by the vibrations within the engine."[21] Lacking either unique claims to expertise or a formal vote in such issues, however, the divisions were powerless to derail the program.

Divisional resistance was to be expected given GM's heritage of divisional autonomy and decentralization. Always attuned to issues of cooperation and consent, however, Sloan remained disturbed by divisional resistance to his new policy of centralization. As the general office took control of what had once been divisional prerogatives, he therefore turned to the task of further modifying GM's governance structure in order to institutionalize the new relations among divisions, headquarters, and owners. In doing so, he sought to attenuate divisional resistance from below while simultaneously reducing the prospect of financial veto from above.

The Transformation of Strategic Planning

The centralization of operations that occurred in conjunction with the product policy of 1934 was accompanied by a transformation of the strategic planning process. This transformation occurred for three reasons, two of which related directly to the new product policy. The first involved continuing efforts to create divisional consent. While the new product policy reduced the need for consent, it was still necessary to engender at least minimal cooperation at the divisional level. Yet the elimination of divisional participation in planning destroyed the most significant means of producing such cooperation, making it desirable to create new institutional mechanisms for doing so. A second and related reason for transforming strategic planning involved the new role of the general office, especially the technical staffs. Prior to the depression, the most powerful actors at GM's headquarters were executives with line authority, especially the president and the group executives. Among staff, only the finance and legal staffs in New York wielded real power; the various technical staffs in Detroit had relatively little influence. In the post-depression era, however, the technical staff would be responsible for an increasing number of decisions. As a consequence, Sloan sought to create a form of strategic planning in which staff took the place of line, displacing divisional representatives and even group executives in influence.

21 Sloan (1964, p. 276).

The third factor behind the transformation of strategic planning came as more of a surprise. Late in December 1933, Lammot du Pont announced his intention to remove owner representatives from GM's Executive Committee.[22] Believing that owners lacked the time and information needed to understand operating strategy, and knowing that new government regulations tended to construe outside involvement in operations as an antitrust issue that could make owners liable for management decisions, Lammot decided that owners should restrict their activities to GM's financial affairs.[23] He stepped down from GM's Executive Committee in February 1934, ordering that no Du Pont representative be appointed to replace him.[24] Sloan worried that without owner representation on the committee, it would be more difficult to convince owners to accept proposed policies. Arguing that representation provided owners with "the opportunity . . . of knowing what we are doing [and] how we are doing it," he accepted Lammot's decision "under protest."[25] Owners' departure from the Executive Committee, along with the debate over the new product policy that occurred late in 1933 and early in 1934, apparently heightened Sloan's worries that owners might intervene in or veto Executive Committee decisions via the Finance Committee. Without owner representatives taking part in Executive Com-

22 See Alfred P. Sloan, Jr., to Lammot du Pont, December 27, 1933. *U.S. v. Du Pont*, GTE #1348, which deals with this issue. Lammot's response to this letter can be found in Lammot du Pont to Alfred P. Sloan, Jr., December 28, 1933. Longwood, 430 (22), First Series, v. 17, p. 5158.
23 The notion that owner participation in operating affairs could have antitrust and liability implications for Du Pont was expressed clearly in a U.S. district court decision involving GM and Du Pont some 35 years later. In that case the court wrote that "the New York courts have frequently held that a dominant or majority stockholder does not become a fiduciary for other stockholders merely by reason of his voting power. It is only when he steps out of his role as a stockholder and begins to usurp the functions of director in the management of corporate affairs that such a duty is imposed." Citing case law dating back to 1919, the court also noted that the New York decisions on this matter had "been cited with approval in Delaware" where GM and Du Pont were incorporated (*Gottesman et al. v. General Motors*. 279 F. Supp. 361, 1967, pp. 383–384). The antitrust environment of the New Deal, along with securities and exchange regulations that emerged at that time, seems to have intensified Du Pont's concern that involvement in GM's operating affairs could increase E. I. du Pont's vulnerability to legal attacks. Indeed, when the U.S. government launched its antitrust case against Du Pont and GM in the 1950s, one of Du Pont's defenses was that there was "a division of responsibility between du Pont and General Motors management" and that "control of finances is not the same thing as control of operations or purchasing" (Dirlam and Stelzer 1958, p. 33).
24 Donaldson Brown and John Pratt were not seen as Du Pont representatives because they were GM employees; they thus continued to sit on GM's Executive Committee. Nonetheless, Brown continued to sit on the Finance Committee and board of E. I. du Pont de Nemours, and he received his position as chairman of GM's Finance Committee in part because he was seen as a guardian of Du Pont interests.
25 Alfred P. Sloan, Jr., to Lammot du Pont, December 27, 1933. *U.S. v. Du Pont*, GTE #1348.

mittee discussions, it would be harder to convince them to accept proposed policies. Moreover, the debate over the 1934 product policy had raised the question of whether the Finance Committee could intervene in Executive Committee decisions when there was a lack of unanimity among Executive Committee members. For both of these reasons, Sloan believed that policy decisions reached by the Executive Committee needed to have the appearance of unanimity. In devising new means for generating divisional commitment to corporate policy and increasing the influence of the general technical staff, he thus sought to create mechanisms whereby the Executive Committee could reach consensus on proposed strategies in order to present a united front to owners and the Finance Committee.

To address these issues, Sloan transformed the strategic planning process by implementing a formal distinction between policy formulation and approval. The primary responsibility for policy formulation rested with a newly created set of functionally defined policy groups.[26] Initially defined as subcommittees of the Executive Committee, each of these groups contained a subset of Executive Committee members. Unlike the interdivisional relations committees that they replaced, the policy groups had no divisional representatives, nor did owners participate. Instead, they were composed almost exclusively of high-level staff and line executives from the general office. They were also charged more specifically with formulating policy recommendations than the interdivisional relations committees had been. The policy groups held neither formal authority to approve policy nor any power to give orders to the divisions. Instead, they formulated policies in specific functional areas and presented them to the Executive Committee in the form of recommendations. The Executive Committee then ratified or voted down these proposals, but had less leeway to modify and reshape policy. Even though the Executive Committee remained legally in charge of approving policy, these modifications made it a judicial body that ratified and modified proposals created in the policy groups.

The policy groups effectively reduced conflict within the Executive Committee by relocating the arena of disagreement from the Executive Committee proper to the various groups, shifting substantive differences from the authorization to the creation phase. Only after disagreements had been thrashed out in the groups would a proposal be offered for a vote. In presenting recommendations, the groups would maintain a unified front, since they had already come to an agreement and expressed

26 The idea of the policy groups probably evolved out of a suggestion from Albert Bradley of GM's finance staff, who suggested that discussions of policy would be expedited by the use of subcommittees. See Sloan (1964, p. 175).

commitment to a line of action.[27] If other Executive Committee members chose to challenge proposed policies, they would be at a factual disadvantage, since policy group participants possessed better information and fuller knowledge of a proposal's implications. Policy group members thus served both as informational gatekeepers and as advocates of their proposals, reducing disagreements within the Executive Committee and the ensuing possibility that owners would use such disagreements as a pretext for intervention.

The policy groups also provided an arena where general office executives could both exercise coercion over and solicit cooperation from the divisions. Once a policy group had decided to endorse a specific policy, an informal meeting would be called between policy group members and divisional personnel. Sloan and his colleagues believed that these seminar-like meetings would help create divisional acceptance of policies in two ways. First, they would allow general office executives to explain proposed policies in a way that demonstrated top management's knowledge and understanding of operating issues. Because divisional acceptance of policies was "dependent largely upon the degree of confidence in the ... judgment and understanding of the authority handing down a policy," these meetings would help gain the confidence of division management.[28] Second, the seminars provided a forum in which divisional representatives could voice their concerns over proposed policies, allowing for at least limited input into strategic planning. Such feedback would also provide policy group members with better information and, at least in principle, could lead to the modification of ill-advised policies. The hope was that through "free and open discussion" and debate, the divisions would understand the reasoning behind policies and would therefore "accept ... the point of policy in the spirit of intended purpose."[29]

Although the policy groups held no formal line authority over the divisions, they could also bring tremendous coercive pressure to bear on operating management. Most important in this regard was the fact that GM's top executives – Sloan, executive vice-president Knudsen, and a few group executives – sat on the groups. Because the groups "had on them the president and other executives [with] line authority," their

---

27 Salancik (1977a; 1977b) points out that public endorsement of a proposal creates commitment and buy-in; when actors express public commitment to a proposal, as policy group members were required to do, they are more likely to become committed to the proposal in subsequent phases of ratification.
28 Donaldson Brown to Alfred P. Sloan, Jr., June 1, 1937, Accession 1334, Box 1.
29 Donaldson Brown to Walter S. Carpenter, July 9, 1957, Accession 542, Box 849. This letter is Brown reflecting back on the functioning of the policy groups many years after the fact.

recommendations were "generally accepted" and were almost never directly challenged by the divisions.[30] Moreover, as centralization increased following the product policy of 1934, Detroit's technical staff took control over decisions once made in the divisions. Even though the heads of the various technical staffs held no line authority over the divisions, they participated in and usually chaired the policy groups in their functional areas, giving them enormous leverage over the divisions. Finally, although the divisions participated in informal meetings with the policy groups, division managers could not cast votes in the policy group seminars as they had in the Operations Committee. While they could voice their objections, it was up to general office executives to decide whether those objections merited attention or even response. The implementation of the policy groups thus made it easier to overlook objections from below. For this reason, however, the new system also increased the possibility that consent would not be forthcoming, for attempts to create cooperation through informal participation and seminars could be circumvented or ignored in a way that direct divisional participation in planning could not. Although the creation of the policy groups was accompanied by some attempts to create divisional consent, overall the new system brought a definite shift toward the use of coercion.

The policy groups were also crucial in building up the influence and auditing capabilities of the nascent technical staff in Detroit. Indeed, they provided the primary mechanisms by which the technical staffs would take over what had once been divisional prerogatives. The first policy groups, instituted around October 1934, were in the areas of engineering and distribution – the two areas most strongly affected by the product policy of 1934. At least one other group, the Price Procedure Policy Group, was also implemented in 1934.[31] To accommodate the creation of these groups, a number of staff executives were named to the board and eventually placed on the Executive Committee so that they could serve as policy group members.[32] As a consequence, the five staff

30 Alfred P. Sloan, Jr., direct testimony. *U.S. v. Du Pont*, pp. 4362–4363 (2469). See also Sloan (1964, p. 182); Alfred P. Sloan, Jr., to Lammot du Pont, April 5, 1945, Accession 542, Box 837.
31 On engineering and distribution groups, see Sloan (1964, p. 182). On the price group, see "Financial and Pricing Policy Groups," internal memo prepared by General Motors counsel on May 29, 1958, Accession 542, Box 849. The latter may have in fact been considered a "distribution" group by Sloan.
32 Richard Grant, Ormond Hunt, and Charles Wilson – vice-presidents of distribution, engineering, and manufacturing, respectively – were added to the board in November 1934 and to the Executive Committee in August 1935. At the same time, James Mooney, group executive in charge of the export division, was also added to the Executive Committee, which grew from seven to eleven members in a single year. The vice-president for finance, Albert Bradley, was made a director in November 1933 and named to the Executive Committee in August 1934. See General Motors Corpora-

members who had once served on the Operations Committee were finally made members of the Executive Committee, cementing general office control of policy. By 1936 there were over a dozen groups in place representing five functional areas: administration, engineering, manufacturing, distribution, and finance.[33] The chairman of each policy group was the Executive Committee member with administrative responsibility for the group's specific area of expertise; in most cases, this was the staff member in charge of that area. Between 1934 and 1936, staff involvement and centrality in strategic planning thus increased significantly.

The policy groups served as the major locus of coordination and control in the post-depression era. Consisting exclusively of general office executives, they involved Sloan and his top assistants in every aspect of strategic planning, giving them enormous influence over areas of decision-making that had once belonged to division managers. They increased the responsibility and power of Detroit's technical staff, giving these men authority over chairing and participating in most areas of policy creation. The groups also functioned to provide a wider range of information to top executives. Executives were often assigned to groups to provide them with information about "the trend of things" rather than to give them "any aggressive part" in making technical decisions.[34] Through informal meetings with operating personnel, the groups also aimed at creating divisional consent to the new setup. Yet the groups also served to change prevailing practices by exerting continual pressure on the divisions. Indeed, Sloan freely admitted that in several cases he assigned specific staff members to the groups because he was "entirely out of sympathy" with prevailing practices and believed that the new staff members would promote different policies.[35] Finally, by making policy a two-stage process of formulation and approval, the groups decreased the likelihood of open dissension within the Executive Committee, thereby reducing the chance that owners would perceive disagreement over proposed policies.

Despite these accomplishments, the policy groups remained largely experimental between 1934 and 1936. Indeed, their efficacy during this period remained very much tied to Sloan's person. Although he believed

tion, "Members of Board of Directors and Principal Executive Offices Held and Officers Who Were Not Directors, 1917–1948." Longwood, 438 (30), First Series, v. 32, p. 9593. General Motors Corporation, "General Motors Corporation Executive Committee," February 12, 1952. Longwood, 441 (33), First Series, v. 32.

33 Alfred P. Sloan, Jr., to Lammot du Pont, attachment, April 14, 1936. Longwood, 430 (22), First Series, v. 20, p. 5836.
34 Alfred P. Sloan, Jr., to Lammot du Pont, April 28, 1936. Longwood, 430 (22), First Series, v. 20, pp. 5825–5829.
35 Alfred P. Sloan, Jr., to Lammot du Pont, April 28, 1936. Longwood, 430 (22), First Series, v. 20, pp. 5825–5829.

that the policy groups were perhaps the most important organizational innovation at GM since the implementation of the M-form in the mid-1920s, he confessed that the only groups making an impact were the ones on which he served; even in 1936 he remained unable "to develop sufficient activity in the other Groups."[36] By 1936 he had begun to take steps that would broaden the power of corporate headquarters even further, institutionalizing its control over corporate resources and solidifying the importance of the policy groups as a governance mechanism.

The Struggle for Control of Finance

The changes that were made between 1933 and the end of 1936 constituted the first phase of administrative centralization. From 1937 to 1941 centralization became even more pronounced, as Sloan and his colleagues set out to bring virtually every aspect of decision-making within the purview of corporate headquarters. There were two factors behind increasing centralization in 1937. The first and more crucial focused on owner control of investment funds. By virtue of their position as liaison between external capital markets and the corporation, and through their subsequent control of the Finance Committee, outside owners could block management policies by refusing to fund them. To ensure that their policies were implemented, Sloan's general office set out to gain greater control over investment funds and weaken owners' veto power. The second factor behind increasing centralization concerned growing labor unrest and state regulation. These forces created a need for more uniform policies, causing headquarters to usurp even more divisional prerogatives.

The primary impetus behind increasing centralization was the desire to loosen ownership control from above. At stake was command of corporate surplus and owners' ability to exercise effective veto power over proposed policies through the Finance Committee. To Sloan, the split between finance and operations was irrational, since the two areas were deeply intertwined. The decision over how best to employ surplus, he believed, should be left in the hands of those who formulated operating policy. This conviction was strengthened by both the withdrawal of owners from the Executive Committee and the emergence of excess

36 Alfred P. Sloan, Jr., to Lammot du Pont, April 28, 1936. Longwood, 430 (22), First Series, v. 20, pp. 5825–5829. On Sloan's assessment of the importance of the policy groups, see Alfred P. Sloan, Jr., to Lammot du Pont, April 14, 1936. Longwood, 430 (22), First Series, v. 20, p. 5836.

capital that eliminated the need to secure investment funds from outside sources.

The desire to loosen owner control of investment funds sprang in large part from headquarters' plans for rapid expansion of plant and capacity. As the country recovered from the depression, demand for new cars outstripped supply. Moreover, the new product policy of offering a wide range of models in the low-priced field actually decreased plant capacity and efficiency, as divisions struggled to produce more models in that price group.[37] The prospect of a shorter work week and possible labor strikes threatened to reduce production further, causing general office executives to conclude that capacity should be increased.[38] Owners were more cautious. Fearing that the country had not fully recovered from the depression, they approved expansion expenditures at a more moderate rate. In 1935 the Finance Committee authorized $50 million in appropriations for increasing capacity; after these funds were exhausted in 1936, further expenditures were not anticipated. Nonetheless, demand continued to outstrip supply, and some divisions remained unable to produce enough cars to meet demand. GM's market share slipped from its 1933 figure of 43.3 percent to only 38.4 percent in 1935.[39] To general office executives, failure to expand further constituted an irrational loss of revenue and market share. The only solution was a "fundamental increase in capacity [that] would require expenditures on a broad front."[40] Yet owners refused to approve such a plan, preferring to take a wait-and-see attitude in order to protect their investments during a time of uncertainty.

The general office's desire to expand more rapidly was linked to slack capital resources created by GM's enormous earning power. The textbook M-form implicitly rested on the assumption that investment funds were a scarce commodity. The Finance Committee was charged with determining what proportion of the corporation's surplus should be consumed as dividends and what portion reinvested in the business. In the latter context, the committee also allocated scarce funds to competing operational projects. In a world of investment shortage, not all projects could be funded. But GM's remarkable earning power undercut these assumptions by creating enormous surplus. The corporation became so profitable that there was more than enough money to fund many projects and still pay generous dividends to owners. Under these conditions,

37 General Motors Corporation, *Annual Report*, 1935, p. 29.
38 Sloan (1964, p. 201).
39 Wolf (1962, p. 479).
40 Sloan (1964, pp. 200–201); General Motors Corporation, *Annual Report*, 1936, p. 7.

there was little question that money for expansion existed. From Sloan's point of view, slack capital resources made it more important that finance and policy be considered together.[41] When investment funds were abundant, the availability and cost of capital were no longer the crucial issues deciding policy. Indeed, many financial decisions became so routine that they could be left to operating personnel. As Sloan later put it:

> ... in a business of our magnitude ... the idea of a Finance Committee dealing with finances and an Executive Committee dealing with the management of the business is misleading. [T]he question of finances per se [is] incidental. The question of business policy in relation to finances [is] paramount. When I went to the Finance Committee [in 1928] and asked for approval [to purchase] Adam Opel AG in Germany, the question of finances did not arise. We all knew that we had the money. We have always had the money in recent years ... to do anything we wanted. [I]t was policy determination ... rather than ... the pure function of finance [that was crucial].
> ... We [also] talk about the Executive Committee administering the business but having nothing to do with finance.... That is not only unrealistic but it is absurd. In a business as big as General Motors ... the great majority of the matters that must be determined ... involve finance.[42]

Lammot du Pont's decision to end owner representation on the Executive Committee also played a role in Sloan's efforts to loosen owner oversight. Sloan believed that owner participation on the Executive Committee made it more likely that the Finance Committee would approve investment projects originating in the Executive Committee. First, such participation provided owners with information and knowledge about operating proposals. If owners did not take part in Executive Committee discussions of policy, they would vote on investment allocations without adequate knowledge of the issues at stake. In this situation,

---

41 Careful readers will note that I support my arguments concerning the consequences of slack capital resources by quoting material from the early and mid-1940s, rather than from the 1937 period. The issues at stake during these two periods were virtually identical: the 1940s memos were written when the du Ponts proposed reversing the changes made in 1937. The later memos reveal a much more powerful and candid Sloan who was willing to challenge owners more directly than he had in 1937. I believe that these materials provide the clearest expression of Sloan's reasons for opposing a distinction between finance and operating policy, and they are consistent with statements made in 1937. See also Alfred P. Sloan, Jr., direct testimony. *U.S. v. Du Pont*, pp. 4342–4343 (2457–2458).

42 Alfred P. Sloan, Jr., to Donaldson Brown, February 2, 1945, Accession 1334, Box 1. See also Sloan, direct testimony. *U.S. v. Du Pont*, p. 4343 (2458); Sloan (1964, p. 185).

Sloan argued, there would be "no relationship of the [stockholders'] interests... with the operating phases. There [would be] a barrier between them."[43] Having such knowledge of operations was particularly crucial in a situation of slack capital resources, when there was more than enough money to fund competing proposals. Second, however, Sloan believed that owner participation in Executive Committee discussions provided the general office with a better opportunity to sell owners on proposed policies. If owners could be convinced to approve proposed policies through participation in the Executive Committee, they would be hard-pressed to oppose them in the Finance Committee. Owner participation on the Executive Committee resulted in a public commitment that created a "buy-in" to proposed policies. Sloan was thus "unalterably opposed to an arbitrary separation between finances and operation" because he believed that it would lead "to some sort of dictatorship, absolute or limited."[44] If management lacked the opportunity to influence owners in Executive Committee discussions, the result was likely to be an arbitrary exercise of Finance Committee veto.

Increased centralization was given additional impetus by the labor unrest of 1937 and growing state regulation. Ironically, GM's vulnerability to organized labor had been increased by the centralization of operations and the policy of forced interdependence that began in 1934. As part of its efforts to create economies by centralizing operations, GM had concentrated final assembly of its autos in two Fisher Body plants. Chevrolet's new all-metal bodies were assembled in Fisher's Cleveland plant, while a majority of Buicks, Oldsmobiles, and Pontiacs were completed in its huge Flint plant.[45] Moreover, GM's decentralized structure left Fisher's management in charge of labor policies; as a consequence, the division remained the "last big stronghold of piecework pay," making it a focus of union hostility.[46] The combination of factors proved disastrous for GM. In 1937 workers at these two facilities began the famous sit-down strike that brought GM's production to a virtual standstill.

The 1937 strike convinced GM management that there was a need for more uniform corporate policies. As GM's experiences with labor dramatically attested, divisional autonomy made it difficult to secure such

43 Alfred P. Sloan, Jr., to Lammot du Pont, April 13, 1942. *U.S. v. Du Pont*, GTE #203. See also Alfred P. Sloan, Jr., to Walter S. Carpenter, April 11, 1942a, Accession 542, Box 837.
44 Alfred P. Sloan, Jr., to Walter S. Carpenter, April 11, 1942a, Accession 542, Box 837. See also Donaldson Brown to Alfred P. Sloan, Jr., January 16, 1945, Accession 1334, Box 1. Note that the document quoted is from a later period than the one being discussed in this section; I believe it is nonetheless representative of Sloan's feelings about the owner-controlled Finance Committee.
45 Cray (1980, p. 295).
46 *Fortune*, "General Motors, Part I of a Study in Bigness," p. 180.

uniformity. Believing that a poor decision or a "misinterpretation of policy on the part of just one of our divisions ... is likely to be used by the opposition as a basis for attack on General Motors," headquarters concluded that further centralization of decision-making was necessary.[47] Further impetus to centralization was prompted by increasing government regulation. The Wagner Act, for instance, compelled GM to negotiate with a single union, rather than allowing its various divisions and plants to deal with autonomous labor organizations.[48] Only months after the sit-down strike ended, Sloan set out to reorganize GM in a way that would put the general office in charge of investment funds while giving it unparalleled authority over virtually every aspect of decision-making.

Reorganizing the M-form

The opportunity to address both the need for uniform policy and top management's desire to extend control over financial decisions came when Lammot du Pont stepped down as GM's chairman of the board early in 1937. Lammot ceded his position to Sloan, who became the first non–du Pont chairman in over two decades. Dissatisfied with existing relations among finance, operations, and policy, Sloan suggested that the change in chairmanship should be accompanied by restructuring at the top of GM's corporate hierarchy. Only in this way, he argued, could GM realize the full potential of the changes that had taken place since the depression.[49] Sloan submitted his plan for reorganization to Lammot du Pont on March 17; the ensuing discussions between owners and managers illuminated the issues at stake and highlighted the different images of the M-form that they held.

Sloan's plan had two components. First, it would weaken owner control over investment funds, thereby reducing owners' ability to oversee management. In addition, it would further curtail divisional power, institutionalizing the ascendance of staff over line and ultimately centralizing a broad range of decision-making authority at the very apex of GM's managerial hierarchy. The proposal called for GM's Finance and Executive Committees to be dissolved and replaced by a Policy Committee and an Administration Committee, respectively. The Policy Committee would oversee all aspects of strategic planning, including financial planning, while the Administration Committee would oversee all aspects

---

47 Donaldson Brown to Alfred Sloan, June 22, 1938, Accession 542, Box 821.
48 See Deposition of Alfred P. Sloan, Jr. *U.S. v. Du Pont*, p. 47 (56–57).
49 Alfred P. Sloan, Jr., to Lammot du Pont, March 17, 1937, Accession 542, Box 821.

of running the business on a day-to-day basis. The new organization would thus replace the split between finance and operations with a distinction between planning and administration. Whereas the old Finance Committee had been composed overwhelmingly of owner representatives, the proposed Policy Committee would be a mix of owners and general office executives, with the latter in the majority. Similarly, the Administration Committee would be composed of a number of staff and line executives from headquarters; it would have neither owner nor divisional representation. General office executives would thus dominate in every aspect of decision-making – strategic, financial, and operating.

In principle the two committees would have clearly delineated areas of jurisdiction: the Policy Committee would not involve itself in daily management issues, and the Administration Committee would not be involved in strategic planning. Yet one provision in the plan militated against this clear separation of functions. In the new setup, the Policy Committee would be clearly superordinate to the Administration Committee and would retain all legal powers of the board. In the old organization, the Finance and Executive Committees were co-equal in the sense that each was delegated specific powers directly from the board. The new plan called for the Policy Committee to be granted complete authority; it would, in turn, delegate power over operational decision-making to the Administration Committee, which would report to the Policy Committee rather than to the board (Table 3.1). There were two reasons for this radical departure from prior practice. First, although Sloan still sought to encourage initiative from below, he wanted to retain ultimate veto power over every aspect of policy and administration. By giving the Policy Committee all powers of the board, any Administration Committee decision could be overturned or modified by the Policy Committee if necessary. Second, by making the Policy Committee completely responsible from a legal point of view, Sloan could circumvent legal restrictions requiring all members of the Administration Committee to be members of the board. Since the Administration Committee was not legally responsible for governance, its members would not have to be board members. This would make it easier for headquarters to put whomever they wanted on the Administration Committee, for owners could no longer block appointments by refusing to place potential Administration Committee members on the board of directors, a tactic that Lammot du Pont had used repeatedly when Sloan had attempted to put division managers on the Executive Committee.

Sloan's plan also called for the board of directors to be reduced from forty members to twenty or twenty-five in order to ensure that the board would have "proper representation" of both operating officials and

Table 3.1. *Responsibilities and Powers of GM's Top Governing Committees, 1933 vs. 1937*

	Finance Committee 1933	Policy Committee 1937
Powers	"The Finance Committee shall have special and general charge and control of all financial affairs of the Corporation.... [It] shall possess and may exercise all the powers of the Board...in the management of the financial affairs of the Corporation...."	"...the policy committee shall possess and may exercise...all the powers of the board of directors in the management and direction of all the business and affairs of the Corporation..., and, if it is deemed desirable, may assume direct charge and control of any of the affairs, activities, positions, officers and employees of the Corporation. It shall have control specifically of the financial affairs and general policies of the Corporation."
Membership	Must be board members. In practice, majority represent outside owners.	Must be board members. In practice, majority are general office executives.
	Executive Committee 1933	Administration Committee 1937
Powers	"...the Executive Committee shall possess and may exercise all the powers of the Board...in the management and direction of all the business and affairs of the Company (except the matters...assigned to the Finance committee)...."	"The administration committee shall actively concern itself with the manufacturing and selling operations of the Corporation, and subject to the policy committee shall have special charge and control of such operations. The administration committee shall make recommendations and reports to the policy committee concerning the operations of the Corporation under its supervision."
Membership	Must be board members.	"The board of directors shall elect from the executive officers of the Corporation and its subsidiaries, an administration committee...and shall designate a chairman of the committee. The members of the administration committee with the exception of the chairman need not be directors."

Source: Information for 1933 is from General Motors Corporation. *By-laws*, as amended to November 1933; information for 1937 is from General Motors Corporation. *By-laws*, as amended to July 1, 1937.

shareholders.⁵⁰ Although the suggestion to reduce the board had originated with Lammot du Pont, Sloan took it as an opportunity to increase management representation at the expense of outside owners. Of the thirteen board members whom Sloan suggested eliminating, eleven represented outside interests, while only two were GM executives.⁵¹ These changes would effectively make the board an instrument of management. Sloan acknowledged that the plan was "quite unusual," but he concluded confidently that it would "promote progress [and] stability in the future management of the Corporation."⁵²

Owners greeted Sloan's proposals with grave reservations. On April 5, 1937, the Finance Committee of E. I. du Pont de Nemours met to discuss the plan.⁵³ The Du Pont group agreed that Sloan's proposal would dilute owner control, commenting that "there was a general feeling of misgiving with respect to discontinuing the present Finance Committee and not establishing some body whose particular function would be handling financial problems of the organization and which would also constitute a concentrated representation of stockholders' opinions on important matters."⁵⁴ They discussed the idea of having three top committees, but dismissed it as too complicated. Lammot then suggested that the board be reduced radically in size so that it could meet monthly and serve as the functional equivalent of a Finance Committee. In this way, the Policy Committee would be staffed by management executives and given responsibility for general operating policies and most financial decisions. However, the new board would retain control over "certain kinds of financial questions," including "purchase, sale, issue or redemption of securities, dividends, general bonus plans, working capital policies, budgets and appropriations in excess of ... ten million dollars, not previously budgeted."⁵⁵ In other words, the new board would retain virtu-

50 Alfred P. Sloan, Jr., to Lammot du Pont, March 17, 1937, Accession 542, Box 821.
51 The suggested deletions were as follows: George Baker of J. P. Morgan; Arthur Bishop, a Flint banker brought onto the board by Durant; Henry F. and Irénée du Pont, of E. I. du Pont de Nemours; William Fisher of GM's Fisher Body division; Louis Kaufman of Chatham and Phoenix National Bank, another Durant ally; Sir Harry McGowan of Nobel Explosives, brought onto the board by Pierre du Pont; J. P. Morgan's Junius Morgan; Fritz Opel of GM's overseas Opel subsidiary; and Seward Prosser, George Whitney, Clarence Woolley, and Owen Young, all brought onto the board as direct or indirect representatives of J. P. Morgan.
52 Alfred P. Sloan, Jr., to Lammot du Pont, March 17, 1937, Accession 542, Box 821.
53 Members of the Du Pont Finance Committee present were Irénée, Lammot, and Pierre du Pont, Walter S. Carpenter, Jr., Donaldson Brown, and Angus Echols. See Lammot du Pont to Alfred P. Sloan, Jr., April 6, 1937. *U.S. v. Du Pont*, GTE #194.
54 Lammot du Pont to Alfred P. Sloan, Jr., April 6, 1937. *U.S. v. Du Pont*, GTE #194. Lammot gave a copy of this memo to Donaldson Brown, asking him to review it and forward it to Sloan. Brown indicated during the antitrust trial that he never gave the memo to Sloan.
55 Lammot du Pont to Alfred P. Sloan, Jr., April 6, 1937. *U.S. v. Du Pont*, GTE #194.

ally all of the powers of the existing Finance Committee. Moreover, the reduced board would have only eighteen members, at least half of whom would represent owners, virtually ensuring that important financial decisions would remain in their hands.[56]

On April 20, 1937, only weeks before the May 3 shareholder meeting at which Sloan wanted to introduce his plan, owners and managers met to discuss their differences.[57] Sloan offered a detailed critique of the Du Pont counterproposal. Although this plan had been favorably reviewed by Du Pont executives, Lammot commented that after Sloan's presentation it "did not meet with unanimous approval; in fact, I don't think anyone had a good word for it."[58] Following a discussion that lasted the rest of the day, the group agreed to a plan that included most of Sloan's original proposals. A Policy Committee would be appointed, consisting of six general office executives and three outside owner representatives. Beneath the Policy Committee, an Administration Committee would be appointed to take charge of daily operations. Sloan would become chairman of the board and retain his position as president, though executive vice-president William Knudsen would "eventually" take over in the latter position. Finally, the board would be reduced to twenty-eight members, but would not take on new responsibilities.

On May 3, 1937, the new organizational structure was formally approved by GM's board of directors (Figure 3.1, Tables 3.2 and 3.3).[59] The new plan contained only minor modifications to the scheme that Sloan and the du Ponts had agreed upon two weeks earlier. The Policy Committee and Administration Committee were both chaired by Sloan, who also took over as chairman of the board and retained the title of chief executive officer. Despite Sloan's desire for a waiting period, Knudsen was appointed president, but absent the title of chief executive officer, Knudsen wielded less power in this position than had Sloan. Indeed, in the new

56 The owner representatives on du Pont's proposed board were as follows: Walter S. Carpenter, Jr.; Irénée, Lammot, and Pierre du Pont; and John Raskob, all of E. I. du Pont de Nemours; and George Baker, Junius Morgan, Seward Prosser, and George Whitney, all of J. P. Morgan. GM members would include the following: Albert Bradley, a vice-president on GM's finance staff; William Knudsen, executive vice-president of operations; James Mooney, group executive in charge of overseas operations; Charles Mott, vice-president; John J. Schumann, head of General Motors Acceptance Corporation; Sloan; J. T. Smith, vice-president in charge of legal affairs, and Charles E. Wilson, vice-president and special assistant to Knudsen. The final member, Donaldson Brown, was GM's vice-president in charge of finance and a former Du Pont executive who served on the Finance Committees and boards of both GM and Du Pont.
57 Those present at the New York meeting were Sloan, Brown, J. T. Smith, John Pratt, John Raskob, and Lammot and Pierre du Pont. See Lammot du Pont to Walter S. Carpenter, April 23, 1937. *U.S. v. Du Pont*, GTE #196.
58 Lammot du Pont to Walter S. Carpenter, April 23, 1937. *U.S. v. Du Pont*, GTE #196.
59 The organization is depicted in General Motors Corporation, "Organization Chart, June 1937." *U.S. v. Du Pont*, DTE #GM5.

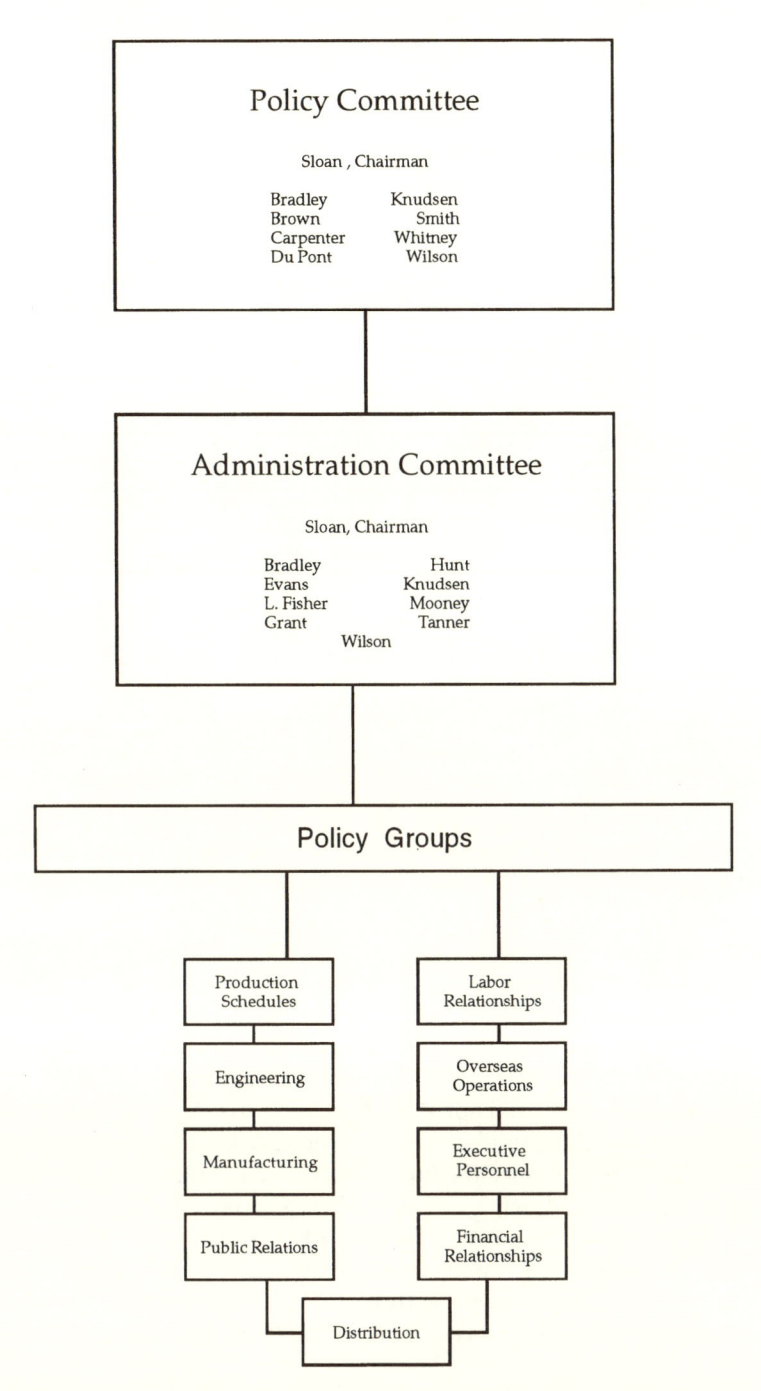

```
                    Policy Committee

                    Sloan, Chairman

              Bradley        Knudsen
              Brown          Smith
              Carpenter      Whitney
              Du Pont        Wilson


                 Administration Committee

                    Sloan, Chairman

              Bradley        Hunt
              Evans          Knudsen
              L. Fisher      Mooney
              Grant          Tanner
                    Wilson


                      Policy Groups
```

Production Schedules	Labor Relationships
Engineering	Overseas Operations
Manufacturing	Executive Personnel
Public Relations	Financial Relationships

Distribution

Figure 3.1. General Motors' top governing committees, 1937

Table 3.2. *Membership of Policy Committee (PC) and Administration Committee (AC), May 1937*

Policy Committee		
Name	Position(s) in Corporation	Staff/Line
Alfred P. Sloan, Jr.	Chairman of the Board, CEO Chairman, Policy Committee Chairman, Administration Comm	Line
Albert Bradley	Vice President, Finance Staff	Staff
Donaldson Brown	Vice Chairman of the Board	Line
Walter S. Carpenter, Jr.	Owner Representative, Du Pont	na
Lammot du Pont	Owner Representative, Du Pont	na
William S. Knudsen	President	Line
John Thomas Smith	Vice President, Legal	Staff
George Whitney	Owner Representative, J. P. Morgan	na
Charles E. Wilson	General Assistant to the President Possibly VP Manufacturing (Staff)	Line

Sources: Information on membership of the two committees and on PC members' positions in the corporation is taken from General Motors Corporation, *Annual Report*, 1937, except for the position(s) of Charles Wilson, which are shown in "C. E. Wilson Employment History with General Motors Corporation," Longwood, Box 417 (9), v. 3.

Information on positions of Administration Committee members is compiled from various sources. Information for all AC members can be surmised from Alfred P. Sloan, Jr., to Members of Policy and Administration Committees, November 11, 1937, Accession 542, Box 821. Information for Evans, Fisher, and Grant can be verified from General Motors Corporation, "Organization Chart," 1941. Information for Hunt can be verified in Sloan (1974, p. 234). Information for Mooney can be verified in General Motors Corporation, *Annual Report*, 1933.

organization Sloan served as chairman of the corporation's top two committees, chief executive officer, and chairman of the board, giving him enormous power over policy, operations, and finance. Donaldson Brown was appointed to the new position of vice-chairman of the board in charge of the financial staff. Though he remained free from any line authority exercised by the president, he was nonetheless subordinate to Sloan. Finally, plans to reduce the board in size were scrapped. Only two directors left the board, while one new director was added.[60]

The reorganization of 1937 gave GM's general office enormous power over all aspects of planning and operations. It greatly weakened owner control of finances, for the three owner representatives on the nine-member Policy Committee – Lammot du Pont, president of E. I. du Pont

---

60 The departing directors were GM's Alfred Swayne and J. P. Morgan's George Baker, who died in the months preceding the reorganization. Swayne was replaced by Marvin E. Coyle, general manager of the powerful Chevrolet division and the only division manager in the new organization to be on the board or hold the title of vice-president. See General Motors Corporation, *Annual Report*, 1937.

Table 3.2. (*Continued*)

Administration Committee		
Name	Probable Position(s) in Corporation	Staff/Line
Alfred P. Sloan, Jr.	Chairman of the Board, CEO Chairman, Policy Committee Chairman, Administration Comm	Line
Albert Bradley	Vice President, Finance Staff	Staff
William S. Knudsen	President	Line
Charles E. Wilson	General Assistant to the President Possibly VP, Manufacturing (Staff)	Line
Ronald K. Evans	Group Executive, Engine Group	Line
Lawrence P. Fisher	Group Executive, Body Group	Line
Richard H. Grant	Vice President, Distribution	Staff
Ormond E. Hunt	Vice President, Engineering	Staff
James D. Mooney	Group Executive, Overseas Group	Line
Floyd Tanner	Vice President, Labor Relations	Staff

de Nemours; Walter S. Carpenter, Jr., a vice-president at Du Pont who later served as president and then chairman; and J. P. Morgan's George Whitney – were in the minority.[61] They could not vote to veto funds for proposed policies without the support of general office executives on the Policy Committee. Moreover, the new organization removed owners from the information flows that would allow them to better assess proposed operating policies, thus diminishing their influence within the Policy Committee. The result was a series of disagreements between owners and managers that continued for decades, causing owners to be increasingly dissatisfied with the new organization over time. On the operating side, the new organization sought to create a clear distinction between policy and administration while increasing the power and influence of the general office technical staff. In fact, however, the new structure thoroughly conflated planning and operations, resulting in extreme centralization in which top executives took over more and more aspects of both strategic and operational decision-making. Unable to draw clear lines of demarcation between policy and administration, headquarters took responsibility for both.

61 It could be argued that Donaldson Brown, who sat on E. I. du Pont's board of directors and Finance Committee, was a Du Pont representative, and indeed he was often sympathetic to owners. Over time, however, Brown's executive position in GM shaped his views, and he became increasingly allied with Sloan and GM's general office.

Table 3.3. *General Motors' Policy Group Membership, November 1937*

	Production	Distribution	Engineering	Manufacturing	PR	Labor	Overseas	Personnel	Financial	Affiliation
Alfred Sloan		•[a]			†[b]		•			PC/AC
Albert Bradley	•	•	•	•	•		•	†	†	PC/AC
Donaldson Brown	•	•					•	•	•	PC
Ronald Evans				•		•				AC
Lawrence Fisher		•	•		•	•				AC
Richard Grant		†	•		•	•		•	•	AC
Ormond Hunt			†							AC
William Knudsen		•	•	•						PC/AC
James Mooney							†			AC
John Smith					•	•		•		PC
Floyd Tanner	†			†		†				AC
Charles Wilson						•		•	•	PC/AC
A.L. Deane[c]		•								division
Composition	3 PC 1 AC	4 PC 2 AC 1 division	3 PC 4 AC	3 PC 2 AC	3 PC 2 AC	3 PC 3 AC	4 PC 1 AC	4 PC 1 AC	4 PC 1 AC	

[a] The bullet symbol (•) denotes Policy Group membership.
[b] The dagger symbol (†) denotes Policy Group chairmanship.
[c] A. L. Deane was head of GM's Motors Holding division, an operation that loaned money to GM's franchise dealers. Although Motors Holding was a division in GM's car and truck group, its functions were financial in nature. Deane was the only member of the Policy Group in 1937 who belonged to neither the PC nor the AC. See Sloan (1964, p. 288); General Motors Corporation, "Organization Chart, 1941."
Source: All information on Policy Group membership is from "General Motors Corporation, Committee Assignments for Policy Purposes," November 9, 1937.

Redefining the Role of Finance

The reorganization of 1937 gave the general office increased control over financial decisions, weakening owner oversight in these areas. In the process, it also subtly redefined the role of finance within GM, accentuating differences between owners and headquarters. Owners' image of finance was rooted in an image of external oversight under hard budget constraints. They assumed that investment funds were scarce and that there was always a need to evaluate whether profit should be consumed as dividends or reinvested in the business. Consequently, they were primarily concerned with financial linkages to capital markets and with questions such as the availability and price of capital, the corporation's credit standing, the value of its securities, and its degree of liquidity and profitability. General office executives had a different view of financial control. Taking it for granted that GM had adequate funds to finance expansion, they were concerned primarily with forecasting market conditions and monitoring divisional performance, and they used the financial process as a means of realizing these goals. Headquarters thus viewed finance not as an end in itself, but as a tool that was subordinate to operating concerns. Owners, on the other hand, believed that if financial considerations were subordinated to operating concerns, the overall standing of the corporation would be imperiled.

These differences were expressed clearly in a debate concerning issues of personnel succession that emerged early in 1941. In June 1940 William Knudsen took a leave of absence from the presidency to serve on the National Defense Advisory Committee. Charles Wilson took over as acting president; when Knudsen elected to resign from GM in January 1941, Wilson was awarded the presidency on a permanent basis. Approaching 66 years of age, Alfred Sloan began to plan for his own retirement. He favored vice-president of finance Albert Bradley as his successor[62] and viewed the appointment of Wilson as an opportunity to make additional personnel changes that would help Bradley qualify as the next chairman of the board. Sloan recommended that Bradley be transferred out of finance and named group executive in charge of the car and truck group. This move would give Bradley a much better grasp of operations than he could obtain in finance, and Sloan believed such knowledge was essential for a chairman serving as the corporation's chief executive officer (CEO).[63]

---

62 Drucker (1978, p. 281).
63 Alfred P. Sloan, Jr., to Walter S. Carpenter, Jr., January 14, 1941, Accession 542, Box 837.

Owners feared that Bradley's reassignment would diminish financial oversight within GM. Although they joined with headquarters executives in approving Bradley's transfer, owners did so only because they believed that GM's general assistant treasurer, Frederic Donner, would be promoted to fill the vacancy created in finance.[64] Much to owners' surprise, however, the public announcement of Bradley's transfer made no mention of a successor. Moreover, the new organization charts drawn up in January 1941 showed the entire finance staff reporting to vice-chairman Donaldson Brown instead of to Sloan and the board.[65] Feeling that Brown had "passed to a more general executive position . . . and Bradley has gone over to the operations end," owners concluded that "there is no one as general financial executive."[66] Anxious to reestablish this function, Lammot du Pont and Walter Carpenter pressured Sloan and Brown to promote Donner.

The ensuing debate over Donner highlighted the different views of finance held by owners and managers. Owners emphasized that the reorganization of 1937 weakened financial oversight by eliminating the owner-controlled Finance Committee. Under the management-dominated Policy Committee, financial oversight was increasingly subordinated to operating concerns, rather than focusing on broad financial issues. Owners saw financial control as ultimately linked to external capital markets. Its primary goal was not simply to facilitate operations, but to acquire scarce capital and to monitor the capital market's assessment of the firm's value. The chief financial executive should review proposals independently of their operating implications, paying attention to financial criteria alone. Insofar as finance became subordinated to operating concerns, this function would be neglected:

> When we had the separate Finance Committee . . . the financial aspects of the Corporation were given more thought than they are today. It seems to me that under our present set-up important decisions are influenced more and more from the operating standpoint, and less and less from the financial

---

64 The decisions on Bradley and Wilson were made at a special meeting of the Policy Committee held in late December 1940. Because the meeting conflicted with a shareholders' meeting at E. I. du Pont de Nemours, Lammot du Pont attended the Policy Committee in Detroit, while Walter S. Carpenter, Jr., presided over the Du Pont meeting in Wilmington. See Lammot du Pont to Donaldson Brown, January 7, 1941, Accession 1334, Box 1; Walter S. Carpenter, Jr., to Donaldson Brown, January 7, 1941. *U.S. v. Du Pont*, GTE #1238; Walter S. Carpenter, Jr., to Donaldson Brown, January 9, 1941. *U.S. v. Du Pont*, GTE #200; Walter S. Carpenter, Jr., to Donaldson Brown, February 13, 1941, Accession 542, Box 837.

65 Walter S. Carpenter, Jr., to Donaldson Brown, February 13, 1941, Accession 542, Box 837.

66 Walter S. Carpenter, Jr., to Donaldson Brown, January 9, 1941. *U.S. v. Du Pont*, GTE #200.

Administrative Centralization of the M-form 111

standpoint. I am afraid that this trend will be accelerated considerably with the [transfer of Bradley and failure to promote Donner]....

Whose job will it be hereafter to consider in the broadest sense the question of the Corporation's credit, the standing of its securities? We can ask some one ... to give us reports on this, but the general subject ... will not ... be anybody's responsibility.[67]

Owners believed that a strong, independent finance staff was imperative in order to maintain accurate audit and control over operations. Such autonomy could be ensured only if the finance staff reported directly to owners; a finance staff that reported to a CEO in charge of operations ran the danger of seeing its monitoring and auditing functions subverted. Failure to replace Bradley would be the final step in undermining the autonomy of the finance staff, a process that had begun with the 1937 reorganization.

Owners also recognized that the subordination of finance to operations rested in part on slack capital resources created by large cash reserves. Excess investment funds made it easier to approve expansion programs while paying less attention to future returns. As budget constraints eased, even operating executives at corporate headquarters failed to evaluate proposed expenditures thoroughly. As one Du Pont representative put it, the "financial position of General Motors today is so strong that ... it is very easy for us to feel that [issues of finance are no longer] critical."[68] Managers who had risen to power under these conditions were especially prone to such negligence. Owners believed that Sloan possessed "a sympathetic appreciation of the financial aspects of the business," due largely to his experiences as an owner-entrepreneur.[69] But they also believed that the situation had deteriorated with the 1937 reorganization and would get worse still under Wilson's presidency, largely because the "broader financial aspects of Mr. Wilson's problems ... have always been provided for."[70] Moreover, they argued, increasing government regulation and the uncertainties created by World War II would revive the importance of finance in the years ahead, making the resurrection of financial oversight and the appointment of a new vice-president of finance all the more crucial.

67 Walter S. Carpenter, Jr., to Donaldson Brown, January 9, 1941. *U.S. v. Du Pont*, GTE #200.
68 Walter S. Carpenter, Jr., to Donaldson Brown, January 9, 1941. *U.S. v. Du Pont*, GTE #200.
69 Walter S. Carpenter, Jr., to Donaldson Brown, January 7, 1941. *U.S. v. Du Pont*, GTE #1238.
70 Walter S. Carpenter, Jr., to Donaldson Brown, January 9, 1941. *U.S. v. Du Pont*, GTE #200.

General office executives had a completely different view of finance that emphasized its role in securing internal control over operations. Taking it for granted that the corporation had more than enough retained earnings to expand virtually at will, corporate headquarters believed that "the most important" aspect of financial control was "forecasting and planning" in the operational sphere.[71] Little concerned with linkages to external capital markets, executives at headquarters focused almost exclusively on the accounting and control systems that allowed them to carry out forward planning and engage in divisional oversight.[72] In their view, profit was created by successful operating practices, not by the manipulation of external capital markets; general office executives saw owners' view of finance as removed from the realities of the business:

> ... effective financial control must rest inescapably upon coordinated thought and application on the part of those in authority.... Surely the financial credit of an industrial concern, or the marketable status of its outstanding securities, cannot be dependent merely upon the existence within its organization of some financial wizard such as [owners] envision.
> ... The record of performance, and the accepted ability to continue creditable [sic] performance is what counts. The desired result cannot be gained by mere oracular pronouncements where the supposed oracle himself may lack understanding of the intricate characteristics of the business, or where his pronouncements may not be accepted and applied by those in authority.[73]

Moreover, general executives did not see the importance of operating issues as evidence of finance's subordination. They emphasized that the finance and operating sides of GM had completely independent reporting lines, with the head of finance reporting to the corporation's vice-chairman and to the Policy Committee. This meant that aside from Sloan, operating executives had no line authority whatsoever over finance. Indeed, Sloan argued that it was this separation that made the transfer of Bradley to operations all the more essential so that the finance staff in New York could "maintain more effective contact" with the operating divisions in Detroit.[74]

71 Donaldson Brown to Lammot du Pont, January 9, 1941, Accession 1334, Box 1.
72 Donaldson Brown to Walter S. Carpenter, Jr., January 8, 1941. *U.S. v. Du Pont*, GTE #199.
73 Donaldson Brown to Walter S. Carpenter, Jr., January–February 1941, Accession 542, Box 837.
74 Alfred P. Sloan, Jr., to Walter S. Carpenter, Jr., January 14, 1941, Accession 542, Box 837.

The general office view of finance also stressed that a knowledge of financial issues alone was not sufficient for making informed financial decisions. Rather, it was essential that the leaders of the finance staff be intimately familiar with operating issues. Without such contact, they would lack sufficient information for evaluating alternative courses of action, since statistical indicators alone did not provide adequate knowledge of how financial decisions affected divisional performance. In addition, absent close contact with operations, finance staff lacked influence with operating personnel: both division managers and general office representatives were apt to resist advice from New York if it failed to manifest an understanding of the operating issues at stake. Financial representatives achieved contact with operations primarily through participation in the policy groups, taking part in meetings with division managers and group executives, and membership on the Administration Committee. Sloan and Brown resisted owners' suggestion that Donner be promoted to vice-president of finance because they felt he lacked such knowledge and therefore would not carry influence with operating personnel:

> [T]he first essential as applying to the financial chief... is that he understand the characteristics of the business with a full sense of practical considerations of an operating nature. The next essential is that he be accepted by the operating executives as entitled to a sympathetic hearing....
> ... When I said Donner was not ripe to assume... charge of finance... it was not with reference to his ability and knowledge of [finance]. The shortcomings of the moment are entirely on the side of contact... with problems of operating character.... One in Donner's position may [have] a perfectly balanced viewpoint on problems requiring coordinated consideration, and yet be regarded as theoretical by operating executives with whom he has not been in intimate contact. It is better far... to give him time to branch out into the field of operating policy considerations and then to move on the matter of his promotion after he has demonstrated ability... to apply his knowledge and experience.[75]

In order to facilitate Donner's preparation, Brown suggested "building up" his influence by involving him in policy group discussions with the divisions and by creating regular contact between Donner and divisional

75 The first paragraph is from Donaldson Brown to Walter S. Carpenter, Jr., January–February 1941, Accession 542, Box 837. The second is from Donaldson Brown to Walter S. Carpenter, Jr., January 8, 1941. *U.S. v. Du Pont*, GTE #199. Brown's admonition that financial executives like Donner were prone to be viewed as "theoretical" by operating men is particularly ironic in light of Donner's later reputation as CEO, described later in Chapter 7.

representatives. Even with these steps, however, Brown suggested that it might take as long as two years before Donner would be ready for promotion.[76]

The different notions of financial control underlying the debate over whether Donner should succeed Bradley as head of finance had important substantive implications. Disagreements over corporate policies toward GM's consumer credit division, General Motors Acceptance Corporation (GMAC), provide a good example. Even before the issue of promoting Donner arose, owner representatives on the Policy Committee had raised the question of whether GM should divest itself of GMAC; GM's competitors had discontinued such programs, fearing that the Justice Department would undertake antitrust action against them. Within the management-dominated Policy Committee, however, owners' concerns had "been set aside with almost no discussion."[77] Owners believed that the issue of GMAC should be reviewed "exhaustively and dispassionately"[78] by a financial chief divorced from operations. Instead, the question of potential legal issues arising out of GMAC was subordinated to operating considerations, and the possibility of divesting GMAC was never seriously considered. As owners feared, the U.S. government filed criminal charges against GM and GMAC in 1938. In 1939 the corporation and GMAC were found guilty of restraint of trade. A government-filed civil suit on related charges followed, and it was not resolved until 1952, when GM signed a consent decree.[79]

The subordination of financial control to operating considerations was not limited to the question of whether GM should continue to own and operate GMAC. Owners believed that government price and production controls instituted because of World War II made it imperative for GMAC to tighten credit to consumers. Because government-imposed production controls would limit the number of cars that GM and other manufacturers produced, demand for automobiles would far outstrip supply; there was thus no need to stimulate demand by offering consumer credit. Moreover, both government controls and reduced stability in consumer purchasing power made it riskier for GM to underwrite consumer purchases. Owners thus concluded that it was rational for GMAC to tighten credit in order to reduce its risk. General office executives on the Policy Committee, however, opposed "doing anything drastic" to curtail credit, for they knew that GM was carrying large inventories that

---

76   Donaldson Brown to Alfred P. Sloan, Jr., January 9, 1941, Accession 1334, Box 1.
77   Walter S. Carpenter, Jr., to Donaldson Brown, January 9, 1941. *U.S. v. Du Pont*, GTE #200.
78   Walter S. Carpenter, Jr., to Donaldson Brown, January 9, 1941. *U.S. v. Du Pont*, GTE #200.
79   See Sloan (1964, p. 309); Cray (1980, pp. 312–313).

needed to be sold to avoid losses.[80] Moreover, they maintained that "the protection of GMAC . . . is paramount" and that curtailing credit would simply cause GMAC to lose business to other financial institutions; they thus concluded that while GMAC should "modify its terms to the extent that" it could, it should not alter them so much that it would lose business to others.[81] From owners' point of view, this was a clear example of corporate executives placing operating considerations of inventory reduction and sales above issues of financial risk.

Different views of the role of finance fueled owner dissatisfaction with GM's 1937 organization. Their dissatisfaction intensified their desire to create a more independent financial staff and to reestablish strong outside control of finances. In the GMAC case, for instance, owners complained that "this [is] the type of thing about which we will always find it difficult to get sympathetic consideration so long as there is no executive . . . whose interest is primarily along financial lines. . . . I am afraid we will not get any solution . . . until the outside members of the Policy Committee insist upon it."[82] Yet outnumbered in the Policy Committee and lacking formal institutional mechanisms for reestablishing control, their complaints went unheeded. As a result, owners became increasingly dissatisfied with the Policy Committee itself. In stressing the need for an independent finance staff overseen by the board, for instance, Du Pont's Walter S. Carpenter commented that "I do not agree that the Policy Committee was ever intended to institute and carry on the financial policies of the Corporation, and I think any attempt to have the Policy Committee run the financial affairs of the Corporation would soon land us in a sorry plight."[83] Owner dissatisfaction over the 1937 organization and disagreements over the role of finance in GM would last for years and helped to shape subsequent reorganizations.

Conflating Policy and Administration

Despite setting out to create a clear distinction between policy and administration, the 1937 organization led to conflation of these issues, eventually resulting in centralization of virtually all decision-making in the general office. Difficulties at this level stemmed primarily from the

---

80 Alfred P. Sloan, Jr., to Walter S. Carpenter, Jr., May 28, 1941, Accession 542, Box 837.
81 Alfred P. Sloan, Jr., to Walter S. Carpenter, Jr., May 28, 1941, Accession 542, Box 837.
82 Walter S. Carpenter, Jr., to Lammot du Pont, June 3, 1941, Accession 542, Box 837.
83 Walter S. Carpenter, Jr., to Donaldson Brown, February 13, 1941, Accession 542, Box 837.

relationship among the Policy Committee, the Administration Committee, and the policy groups, and from the fact that the new organization embodied contradictory goals. On one hand, the 1937 structure was designed to create a superordinate Policy Committee with clear authority to intervene in all aspects of the business if necessary. On the other hand, Sloan also insisted that he wanted to delegate authority for running the business to the group executives and general office staff composing the Administration Committee. When fulfilling both of these goals proved problematic, increasing centralization resulted.

The desire to create a superordinate Policy Committee was rooted in headquarters' relations with both owners and operating management. As outlined earlier, one goal in establishing the Policy Committee was to minimize owner control from above, especially owners' ability to exercise financial veto power. Here, the creation of the Policy Committee replaced a division of powers between owners and managers with a more unified control over financial and operating policy in which general office executives dominated in both numbers and influence. At the operating level, the Policy Committee was designed to oversee the new conditions created by the product policy of 1934. As we saw earlier, forced interdependence between divisions was predicated on the assumption that headquarters would be responsible for specifying both technical aspects of operations and more general relations between the divisions. Because the general office therefore needed to be "in a position to deal frankly and aggressively" with the divisions, Sloan believed that the Policy Committee should have the capacity to involve itself in operating matters and issue orders to the divisions if necessary.[84] In this regard, the new structure marked a deliberate effort to give headquarters direct power over operating issues that had once been in the divisional domain. For both financial and operating reasons, then, Sloan believed that "the top Committee should be the top Committee ... and not one having only equal power with the other Committees."[85]

Yet the desire for Policy Committee control over operations was tempered by the conviction that, insofar as possible, the new Administration Committee should be given the authority to run the business. This would give the group executives and technical staff on the Administration Committee increased responsibility for overseeing operations and help groom them for future positions of power. Insisting that the "last thing I want to convey is that [the Policy Committee] is an Executive Committee," Sloan argued that it should be up to the Administration Committee to take on the responsibilities formerly assigned to the Executive Committee.[86] Indeed, Sloan went so far as to say that it should really be

84 Sloan (1964, p. 178).
85 Alfred P. Sloan, Jr., to Lammot du Pont, April 13, 1942. *U.S. v. Du Pont*, GTE #203.
86 Alfred P. Sloan, Jr., to Lammot du Pont, March 17, 1937, Accession 542, Box 821.

up to the Administration Committee, in conjunction with the policy groups, to formulate operating policy. The Policy Committee would simply serve as a review board to oversee, ratify, and, if necessary, alter strategic plans worked up in the Administration Committee. As Donaldson Brown put it, "the ideal would be ... if the Policy Committee ... never found the need to take the initiative in the formulation of policies, but rather found that [this] was being done by the Administration Committee."[87] In this scenario, the Policy Committee would be loath to actually exercise its power and would act primarily in an advisory capacity to the Administration Committee, which would carry out most aspects of strategic planning.

Both legal considerations and the nature of the relations among Policy Committee, Administration Committee, and policy groups militated against the Administration Committee serving as an effective governing body. Because the Policy Committee held all legal authority in the corporation, it was required to endorse any action taken by the Administration Committee. This meant that the Administration Committee could not formulate policy without Policy Committee approval; the Policy Committee was legally bound to review and approve every decision made by the Administration Committee, whether it pertained to policy or operations. Moreover, the Policy Committee held the power to "assume direct charge and control of any of the affairs, activities, positions, officers and employes of the Corporation."[88] This meant that the Policy Committee could overturn or modify Administration Committee recommendations whenever it desired; indeed, it could issue direct orders to the Administration Committee and its members. The unchallenged authority of the Policy Committee undoubtedly made it difficult for top officers to delegate initiative, for it made it all too easy for those executives to intervene in decisions and policies with which they did not agree. Finally, the Administration Committee was itself chaired by either Sloan or president William Knudsen, who took over as chair on May 1, 1939.[89] Through their chairmanship of the Administration Committee, they were able to influence the agenda and scope of the Administration Committee's activities.

The role of the policy groups in the new organization made it even less likely that the Administration Committee could function to articulate policy in an independent manner. Prior to 1937 the policy groups were subcommittees of the Executive Committee; all policy group members sat on the Executive Committee and on GM's board. After the

87 Donaldson Brown to Alfred P. Sloan, Jr., June 1, 1937, Accession 1334, Box 1. See also General Motors Corporation, *Annual Report*, 1937, p. 38.
88 General Motors Corporation, *By-laws*, as amended to July 1, 1937, p. 7.
89 General Motors Corporation, "Members of Board of Directors and Principal Executive Offices Held and Officers Who Were Not Directors, 1917–1948." Longwood, 438 (30), First Series, v. 32, p. 9593.

reorganization, the responsibilities of the old Executive Committee were divided between the Policy and Administration Committees. Under the new arrangement, the policy groups reported to the Administration Committee, but they were composed of both Policy Committee and Administration Committee representatives.[90] Rather than simply being subcommittees of a single governing body, the policy groups now constituted an arena in which members of two distinctly unequal committees met to formulate policy. Within the groups, top executives from the Policy Committee dominated in both numbers and influence. Of the eight groups, only one, engineering, had a majority of members who served solely on the Administration Committee.[91] Because Policy Committee members usually held line authority over such men, they could exert subtle pressure on them. As Sloan later remarked:

> ... with our organization set-up only a very small percentage of the broader problems have to go to the Administration Committee, simply because they are authoritatively dealt with by the Policy Groups.... And in these [groups] the President, the Executive Vice President or myself always participate.[92]

At both the formulation and ratification stages of the decision-making process, Administration Committee members participated with and were often outnumbered by more prestigious executives who held line authority over them. In this environment, Administration Committee members were much more likely to defer to their superiors instead of taking the initiative in policy matters.

The relationship among the Policy Committee, Administration Committee, and policy groups had two important consequences for planning and decision-making at GM. First, it gave enormous power to the corporation's top executives, especially Sloan, and it involved those men in every aspect of decision-making. As a result, the 1937 organization put a handful of men in control of every aspect of decision-making, including both strategic planning and more routine administration. Four of the general office executives on the Policy Committee – Sloan, Albert Bradley, William Knudsen, and Charles Wilson – also sat on the Admin-

90 Only one group had a member who belonged to neither the Policy Committee nor the Administration Committee. The Distribution Group's Albert L. Deane served as division manager of General Motors Holding Division, an operation that loaned money to GM's franchise dealers. Although he was a division manager, Deane's operation was exclusively financial in nature.
91 "General Motors Corporation, Committee Assignments for Policy Purposes," November 9, 1937, attachment to Alfred P. Sloan, Jr., to Members of Administration and Policy Committees, November 11, 1937, Accession 542, Box 821.
92 Alfred P. Sloan, Jr., to Lammot du Pont, April 5, 1945, Accession 542, Box 837. See also Sloan (1964, p. 182); Sloan, direct testimony. *U.S. v. Du Pont*, pp. 4362–4363 (2469).

istration Committee. In addition to collaborating on policy issues, the Administration Committee was charged with administering more routine operating matters. By virtue of their participation on the Administration Committee, these four top executives thus became deeply involved in administering operations, creating an opportunity for them to intervene in divisional affairs. Top involvement in operating matters was intensified by corporate by-laws requiring that all Administration Committee decisions, whether pertaining to policy or administration, be formally reviewed and approved by the Policy Committee. Over time, the Policy Committee virtually took over both strategic planning and administrative decision-making. Instead of delegating authority to technical staff and group executives, the new organization thus created extreme centralization.

The second consequence of the 1937 setup was that it created information asymmetries that made it extremely difficult for owners to participate effectively in governance. General office executives on the Policy Committee participated in policy group discussions of policy, and four of these men also sat on the Administration Committee. Only the three Policy Committee members who represented outside owners – Walter S. Carpenter, Jr., Lammot du Pont, and George Whitney – sat on neither the Administration Committee nor the policy groups. As a result, the general office men were much more knowledgeable about both policy and administration issues than were owners. Because they participated in neither the policy groups nor the Administration Committee, owners were cut out of informational loops, leaving them ill-equipped to evaluate Administration Committee recommendations and ill-prepared to understand the implications of policies developed in the policy groups. Owners thus remained unable to match the influence of general office executives in Policy Committee discussions, and more often than not they saw their opinions go unheeded by management. Despite owners' representation on the Policy Committee, the new organization diminished their ability to exercise influence on that committee.

Centralization Completed

While the goal of the 1937 structure was to create "a sensible, sane and orderly segregation of policy from problems of administration,"[93] it had the effect of thoroughly confusing the two functions. Unable to draw clear distinctions between the two spheres, the Policy Committee devoted

---

93 Donaldson Brown to Walter S. Carpenter, Jr., September 8, 1938, Accession 542, Box 821.

more and more of its time to operating issues, paying little attention to policy proper. This development was particularly alarming to owners, who quickly concluded that the new organization was not working properly. By the time the new structure was a year old, owners were charging that the Policy Committee had "failed of its purpose in large part."[94] Their objections were threefold: the Policy Committee did not keep its members abreast of crucial information, which resulted in perfunctory and uninformed decision-making; the Policy Committee subordinated financial issues to operating considerations, failing to allow for independent analysis; and the Policy Committee became increasingly involved in operating issues, forsaking its mission of strategic planning and involving itself in details of the business better decided at a lower level of the organization.[95] General office executives did not agree with these criticisms, but they conceded that each contained at least an element of truth.

Owners' charge that the Policy Committee made decisions in a perfunctory manner was related in large part to their exclusion from the policy groups and the Administration Committee. As outlined earlier, policy proposals were formulated in the policy groups, then reviewed, debated, and sometimes modified in Administration Committee meetings and in less formal seminars with divisional representatives. Owners did not participate in any of these meetings – they received only the final reports on proposed policies prepared by the Administration Committee. When the Policy Committee met to approve policies, it received "numerous and voluminous" reports from the Administration Committee on relatively short notice; owners charged that in discussing these reports, Policy Committee members would "get side-tracked on two or three questions, and then practically receive and accept the reports en masse."[96] Owners thus believed that there was insufficient time to review reports on proposed policies and that Policy Committee discussion of such proposals was haphazard and unsystematic. Du Pont's Walter S. Carpenter, Jr., quickly became so frustrated with this lack of information that he "found it desirable to go over . . . reports with Mr. Bradley [of GM's finance staff] and others . . . with the idea of acquainting myself on certain subjects."[97]

General office executives on the Policy Committee were not bothered by having to vote on reports and recommendations without discussion, because they had played leading roles in preparing those reports through

[94] Walter S. Carpenter, Jr., to Donaldson Brown, July 5, 1938, Accession 542, Box 821.
[95] Owners later worried that the Policy Committee's involvement in operating matters would make owner representatives legally liable for operating decisions, but this does not appear to have been a concern prior to 1942. See Chapter 4 herein.
[96] Walter S. Carpenter, Jr., to Donaldson Brown, July 5, 1938, Accession 542, Box 821.
[97] Walter S. Carpenter, Jr., to Donaldson Brown, July 5, 1938, Accession 542, Box 821.

Administrative Centralization of the M-form 121

their participation in the policy groups and the Administration Committee and were thus well versed in the issues.[98] As Carpenter put it, general office executives were "necessarily so conversant with the Corporation[']s affairs that you do not feel the absence of a discussion of the important matters involving the Corporation, whereas some of us are in a quite different position."[99] Top executives could only agree that their knowledge made them "apt to minimize the importance" of discussions within the Policy Committee, and to address owners' concerns, Sloan suggested devoting a portion of each meeting to "keeping the members . . . in touch with what is happening in the business."[100] Despite this move, however, owners continued to be at an informational disadvantage, and they continued to see Policy Committee meetings as perfunctory and unsystematic.

Better information alone could not resolve owners' complaints, for managers and owners continued to adhere to different notions of the definitions of and relationships among policy, finance, and administration. Despite the elimination of the old Finance Committee, owners still envisioned policy-making as a financial review in which the Policy Committee would oversee operations through controlling appropriations and allocating scarce investment funds. They thus clung to the notion that the crucial issue guiding decisions should be the availability of funds and the prospective costs and returns of proposed policies. Many of their complaints concerning the perfunctory nature of Policy Committee meetings were grounded in what they saw as a failure to subject proposed policies to adequate financial analysis. In this sense, they maintained, policy and administration should both be subject to finance. But increasingly, Sloan and the general office turned this edict on its head, as financial decision-making became subject to operations. Indeed, budget constraints softened to such an extent that corporate headquarters came to regard appropriations as "a purely operating matter"[101] to be decided in the Administration Committee and approved later by the Policy Committee. Although information asymmetries played a part in owners' complaints about financial control, simply providing better information to owners would not resolve these differences. At their heart, these disagreements were rooted in different views of how proposed policies should be evaluated.

---

98 See Donaldson Brown to Walter S. Carpenter, Jr., May 9, 1938, Accession 542, Box 821.
99 Walter S. Carpenter, Jr., to Alfred P. Sloan, Jr., February 20, 1939, Accession 542, Box 821.
100 Alfred P. Sloan, Jr., to Walter S. Carpenter, Jr., March 20, 1939, Accession 542, Box 821.
101 Alfred P. Sloan, Jr., to Walter S. Carpenter, Jr., April 11, 1942b, Accession 542, Box 837.

Owners' concerns that expenditures and financial control received inadequate attention in the new organization became apparent when Du Pont's Walter Carpenter wrote a long letter to Alfred Sloan in which he excoriated the Policy Committee, charging that it was abrogating its financial responsibilities. In the Policy Committee meeting of November 1938, for instance, Carpenter charged that the committee "had a long list of important items to cover [including] declaring some thirty or forty millions of dollars in dividends."[102] Although owners were vitally interested in these issues, the Policy Committee spent no more than 30 minutes discussing the entire list of agenda items, focusing instead on a proposed "Labor Loan Plan" that would allow employees to borrow money from GM. The latter plan required "commitments which ... might mount to millions of dollars," involved complicated mathematical formulas, and had "been under discussion by Corporation executives for months," yet no advance written report on the topic had been submitted to the Policy Committee. Similarly, the January 1939 Policy Committee meeting faced "a large accumulation of reports ... involving ... huge appropriations." Yet once again, the committee spent most of its time considering "a mathematical formula involving the distribution of the bonus available [to] various departments," with no advance written reports to expedite the discussion. Consideration of the bonus took up so much time that the Policy Committee was forced to cover other agenda items "as the meeting waxed toward the close," leaving "a large number of important items ... and huge sums involved with no time for discussion." To owners' horror, tens of millions of dollars were committed virtually without comment. Owners concluded that the problems with the 1937 structure went beyond the need for better information; they believed that the Policy Committee was failing to exercise adequate financial oversight or to engage in effective strategic planning. General office executives conceded that the Policy Committee had "not entered the field of policy determination to the extent [originally] conceived as desirable," but they remained relatively unconcerned over this situation.[103]

While owners believed that the Policy Committee had abrogated its financial and strategic planning responsibilities, they also charged that it had become too involved in operations, causing headquarters to become deeply enmeshed in administrative decision-making. As outlined earlier, Policy Committee involvement in administration and operational decision-making was encouraged both by the product policy of 1934 and by the organizational and legal features of the new structure. The new

[102] Walter S. Carpenter, Jr., to Alfred P. Sloan, Jr., February 20, 1939, Accession 542, Box 821. All quotes in the paragraph are from this source.
[103] Donaldson Brown to Walter S. Carpenter, Jr., May 9, 1938, Accession 542, Box 821.

Administrative Centralization of the M-form 123

product policy made headquarters responsible for many operating decisions, and by 1938 the general office technical staff had taken over most decision-making in the areas of styling, engineering, manufacturing, and sales. Divisions that had once been responsible for designing their own car bodies, for instance, had seen their range of discretion over styling limited to areas like "hoods, cowling, and radiator grilles."[104] Similarly, engineering decisions were moved out of the divisions and into the general office technical staff, while sales became so centralized that division managers could no longer even add or replace dealers without permission from the general office sales and distribution staff.[105] The centralization of operating decisions was carried out by the technical staffs working through the policy groups and the Administration Committee. Yet because Administration Committee decisions on these matters had to be approved by the Policy Committee, top executives also became involved. Over time, these men took over almost every level of decision-making.

Finally, owners' doubts about the new structure may have been intensified by GM's performance during this period. Pointing to the fact that GM did not report a single loss during the years of the depression, most analysts have emphasized GM's success relative to the disastrous performance of Ford during the 1930s.[106] What these comparisons fail to note is that after 1934, GM was consistently outperformed by Chrysler. Moreover, as owners were well aware, GM's inability to match Chrysler's performance was linked directly to the financial and operating policies promulgated by the Policy Committee. Recall that one of the central issues leading to the reorganization of 1937 was headquarters' desire to increase capacity. Following the 1937 reorganization, general office executives on the Policy Committee quickly authorized a $60 million expansion program.[107] While the expansion that resulted led to an increase in production and sales, GM's profits remained well below their pre-depression levels. This was partly a result of higher taxes that cut into profit margins. But GM's poor performance was also linked directly to the decision to increase capacity. Data for return on net investment – GM's own preferred yardstick for evaluating performance – show that Chrysler consistently outperformed GM during this period (Figure 3.2). Between 1935 and 1940, Chrysler's return on investment regularly and sometimes dramatically surpassed GM's. Chrysler's superior performance was due primarily to its much higher turnover rates; by

104 *Fortune*, "General Motors, Part I of a Study in Bigness," p. 156; this passage was brought to my attention by Kuhn (1986, p. 125).
105 Kuhn (1986, pp. 126, 134–135).
106 See, for example, Kuhn (1986, Chapters 11 and 14).
107 General Motors Corporation, *Annual Report*, 1937, pp. 7–8; Sloan (1964, p. 201).

General Motors

Year	1. Net Income/ Net Sales	2. Net REP Turnover	3. Net Working Cap. Turnover	4. Net Total Turnover	5. Net ROIC
1934	12.77%	2.94189	3.15795	.98229	12.55%
1935	17.02%	3.62068	3.61182	1.22174	20.79%
1936	19.60%	3.70749	4.23711	1.45150	28.45%
1937	15.28%	3.93371	4.62764	1.55800	23.81%
1938	12.20%	2.69205	2.75530	1.01412	12.37%
1939	16.57%	3.56821	3.17115	1.26342	20.94%
1940	17.86%	4.45816	3.75557	1.57563	28.15%
1941	20.09%	5.94524	4.87338	2.03179	40.83%

Chrysler

Year	1. Net Income/ Net Sales	2. Net REP Turnover	3. Net Working Cap. Turnover	4. Net Total Turnover	5. Net ROIC
1934	3.14%	6.10304	7.33277	2.98710	9.39%
1935	8.50%	9.64641	8.43074	4.08209	34.68%
1936	11.41%	11.07656	10.26844	4.92192	56.15%
1937	8.19%	11.65237	10.39511	5.12765	41.98%
1938	5.44%	5.90510	5.28229	2.64701	14.41%
1939	8.25%	8.12434	5.80322	3.20074	26.42%
1940	8.23%	11.74337	6.44296	3.84422	31.65%
1941	7.75%	15.23940	6.98203	4.53510	35.13%

Figure 3.2. Return on invested capital (ROIC) and related performance indicators, GM and Chrysler, 1934–1941. Net real estate and plant (REP) turnover (2) is defined as the value of net sales divided by the value of net real estate and plant (i.e., real estate and plant after subtracting depreciation reserves). Working-capital turnover (3) is defined as the value of net sales divided by the value of net working capital (gross working capital minus current liabilities). Total net turnover (4) is defined as the value of net sales divided by the value of net working capital (cash; securities and tax notes; accounts receivable; inventories) plus net fixed capital (investments in other companies; other investments; miscellaneous assets; capital stock in treasury; prepaid expenses and deferred charges; net real estate, plant, and equipment). (All figures calculated from the annual reports of General Motors Corporation and Chrysler Corporation.)

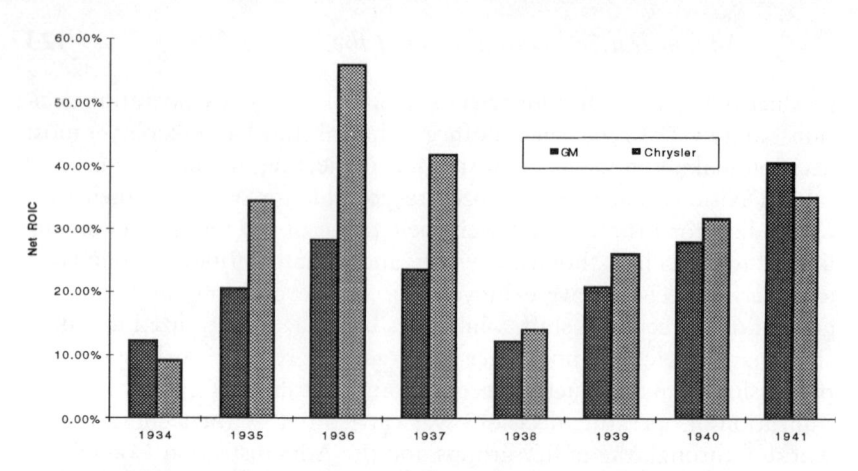

Administrative Centralization of the M-form

maintaining lower capacity and using its plant and working capital more intensively, Chrysler was able to surpass GM's performance. Because of its larger (and growing) investment in plant and capacity, GM had much lower turnover rates. The comparison with Chrysler probably fueled owners' fears that headquarters was expanding too rapidly, thereby increasing market share at the expense of profit.

Even after the expansion program finally began to pay off in 1941, when sales exceeded pre-depression levels and return on net investment finally exceeded the 30 percent target, owners continued to believe that the new organization was too centralized. In 1942 they complained that "as the years have gone on, the Policy Committee has become stronger, and the Administration Committee has become of gradually lesser importance."[108] Even Sloan was eventually forced to confess that "we have reached the point where practically everything of any importance involving 'running the business' goes to the Policy Committee."[109] As the extent of centralization became apparent, even financial success could not quell owners' doubts about the new organization. As Walter Carpenter put it:

> ... I am of the feeling that the present form of organization ... functions merely because of the individuals involved and because of the evolution of the organization. ... I have some doubt whether the Administration Committee itself serves much, if any, useful purpose. ... There is a good deal of discussion about a decentralized management in General Motors, though, it seems to me that ... there is too much centralization of authority ... in the Policy Committee [and thus] in a very few individuals.[110]

With policy, administration, and financial decision-making all within the purview of the general office, the 1937 organization completed the process of administrative centralization that had begun in 1934.

Summary

Between 1934 and 1941, GM became extremely centralized, giving its top executives control over both strategic planning and administrative

---

108 Walter S. Carpenter, Jr., to Alfred P. Sloan, Jr., April 8, 1942. *U.S. v. Du Pont*, GTE #201.
109 Alfred P. Sloan, Jr., to Donaldson Brown, December 28, 1944. *U.S. v. Du Pont*, DTE #GM7. Note that this document is out of temporal sequence; it reflects Sloan looking back on the prewar (i.e., pre-1942) structure.
110 Walter S. Carpenter, Jr., to Lammot du Pont, March 28, 1945, Accession 542, Box 837. This document is out of temporal sequence.

decision-making. Administrative centralization occurred in two stages. Between 1934 and 1936, the general office centralized operations, reducing divisional autonomy, virtually eliminating the mechanisms for creating divisional consent, and taking control of operating decisions once made in the divisions. Headquarters' centralization of operations rested in part on better information. The reduced uncertainty in manufacturing and engineering that resulted from the depression made the general office less reliant on divisions for information, increasing its ability to make informed operating decisions. But centralization also rested on a social transformation that undermined divisional autonomy. The product policy of 1934 destroyed expertise based in market segmentation by putting the automobile divisions in direct competition within the same market. It is important to realize that the decision to put the divisions in competition with one another was not simply an efficient response to an undifferentiated market. The efficient response to such conditions, as GM's own financial staff argued, was to reduce internal differentiation by maintaining fewer divisions. Indeed, the decision to return to five car divisions created additional complexity and probably increased costs. But it also reduced the need for divisional consent, thereby allowing the general office to take over what had once been divisional prerogatives and eliminate participative decentralization. Without jurisdiction over specific markets, division managers could not claim unique expertise and therefore could not justify their inclusion in the strategic planning process.

Administrative centralization was completed only when the general office weakened owners' ability to exercise financial veto and took control of investment surplus following the reorganization of 1937. Huge profits created surplus capital. Under these conditions, proposed policies could no longer be vetoed simply on the ground that funds did not exist. Instead, any number of proposals could be funded, and the evaluation of proposed policies was tied more closely to an assessment of their prospective consequences. As a result, financial decision-making became much more closely tied to knowledge of the various trade-offs embodied in prospective policies. Because owners lacked detailed knowledge of operations and were not included in key information loops, their influence over both policy and finance was reduced, and the general office took control of these functions. The 1937 reorganization was thus the final step in the process of administrative centralization, and it left GM's corporate headquarters in command of almost every aspect of planning and operations.

4

Participative Decentralization Redefined: Mobilizing for War Production, 1941–1945

The outbreak of World War II changed the conditions that had led to administrative centralization and introduced extreme uncertainty for GM and other manufacturers. Virtually overnight GM ceased manufacturing automobiles and converted to the production of military equipment. The uncertainties associated with war production imposed contradictory organizational imperatives that taxed GM's existing structure. On the one hand, this abrupt change called for greater decentralization and increased the need for divisional consent. The need to design, modify, and produce a large number of new and diverse products in a limited amount of time greatly increased uncertainty in the areas of manufacturing and engineering. Moreover, the fact that the different divisions were making extremely diverse and dissimilar products meant that each was again producing for a separate "market." The technical uncertainty and market differentiation created by wartime production increased the importance of divisional knowledge and consent. Yet in other areas, the war created a need for greater centralization. The conversion to military production intensified the need for quick decision-making and uniform policy. GM's method of formulating and approving policies through review and discussion in a number of committees proved to be too cumbersome and slow for wartime conditions and would have to be streamlined.

In order to address the contradictory imperatives imposed by the war, GM modified its organizational structure several times during the period between 1942 and 1945. Except for a brief period of extreme centralization in 1942, most of the changes made during the war marked a return to and transformation of participative decentralization. At the heart of this transformation was the distinction between policy formulation and policy approval that had been introduced in 1937. During the war, GM increased divisional participation in the policy approval phase of strategic planning, leaving policy formulation largely in the hands of the general office. As a result, the corporation was able to reorganize the balance between coercion and consent. By giving top executives control over policy formulation, the new organization allowed headquarters to control the premises of decision-making and to retain hegemony over the strategic planning and resource allocation process.[1] But by giving division managers a formal vote in the policy approval stage of strategic planning, it also gave the divisions limited but real power in that process, thereby eliciting their consent to corporate policies. Wartime reorganization thus created a new form of participative decentralization that attempted to balance general office control with divisional consent.

Contradictory Imperatives of Defense Production

Even before the United States entered the war, GM's increasing military production began to create strain on its organization, foreshadowing the changes that would occur following all-out conversion to defense production. Between 1940 and 1941, the U.S. government increased its national defense program dramatically, and by January 1941 GM had acquired over $683 million worth of domestic and foreign defense contracts.[2] The extreme uncertainty associated with these contracts put enormous pressure on GM's organizational capabilities. Most defense contracts involved the manufacture of new products for which technology and costs were uncertain, leading to questions over how to evaluate and allocate contracts and how to carry out production. Moreover, many of these contracts required the rapid construction or deployment of new manufacturing facilities, raising issues of how to finance investment in war-related plant. Finally, despite the uncertainties associated with defense production, decisions on these issues had to be made very quickly, leaving little time for complex analyses of contracts or for debating and passing proposals in a number of committees. These strains were further exacerbated by important personnel changes. On September 3, 1940, following a six-month leave of absence, William Knudsen resigned his position as president and stepped down as a member of GM's board, leaving Charles E. Wilson in charge as acting president and chair of the Administration Committee.[3] This in turn set off a series of promotions

---

1 On the importance of controlling the premises of decision-making, see Simon (1976, especially Chapter 11); Simon (1991, p. 32).
2 General Motors Corporation, *Annual Report*, 1940, p. 21.
3 Cray (1980, p. 316). General Motors Corporation, *Annual Report*, 1940. Knudsen began a leave of absence in June 1940 to serve on the U.S. government's National Defense Advisory Committee. The timing was unfortunate from GM's point of view, for government orders reached a record high that month, following the fall of France. Perhaps for that reason, Sloan opposed the move, but corporate regulations allowed Knudsen to take a ninety-day leave without Policy Committee approval. Wilson was

and reassignments at the top of GM's corporate hierarchy that put a number of key executives in new jobs.[4]

The initial reaction to the growing importance of defense contracting was increased centralization in that area. In June 1940 Sloan created a new Defense Materials Relationships Committee (DMRC) that reported directly to the Policy Committee. Chaired by James Mooney, executive assistant to the president, the purpose of the new committee was to formulate policies regarding defense contracting.[5] In principle the group was to make recommendations to the Policy Committee and was subject to reversal by that body. But in fact, the DMRC contained the entire membership of the Policy Committee, minus its three owner representatives.[6] In effect, the new arrangement simply turned all defense-related policy decisions over to general office members of the Policy Committee, thereby removing owners from involvement in such decisions. A similar centralization took place in the realm of non-defense-related operating policy, where Wilson, Albert Bradley, and Ormond Hunt "were made a 'triumvirate' to handle all operations policy,"[7] putting planning in that domain in the hands of a small number of top executives.

Formal centralization was accompanied by informal practices that bypassed established lines of authority and gave even more power to a small number of executives. On June 27, 1940, little more than a week after Wilson took over as acting president, Sloan held an informal meeting with Wilson, Brown, "and perhaps some others" to discuss problems raised by the sudden increase in defense contracts.[8] Working independently of both the Policy Committee and the DMRC, this group of men adopted a tentative "Defense Materials Policy" to govern the pro-

---

named acting president and chairman of the Administration Committee on June 18. When Knudsen's ninety-day period expired, he resigned in order to work full-time for the government's war effort, leaving Wilson in charge. In addition to the foregoing sources, see Beasley (1947, p. 234).

4 Albert Bradley, Ormond Hunt, and James Mooney were all named executive assistants to Wilson. Bradley was also named group executive in charge of the car and truck group (see Chapter 3), while Hunt and Mooney relinquished their respective positions as staff vice-president in charge of engineering and group executive for overseas operations. Hunt was also appointed to the Policy Committee. See General Motors Corporation, "Organization Chart, August 1941." Mooney resigned on January 5, 1942, to serve in the U.S. government.
5 General Motors Corporation (1943, Section IV, p. 2).
6 The members of the DMRC were as follows: Mooney; Albert Bradley, group executive in charge of the car and truck group and executive assistant to Wilson; vice-chairman of the board Donaldson Brown; Ormond Hunt, executive assistant to Wilson and head of the patents staff; Alfred Sloan, chairman of the board and CEO; vice-president of legal affairs John Thomas Smith; and Charles Wilson, acting president of the corporation. Of this group, only Mooney was not also a member of the Policy Committee. See General Motors Corporation (1943), organization chart for 1940.
7 Sloan (1964, p. 378).
8 Charles Wilson to Alfred P. Sloan, Jr., September 19, 1940, Accession 542, Box 837.

curement of government contracts. Intended to serve as a tentative guideline until government laws and requirements were clarified, the policy does not seem to have been cleared through the Policy Committee. Instead, it was agreed upon and implemented through informal discussions among Sloan, Wilson, Bradley, and Mooney. This group of four thus outlined the policy that would be used in making commitments for government contracts worth hundreds of millions of dollars.

The defense materials policy focused on determining which defense "markets" GM should enter and what proportion of the corporation's resources should be devoted to these new markets. It stated that the corporation should attempt to obtain orders for between 10 and 15 percent of GM's annual capacity – some $150,000,000 to $200,000,000 worth of work annually.[9] This move was made because Sloan and his colleagues feared that the war might cause GM's auto sales to be curtailed, making it necessary to have other business to take up the slack.[10] The policy further specified that contracts should be for larger and more complex products rather than for those that were easily designed and built.[11] Executives later reported that this policy was initiated in order to make the best use of GM's experience and skills, but contracts for more complicated products were almost always more profitable. For instance, Oldsmobile made "only 44 of the 862 parts in its four guns [but] fabrication of these 44 parts, together with assembly, proof-firing and packing, account for approximately 48 percent of the total cost of the guns."[12]

The defense materials policy also recommended that GM obtain defense contracts for all of its plants or plant cities as a means of avoiding worker layoffs. This decision was based on an erroneous projection by the general office sales staff, which predicted that car sales for 1941 would fall well short of the 1940 peak, requiring GM to lay off some 20,000 workers. Defense contracts would allow the corporation to keep those workers on the payroll, making it less susceptible to possible labor shortages brought on by the war.[13] Finally, the executives who imple-

9 "Defense Material Policy," June 27, 1940, as quoted in Charles Wilson to Alfred P. Sloan, Jr., September 19, 1940, Accession 542, Box 837.
10 The rationale behind the various aspects of the policy is given in "Defense Material Policy." Sloan indicated that in an expansion of the defense program that led to government regulation of materials and markets, GM would be hurt "more ... than any other non-defense industry," unless they took part in defense production. See Alfred P. Sloan, Jr., to Walter S. Carpenter, Jr., May 28, 1941, Accession 542, Box 837.
11 General Motors Corporation (1943, Section IV, p. 29). See also Sloan (1964, p. 280); Drucker (1972, p. 76).
12 General Motors Corporation (1943, Section IV, p. 39). A number of similar examples are given in this document.
13 Charles E. Wilson to Alfred P. Sloan, Jr., September 19, 1940, Accession 542, Box 837. As it turned out, GM's automobile production for 1941 reached an all-time high. The corporation could not keep up with demand in the first half of that year, and its

Participative Decentralization Redefined 131

mented the defense materials policy decided that the corporation's top defense priority would be the Allison division's production of airplane engines and that two top general office executives would devote all of their time to Allison until production of the engines was under way.[14] Between late June and September 1940, these guidelines served as the corporation's general policy regarding defense contracting, even though they apparently had never been formally approved by the Policy Committee.

Although defense production led to increased centralization in the policy area, it also increased divisional participation at other levels, particularly in the area of defense contract allocation. Decisions over whether the corporation should take on prospective defense contracts were subject to general office review and control in two ways. First, they were discussed in the Administration Committee by the top executives and general office staff men who constituted that body. Second, before any definite commitments were made, contracts were reviewed by New York's financial and legal staffs. Yet because work would have to be carried out in the various divisions, divisional personnel were also deeply involved in the contract allocation process. James Mooney and his staff served as liaisons with the operating divisions to discuss prospective contracts. Each of the divisions appointed a contact man for defense-related work, and "no projects [were] given serious consideration unless they were interesting to the managers of the divisions who would make the products."[15] Indeed, Mooney's staff sought to put the divisions directly in contact with government agencies so that operating men and government representatives could discuss and negotiate contracts directly, with a minimum of general office intervention. Thus, although the general office continued to oversee project allocation, war conditions made it more important to involve division managers in the decision-making process. These pressures would increase following conversion to all-out war production.

The contradictory imperatives created by defense-related production undermined the authority of the Policy Committee and further diminished owner control. The need for quick decision-making caused defense-related policies to be centralized in the DMRC or to be carried out informally by a handful of top executives. The Policy Committee did

market share slipped in spite of record sales. See General Motors Corporation, *Annual Report*, 1941, pp. 8–10. Shortage of capacity was probably due in part to the general office's erroneous prediction that 1941 sales would fall below 1940 levels.

14 Charles E. Wilson to Alfred P. Sloan, Jr., September 19, 1940, Accession 542, Box 837. The men in question were Ormond Hunt, one of Wilson's executive assistants, and Ronald K. Evans, group executive in charge of the Engine Group.

15 Charles E. Wilson to Alfred P. Sloan, Jr., September 19, 1940, Accession 542, Box 837.

little more than rubber-stamp initiatives approved by the DMRC, and in some cases defense-related decisions were not even reviewed by the Policy Committee. As a consequence, owner representatives on the Policy Committee knew relatively little about GM's defense-related decisions. The decentralization of contract allocation decisions meant that the Policy Committee did not become involved in such questions unless issues of investment and finance were at stake, and even in these instances it let the Administration Committee take the lead. In August 1940, for instance, the Administration Committee moved to clarify procedures for financing government projects. On August 15, it recommended that GM finance facilities used for defense production only in cases where the government would "fully protect the Corporation against loss of capital" in the event that production was suspended.[16] When the government would not agree to such conditions, or when expansion involved the construction of facilities that could not be used for the production of automobiles, the government would have to provide capital before GM would accept the contract. The Policy Committee approved these recommendations on August 20, 1940, but even the fact that they originated with the Administration Committee marked a departure from earlier practice. The need for rapid decision-making and the growing importance of divisional expertise meant that policy initiatives increasingly emerged from below, even when broad financial issues were at stake.

As the Administration Committee and the divisions took over contract allocation, owner representatives objected that defense projects were not receiving proper scrutiny and clearance from the Policy Committee. Allowing defense contracts to clear through the Administration Committee and the divisions subverted formal organizational structure, they complained, especially financial oversight. At the Policy Committee meeting of September 18, 1940, for instance, owners complained that the Allison division and corporate executives had signed a contract to produce airplane engines and had made enormous commitments to the government. Yet contrary to accepted procedures, the contract had been approved without an analysis of how it would affect GM's finances and profits, return on investment, or capital requirements. Indeed, the Allison agreement had never been approved by the Policy Committee. Acting president Wilson could only admit that "considering the magnitude of the business, its importance from a defense angle, and its possible effects on ... profits, such a report should have been made."[17] Similar problems existed with regard to a large contract for machine guns, where general

---

16 Administration Committee resolution quoted in Charles E. Wilson to Alfred P. Sloan, Jr., September 19, 1940, Accession 542, Box 837.
17 Charles E. Wilson to Alfred P. Sloan, Jr., September 19, 1940, Accession 542, Box 837.

office executives took the position that because facilities were being financed by the government, prior Policy Committee approval of expenditures was not required. Owners also complained that centralization of defense-related policy in the DMRC subverted Policy Committee oversight. DMRC chairman James Mooney had unilaterally announced that he was issuing a report outlining the corporation's defense policy, owners complained, even though the existing rules of procedure clearly indicated that he could not do so without first having any proposed policies reviewed by both the Administration Committee and the Policy Committee.

Wilson acknowledged that the Policy Committee had not yet approved definite policies and procedures on many defense matters and that existing procedures had not been implemented consistently, but he attributed these difficulties to the "hurry and rush with which projects are being handled by the Government." To satisfy owner demands for Policy Committee oversight, he agreed that commitments on capital expenditures over $500,000 or sales to the government over $1 million would not be made without obtaining prior approval from the Policy Committee, even in cases where the government was to provide all of the investment required to carry out the project. He also agreed to draw up reports on existing projects that would be submitted to the Policy Committee for review and approval; these would include analyses of capital requirements, sales volume, projected profits and return on investment, number of employees required, tax implications, and potential legal issues. Prospective projects involving sales over $1 million were to be reviewed by the DMRC and the Administration Committee, and Mooney was advised that he could not make recommendations to either the Administration Committee or Policy Committee without first clearing them through the DMRC. Finally, Wilson agreed that Donaldson Brown would draw up a report to the Policy Committee, making recommendations for policies to guide future defense contracts. In any situation involving immediate decisions, Brown would gain advance approval of Policy Committee members before action was undertaken. Taken together, these moves served to forestall the objections of owner representatives.

The events of 1940 highlight the contradictory strains created by defense production. The need for quick decision-making under conditions of high uncertainty led GM's general office to centralize many aspects of governance. Guidelines concerning the types and extent of GM's commitments were made by management representatives from the Policy Committee acting primarily through the DMRC. Because there was not time to clear decisions through a number of committees nor to draw up extensive reports and analyses, many of these guidelines were not even cleared through the DMRC, but were worked out informally between a handful of top executives. While these men kept in touch with defense problems through their participation in the DMRC and informal discussions, owners were cut off from detailed knowledge of such issues unless those issues came before the Policy Committee. The pressures of defense contracting caused other types of decision-making, including the process of making financial commitments to prospective projects, to become quite decentralized. While the general office had appointed a trio of top men empowered to declare policy unilaterally, decisions of contract allocation nonetheless devolved into the divisional domain. Contractual commitments were thus being made at a rapid pace by divisional personnel working in cooperation with general office men. Because the corporation needed to get projects under way before the extent and sources of required funding and prospective returns were known with any degree of certainty, these projects cleared either through the Administration Committee or the DMRC. Once again, general office executives could keep in touch with these developments through their positions on these committees, but owners could not.

Finally, the events of 1940 may have served to solidify owner unhappiness with both Charles Wilson and GM's organization structure. Only days before the Policy Committee meeting of September 18, 1940, owner representatives wrote to Sloan to suggest that Wilson's tenure as acting president be cut short and that Sloan reassume the presidency in order to expedite Knudsen's return after his service with the government ended.[18] Although Sloan vetoed the plan, the controversy within the Policy Committee over war contracts probably heightened the du Ponts' uneasiness with Wilson, which became apparent in later years.[19]

Organizing for War

The most dramatic changes in GM's organization occurred only after the United States entered World War II. Prior to that time, defense contracts accounted for a relatively small proportion of GM's overall business. Following Japan's attack on Pearl Harbor, however, the U.S. government ordered a complete halt in the production of civilian vehicles.[20] For the duration of the war, GM's entire capacity would be devoted solely to military production. These changes created radical uncertainty at almost every level of the corporation, as the relative stability that had prevailed

18 Walter S. Carpenter, Jr., to Alfred P. Sloan, Jr., September 12, 1940. Longwood, 430 (22), First Series, v. 24, pp. 7499–7500.
19 Alfred P. Sloan, Jr., to Walter S. Carpenter, Jr., September 17, 1940, Longwood, 430 (22), First Series, v. 24, pp. 7501–7503.
20 General Motors Corporation, *Annual Report*, 1942, pp. 1–2.

Participative Decentralization Redefined

prior to 1941 was shattered. Just as in 1940, the most immediate uncertainty was over how to coordinate the allocation of new contracts. Commitments for the production of war materials were growing at a phenomenal rate. In the first ten days of 1942, for instance, General Motors divisions made nearly $800 million worth of commitments for the production of war-related materials.[21] Some method of allocating these contracts had to be found, in case the divisions overextend corporate commitments or take on more work than they could actually carry out.

The short-term response to these issues was even more extreme centralization. On January 5, 1942, the DMRC was replaced by a seven-man War Emergency Committee (WEC) that was essentially empowered to carry out the functions of both the Policy and Administration Committees.[22] Like its predecessor, the new committee was composed of all the non-owner representatives from the Policy Committee. Indeed, the only difference between the WEC and the DMRC in terms of membership was that vice-president of finance Frederic Donner replaced James Mooney as the sole non–Policy Committee member.[23] But the WEC was much more powerful than its predecessor; corporate by-laws stipulated that the new committee had "all the powers of the policy committee in the management and direction of all the business and affairs of the Corporation."[24] Between Policy Committee meetings, the WEC carried total authority in the corporation, subject only to the restriction that its actions would be reported to the Policy Committee for approval after the fact. Moreover, the WEC was more active than either the Policy Committee or the DMRC, meeting at least once a week and often even more frequently. Between January and April 1942, the WEC ran the corporation.[25] The Policy Committee continued to exist, but it no longer played an active role in planning; insofar as it approved policy, it did so after the fact, rubber-stamping decisions made in the WEC. The Administration Committee became inactive and "more or less passed out of existence" as a governing committee during this period.[26]

21 General Motors Corporation (1943, Section IV, p. 4).
22 Sloan (1964, p. 185). General Motors Corporation (1943, Section IV, p. 3).
23 Sloan identifies the WEC as a six-man body, but corporate documents show the number was seven, counting Sloan himself. See Sloan (1964, p. 185). General Motors Corporation, "General Motors Corporation Administration Committee." Document prepared by GM legal staff for U.S. antitrust trial, December 17, 1951. Longwood, 441 (33), First Series, v. 32. The members of the WEC were Albert Bradley, Donaldson Brown, vice-president of finance Frederic Donner, Ormond E. Hunt, Alfred Sloan, John Smith, and Charles Wilson.
24 General Motors Corporation, *By-laws*, as amended to January 1942, Section 3(b), p. 8.
25 Sloan (1964, p. 185).
26 Walter S. Carpenter, Jr., to Alfred P. Sloan, Jr., April 8, 1942. *U.S. v. Du Pont*, GTE #201. Lammot du Pont to Alfred P. Sloan, Jr., April 10, 1942. *U.S. v. Du Pont*, GTE #202.

The most immediate problem facing the WEC was to design a new set of statistical and financial controls appropriate for wartime production. During the period from 1921 to 1925, GM had devised and refined a series of controls that allowed top executives to project demand, determine return on investment for the various divisions, set prices, analyze the constituent elements of profit, project capital needs, and tie production to demand.[27] Under this prewar system, production was guided by a measure of "standard volume" indicating the costs, price, and annual output that a division or plant would have to achieve in order to realize a "normal" profit on a given level of investment. Yet the financial figures that went into determining standard volume – projected costs, demand at a given price, output with a given level of plant, required investment – were based largely on past operating experience.[28] Most existing controls were thus virtually useless for regulating wartime production, for after 1942 the corporation was manufacturing new products for which such data did not exist. Moreover, wartime production also occurred under conditions of intense government regulation, giving GM far less flexibility over matters like pricing and manufacturing standards. Consequently, it was "impossible to predict with any degree of certainty what the operating results of particular contracts might be,"[29] and the WEC turned quickly to addressing this problem.

The first area of financial control addressed by the WEC was the formulation of guidelines for the allocation of defense contracts. With the corporation rapidly taking on hundreds of millions of dollars' worth of contracts for entirely new products, some method for allocating work among the various divisions and plants had to be found. The WEC developed a "Load Distribution Plan" designed to address this issue. In essence, it set an upper limit on the amount of defense work a division could take on; this limit was based solely on the availability of labor. Prior to U.S. entry into the war – probably as a result of the studies carried out by Donaldson Brown and the New York financial staff in response to the problems of defense contracting that arose in 1940 – GM "had decided that labor supplies would be the initial and controlling factor in the war program."[30] The Load Distribution Plan estimated the labor supply that would be available for each GM plant, and it assigned each division a maximum contract load based on the labor available in its various plant locations. This decision reflected the fact that labor supply was the least certain factor of production in the wartime

27 See Sloan (1964, Chapter 8); see also the essays in Chandler (1979).
28 Sloan (1964, pp. 142, 144).
29 General Motors Corporation (1943, Section I, p. 2).
30 Drucker (1972, p. 76). Studies of available labor were largely completed by fall 1941, but at the time of Pearl Harbor there was still no method for determining how many laborers would be needed to carry out a given contract.

economy. The U.S. government provided guaranteed demand for products, it stipulated the prices that would be paid for those goods, and it furnished much of the capital needed for producing them.[31] From the producer's point of view, availability of labor thus posed the most significant constraint on production.

The WEC devised a simple method for estimating the amount of labor that each government contract would require. Corporate executives first determined the "annual peak value" of a contract, defined as the dollar value "of twelve months' output at the peak monthly capacity required by the contract."[32] This figure allowed comparisons across contracts of different durations, and since each contract specified both a peak monthly output and a negotiated price, this value could easily be determined. After determining the annual peak volume of a given contract, executives subtracted from that figure the total value of expenditures for materials and supplies that would be required to carry out the contract. This left a "net load" figure that indicated the dollar proportion of each contract that actually had to be produced by a particular division. This net load figure was used to estimate the number of hourly laborers that each contract would require at peak production, and divisions could determine whether a given contract would fit within their maximum load limit.[33] The Load Distribution Plan thus served as a mechanism to ensure that divisions did not overextend corporate commitments by taking on more contracts than they could handle.

Only after developing the Load Distribution Plan did the WEC turn to the issue of how to ensure profits and encourage cost-effective production in the wartime environment. This entailed outlining an entirely new strategy for maintaining return on investment and devising a new system of financial controls and incentives appropriate to a non-market context. The need to develop a new strategy for maximizing returns was linked to government regulations that capped corporate profits for the duration of the war. In March 1942, anticipating forthcoming government regulations, GM's Policy Committee approved a voluntary limitation on corporate profits that restricted "profits on the over-all manufacturing operations of the company, before taxes but after all other charges including [depreciation] reserves, . . . to 10% of total sales [by value]."[34] On the face of it, this move seemed to place severe constraints

---

31   GM spent $911 million for new plant and equipment during the war years, of which $809 million was provided by the U.S. government. See Cray (1980, p. 318).
32   General Motors Corporation (1943, Section IV, p. 7).
33   The Load Distribution Plan is described in General Motors Corporation (1943, Section IV, pp. 7–18). See also Sloan (1964, pp. 381–382).
34   General Motors Corporation (1943, Section I, p. 3). A similar limitation on profit margin was adopted by the U.S. government later in 1942 to govern its war contracts with all manufacturers.

on profits from defense production. In 1941, for instance, GM's total after-tax profits were slightly over 20 percent of its net sales by value; the new profit cap would cut that figure in half. As top executives well understood, however, the limitation was not as severe as it seemed. Rather, it called for a new strategy of maximizing return on invested capital.

The key to GM's strategy for maximizing return on investment under wartime conditions was to increase capital turnover. As Donaldson Brown's pioneering work in financial controls had made clear, return on invested capital was composed of two parts: the profit margin on sales and the rate of capital turnover.[35] Return on investment could therefore be increased either by increasing profit margins or by improving capital turnover. Government regulations affected only one half of this equation, restricting GM's profit margin to 10 percent of net sales, but placing no limit on turnover.[36] If GM could increase capital turnover sufficiently, it would therefore be possible to maintain or even improve return on investment despite the 10 percent limitation on profit margins. Du Pont's Walter Carpenter pointed this out dramatically when he questioned GM's adoption of the 10 percent limit on profit:

> Should not the amount of the investment used in the manufacture of [defense] products influence the rate of profit? ... [I]n the manufacture of automobiles the investment base is the foundation of our entire price structure. As a part of this same factor is the rate of turnover. For instance the [1941] 12% profit on [defense] sales seems low enough with a turnover once a year, but if the turnover [was] five to ten times a year the rate of return on the investment might be unconscionable.[37]

A 12 percent profit margin with a turnover of five times would create a 60 percent return on investment; a capital turnover of ten would result in a 120 percent return on investment.

35 In mathematical terms, the rate of return on investment (R) is equal to profit margin on sales (P) times turnover (T): $R = PT$. Profit margin is defined as the value of profits divided by the value of net sales; turnover is defined as the value of net sales divided by the value of capital employed in the business. See Brown (1924), reprinted in Chandler (1979).
36 The form of profit restriction adopted by the government was not accidental. When various types of profit limitations were being considered by the government, GM executives lobbied heavily against restrictions that would cap return on investment. See, for example, "Notes to Conversation between Mr. Donaldson Brown and Senator Walter F. George," March 6, 1942, Accession 542, Box 837; "Notes to Conversation between Mr. Donaldson Brown, S. M. DuBrul and Colin F. Stam, Chief of Staff, Joint Committee on Internal Revenue Taxation," March 6, 1942, Accession 542, Box 837.
37 Walter S. Carpenter, Jr., to O. E. Hunt, December 15, 1941, Accession 542, Box 837.

Increased turnover above prewar levels was virtually ensured by conditions unique to defense production. First, defense contracting actually created more predictable demand than GM had experienced in the automobile market. Sales of war materials were mediated through contractual agreements with the government and were not subject to the seasonal fluctuations in sales that characterized the market for automobiles. Peacetime demand for automobiles fluctuated enormously from month to month. Such irregular demand decreased turnover, since GM's strategy was to carry sufficient capacity to produce enough cars for the highest months of demand – capacity that would be idle during periods of lower demand.[38] Defense contracts, on the other hand, stipulated the precise number of units that the government would buy within a given period. This meant that, in principle, defense production could be carried out at a much steadier rate, without the need for excess capacity, thereby increasing turnover. Table 4.1, which breaks net turnover down into its constituent elements, shows that inventory turnover increased substantially during the war, indicating that GM was indeed able to increase turnover because of more predictable demand. Ironically, even though delivery schedules and specifications for product mix could and sometimes did change precipitously during the war,[39] government-regulated defense contracting proved more predictable than coordination via the market.

Turnover was also effectively "improved" by the unique conditions governing investment in facilities used to manufacture war materials. Most important in this regard was the fact that a significant proportion of GM's war production was carried out using government-owned facilities. This allowed the corporation to realize return on plant and other capital that it neither owned nor paid for.[40] Table 4.1 shows that this policy resulted in an enormous increase in net real estate and plant turnover during the war years. This increase is a statistical illusion, of course – if the $400 million to $650 million worth of government-owned facilities were included in GM's real estate and plant figures, the turnover figure would decline below prewar levels.[41] But since GM did not pay

---

38 See Bradley (1926a), reprinted in Chandler (1979).   39 Sloan (1964, p. 380).
40 The corporation's official policy, approved on August 20, 1940, was to allow the government to pay for those facilities that could not be redeployed for civilian production. If facilities were redeployable, GM would pay for them. See "Policy re Financing Facilities for War Orders," in Charles E. Wilson to Alfred P. Sloan, Jr., September 19, 1940, Accession 542, Box 837. Evidence suggests that there were important deviations from this policy, however: see the later discussion of financing diesel locomotives.
41 The gross value of government-owned facilities was $428,726,155 in 1942, $631,589,862 in 1943, $649,539,159 in 1944, and $507,671,844 in 1945. See General Motors Corporation, *Annual Reports*, 1942, p. 75; 1943, p. 45; 1944, p. 36; 1945, p. 36. No information is given concerning depreciation of government-owned facilities.

Table 4.1. *General Motors Corporation: Turnover Broken Down into Constituent Elements, 1937–1941 versus 1942–1945*

Year	Inventory Turnover[a]	Net Real Estate & Plant[b] Turnover	Net Working Capital Turnover	Net Total Turnover[c]
1937	5.75608	3.93371	4.62764	1.55800
1938	6.07583	2.69205	2.75530	1.01412
1939	5.88980	3.56821	3.17115	1.26342
1940	6.77333	4.45816	3.75557	1.57563
1941	7.32153	5.94524	4.87338	2.03734
Avg.	6.43864	4.13463	3.93371	1.50357
-excl 1938	6.49600	4.49046	4.10114	1.61912
1942	4.82675	6.05828	3.45004	1.77487
1943	6.72579	11.60077	4.57783	2.73831
1944	8.54623	14.27651	4.71796	3.00891
1945	8.98624	8.94210	4.03485	2.29465
Avg.	7.15683	9.97493	4.25189	2.47274
-excl. 1945	6.74047	10.33721	4.32244	2.53237

[a] Inventory turnover is defined as the value of net sales divided by the value of inventories at the end of the fiscal year.
[b] Net real estate and plant turnover is defined as the value of net sales divided by the value of GM-owned real estate and plant after deduction of depreciation reserves.
[c] Net turnover is defined as the value of net sales divided by the value of net working capital (gross working capital minus current liabilities) plus net fixed capital (investments in other companies; other investments; miscellaneous assets; capital stock in treasury; prepaid expenses and deferred charges; GM-owned real estate, plant, and equipment after deduction of depreciation reserves). Figures for net investment do not deduct other liabilities and reserves, which include funds set aside for postwar rehabilitation and bonus plan; if these numbers were deducted from net investment, net turnover figures would be higher still.
Source: All figures calculated from General Motors' annual report, 1937–1945. The second set of averages excludes figures for 1938 (a recession year) and 1945 (when GM experienced significant cancellations of defense contracts).

These calculations adhere as closely as possible to the formula for determining return on investment outlined by GM's Donaldson Brown (1924). Those articles are reprinted in Chandler (1979).

for purchase or upkeep of these facilities, there was no need to include them in calculations for turnover and return on investment. In effect, GM was realizing returns on this plant without incurring costs. Turnover also improved because of changes in the tax code that allowed for accelerated depreciation of plant.[42] Because depreciation reduced net investment in plant, turnover (the ratio of net sales to net investment) improved. As Table 4.2 shows, the strategy of increasing turnover allowed GM to maintain return on investment during the war at a much

---

42 For an interesting discussion of such tax issues, see Frederic Donner to Walter S. Carpenter, Jr., July 8, 1942, Accession 542, Box 837.

Table 4.2. *General Motors Corporation: Return on Invested Gross and Net Capital, 1937–1941 versus 1942–1945*

Year	1. Net Income/ Net Sales[a]	2. Gross Turnover[b]	3. Net Turnover[c]	4. Gross ROIC (1*2)	5. Net ROIC (1*3)
1937	15.28%	1.05964	1.55800	16.19%	23.81%
1938	12.20%	0.68940	1.01412	8.41%	12.37%
1939	16.57%	0.83111	1.26342	13.77%	20.94%
1940	17.86%	0.94610	1.57563	16.90%	28.15%
1941	20.09%	1.14110	2.03734	22.93%	40.94%
Avg.	16.40%	0.93347	1.50357	15.64%	25.242
-excl 1938	17.45%	0.99449	1.61912	17.35%	28.07%
1942	11.59%	0.92578	1.77487	10.73%	20.56%
1943	10.50%	1.36896	2.73831	14.38%	28.76%
1944	10.22%	1.54932	3.00891	15.83%	30.74%
1945	6.79%	1.27699	2.29465	8.68%	15.59%
Avg.	9.78%	1.28020	2.47274	12.41%	23.91%
-excl. 1945	10.77%	1.28135	2.53237	13.8%	27.00%

[a] Net income/net sales figures include income from nonmanufacturing sources and can thus exceed 10% for the war years.
[b] Gross turnover is defined as the value of net sales divided by the value of gross working capital (cash; securities and tax notes; accounts receivable; inventories) plus gross fixed capital (investments in other companies; other investments; miscellaneous assets; capital stock in treasury; prepaid expenses and deferred charges; GM-owned real estate, plant, and equipment prior to deduction of depreciation reserves).
[c] Net turnover is defined as the value of net sales divided by the value of net working capital (gross working capital minus current liabilities) plus net fixed capital (investments in other companies; other investments; miscellaneous assets; capital stock in treasury; prepaid expenses and deferred charges; GM-owned real estate, plant, and equipment after deduction of depreciation reserves). Figures for net investment do not deduct other liabilities and reserves, which include funds set aside for postwar rehabilitation and bonus plan; if these numbers were deducted from net investment, turnover and return on investment figures would be higher still.
Sources: All figures calculated from General Motors' annual reports, 1937–1945. The second set of averages excludes figures for 1938 (a recession year) and 1945 (when GM experienced significant cancellations of defense contracts).

These calculations adhere as closely as possible to the formula for determining return on investment outlined by GM's Donaldson Brown (1924). Those articles are reprinted in Chandler (1979).

higher level than has generally been realized, despite the 10 percent limitation on profits.[43]

Having decided on the strategy of increased turnover, the WEC also set out to create incentives that would encourage division managers and operating personnel to improve turnover figures in production. Concomitant

---

43 The larger differences between gross and net return on investment during the war years are due primarily to accelerated depreciation allowed under special tax laws in effect for the duration of the war.

with the decision to limit profit margin to 10 percent, the WEC ordered that all government contracts should be carried out on a fixed-price basis rather than a cost-plus basis.[44] Cost-plus contracts guaranteed a specified profit margin by allowing the divisions to charge the government the actual cost of production plus a fixed percentage. Yet such contracts actually discouraged improvements in turnover, since any increases would result in a lower production cost and would thus lower the absolute level of profits. In fixed-price contracts, on the other hand, profits would result only to the extent that production costs dropped below the fixed price negotiated between GM and the government. In order to establish information about costs, initial production was often carried out on a cost-plus basis; as soon as costs were known with some certainty, a fixed-price contract would be established.[45] Once a fixed price had been established, return on investment could be increased primarily by improving turnover. Contracts were subject to price renegotiations that could lower the price paid by the government, but such renegotiations considered only changes in the price of supplies and labor, not changes in cost due to better turnover. Indeed, in discussions with government officials, GM executives were adamant that price renegotiations should be based only on "procurement" considerations and not turnover.[46]

The centralization that occurred when the WEC was instituted in January 1942 was primarily due to the need for quick decisions under conditions of extreme uncertainty. The WEC's most important work was to devise guidelines for allocating defense contracts and to create a new system of financial controls appropriate for wartime conditions. Yet the WEC itself was not viable over the long run. The immense size and diversity of GM's defense-related programs meant that a small group of general executives could not hope to oversee all aspects of planning and administration. Thus, once the Load Distribution Plan and incentives for increasing turnover had been formulated, GM management began to search for a new governance structure capable of coordinating defense production over the long run.

Participative Decentralization Reestablished

Over the longer run, wartime conditions led to the reemergence of participative decentralization, for adaptation to these new conditions

[44] General Motors Corporation (1943, Section I, pp. 2–6). Sloan (1964, p. 383).
[45] See General Motors Corporation (1943, Section I, pp. 1–6). See also O. E. Hunt to Robert Patterson, undersecretary of war, May 8, 1942, as quoted on p. 4 of the foregoing document. Obviously, the more "slack" there was in the negotiated price, the more room for increasing profits through improving turnover.
[46] See General Motors Corporation (1943, Section VIII).

Participative Decentralization Redefined

required the technical knowledge controlled by the divisions. Most of the uncertainty caused by the war centered on technical issues of manufacturing and engineering. In a matter of weeks the corporation had to shift from production of some 250 components used in cars to the manufacture of over 3,000 military products.[47] GM had little or no experience in producing these items, and many had never been mass-produced at all. "In many cases drawings and specifications were not immediately available, and, in some cases ... there existed no adequate basis for estimating costs."[48] Moreover, the wide range of products to be manufactured enhanced divisional autonomy by making it untenable for top management to maintain forced interdependences between operating units. Because the divisions would have to produce a wide number of distinct products, there "could be no production policy, no [price] 'range' planned and imposed by central management. The most that could be done was to prevent divisions from competing against each other, and to promote subcontracting between them whenever possible."[49] As a result, decision-making could no longer be centralized as it had been under the 1937 structure.

Alfred Sloan argued that wartime conditions made it advisable to increase divisional participation in strategic planning and resource allocation. As in the past, this belief rested on both technical and social considerations. On the technical side, the radical uncertainty created by defense production meant that operating management now controlled crucial information necessary for strategic planning and decision-making. Product pricing, for instance, rested on divisional expertise and required the intimate involvement of operating personnel: because "there was no ready-made yardstick against which the Corporation could measure proposed prices" for new products, it was "necessary to rely largely upon the judgment of the several general managers of the operating divisions and the Government contracting officers" in making pricing decisions.[50] Similarly, judgments about whether or not to accept new defense contracts – the wartime equivalent of whether to enter new lines of business – often turned on technical information controlled by the divisions. As a result, a "very large part of the war orders was accepted by the divisional managers on their own, often without any consultation with central management."[51] During the first ten days of 1942 alone, the divisions accepted defense contracts worth some $769 million.[52] Top executives could not hope to stay abreast of the technical

---

47 Drucker (1972, p. 82).   48 General Motors Corporation (1943, Section IV, p. 4).
49 Drucker (1972, p. 82).   50 General Motors Corporation (1943, Section I, p. 2).
51 Drucker (1972, p. 79). Drucker also reports, however, that headquarters sometimes encouraged divisions to take specific contracts.
52 General Motors Corporation (1943, Section IV, p. 4).

issues involved in such decisions and thus relied increasingly on divisional knowledge and discretion.

Sloan's belief that divisional participation in planning should be implemented also rested on social structural factors that increased the need for consent. Wartime conditions re-segmented market demand: as the divisions took on new and diverse types of defense contracts, they once again began to serve separate markets, rather than competing against one another in the same market. As a result, division management again developed distinct spheres of jurisdiction and claims to unique expertise within the firm. Sloan's response to these developments was to stress that structurally autonomous division managers would be more likely to understand policies and enact them in consummate fashion if they took part in creating those policies. In a striking departure from his later claim that "the top operating committee should be a policy group detached from the interests of specific divisions," Sloan now argued that technical and social factors combined to make divisional representation essential:[53]

> I hold very strongly to the belief that those who are doing the actual work and hence are in direct contact with the problems involved should be those who pass on and finalize the Corporation's policies.... I do not believe in legislation without representation. I believe that [the division managers] can do a much better job for the Corporation as a whole when they act both as to their own direct executive responsibility and for the Corporation as well. [Divisional participation in planning is preferable to having] some supermen determining policies from above which others must accept and work to underneath. To me that is poor psychology; wrong in principle; contrary to the philosophy of decentralized management, and does not promote democracy and cooperation.[54]

In April 1942, Sloan recommended a number of organizational changes to improve corporate governance during the war. First, because the need for quick decision-making continued to make a single committee system desirable,[55] he recommended a change in the corporation's top committee structure. The Administration Committee would become the

53 Sloan (1964, p. 113).
54 Alfred P. Sloan, Jr., to Walter S. Carpenter, Jr., June 14, 1945, Accession 542, Box 837. This document is out of temporal sequence; in it, Sloan explains his rationale for the participative decentralization that arose during the war.
55 See, for instance, Alfred P. Sloan, Jr., to Lammot du Pont, Walter S. Carpenter, Jr., and George Whitney, June 10, 1943, Longwood, 438 (30), First Series, v. 27, pp. 8156–8159.

active top committee and would have full authority to run the corporation; Sloan would take over from Wilson as chair of the Administration Committee.[56] The Policy Committee would continue to exist, but for the duration of the war it would play a less active role, relinquishing much of its power to the Administration Committee. Second, to increase divisional participation in planning, Sloan recommended a transformation of Administration Committee membership. Arguing that "the function of the staff should be to assist" the divisions and not take their place in the strategic planning process, he maintained that GM had "gone off the track" in substituting general office staff executives for division managers in the strategic planning process.[57] He therefore recommended that staff men on the Administration Committee be replaced with operating men holding line authority, including some division managers. Finally, all seven members of the WEC would be placed on the Administration Committee, making it a group where top executives and operating management came together to oversee corporate governance. In order to carry out this transformation, Sloan proposed replacing six staff men and three group executives on the Administration Committee with three division managers and two top general office executives[58] (Table 4.3). This move would reduce staff representation enormously, making planning the province of line managers and general office executives.

Owners disagreed with Sloan's suggestions and responded by advocating a return to a more traditional M-form in which the general office would make operating policy subject to owner financial veto. Early in April 1942, Sloan visited Wilmington to discuss these changes with the du Ponts. They responded to Sloan's suggestions by urging that the Policy Committee and Administration Committee be replaced by Finance and Executive Committees with responsibilities similar to those held prior to 1937. In making these counterproposals, owners repeatedly emphasized

---

56 See Alfred P. Sloan, Jr., to Walter S. Carpenter, Jr., April 11, 1942, Accession 542, Box 837. For later confirmation that Sloan intended to increase the Administration Committee's powers in 1942, see Alfred P. Sloan, Jr., to Donaldson Brown, December 28, 1944. *U.S. v. Du Pont*, DTE #GM7; Alfred P. Sloan, Jr., to Donaldson Brown, February 2, 1945, Accession 1334, Box 1.

57 Alfred P. Sloan, Jr., to Walter S. Carpenter, Jr., April 11, 1942a, Accession 542, Box 837.

58 The personnel changes that Sloan recommended verbally can be discerned through a careful reading of Walter S. Carpenter, Jr., to Alfred P. Sloan, Jr., April 8, 1942. *U.S. v. Du Pont*, GTE #201. Deletions can be determined by comparing this list to General Motors Corporation, "General Motors Corporation Administration Committee." Note that even though Sloan recommended removing R. Evans and W. Williams from the Administration Committee, they survived as members of the WAC. Titles for committee members can be determined by comparing organization charts for 1941 and 1943. In the cases of Harry Anderson, Bayard Kunkle, and Floyd Tanner, several job reassignments in a short space of time make titles at the time of reorganization somewhat uncertain.

Table 4.3 *Membership of Administration Committee, 1941, and Membership of War Administration Committee, 1942*

Administration Committee, 1941		
Name	Position(s) in Corporation	Staff/Line
Charles E. Wilson	President, Chair AC; Member, WEC	Line
Alfred P. Sloan, Jr.	Chairman of the Board, CEO Chairman, Policy Comm., Vice Chairman, AC; Chair WEC	Line
Albert Bradley	Group Exec, Car & Truck Executive Asst to President; Member WEC Policy Comm member	Line/ Group Exec
Ernest Breech (left AC 2/24/42)	Group Executive, Household Appliances Group	Line/Group Exec
Frederic Donner (added July 1941)	Vice President, Finance; Member WEC	Staff
Ronald K. Evans	Group Executive, Engine Group	Line/Group Exec
Lawrence Fisher	Group Executive, Body Group	Line/Group Exec
Richard Grant	Vice President, Distribution	Staff
Henry Hogan	Vice President, Detroit Legal	Staff
Ormond E. Hunt	Exec Asst to President; VP Patents PC member; WEC member	Line
Bayard Kunkle	VP Manuf/Personnel	Staff
Charles Mc Cuen	Vice President, Engineering	Staff
James Mooney (left AC 1/5/42)	Executive Asst to President, Chair, DMRC	Line
Floyd Tanner	VP, Labor and/or Manufacturing	Staff
William Williams	Group Executive, Accessory	Line/Group Exec
Harry Anderson (added 1/5/42)	Vice President, Personnel	Staff

two points. First, they believed that the "top" committee within GM should have a strictly financial responsibility; this would make for a clearer demarcation between the committees' spheres of jurisdiction and would make it unnecessary for owners to have detailed knowledge about or involvement in operating matters. Second, the du Ponts argued that the committee in charge of operations and operating policy should not include operating men with line authority, especially division managers. Instead, it should be composed of staff executives who lacked line authority and partisan interests in particular divisions or groups.

Owners wanted a Finance Committee primarily because it would restore their ability to steer operating policy by exercising financial veto. They recommended a seven-man Finance Committee that would increase owner representation at the expense of management.[59] Owners also

[59] Owners suggested a Finance Committee consisting of Walter Carpenter, Lammot du Pont, and George Whitney (the three shareholder representatives on the Policy Committee), Sloan, J. T. Smith, and Charles Wilson (three of the top GM management executives on the committee), and Donaldson Brown, who served both as a top GM

Table 4.3 (*Continued*)

War Administration Committee, May 5, 1942		
Name	Position(s) in Corporation	Staff/Line
Charles E. Wilson	President; Vice Chair, WAC	Line
Alfred P. Sloan, Jr.	Chairman of the Board, CEO Chairman of Policy Committee Chairman, WAC	Line
Albert Bradley	Executive Vice President Policy Committee member	Line
Frederic Donner	Vice President, Finance	Staff
Ronald K. Evans	Group Executive, Engine Group	Line/Group Exec
Ormond E. Hunt	Executive Vice President Policy Comm member	Line/Executive
William Williams	Group Executive, Accessory	Line/Group Exec
Donaldson Brown (added 5/4/42)	Vice Chairman of Corp. Vice Chair, Policy Comm	Line
Marvin Coyle (added 5/4/42)	Division Manager, Chevy Group Exec, Chevy	Line/Division/ Group Exec
Harlow Curtice (added 5/4/42)	Division Manager, Buick Group Exec, Buick	Line/Division/ Group Exec
Edward Fisher (added 5/4/42)	Division Manager, Fisher Group Exec, Fisher	Line/Division/ Group Exec
John Thomas Smith (added 5/4/42)	VP Legal; Policy Comm member	Staff
E. F. Johnson (added 11/42)	Group Executive, Eastern/Dayton Aircraft	Line/Group Exec

executive and as a representative of Du Pont. See Walter S. Carpenter, Jr., to Alfred P. Sloan, Jr., April 8, 1942. *U.S. v. Du Pont*, GTE #201. Lammot du Pont suggested that Carpenter be taken off GM's Finance Committee so that he could devote his time to running Du Pont during the war. Lammot further suggested that Carpenter's place be filled by Henry Belin du Pont "not because he is a substitute for Walter in financial experience, or other business experience, but [because] he is equally competent to represent the largest single stockholder in General Motors ... and is generally in accord with the thinking of du Pont management." See Lammot du Pont to Alfred P. Sloan, Jr., April 10, 1942. *U.S. v. Du Pont*, GTE #202.

argued that the existing Policy Committee suffered from two additional weaknesses. First, its functions were not adequately distinguished from those of the Administration Committee. Walter Carpenter noted that even before the war it had been "very difficult for us to distinguish between questions which should have been matters for the Policy Committee and questions which should have been properly within the sphere of the Administration Committee [because] it is inherently difficult to distinguish between matters of policy and administration."[60] As a consequence, the Policy Committee had increasingly encroached into operating matters, and its decisions often turned on highly technical issues. The war would only exacerbate these tendencies, since it created unprecedented new technical uncertainties. Second, because the Policy Committee was dominated by general office executives who possessed a greater knowledge of operations, owners' influence within that body was not great. A Finance Committee/Executive Committee setup would eliminate both of these problems, since all planning for operations would be carried out in the Executive Committee, and only proposals involving expenditures above a specified amount would go on to the Finance Committee for approval. In this context, the primary criterion for membership on the Finance Committee was not a knowledge of operations, but expertise in financial matters and the ability to "properly represent large stockholders."[61]

Owners also opposed Sloan's proposed changes in Administration Committee membership. They maintained that operating policy should be made by staff executives serving in an advisory role, rather than by operating men with line authority, and they were particularly unhappy with Sloan's desire to add three division managers to the Administration Committee. Owners believed that if division managers served in dual roles as operating executives and Administration Committee members, one of these jobs would be slighted. They thus argued that division managers serving on the Administration Committee should "be entirely relieved of their divisional duties" within "a reasonable length of time."[62] Perhaps more important, they argued that divisional men possessed partisan "interests and responsibilities [that were] primarily departmental or sectional rather than general."[63] Letting these men take charge of

60 Walter S. Carpenter, Jr., to Alfred P. Sloan, Jr., April 8, 1942. *U.S. v. Du Pont*, GTE #201.
61 Lammot du Pont to Alfred P. Sloan, Jr., April 10, 1942. *U.S. v. Du Pont*, GTE #202.
62 Lammot du Pont to Alfred P. Sloan, Jr., April 10, 1942. *U.S. v. Du Pont*, GTE #202. In keeping with their desire to change GM's top committee setup, owners continually referred to the Administration Committee as the Executive Committee and to the Policy Committee as the Finance Committee. I have used the names Policy Committee and Administration Committee to avoid unnecessary confusion. Keep in mind, however, that owners' advice about who should serve on committees was always coupled with a different definition of committee responsibilities, i.e., financial decisions and operational policy-making.
63 Walter S. Carpenter, Jr., to Alfred P. Sloan, Jr., June 7, 1945. *U.S. v. Du Pont*, GE #161.

strategic planning would thus lead to subgoal pursuit rather than the formulation of policies in the interest of the corporation as a whole. Owners also opposed plans to add more high-level general office men to the Administration Committee. Du Pont's Walter Carpenter advised against adding vice-president of legal affairs J. T. Smith, for instance, because he believed that Smith could not provide objective legal opinions on policies that he had helped formulate and approve.[64] Moreover, Carpenter argued, the Administration Committee would be extensively involved in operating matters, whereas Smith's talents were in other areas.[65] Similarly, Lammot du Pont saw "no particular reason" to add vice-chairman of the board Donaldson Brown to the Administration Committee, believing that top executives like Brown and Smith should serve on the Policy Committee.[66]

In responding to owner criticisms and counterproposals, Sloan remained adamant that wartime conditions required participative decentralization. He bluntly told owners that there was "no room in the General Motors scheme of things" for an Administration Committee composed of general executives lacking line authority.[67] He emphasized that the inclusion of division managers on the Administration Committee would not lead to the partisan politics that owners feared, since the Administration Committee approved policies but did not formulate them. The task of policy formulation was carried out by general executives and general office staff working together in the policy groups. These groups made policy recommendations to the Administration Committee, which discussed them briefly and then voted to ratify or reject them. The Administration Committee thus served as a "judicial body" rather than a "creative" one, and in this context the inclusion of divisional and operating men proved no great threat.[68] These men would not have to take large amounts of time away from their operating responsibilities, nor would they be able to unduly influence policy. Yet their participation would help create acceptance of policies and would provide general office executives on the Administration Committee with more detailed information if objections to specific recommendations did arise.

Sloan also strongly reiterated that he was "unalterably opposed" to reviving a Finance Committee capable of exercising financial "dictator-

---

64 Walter S. Carpenter, Jr., to Alfred P. Sloan, Jr., April 22, 1942, Accession 542, Box 837.
65 Walter S. Carpenter, Jr., to Alfred P. Sloan, Jr., April 8, 1942. *U.S. v. Du Pont*, GTE #201.
66 Lammot du Pont to Alfred P. Sloan, Jr., April 10, 1942. *U.S. v. Du Pont*, GTE #202. The only difference of opinion between du Pont and Carpenter was whether owners should have a representative on the Administration Committee, a move that Carpenter favored but Lammot opposed.
67 Alfred P. Sloan, Jr., to Lammot du Pont, April 13, 1942. *U.S. v. Du Pont*, GTE #203.
68 Alfred P. Sloan, Jr., to Lammot du Pont, April 13, 1942. *U.S. v. Du Pont*, GTE #203.

ship" from above.[69] The crux of his objection was clear: because important questions of operating policy always involved financial issues and often required significant capital outlays, an owner-controlled Finance Committee had too much power to strike down proposed policies by fiat. Understandably, he tried to sell this conclusion to the du Ponts by arguing that the organization he advocated was actually more in accord with owner interests than the one they favored. He maintained that financial oversight and even financial dictatorship could not ensure effective and efficient policies, for "if the operations of the Corporation are not intelligently and aggressively conducted, then the financial departments can do very little about it."[70] The power to create efficiency rested with the committees that formulated operating policy. For this reason, "the major interests of the stockholders are involved in the operations department," and any committee set up to provide stockholder oversight should be involved in matters of operating policy.[71] Such involvement was particularly important as owners became more distant from and less knowledgeable about the details of operations. At Du Pont, owners came up through management ranks and thus possessed operating knowledge; ownership and management were thus "closely tied in together."[72] But at GM, owners were outsiders who were increasingly out of touch with the business. Here they could not "afford to be represented" only on a Finance Committee, for such a group would lack knowledge of operating issues and would be out of touch with problems that arose on the operating side of the business.[73] Sloan argued that in GM, owners needed a top committee that would consider issues of both finance and policy.[74]

The conversion to war production left little time for extended discussions, and owners chose to let Sloan have his way. On May 4, 1942, the WEC was disbanded, and a new Administration Committee – renamed

69 Alfred P. Sloan, Jr., to Walter S. Carpenter, Jr., April 11, 1942a, Accession 542, Box 837.
70 Alfred P. Sloan, Jr., to Lammot du Pont, April 13, 1942. *U.S. v. Du Pont*, GTE #203.
71 Alfred P. Sloan, Jr., to Lammot du Pont, April 13, 1942. *U.S. v. Du Pont*, GTE #203. See also Alfred P. Sloan, Jr., to Walter S. Carpenter, Jr., April 11, 1942a, Accession 542, Box 837.
72 Alfred P. Sloan, Jr., to Lammot du Pont, April 13, 1942. *U.S. v. Du Pont*, GTE #203.
73 Alfred P. Sloan, Jr., to Walter S. Carpenter, April 11, 1942a, Accession 542, Box 837.
74 To support his view that operating policy constituted the most important work of the Policy Committee, Sloan analyzed all the decisions that the committee made between 1937 and 1941. His figures showed that out of 1,864 decisions made by the Policy Committee, "711 [38.1%] were entirely matters of major policy. 707 [38.0%] were purely financial. 383 [20.6%] dealt with budget matters and appropriations." Rather than concluding that finance and budget questions constituted almost 60% of the Policy Committee's business, however, Sloan averred that budget and appropriations were operating matters that should be decided at a lower level. See Alfred P. Sloan, Jr., to Walter S. Carpenter, Jr., April 11, 1942b, Accession 542, Box 837.

Participative Decentralization Redefined 151

the War Administration Committee (WAC) for the duration of the war – took over most aspects of running General Motors.[75] The change in the WAC's authority was reflected in corporate by-laws, which explicitly granted the new group the power to run the corporation.[76] The membership of the WAC incorporated most of the suggestions made by Sloan only a month earlier. It consisted of all seven members of the former WEC (six of whom served on the Policy Committee), two group executives, and the managers of GM's three largest divisions. The addition of the latter three men – Buick's Harlow Curtice, Marvin Coyle of Chevrolet, and Fisher Body's Edward Fisher – involved a compromise with owners. For the duration of the war, the divisions under their command were redefined as "groups," and these men served simultaneously as group executives and division managers.[77] Despite the new titles, they continued to serve as the active managers in charge of operations, and both headquarters and owners continued to refer to them as division managers. The creation of the WAC put governance and strategic planning in the hands of a combination of top executives and operating men. At Lammot du Pont's suggestion,[78] Sloan chaired the new committee, probably because owners were not entirely comfortable letting Wilson and "Detroit" oversee corporate governance.

Years later, Sloan explained the return to participative decentralization embodied in the WAC as an outgrowth of the war, and he implied that such a setup would not be appropriate under normal conditions. Specifically, he maintained that the WAC was able to run GM "because our wartime policy was set and nearly all the corporation's work was war

---

75 Sloan (1964, pp. 185–186). The new organization is depicted in General Motors Corporation, "Organization Chart, February 1943" (1943, Section IV).
76 Corporate by-laws stipulated that the WAC would "possess and may exercise all the powers of the board of directors in the management and direction of all the business and affairs of the Corporation (except the matters assigned ... to the policy committee)." In comparison with prewar by-laws specifying that the Administration Committee was authorized only to "actively concern itself with the manufacturing and selling operations of the Corporation" subject to Policy Committee control (see Table 3.1), this suggests a great increase in the Administration Committee's legal powers. Yet wartime by-laws continued to delegate "all the powers of the board" to the Policy Committee. In effect, GM's wartime by-laws were contradictory, probably because not all Administration Committee members were on the board, making it technically illegal for this subcommittee to assume all the powers of the board. In practice, the Administration Committee took over many functions previously carried out by the Policy Committee. The latter committee ratified WAC decisions after the fact, in order to make them legal. See General Motors Corporation, *By-laws*, as amended to April 1942, Article IV, Sections 1–4; Sloan (1964, pp. 185–186, 378).
77 On the fact that the general managers of these divisions also served as group executives, see General Motors Corporation (1943, Section I, pp. 1–2) and General Motors Corporation, "Organization Chart, February 1943."
78 See Alfred P. Sloan, Jr., to Lammot du Pont, Walter S. Carpenter, and George Whitney, June 10, 1943. Longwood, 438 (30), First Series, v. 27, pp. 8156–8159.

production. Aside from the technical problems of production, our policy decisions were concerned primarily with our relationships with various departments."[79] He thus implied that the decision-making carried out by the WAC did not really constitute strategic planning in the true sense. Yet, as will be shown later, Sloan actually strove to increase divisional participation in planning as the war began to wind down. Moreover, even during the war years, the WAC directly involved division managers in some of the most significant policy decisions in GM's history, including planning for postwar growth – the largest expansion the corporation had ever carried out.

Participative Decentralization Redefined

The 1942 reorganization implemented a new form of participative decentralization. Unlike the informal participative decentralization of the 1920s, the new structure gave the managers of GM's three largest divisions formal representation in and responsibility for strategic planning and resource allocation. Through their positions on the WAC, these men took part in discussing and approving virtually all of the corporation's policies during this period, including those involving crucial areas such as product pricing and postwar planning. Despite divisional representation in strategic planning, however, the new organization also allowed the general office to retain greater control over policy than had been possible under previous forms of participative decentralization. The key to this control was the distinction between policy formulation and policy approval that had been introduced in the 1937 organization. Policy formulation took place in the various policy groups, and division managers were not members of these bodies. After tentative policies were worked out, they were forwarded to the WAC for discussion, modification, and approval. Rather than creating a situation in which the divisions exercised relatively direct control over policy, the separation of policy formulation and approval allowed headquarters to extract both information and consent from the divisions while maintaining general office hegemony. Headquarters' control over the policy formulation process went a long way toward allowing top executives to control or shape the premises of decision-making.[80]

Divisional discretion seems to have been at its highest during the first half of 1942, when the uncertainties created by reconversion were at their peak. During this period, the WAC took direct charge of product

79   Sloan (1964, p. 186).
80   See March and Simon (1993). As we will see later, headquarters' ability to shape decision premises was imperfect at best; the divisions still retained significant power to resist general office directives, and this power probably grew greater over the years.

development, meeting frequently in an attempt to keep up with "the rapid evolution of events."[81] Division managers were free to accept orders for defense materials up to a specified limit; orders beyond the maximum level had to be cleared through the WAC, where the general managers of Buick, Chevy, and Fisher were represented directly.[82] Working in this fashion, division managers committed the corporation to billions of dollars' worth of defense contracts.[83] Their discretion in accepting or rejecting orders for new products was so great that one division manager went against "the almost unanimous opinion" of top executives "and agreed to the cancellation of the largest war contract... held at that time and to its replacement by a contract for an entirely new product, without even informing [headquarters] before he signed."[84]

During the early months of the war, the divisions also reestablished control over manufacturing, engineering, and purchasing decisions that had been carried out by the general office staff under the administrative centralization that occurred between 1934 and 1941.[85] Whereas centralization created forced interdependences from above by ordering divisions to share parts and designs, the rapid conversion to defense production created parts and materials shortages that gave divisions almost complete control over design and purchasing. Because reliable sources of supply became so scarce that divisional "purchasing departments... doubled and even trebled in size,"[86] divisions often took on not only the task of locating parts but of designing them and teaching suppliers to produce them as well. Under these conditions, the creation of forced interdependence from above was not viable, and division managers took control of decisions previously carried out by the general office staff. While the technical staffs assisted where they could, the division manager "decided what to produce, where and how [to produce it], ... priced his products for the Government, worked out delivery schedules, ... was responsible for the methods of production, ... decided what new plants and ... equipment he would need and how the load of war work would be distributed between the plants."[87]

As the uncertainties of conversion to war production became more manageable, divisions came to exercise less direct control over questions of broad policy, yet they continued to participate in the process of strategic planning. The key to this transformation was the distinction between the formulation and final approval of policy that had been introduced

---

81 Alfred P. Sloan, Jr., to Lammot du Pont, March 29, 1945, Accession 542, Box 837.
82 Drucker (1972, p. 78).
83 General Motors Corporation (1943, Section III, pp. 1–3).
84 Drucker (1972, p. 80).
85 See General Motors Corporation (1943, Section IV, pp. 28–39).
86 General Motors Corporation (1943, Section IV, p. 32).   87 Drucker (1972, p. 78).

in 1937. The WAC served as a "judicial body" that approved or vetoed policies worked out in the functionally defined policy groups.[88] During the early months of the war, the need for quick decisions caused the WAC to take over both the formulation and approval of policy, but as war production became more routine, the policy groups became active once again. New groups were created to oversee postwar planning, legal issues, and finance and pricing; by February 1943 there were ten active policy groups.[89] In addition, a number of "product groups" were created to study the design and manufacture of both existing and prospective war products.[90] Responsibility for formulating policies and designing war products – tasks that the WAC had carried out directly in the early months of the war – were gradually taken over by the policy and product groups respectively. The policy groups were made up of top executives and general office staff representatives, and each group was chaired by a staff member. Indeed, in several cases, staff representatives to the policy groups were the men who had been removed from the WAC only months earlier. The seven top executives who had composed the WEC constituted the majority on most of the groups, and Sloan and Wilson sat on every group as *ex officio* members (Table 4.4). The three division managers on the WAC were not members of any policy groups, although they may have participated informally in group meetings.

The division of labor between the WAC and the policy groups created an organization that allowed for divisional participation in strategic planning without relinquishing general office hegemony over that process. The task of formulating plans was carried out by the general office executives and staff who composed the policy groups. Once these men agreed on a proposed policy, it was forwarded to the WAC for approval. The WAC could veto policies that it did not support, and it held limited power to modify policy proposals. Yet the WAC did not have unencumbered control over the strategic planning and resource allocation process. First, it could apparently only fine-tune proposed policies; in principle it could not rewrite them completely. The new system thus allowed headquarters to shape decision-making premises,

88 Alfred P. Sloan, Jr., to Lammot du Pont, April 13, 1942. *U.S. v. Du Pont*, GTE #203.
89 General Motors Corporation, "Organization Chart, February 1943." The groups were in the areas of finance and pricing; legal; public relations; postwar planning; general engineering; manufacturing; distribution; labor; executive personnel; and overseas. Organization charts showed four of these groups (public relations, postwar planning, legal, and finance and pricing) reporting directly to the Policy Committee rather than to the Administration Committee. Evidence suggests that like the other groups, they in fact made recommendations to the WAC. See the later discussion of postwar planning. Beginning in 1944, organization charts showed all policy groups reporting to the Administration Committee.
90 General Motors Corporation (1943, Section V, p. 17). Alfred P. Sloan, Jr., to Walter S. Carpenter, Jr., March 29, 1945, Accession 542, Box 837.

Table 4.4. *General Motors Policy Group Membership, February 1943*

	Finance	Legal	PR	Postwar Planning	Engineering	Manufacturing	Distribution	Labor	Executive Personnel	Overseas	Affiliation/Position
Alfred Sloan	△	△	△	†△	•△	△	△	△	△	△	Chairman, CEO
Charles Wilson	△	△	△	•△	•△	△	△	△	△	†	President
Albert Bradley	•	•	•	•		•	•		†	•	Exec VP
Donaldson Brown	†	•	•	•			•	•	•	•	Vice Chairman
Frederic Donner	•						•	•			VP, Legal NY
Ronald Evans					•	•					Grp Exec, Engine
Ormond Hunt	•	•		•	•	•			•		Exec VP
Bayard Kunkle					•	†	•			•	Group/Staff (Dual Position)
John T. Smith	•	†	•	•				•		•	VP, Legal
William Williams						•					Grp Exec, Accessory
Harry Anderson								†	•		VP, Personnel
Lawrence Fisher			•				•	•			VP Special Asgnmt
Paul Garrett			†								VP, Public Rel
Richard Grant			•				†		•		VP, Distribution
Henry Hogan		•					•				VP, Detroit Legal
Charles Kettering				•	•						VP, Research
Charles McCuen				•	†						VP, Engineering
Edward Riley										•	Div Mgr, Overseas

Notes: The dagger symbol (†) denotes Policy Group chairmanship; the bullet symbol (•) denotes membership; the triangle (△) denotes *ex officio* membership. Bayard Kunkle served simultaneously as group executive over the "other car divisions" group (a line position) and as vice-president of manufacturing (a staff position). Names above the double line were members of the WAC; those below the double line were not members of the WAC. Four WAC members did not serve on any policy groups: Harlow Curtice (Buick division manager); Marvin Coyle (Chevrolet division manager); Edward Fisher (Fisher division manager); and Earle Johnson (group executive, Aircraft Group). Edward Riley (overseas division) was thus the only division manager serving on the policy groups at this time.

Source: All information on Policy Group membership is from General Motors Corporation, "Organization Chart," February 1943.

thereby limiting the scope of divisional action. Moreover, since Sloan or his top assistants sat on all of the groups, WAC members were under considerable informal pressure to ratify policy proposals. Operating men who opposed proposed policies would have to confront top executives directly in WAC meetings. Given the far greater power of executives and the small number of divisional men on the WAC, it was unlikely that operating men would triumph in such a confrontation. If the divisions were to strike down proposed policies, they would have to convince top executives that there were good reasons for doing so. The formal participative decentralization of 1942 thus gave division managers real input into and power over the planning process, but it limited the extent to which they could engage in partisan politics by shaping policies to their own ends.[91]

Postwar planning provides a good example of how this new form of participative decentralization worked. By mid-1943 war production had become sufficiently routinized that the corporation began to plan for the conversion back to a peacetime economy. Formal responsibility for formulating plans fell on the postwar planning policy group, composed of six general office members of the WAC and two staff representatives.[92] The group drew up a list of immediate and longer-range issues that would face GM after the end of the war. This list did not involve any policy recommendations *per se*, but outlined the general types of policy decisions that would have to be made and the factors that would influence those decisions.[93] The actual task of formulating specific policies – determining postwar production capacity, product mix, and capital requirements – was carried out "in close consultation with divisional

---

91 Peter Drucker, who sat in on meetings of GM's top governing committees from fall 1943 until spring 1945, reports that the policy groups included divisional representation. It is probable, however, that divisional men did not become formal policy group members until further organizational changes were made in 1945 (as discussed later), as official organization charts do not show any divisional men serving on the policy groups. Divisional representatives were probably represented on the new product groups; the membership of these groups was not shown on organization charts. See Drucker (1972, pp. 44, 60). General Motors Corporation, "Organization Chart, February 1943."

92 The members were Albert Bradley, Donaldson Brown, Ormond Hunt, Alfred Sloan (who chaired the group), John Smith, and Charles Wilson – all of whom also sat on the Policy Committee – plus vice-president of research Charles Kettering and vice-president of engineering Charles McCuen. See General Motors Corporation, "Organization Chart, February 1943." The inclusion of Kettering seems to have been motivated more by Sloan's desire to prepare him for future membership on the Policy Committee than by a belief that his contributions were necessary for postwar planning. See Alfred P. Sloan, Jr., to Lammot du Pont, May 29, 1943. *U.S. v. Du Pont*, GTE #205.

93 See "General Motors Immediate Post-Armistice Problems" and "General Motors Longer Range Post-War Problems," both undated, but probably early to mid-1943, Accession 542, Box 837. The former document lists ten "immediate" policy decisions to be made: determination of postwar capacity; product mix; analysis of actual and

executives but independently of them."⁹⁴ Divisional and group representatives were called in to policy group meetings to discuss postwar plans and to voice their preferences and concerns. Divisions were also responsible for working out preliminary projections for capacity, demand, product mix, and capital requirements, which were then reviewed by the financial staff. Based on these discussions and projections, the postwar planning group decided in mid-1943 that to meet pent-up demand and maintain market share in the postwar automobile market, GM would need to enlarge its productive capacity by an additional 50 percent. The group estimated that this expansion would require an outlay of some $500 million for new plant and equipment.⁹⁵

Following the policy group recommendation, the postwar expansion plan was forwarded to the WAC for approval. Within the WAC, many aspects of the expansion plan remained open to debate and modification. The WAC modified the product mix, for instance, cutting back proposed capacity for some divisions and expanding capacity for others.⁹⁶ Such changes involved increasing or cutting capital allocations to specific divisions and groups, and divisional representatives and group executives on the WAC took part in these decisions. Indeed, by the time that the postwar plan was finalized in early 1944, the combined number of group executives and division managers on the WAC was equal to the number of general executives on the committee, providing ample opportunity for self-interested policy-making.⁹⁷ The final program approved by the WAC also increased the scope of expansion beyond that recommended by the postwar planning policy group.⁹⁸ Despite these changes, however, headquarters retained control over the general parameters of the postwar program. The postwar planning group's decision to operate "with two eight-hour shifts, five days per week for a 210-day year," for instance, effectively limited the scope of the expansion program.⁹⁹ While the WAC was able to modify the scope of the program slightly, it could hardly hope to alter it dramatically. Indeed, when the Policy Committee approved the WAC's recommendations on September 14, 1944, it cut

> potential competitive factors; plant re/location; analysis of labor situation; personnel reorganization; advance orders for supplies; distribution facilities; capital requirements for undertaking full production; pricing and profit policies. Longer-term policies requiring ongoing study were listed in the second document: market analyses and forecasts; capital requirements; pricing and profit policies; vertical and horizontal expansion; personnel; technical research; procurement policies and supplier relations; distribution policies; cooperation with other manufacturers; government relations; public relations programs to assess and influence public opinion.

94 Drucker (1972, p. 81).
95 Sloan (1964, pp. 384–385). Cray (1980, p. 319).
96 Drucker (1978, pp. 286–287). On changes to Chevrolet's portion of the product mix, see Albert Bradley to C. E. Wilson, June 6, 1947, Accession 542, Box 838.
97 General Motors Corporation, "Organization Chart, February 1943."
98 Albert Bradley to C. E. Wilson, June 6, 1947, Accession 542, Box 838.
99 Albert Bradley to C. E. Wilson, June 6, 1947, Accession 542, Box 838.

postwar capacity back from the 2,300,000 units approved by the WAC to 2,100,000 units.[100]

In some cases, disagreement over proposed policies allowed operating men on the WAC to form alliances with general office executives. As part of its postwar planning, for instance, GM considered whether it should continue to compete in the diesel locomotive market. GM's Electro-Motive division had been the only company to produce commercial diesel freight locomotives prior to the war, and it remained the largest manufacturer of diesel locomotives for the government.[101] Yet the finance staff recommended against participation in the postwar diesel market, arguing that locomotives had not proved particularly profitable and noting that current financial projections showed that return on investment in the diesel business would decline to the point of unprofitability over the long run.[102] Division managers, on the other hand, argued that diesel sales would be strong following the war and that any decline in return would be slow to materialize because of GM's head start over other manufacturers. Owners complained that such divisional conclusions were biased by partisan participation and rested on a "protagonist's belief in favor of it rather than a careful analysis of all sides of the question."[103] Sloan acknowledged that the divisions were overly optimistic about the postwar era, but he nonetheless supported the recommendation to expand diesel production after the war. Arguing that profits in the locomotive business would be more than satisfactory if GM could capture the market for servicing diesels, Sloan insisted that "we must do the things that will prevent the servicing of [locomotives] or the rebuilding of them... being undertaken by the railroads."[104] With Sloan's sponsorship, the proposal to expand postwar diesel capacity passed, against the advice of owners and finance staff.

Although the new organization increased divisional autonomy and participation in most types of planning, decisions in some areas remained highly centralized. Labor policy, for instance, was the province of a few top executives. During the war, GM's workforce grew enormously, from 249,386 workers in 1940 to 465,617 in 1944.[105] Because this expansion took place at a time when labor was in extremely short supply and work

---

100 This was not the end of the story, however. Following the war, a struggle emerged as president Charles Wilson and the divisions attempted to increase expansion further. See Chapter 6 herein.
101 Sloan (1964, p. 352).
102 Alfred P. Sloan, Jr., to Walter S. Carpenter, Jr., April 13, 1942. *U.S. v. Du Pont*, GTE #203.
103 Walter S. Carpenter, Jr., to Alfred P. Sloan, Jr., April 7, 1942, Accession 542, Box 837.
104 Alfred P. Sloan, Jr., to Walter S. Carpenter, Jr., April 13, 1942. *U.S. v. Du Pont*, GTE #203.
105 General Motors Corporation, *Annual Report*, 1944, p. 49.

stoppages would prove especially costly, top management was particularly fearful of strikes and kept labor decisions more centralized than ever.[106] Certain types of financial decisions also remained highly centralized during the war. The issue of how to pay for expansion, for instance, was left almost completely in the hands of the New York financial staff. There was no need to go to outside financial markets for capital, because the government was willing to provide money for the construction of plant and facilities. The question of how to pay for expansion thus turned on an analysis of the trade-offs involved in reinvesting earnings and retaining ownership of plant versus using government funds and giving up ownership.[107] Projections on such issues were made by the financial staff. In the Electro-Motive case, for instance, New York's finance staff and top executives decided to finance Electro-Motive's expansion with government funds. This decision turned on tax considerations and laws governing depreciation; the divisions had little to say in such matters.

Overall, the 1942 organization increased divisional participation in both planning and resource allocation. Division managers serving on the WAC were given a formal vote in these matters. Unlike the informal participative decentralization that occurred between 1924 and 1933, the new organization thus incorporated divisional influence more directly into the planning process. Yet the new organization also constrained divisional participation in ways that informal participative decentralization had not. First, relatively few division managers were represented on the WAC in the initial stages of the war. Second, the distinction between policy formulation and policy approval meant that the influence of the divisions on policy was limited. General executives controlled the formulation of policy through the various policy groups. This gave them considerable control over the premises of decision-making. Nonetheless, it is important to recognize that this control was far from complete. Divisions could and evidently did use their positions on the WAC to enact self-interested agendas; such behavior became more pronounced as the degree of divisional representation increased following the war. Finally, divisional discretion was also limited by the fact that a number of areas of decision-making remained relatively centralized in the hands of headquarters. In addition to financial decisions, discussed earlier, one realm

---

106 Drucker (1972, p. 82).
107 Such decisions were heavily influenced by new laws concerning taxation and depreciation. The excess-profits tax of 1942 put a heavy tax on corporate profits. Yet this law also allowed corporations to realize enormous tax savings on the value of plant that was not recovered through normal depreciation. Investing retained earnings in plant might be worthwhile if the plant was redeployable and its value could be recovered through a combination of normal depreciation and tax breaks. See Frederic Donner to Walter S. Carpenter, Jr., July 8, 1942, Accession 542, Box 837.

of decision-making that remained centralized was that of legal issues. In the following section, I turn to a brief discussion of the growing importance of legal issues during the war years.

Growing Importance of Legal Decisions

Legal issues came to play a special role during the war years, and as they grew in importance, their oversight became more centralized. Such issues grew in importance primarily because in the wartime economy contractual stipulation took the place of market exchange.[108] Every contract negotiated with the government needed to be analyzed from the legal angle before it was put into writing, and the legal ramifications of defense-related policies had to be explored before those plans were finalized. Such analyses included not only considerations of price, delivery, production scheduling, and payment, but product performance and liability after delivery as well. As a result of such considerations, vice-president of legal affairs John Thomas Smith was placed on six of GM's ten policy groups in order to oversee legal issues.[109] Through his positions on these groups, the WAC, and the Policy Committee, Smith took part in both formulating and approving corporate policy, exercising almost complete control over legal strategy.

An example of the potential problems arising from defense contracts can be seen in the case of airplane engines produced by GM's Allison division. A government report criticized the performance of Allison engines in P-40 airplanes on the English front, saying they did not perform adequately at high altitudes, while competing Lockheed engines did. Alfred Sloan complained that when development of the P-40 engine had begun, the government had not specified altitude as a criterion of performance. The Allison met all the standards that the government had specified:

> You might just as well criticise the Cadillac car because it will not go a thousand miles an hour. It was never designed to go a thousand miles an hour. The real test of the P-40 and the Allison engine is whether it operates successfully within the area in which it was designed to operate. The answer to that is very definitely "yes." ... The fact that it is not a serviceable plane on the English front where altitude is essential ... is entirely beside the point.[110]

108 See Alfred P. Sloan, Jr., to Lammot du Pont, September 8, 1942, Accession 542, Box 837.
109 See General Motors Corporation, "Organization Chart, February 1943."
110 Alfred P. Sloan, Jr., to Henry Belin du Pont, October 26, 1942. Longwood, Box 438 (30), v. 26, p. 7963. Differences in altitude performance were due to the fact that

Nonetheless, defense contracts stipulated that manufacturers were liable for "latent defects, fraud, or such gross mistakes as amount to fraud," and GM executives worried that because the term "latent defects" could not be clearly defined *ex ante*, the government might seek to hold GM liable in cases like that of Allison.[111] As a consequence, every government contract had to be reviewed by GM's legal staff before it was given final approval. In this way, the corporation hoped to minimize potential legal problems.

Legal issues also increased in importance for reasons unrelated to the war. On April 10, 1942, a U.S. federal court in New York ruled against GM in a small-stockholders' suit that had been brought before the court in 1936.[112] The decision involved the administration of GM's bonus plan between 1930 and 1940, charging that top officers and directors had wasted corporate assets in calculating and dispersing bonus payments.[113] These men were ordered to repay the corporation some $4.3 million in principal and another $2.3 million in interest. One of the issues in the ruling against them was that many of these men had participated both as administrators over and as beneficiaries of the bonus plan. Moreover, Smith had made decisions concerning the legality of the transactions in question, even though he himself had benefited from the plan. Immediately following the court's decision, owners objected to Smith's increased participation in policy formulation and approval, arguing that such involvement would make it difficult for him to assess the legality of those policies in an unbiased manner.[114] They called for policies to be reviewed instead by independent counsel in order to avoid any potential conflicts of interest.[115]

The U.S. government's pending lawsuit against GM and GMAC further increased both the importance of legal decisions and owners' unhappiness with centralization of such decisions. The suit charged that GM and GMAC had conspired together in restraint of trade to prevent other finance companies from having an equal opportunity to finance customer purchases of GM automobiles.[116] Since GMAC, unlike the

> the Lockheed engine was supercharged, while the Allison was not. Allison had chosen to forgo a supercharged design in order to get the engine into production as quickly as possible.

111 General Motors Corporation (1943, Section VI, p. 7).
112 *Winkelman et al. v. General Motors Corporation et al.* 44 F. Supp. 960, April 10, 1942. See also *New York Times*, April 12, 1942, A-1. General Motors Corporation, *Annual Report*, 1942, pp. 46–51. Cray (1980, pp. 321–322).
113 Those charged in the suit were as follows: GM executives Albert Bradley, Donaldson Brown, James Mooney, Alfred Sloan, and John Smith; J. P. Morgan's Junius Morgan and George Whitney; and long-time board member Seward Prosser.
114 Walter S. Carpenter, Jr., to Alfred P. Sloan, Jr., April 22, 1942, Accession 542, Box 837.
115 Lammot du Pont to George Whitney, Walter S. Carpenter, Jr., John Raskob, and John Pratt, June 12, 1942, Accession 542, Box 837.
116 *United States of America v. General Motors Corporation*, #7146, 7th Circuit, 1940.

operating divisions, was a nominally independent corporation – wholly owned by GM, but with its own board of directors – there was a strong possibility that conflict-of-interest issues would arise in this case as well.[117] Smith recommended that GM simply absorb GMAC entirely, since "we were charged with conspiring with GMAC, whereas we could not be charged with conspiring against [sic] ourselves."[118] But owners worried that the outright acquisition of GMAC would damage GM's credit rating and its ability to borrow in the short-term credit market, since GMAC held a much higher ratio of short-term debt than GM. Equally important, Du Pont counsel disagreed with Smith's legal analysis: they argued that acquiring GMAC not only would fail to help GM's case but also would anger government prosecutors and make for bad public relations.[119] This only strengthened owners' conviction that it was unwise for GM to involve its own legal department in policy decisions.

The need for quick action under wartime conditions won out over owner concerns about Smith's inclusion in the planning process, but the bonus suit and the GMAC case nonetheless had a lasting impact on organization structure. Arguing that the legal aspects of strategic planning could not be left to outside counsel "without loss of time and effectiveness," Sloan convinced owners that it was necessary for Smith to remain on the policy groups, the WAC, and the Policy Committee.[120] If conflict of interest was involved, or if legal questions remained after policy decisions had been made, outside counsel could review these matters after the fact, but the need for quick decisions required continued involvement of in-house counsel.[121] Sloan nonetheless agreed with owners that GM needed to examine new ways of handling legal matters that would help to prevent future litigation.[122] To minimize conflict-of-interest charges like those that had arisen in the bonus suit, corporate by-laws were amended to put salary, bonus, and audit oversight into the hands of two subcommittees of the board – the Bonus and Salary Committee and the Audit Committee.[123] While both committees had existed prior to 1942, this was the first time they were made standing subcommittees of the

---

117 Alfred P. Sloan, Jr., to Walter S. Carpenter, Jr., July 27, 1942, Accession 542, Box 837.
118 John Thomas Smith, as paraphrased in Walter S. Carpenter, Jr., to Alfred P. Sloan, Jr., October 22, 1942, Accession 542, Box 838.
119 John Eckelberry to H. C. Haskell, December 21, 1942, Accession 542, Box 838.
120 Alfred P. Sloan, Jr., to Lammot du Pont, August 27, 1942, Accession 542, Box 837.
121 Alfred P. Sloan, Jr., to Lammot du Pont, August 27, 1942, Accession 542, Box 837. See also Donaldson Brown to Alfred P. Sloan, Jr., August 21, 1942, Accession 542, Box 837.
122 Alfred P. Sloan, Jr., to Lammot du Pont, August 27, 1942, Accession 542, Box 837.
123 General Motors Corporation, *By-laws*, as amended to November 1942.

board. Moreover, the new by-law provisions addressed conflict-of-interest issues by preventing members of these bodies from being eligible for bonus allotments; in the case of the Audit Committee, members could not be officers of the corporation, nor could they serve on the Policy Committee or Administration Committee.

The growing importance of legal issues and the continuing threat of litigation also served to increase owners' unhappiness with GM's organization and their resolve to change that structure. Following the ruling in the bonus suit, Du Pont representatives became concerned that their own participation on the Policy Committee might make them liable for damages in future lawsuits, and they became even more determined to keep that body out of operational decision-making.[124] Moreover, fearing that management representation on the board of directors might leave that body open to conflict-of-interest charges, they called for an increase in the number of outside directors on the board in order to retain owner control.[125] To avoid conflict-of-interest charges, more issues "had to be determined by those outside the ... operating organization itself."[126] Similarly, because bonus and audit committees could not be staffed by management executives, the corporation had to find more outside directors who could sit on these committees.

Participative Decentralization in the Postwar Era

The participative decentralization that emerged during the war persisted and increased as the war drew to a close. Sloan was convinced that the inclusion of divisional executives on the WAC made it "the best set-up that we have ever had."[127] He therefore sought to extend participative decentralization in the postwar era by giving all the car- and truck-producing divisions direct representation on the WAC. Once again, however, sharp disagreements emerged with owners, who continued to favor an organization that would put operating policy in the hands of executives without line authority. The outcome of this ongoing disagreement was an inability to reach accord on a postwar organization

124 Alfred P. Sloan, Jr., to Donaldson Brown, December 28, 1944. *U.S. v. Du Pont*, DTE #GM7. Alfred P. Sloan, Jr., to Donaldson Brown, February 2, 1945, Accession 1334, Box 1.
125 Lammot du Pont to Alfred P. Sloan, Jr., February 23, 1943. Longwood, 438 (30), First Series, v. 27, pp. 8100–8104. Walter S. Carpenter, Jr., to Alfred P. Sloan, Jr., April 8, 1943. *U.S. v. Du Pont*, GTE #204.
126 Alfred P. Sloan, Jr., to Lammot du Pont, June 1, 1944. Longwood, 438 (30), First Series, v. 28, pp. 8509–8511. See also Walter S. Carpenter, Jr., to Alfred P. Sloan, Jr., April 8, 1943. *U.S. v. Du Pont*, GTE #204.
127 Alfred P. Sloan, Jr., to Lammot du Pont, Walter S. Carpenter, Jr., and George Whitney, June 10, 1943. Longwood, 438 (30), First Series, v. 27, pp. 8156–8159.

plan. While owners grudgingly allowed Sloan to increase divisional representation in the short run, they remained adamant that the structure he had created should not be carried over into the postwar era. Between late 1944 and early 1946, long-term organization plans were "taken up more or less actively and discussed and then dropped... without anything being accomplished."[128]

The issue of organization arose again late in 1944, as war production reached a plateau. With the pressures of conversion past, it was no longer necessary for the WAC to oversee both production and governance. Sloan wanted to return to something like the pre-1942 structure in which the Policy Committee would play a more active role than it had during the war years. Yet even though he remained "very enthusiastic" in his support for a clearly superordinate top committee, he now acknowledged that the Policy Committee had become too involved in operations prior to the war.[129] He therefore sought to create an organization that made the Administration Committee "the management body in fact, headed by the President," but that also allowed for a superordinate Policy Committee with the power to determine broad issues of policy.[130] Moreover, the functioning of the WAC had convinced Sloan that it was desirable to maintain and increase divisional representation on that committee. Finally, these questions of postwar organization were intimately bound up with personnel matters, for like several of his most experienced managers, the sixty-nine-year-old Sloan planned to retire after the war, making it necessary to decide who would succeed him.

Sloan's initial attempts to implement changes were thwarted by owner resistance. On September 18, 1944, he traveled to Wilmington to discuss postwar organization and his intention to retire. Owners countered with a predictable response, advocating a return to the old Finance–Executive Committee arrangement. Walter Carpenter outlined a tentative organization plan that offered only two changes from the one he had put forth in 1942. First, in deference to Sloan's and Wilson's repeated entreaties that the president should head the committee in charge of operating policy, Carpenter proposed a by-law amendment that would automatically make the corporation's president chairman of the proposed Executive Committee. Second, he suggested that Sloan stay on as chairman of the board in the postwar organization, but turn the title of CEO over to the president. This would allow Sloan to reduce his responsibilities while staying on "to observe the workings of the Corporation under the new regime."[131]

128 Walter S. Carpenter, Jr., to Lammot du Pont, March 28, 1945, Accession 542, Box 837.
129 Alfred P. Sloan, Jr., to Donaldson Brown, December 28, 1944. *U.S. v. Du Pont*, DTE #GM7.
130 Alfred P. Sloan, Jr., to Donaldson Brown, February 2, 1945, Accession 1334, Box 1.
131 Walter S. Carpenter, Jr., to Alfred P. Sloan, Jr., September 22, 1944, Accession 542, Box 837.

Faced with owners' different vision of postwar organization, Sloan delayed and then dropped scheduled meetings with the du Ponts concerning long-range plans and opted instead to make less extensive short-term changes.[132] On November 6, 1944, the WAC was officially renamed the Administration Committee, and its powers and responsibilities were reduced to prewar levels. The Administration Committee no longer served as the primary locus of decision-making, nor was it authorized to exercise all the powers of the board.[133] Instead, its actions were explicitly subject to review and revision by the Policy Committee, which reemerged as the active locus of corporate control. Yet the membership of the Administration Committee remained unchanged, and several division managers continued to sit on that body. Sloan knew that owners would continue to object to this arrangement, so he began to rethink the relationship between GM's top two committees in hopes of outlining a new organization that could be put into effect at the annual shareholder meeting scheduled for May 1945. Turning to Donaldson Brown for advice and cautioning him to "keep the matter within ourselves,"[134] Sloan sought to "work out something that would not limit the present scheme of things [but that would still] meet the viewpoint of [owners]."[135]

Sloan was unable to come up with a plan that would placate owners, in large part because he overlooked or misunderstood some of their criticisms. He believed that the crux of owner objections centered on the role of the Policy Committee and the fact that it was "asked to pass on too many details of administering the business, concerning which [owners] could not possibly be familiar."[136] This concern had become even more pronounced following the bonus suit, when owners began to worry that their participation on the Policy Committee would leave them legally liable for any decisions made by that body. Lacking an in-depth knowledge of the automobile business, owners worried that their representation on the Policy Committee gave them legal responsibilities that they could not "adequately make good on" because they could not "possibly be expected to know about the ramifications" of the operating issues that the Policy Committee approved.[137] To meet these objections,

---

132   Walter S. Carpenter, Jr., to Lammot du Pont, March 28, 1945, Accession 542, Box 837.
133   See General Motors Corporation, *By-laws*, as amended to November 1944, Sections 36 (Policy Committee) and 37 (Administration Committee), pp. 7–8. Following the changes, the Administration Committee was given "general charge of the manufacturing and selling activities of the corporation," and all of its actions were "subject to revision by the policy committee."
134   Alfred P. Sloan, Jr., to Donaldson Brown, February 2, 1945, Accession 1334, Box 1.
135   Alfred P. Sloan, Jr., to Donaldson Brown, December 28, 1944. *U.S. v. Du Pont*, DTE #GM7.
136   Alfred P. Sloan, Jr., to Donaldson Brown, December 28, 1944. *U.S. v. Du Pont*, DTE #GM7.
137   Alfred P. Sloan, Jr., to Donaldson Brown, February 2, 1945, Accession 1334, Box 1.

Sloan proposed two key changes. First, he would give the Administration Committee clear authority to "run the business."[138] This would prevent the Policy Committee from becoming embroiled in technical debates. Second, in order to minimize Policy Committee interference, he would delegate Administration Committee authority directly from the board rather than through the Policy Committee. This would mean that Policy Committee members would no longer be potentially liable for decisions made in the Administration Committee. Sloan hoped that these changes would allow him to meet owner objections while retaining the basic 1937 structure. He was especially concerned to retain a Policy Committee that had authority over "matters of broad policy... financial and otherwise," rather than an owner-dominated Finance Committee that exercised financial veto.[139]

Sloan saw the delegation of authority to the Administration Committee from the board as a legalistic maneuver designed to win owner approval, rather than a substantive change in how the organization would actually function. Based on discussions with Brown, he concluded that there would always be some areas of overlap in the responsibilities of the top governing committees. Brown pointed out that even within Du Pont there was duplication of responsibility between the Finance Committee and Executive Committee; conflict was avoided through custom rather than through legal restrictions imposed by corporate bylaws.[140] Owners favored a Finance Committee/Executive Committee setup, Sloan concluded, because it was more deeply embedded in convention, not because it led to a clearer delineation of responsibilities.[141] But if owners believed that the delegation of authority from the board rather than from the Policy Committee would make a difference, Sloan was willing to modify that aspect of GM's organization. Despite Sloan's conviction that this legalistic maneuver would create a satisfactory compromise, however, significant problems remained.

Sloan's plan to delegate increased powers to the Administration Committee from the board failed to address owner objections to participative decentralization. Owners had emphasized repeatedly that they opposed the inclusion of division managers and even group executives on governing committees because they feared that such men would use their positions to pursue partisan interests. Increasing the Administration Committee's authority over operations only served to heighten this

138   Alfred P. Sloan, Jr., to Donaldson Brown, December 28, 1944. *U.S. v. Du Pont*, DTE #GM7; Alfred P. Sloan, Jr., to Donaldson Brown, February 2, 1945, Accession 1334, Box 1.
139   Alfred P. Sloan, Jr., to Donaldson Brown, December 28, 1944. *U.S. v. Du Pont*, DTE #GM7.
140   Donaldson Brown to Alfred P. Sloan, Jr., January 16, 1945, Accession 1334, Box 1.
141   Alfred P. Sloan, Jr., to Donaldson Brown, February 2, 1945, Accession 1334, Box 1.

concern, a fact that both Sloan and Brown seemed to overlook. In February 1945, Brown traveled to Wilmington at Sloan's request to discuss GM's organization with the du Ponts.[142] Lammot du Pont and Walter Carpenter reiterated their position that a committee containing divisional representation was not appropriate to be in charge of operations. Brown "found it difficult to give Lammot and Walter a picture of the [relationships between] standing committees, policy groups and operating executives so that they might understand better how questions of policy are considered and dealt with in General Motors."[143] Indeed, following the meeting, Lammot again voiced reservations about the Administration Committee, while Carpenter indicated that, in his view, the inclusion of division managers on the Administration Committee meant that it "conceivably may be a net loss to the Corporation."[144]

Sloan and Brown emphasized that they regarded divisional representation on the Administration Committee as essential, and both stressed that such representation played a crucial role in creating divisional cooperation and consent. Sloan assured owners that GM's organization would not lead to partisan policy-making, because of the distinction between policy formulation and policy approval that had been institutionalized in the relationship between the policy groups and the Administration Committee. Using a number of examples, he tried to show that the Administration Committee did not formulate policy, but served as a "clearing committee" for policies worked out in the groups.[145] Policy was formulated by general office executives, and only seldom did the Administration Committee make any changes to the recommendations put forth. The general office thus retained control over policies, but divisional approval created consent and acceptance. Brown emphasized even more strongly that divisional participation did not mean the absence of general office control. While he acknowledged that it "is difficult to enjoy full freedom of discussion when there is participation [on governing committees] by ... executives whose own operations are or should be the subject of critical analysis," he nonetheless insisted that "the operations of our divisions are under continual scrutiny," and there was thus "no loss of ... critical analysis of operations on account of the way in which the Administration Committee is constituted."[146] These efforts appear

---

142 Donaldson Brown to Alfred P. Sloan, Jr., February 7, 1945, Accession 1334, Box 2. Donaldson Brown to Alfred P. Sloan, Jr., April 12, 1945, Accession 1334, Box 2.
143 Donaldson Brown to Alfred P. Sloan, Jr., April 12, 1945, Accession 1334, Box 2.
144 Walter S. Carpenter to Lammot du Pont, March 28, 1945, Accession 542, Box 837. The letter from Lammot is not available, but Sloan's reply can be found in Alfred P. Sloan, Jr., to Lammot du Pont, April 5, 1945, Accession 542, Box 837.
145 Alfred P. Sloan, Jr., to Lammot du Pont, April 5, 1945, Accession 542, Box 837.
146 Donaldson Brown to Alfred P. Sloan, Jr., April 12, 1945, Accession 1334, Box 2.

to have made little impression on owners, who continued to oppose participative decentralization.

Sloan's plan to make the Administration Committee responsible for running the business, with its powers delegated directly from the board, also failed to address the continuing inability to distinguish between policy and administration in a systematic way. Sloan himself admitted that "it is difficult to decide what is broad policy and what is not – it is a matter of interpretation."[147] The inability to distinguish clearly between policy and administration was exacerbated by the fact that many functions that Sloan referred to as "running the business" – appropriations, engineering and manufacturing decisions, production levels, product mix – had previously been defined as issues of financial and operating policy. Indeed, he went so far as to argue that the 1928 decision to buy Germany's Adam Opel A.G. was the sort of issue that should be left up to the Administration Committee; the role of the Policy Committee in such issues of expansion was merely to decide "whether as a matter of broad policy" GM should operate in Germany.[148] Moreover, as long as the Policy Committee held responsibility for finalizing broad policies, it remained likely that conflation between policy and administration would continue: the Policy Committee would intervene in Administration Committee decisions and operating affairs, claiming that issues of policy were at stake. Donaldson Brown recognized this fact and warned that delegating power to the Administration Committee from the board would only complicate matters by creating "dual responsibilities."[149] If the Policy Committee was to remain superordinate, as both Brown and Sloan believed it should, then it needed to continue to have all the powers of the board. Only in this way could its power over the Administration Committee be ensured.

Because Sloan's plan did not adequately address owner objections, he was unable to convince them to approve his proposed postwar changes. Indeed, after discussions with Sloan and Brown in the spring of 1945, owners insisted even more strenuously that GM's organization was not appropriate for the postwar era. Clearly believing that Sloan was delaying action on the matter in an attempt to get his own way, Walter Carpenter urged Lammot du Pont to resolve questions over GM's organization once and for all by appointing a committee of Lammot, Sloan, and Wilson to come up with a new organization plan. In order to avoid further delay by Sloan and to make organization design a formal rather than informal function, he suggested that this three-man committee be

---

147   Alfred P. Sloan, Jr., to Donaldson Brown, December 28, 1944. *U.S. v. Du Pont*, DTE #GM7.
148   Alfred P. Sloan, Jr., to Donaldson Brown, February 2, 1945, Accession 1334, Box 1.
149   Donaldson Brown to Alfred P. Sloan, Jr., February 7, 1945, Accession 1334, Box 2.
      Donaldson Brown to Alfred P. Sloan, Jr., January 16, 1945, Accession 1334, Box 1.

formally appointed by the Policy Committee, with firm deadlines for outlining a new organization structure.[150] Lammot declined to do so, evidently still hoping that owners and managers could reach an agreement on postwar organization.

Having failed to reach agreement on a postwar structure, owners reluctantly allowed Sloan to implement changes that increased participative decentralization in the short run. At the annual board meeting held on June 4, 1945, the board approved extensive changes in Administration Committee membership recommended by Sloan[151] (Table 4.5). The changes added six new men – four division managers and two group executives.[152] Sloan, Brown, and Smith stepped down from the Administration Committee, making it an eighteen-member body chaired by Wilson and made up of seven division managers, six group executives, and five general office representatives. While these changes did not address the responsibilities of the Administration Committee nor its relationship to the Policy Committee, they clearly increased divisional participation in policy approval. Moreover, at least one source indicates that following these changes, division managers gained representation on at least some of the policy groups, involving them directly in the formulation of strategic plans.[153] Together these changes clearly indicated Sloan's continuing commitment to the form of participative decentralization that had emerged under wartime conditions.

Although they evidently approved the changes made in June 1945, owners wasted no time in arguing that the new Administration Committee was entirely inappropriate to serve as a governing committee. Only three days after the changes were made, Du Pont's Walter Carpenter charged that the Administration Committee was beset by partisan bargaining that stemmed from the presence of division managers and group executives. He maintained that when appropriations requests and issues of salary were brought before the Administration Committee for approval, "each member wonders what effect his action on that case might have upon the next case he may bring."[154] Administration Committee members with interests in specific divisions or groups were thus

150 Walter S. Carpenter, Jr., to Lammot du Pont, March 28, 1945, Accession 542, Box 837.
151 The meeting was delayed one month from its scheduled date in May, probably because of America's victory over Germany on May 4, 1945.
152 General Motors Corporation, "General Motors Corporation Administration Committee." General Motors Corporation, *Annual Report*, 1945. General Motors Corporation, "Organization Charts," 1944, 1946.
153 Drucker (1972, pp. 44, 60). Organization charts published after October 1944 did not identify the members of the policy groups, making it impossible to verify Drucker's claim. Because he sat in on meetings of the Administration Committee and other top-level committees during this period, Drucker was in a position to have access to such information, however.
154 Walter S. Carpenter, Jr., to Alfred P. Sloan, Jr., June 7, 1945. *U.S. v. Du Pont*, GE #161.

Table 4.5. *Membership of War Administration Committee, 1944, and Membership of Administration Committee, 1945*

War Administration Committee, 1944		
Name	Position(s) in Corporation	Staff/Line
Charles E. Wilson	President, Vice Chairman WAC	Line
Alfred P. Sloan, Jr.	Chairman of the Board, CEO Chairman, PC; Chairman, AC	Line
Albert Bradley	Executive Vice President PC member	Line
Donaldson Brown	Vice Chairman of Board Vice Chairman, PC	Line
Marvin Coyle	Division Manager, Chevrolet Group Exec, Chevrolet	Line
Harlow Curtice	Division Manager, Buick Group Exec, Buick	Line
Frederic Donner	Vice President, Financial	Staff
Ronald Evans	Group Executive, Engine	Line
Edward Fisher to 8/7/44	Division Manager, Fisher Group Executive, Fisher	Line
Ormond Hunt	Executive Vice President PC Member	Line
Earle Johnson	Group Executive, Aircraft	Line
Bayard Kunkle	Group Executive, Other Car & Truck Group	Line
William Williams	Group Executive, Accessory	Line
Thomas Archer (added 8/7/44)	Division Manager, Fisher Group Executive, Fisher	Line

deciding appropriations and salary issues from a self-interested point of view, indicating "an inherent weakness in the constitution of the Administration Committee."[155] Carpenter argued that GM's record of success had been achieved despite the corporation's organization, not because of it: the critical functions of the Administration Committee had been carried out by an informal group of Sloan and five top executives in New York and Detroit. Although Carpenter admitted that he was hesitant to insist on change, given Sloan's belief "that you have the ideal type of organization," he nonetheless hinted that it was time for owners to insist that participative decentralization be ended.[156]

155 Walter S. Carpenter, Jr., to Alfred P. Sloan, Jr., June 7, 1945. *U.S. v. Du Pont*, GE #161.
156 Walter S. Carpenter, Jr., to Alfred P. Sloan, Jr., June 7, 1945. *U.S. v. Du Pont*, GE #161. Carpenter charged that one of the policy groups – the Policy Executive Group – informally carried out the critical functions of the Administration Committee. The

Table 4.5. (*Continued*)

Administration Committee, June 1945		
Name	Position(s) in Corporation	Staff/Line
Charles E. Wilson	President; Chairman, AC	Line
Albert Bradley	Executive Vice President PC member	Line
Marvin Coyle	Division Manager, Chevrolet	Line
Harlow Curtice	Division Manager, Buick	Line
Frederic Donner	Vice President, Financial	Staff
Ronald Evans	Group Executive, Engine	Line
Ormond Hunt	Executive Vice President PC Member	Line
Earle Johnson (to 12/45)	Group Executive, Aircraft	Line
Bayard Kunkle	Group Executive, Other Car & Truck Group	Line
William Williams (to 11/45)	Group Executive, Accessory	Line
Thomas Archer	Division Manager, Fisher	Line
James Mooney (3/5/45 to 12/31/45)	Probably Group Executive, Canadian and Overseas ???	Line ???
Francis Burke	Group Executive, Accessory (to 12/45)	Line
Morgan Douglas	Division Manager, GM Truck	Line
Nicholas Dreystadt	Division Manager, Cadillac	Line
Louis Goad	Group Executive, BOP Assembly, Appliance, Dayton Group	Line
Harry Klingler	Division Manager, Pontiac	Line
Sherrod Skinner	Division Manager, Oldsmobile	Line

Sloan's response again emphasized that participative decentralization produced divisional consent and led to more knowledgeable decision-

<blockquote>
policy executive group was composed of Brown, Bradley, Donner, Hunt, Sloan, Smith, and Wilson; all but Donner were on the Policy Committee. See Donaldson Brown to Alfred P. Sloan, Jr., April 30, 1946, Accession 542, Box 838; Alfred P. Sloan, Jr., to Walter S. Carpenter, Jr., May 1, 1946, Accession 542, Box 838; General Motors Corporation, "Organization Chart," October 10, 1944.
</blockquote>

making, making it indispensable in the postwar era. He denied that bargaining had taken place within the Administration Committee, arguing that salaries and appropriations were always analyzed by the financial staff, which made recommendations to the Administration Committee based on its analysis. This was sufficient to prevent abuse. Nonetheless, Sloan conceded that Administration Committee members had particularistic interests that could potentially lead to conflict and bargaining. Despite the possibility of such partisan behavior, however, he believed that the benefits of participative decentralization outweighed its potential problems. There were adequate means for preventing such behavior, and even when subgoal pursuit did occur, the benefits of participative decentralization outweighed the costs of partisan self-interest-seeking. In a hauntingly prescient passage, Sloan argued that the textbook M-form advocated by owners would lead only to failure; divisional participation in planning was necessary to create consent and improve information:

> ... I accept the fact that there are on the Administration Committee executives who [have conflicting interests]. However, I believe ... it is far better to have differences ... identified, laid on the table face up and discussed. No good is ever accomplished by trying to keep differences away from people because they always know about them anyway. It leads to suspicion and lack of confidence.
> ... [Y]ou urge that we set up a group of supermen who have no direct operating responsibility but who do lay down the major policies of the Corporation. As I said before, that is legislation without representation. ...
> ... No group of supermen are [sic] so super that they know all the answers to all the intricate problems involved in a business of the magnitude of General Motors. If we set up an organization of supermen, you will find, as sure as night follows day, that this super-organization ... will become more and more separated from what is going on in the business. ... That gets to the point that we have not only legislation without representation, but legislation without knowledge. And that is worse. ... [S]uch supermen would, of necessity, become academic, hence would be a greater liability to the business than an asset.[157]

Dismissing Carpenter's charge that top executives informally carried out the task of overseeing operations, he emphasized that any recommenda-

157 Alfred P. Sloan, Jr., to Walter S. Carpenter, Jr., June 14, 1945, Accession 542, Box 837.

tions made by the policy groups still had to be approved by the Administration Committee. It was thus the inclusion of divisional men in the planning process that accounted for GM's success.

Sloan's repeated emphasis on the importance of consent did not go unnoticed by owners, but neither did it convince them. Differences over the role of the Administration Committee were summed up succinctly by Lammot du Pont, who advised Sloan that "the governing committee of a corporation is not... set up to secure cooperation, but is ... set up to *rule* the business of the corporation."[158] Continuing to operate on an image of decentralization that centered around fiat from above, owners remained opposed to the GM scheme. Despite repeated discussions on the topic of organization, little progress had been made. With the war in Germany over and victory in Japan only months away, managers and owners found themselves unable to agree on a postwar organization.

Summary

The war years created a return to and transformation of participative decentralization at General Motors. The overwhelming technical uncertainties of war production made divisional knowledge and expertise much more important than they had been during the 1930s. In addition, the production of a vast number of new and diverse products meant that the various operating divisions were no longer competing against one another in a single, undifferentiated market, but rather specialized in the design and production of specific goods for separate markets. In response to these developments, GM restored divisional participation in the planning and resource allocation process. Sloan was quite clear that the inclusion of division managers occurred both to elicit consent from these men and to ensure that decisions were made by those with a knowledge of technical facts. He acknowledged that participative decentralization might, in some instances, lead to self-interested behavior on the part of the divisions, but he believed that the benefits of divisional participation in planning outweighed the costs.

The form of participative decentralization that emerged during the war was quite different from what had prevailed in the 1920s, when divisional participation in planning was largely informal. The distinction between policy formulation and policy approval allowed the general office to exercise substantial control over strategic planning. Headquarters' dominance in the policy formulation process essentially allowed them to shape decision premises at lower levels of the organization. In

---

[158] Lammot du Pont to Alfred P. Sloan, Jr., August 8, 1945, Accession 542, Box 837. Emphasis in original.

addition, the outbreak of the war was accompanied by a brief period of extreme centralization in which the top officers in the corporation designed a new set of controls and a new strategy for making profit during the war. Although these new systems allowed divisions much more discretion than they had experienced during the 1930s, they nonetheless set minimal constraints on divisional behavior. But the divisions did enjoy real power in the planning and resource allocation process through their participation on the WAC, and this power increased as the war came to a close. Because they were given a voice and a vote in policy approval and implementation, the divisions were able to shape and sometimes veto policies. In addition, by forging coalitions with other actors – especially group executives or top officers – they could promulgate new policies or reshape proposals coming from the policy groups.

The developments of the war caused owners to become even more unhappy with the GM organization. The effective suspension of Policy Committee activities meant that owners lost the last vestiges of veto power that they had once controlled; decisions were now made by a coalition of top executives, operating officers, and support staff on the WAC and in the policy groups. Owners were not represented at any of these levels. Growing legal concerns and the fear that they would be held legally liable for operating decisions further fueled owner unhappiness with GM's organization. Finally, they were vehemently opposed to the revival of participative decentralization and the inclusion of divisional personnel on top governing committees. Indeed, owners now argued that even group executives were not appropriate to sit on these committees, as they had become too identified with specific operational interests. While owners allowed Sloan to increase participative decentralization through short-term changes in GM's organization, they refused to accept it as an appropriate governance structure for the postwar era.

5

The Split between Finance and Operations: Postwar Problems and Organization Structure, 1945–1948

The postwar era brought unprecedented opportunities for profit and expansion in the automobile industry. Because no new cars had been produced for civilian use during the United States' participation in the war, there was an enormous pent-up demand for new automobiles that would remain unsatisfied until 1949.[1] Over the long run, the decade following the war also saw significant growth in consumer income and purchasing power, further stimulating demand and ultimately leading to the production of larger cars with more accessories and higher profits per unit.[2] These trends would put the automobile industry at the center of postwar growth in the American economy. But before long-range prosperity could be realized, a number of difficulties and uncertainties had to be resolved.

The most immediate problem facing GM and other automobile producers was the process of reconversion itself. Victory over Japan was accompanied by "an avalanche of contract terminations amounting to approximately $1.75 billion of war orders."[3] Government-owned inventories, equipment, and machinery had to be removed from GM's plants, generating some 17,000 freight-car loads of material. After being stripped down, existing plants had to be redesigned and refurbished with new equipment, and many new plants were built to increase productive capacity. Reconversion and expansion had to be carried out under conditions of high inflation, shortages of critical materials, and governmental controls that set prices and limited access to steel and other critical supplies. A number of strikes also interrupted production both inside and outside of GM. One source reported "143 strikes in General Motors' suppliers' plants as of May 20, 1946,"[4] and production lines within all GM plants came to a halt for some five months during a "united auto workers" (UAW) strike against GM lasting from November 21, 1945, until March 13, 1946.[5] Although Alfred Sloan would later recall that

---

1 White (1971, pp. 10–13).   2 Cray (1980, pp. 361–362).
3 Sloan (1964, p. 385).   4 White (1971, p. 10).
5 General Motors Corporation, *Annual Report*, 1946, p. 19; Cray (1980, pp. 337–341).

"our first automobile was produced and shipped about forty-five days after V-J Day," it was years before the corporation returned to normal operations.[6] During this period, the remaining independent auto producers gained market share on the big three, at least temporarily.[7]

The strains of reconversion exacerbated disagreements between owners and managers concerning how to reorganize GM's governance structure. As the process of reconversion got under way, owners and managers still had not reached agreement over GM's postwar organization. The process of reconversion quickly fueled differences of opinion around two key issues. The first involved finance. Despite its postwar planning efforts, GM found that its proposed $500 million expansion plan would require the corporation to go to the capital markets in an extensive way for the first time in decades. While the original plan called for GM to finance expansion through retained earnings, postwar inflation and an extended strike made this impossible. By the end of 1945 it was apparent that expansion would require extensive borrowing or new equity issues.[8] The surplus investment funds that GM enjoyed for decades had disappeared seemingly overnight. As a result, owners became much less willing to delegate jurisdiction over financial matters to the general office, and they redoubled their efforts to reestablish owner veto power over investment decisions.

The second area of contention involved the issue of participative decentralization and divisional participation in the strategic planning and resource allocation process. Believing that GM's postwar financial woes were due in part to the self-interested behavior of operating men, owners also increased their opposition to participative decentralization. Sloan, on the other hand, continued to see such divisional participation as essential, particularly in light of postwar personnel changes. Anticipating his own retirement, Sloan wanted the operating side of the organization to take on more authority and responsibility in the governance process. He saw participative decentralization as an integral part of this process and was thus loath to give in to owners on the matter. Moreover, to strengthen the operating side of the organization, Sloan had decided that the title of chief executive officer should return to president Charles E. Wilson in Detroit, rather than remaining with the chairman of the board in New York. As a result, questions of participative decentralization became deeply intertwined with personnel issues, creating both personal resentments and organizational questions about the relationship between the financial and operating sides of the corporation. Ultimately,

6 Sloan (1964, pp. 385–386).   7 White (1971, p. 11).
8 Sloan (1964, pp. 206–209).

these differences created a deep rift between the financial and operating sides of GM's management that led to a realignment of coalitions within the firm.

The new organizational structure that finally emerged in 1946 was the result of political compromise at the levels of both financial control and operating policy. While this governance structure led GM to the most prosperous period in its history, it continued to entail significant conflation between strategic and tactical planning. Moreover, despite the financial success achieved in the postwar era, the split between finance and operations created by the new organization would plague the corporation for decades to come.

Hard Budget Constraints and Owner Control of Finance

The struggle to devise a new governance structure was deeply influenced by a temporary return to hard budget constraints. The expansion plan that had been formulated in 1944 estimated that postwar growth would cost about $500 million. By the end of 1945, however, it had become apparent that the costs of the expansion program were ballooning. The ongoing UAW strike had brought production to a standstill, leaving the corporation with no income to cover its high fixed costs. Moreover, by the beginning of 1946 the nation was experiencing rapid inflation that dramatically increased the need for working capital and cash to carry out production: materials and equipment for expansion had to be purchased at high prices, inventory commitments rose, and the cost of labor was increasing. Under these conditions, the $500 million estimate proved far too low, and by March 1946, GM had begun looking into sources of additional capital.[9]

GM's capital shortage led to intensified struggle between owners and managers. Management seemed relatively unalarmed by rising costs and saw little need to curtail expansion. Instead, they sought to meet the problem by obtaining new capital through borrowing and other forms of debt financing. Owners, on the other hand, were deeply concerned about GM's apparent capital shortage. In response, they sought to reevaluate the scope of the expansion program and cut it down to more modest levels, a tactic that brought them into direct conflict with operating management. Because owners lacked the ability to exercise financial veto

---

9 Sloan (1964, p. 207).

power, they were unable to curtail expansion. When it became clear that they would not be able to rein in management spending, owners insisted on an organization that would once again allow them to exercise veto power over financial decisions.

In their attempt to curtail expansion, owners sought to eliminate programs that were highly valued by management. Owners first sought to reduce overall capacity below the levels called for in the postwar expansion plan. This proved to be impossible, however, for construction had already begun on many projects. The corporation could not simply abandon expansion that had already begun. The situation was similar to the one that had arisen in the 1920s: commitments had been made and had to be carried through, yet the corporation found itself strapped for cash. Moreover, reductions could not be made in one part of the plan without creating an adverse impact on other parts of the program.[10] Owners thus began to look for items that could be eliminated without seriously affecting the overall expansion plan. The items they identified as suitable for elimination included "the new ball bearing plant, the new assembly plants, the new technical center, and the small car."[11] Owners thus sought to reduce or eliminate programs supported by Charles Wilson and the operating divisions, leading to direct conflict with operating management.

The most important target of owners' cost-cutting plans was the so-called small car, later dubbed the Chevrolet Cadet. General Motors had been researching the idea of introducing a small, lightweight vehicle since at least the late 1930s. In 1939, the corporation had gone so far as to make plans for such a car to be produced by Chevrolet but marketed under a new name.[12] The car was not put into production at that time, in part because Chevrolet division manager Marvin Coyle opposed the program and believed that it would take sales away from his division.[13] Even more problematic was the fact that no amount of forward planning could determine with any degree of accuracy whether the car would be profitable. Despite its much-vaunted strategic planning capabilities, GM remained unable to determine how much the small car would cost to produce, how many units it was likely to sell, how its sales would affect those of the other divisions, or what its returns might be. As Alfred Sloan admitted in 1946,

10 Walter S. Carpenter, Jr., to Policy Committee, February 25, 1946, Accession 542, Box 838.
11 Lammot du Pont to Charles E. Wilson, February 15, 1946, Accession 542, Box 838.
12 See Walter S. Carpenter, Jr., to Albert Bradley, September 8, 1939, Accession 542, Box 821, and Albert Bradley to Walter S. Carpenter, Jr., September 15, 1939, Accession 542, Box 821.
13 Coyle recounted his position in Marvin E. Coyle to Walter S. Carpenter, Jr., March 1, 1946, Accession 542, Box 838.

The Split between Finance and Operations

> We have been discussing this [small car] problem among ourselves for about ten years. We have had at least three very complete engineering studies made on the subject. We have spent many hundreds of thousands of dollars in engineering development work to learn more about the possibilities. We have, however, been unable to come to a decision that we ought to go ahead simply because the facts upon which the decision should be based are not available and probably never will be available unless we produce the car and have them determined by the car itself.[14]

For almost a decade, GM had remained unable to determine whether it should develop and introduce a small car.

By early 1945 new conditions had convinced GM to enter the small-car market. On the surface, postwar conditions seemed to work against introduction of the small car. The enormous pent-up demand for new automobiles meant that manufacturers could sell every car they were able to produce. The hunger for cars was so great that most automakers did not even bother to introduce new models after the war, but reverted to production and sale of cars designed in the 1930s, thus eliminating the costs associated with model changeovers.[15] In this environment, it did not seem to make sense to undertake the trouble and expense associated with bringing out an entirely new car, especially when its sales potential remained unknown. Yet it was not only the new-car market where demand outstripped supply: because no new cars had been produced during the war, there was a severe shortage of used automobiles as well. The shortage of used cars played a key role in GM's final determination to enter the small-car market.

The decision to proceed with the small car was made in an attempt to protect Chevrolet's market share, not because of the new car's profit potential. Postwar price and material controls favored the remaining independent auto producers – Crosley, Hudson, Kaiser-Frazer, Nash, Packard, and Studebaker – and had enabled them to make inroads into the market shares of the "big three."[16] GM management worried that if

---

14 Alfred P. Sloan, Jr., to Walter S. Carpenter, Jr., March 5, 1946, Accession 542, Box 838.
15 White (1971, pp. 11–12). GM was no exception to this rule, and its postwar models were based on 1937 designs. See Marvin E. Coyle to Walter S. Carpenter, Jr., March 1, 1946, Accession 542, Box 838. GM was the first of the big three to return to annual model changes, which it did in 1948. See Frederic Donner to Walter S. Carpenter, Jr., April 10, 1947, Accession 542, Box 838.
16 White (1971, pp. 10–11). See John Felli to Donaldson Brown, August 14, 1946, Accession 542, Box 838, for evidence that the independents were able to increase their existing market share because of material and price controls, thus allowing them to reinvest more earnings and increase their productive capacity.

one of these companies was able to capture the "used-car" market by selling stripped-down new automobiles, it could eventually make real inroads into Chevrolet's price class. They decided that GM should produce a small car in order to protect Chevrolet's markets, even if it meant losing money on that model. Chevrolet's M. E. Coyle summed up management's thinking:

> It may appear that two or three hundred thousand cars annually [the projected market for the small car] is not much in relation to the total industry volume. That is true – but when you add that two or three hundred thousand to the volume of some other manufacturer who already has even a basic volume, he can become an important competitor, looking down the road. . . .
> . . . we must realize that Chevrolet, together with Chevrolet business from the related Corporation Divisions, represents about one-half of both the gross and net profit of General Motors. That position should be protected and I believe we are justified in spending a substantial insurance premium to be certain that it is protected.[17]

Convinced that postwar conditions made this "insurance policy" necessary, operating management voted to proceed. On May 15, 1945, president Charles Wilson announced GM's plans to enter the small-car market following the war, emphasizing that "the car is only in the idea stage, and therefore . . . cannot be placed into production until a considerable period of time after the close of the war with Japan."[18]

As costs for the postwar expansion program mounted, owners put pressure on GM's management to drop the small-car program. They first attacked the small car as unprofitable. Because it was designed to protect markets during a period when there was a shortage of used cars, the life of the small-car program would be relatively short. When the supply of used cars improved two or three years down the road, the small-car program would have to be "abandoned or merged into the standard car line."[19] This made it unlikely that the car would be in production long enough to recover costs of development and production, particularly since labor and materials shortages meant that the car was unlikely to go into production before the 1948 model year. By that time, the short-

---

17 Marvin E. Coyle to Walter S. Carpenter, Jr., March 1, 1946, Accession 542, Box 838.
18 Charles E. Wilson, as quoted in Ludvigsen (1974, p. 16).
19 Walter S. Carpenter, Jr., to Charles E. Wilson, February 13, 1946, Accession 542, Box 838.

The Split between Finance and Operations

age of used cars would already be starting to dissipate.[20] Moreover, the projected costs of the small car kept climbing. Originally slated to sell for under $1,000, the estimated costs of the car rose until they were virtually identical with those of the standard Chevrolet.[21] Owners complained that this would make it nearly impossible to turn a profit on the project, arguing that if "it is true that we cannot expect to make this new car at very much, if any, lower cost than the standard Chevrolet, and if it is sold at a price lower than the Chevrolet, is it not expecting a good deal to hope that we may be able to recover our investment during the [approximately five-year] life of the project?"[22]

Owners also maintained that the small car should be eliminated in order to reduce costs, regardless of its profit potential. Like the expansion program as a whole, the projected costs of fixed and working capital associated with the small program were rising. Initial estimates earmarked $50 million for the project, though "it was at all times recognized that no careful estimate had been made in the preparation of that figure," which had been "more or less picked out of the air."[23] By early 1946, the projected costs had risen to $72 million and were expected to climb still further. The ultimate cost of the small car might run upwards of $100 million, owners warned, with little assurance of a profit ever being made. This would indeed be a "substantial insurance premium" for protecting Chevrolet's markets – one that owners believed would be excessive. They thus sought to eliminate the small car in order to cut down on the increasing cost of the expansion program, seeing it as "substantially the only item ... left ... for discussion in the interest of reducing our commitments."[24]

The first real test for the small-car program came at a March 4, 1946, meeting of the Policy Committee. With a number of owners unable to attend the meeting because of scheduling conflicts, Du Pont's Walter Carpenter sent committee members a long letter outlining owner objections to the program and recommending that it be deferred. He noted that the report to the Policy Committee on the small car highlighted the program's problems: it included an explicit statement from GM's vice-president of finance that "from the standpoint of profit and return on

---

20 Walter S. Carpenter, Jr., to Policy Committee, February 25, 1946, Accession 542, Box 838.
21 Ludvigsen (1974, p. 18).
22 Walter S. Carpenter, Jr., to Charles Wilson, February 13, 1946, Accession 542, Box 838.
23 The first passage is from Walter S. Carpenter, Jr., to Policy Committee, February 25, 1946, Accession 542, Box 838; the second phrase is from Walter S. Carpenter, Jr., to Charles Wilson, February 13, 1946, Accession 542, Box 838.
24 Walter S. Carpenter, Jr., to Charles Wilson, February 13, 1946, Accession 542, Box 838.

investment, it is, of course, impossible at this time to make any estimates, either as to the cost of the car or as to the eventual selling price."[25] Carpenter argued that it was ludicrous to undertake a project of uncertain return that might not get cars into production before the demand had already disappeared; the small car would simply sap resources from other portions of the expansion project. Finally, Carpenter emphasized the need to reduce expenditures, noting that the cost of GM's postwar expansion had grown so rapidly that "it may present a considerable item for even so great a company as General Motors."[26]

Despite owner objections and despite the lack of solid financial data on the new car's expected earnings, the Policy Committee voted to continue the program.[27] Operating management strongly supported the small car, and Chevrolet's Coyle again emphasized the need to protect his division's market share. He stressed that the decision should be made quickly in order to ensure such protection. Indeed, Coyle went so far as to argue that if the Policy Committee acted to defer the program, it should go ahead and kill it entirely. Postwar market conditions were unique, Coyle maintained, and it was "unwise to bring out a car of this type on normal markets."[28] Therefore, the Policy Committee should either approve the program or eliminate it entirely. In the end, the Policy Committee showed more faith in the judgment of the divisions than sympathy for owners' concerns over finances; with owner representatives absent, continuation of the small car was unanimously approved. Owners had been unable to curtail expansion in order to reduce the costs of the postwar program.

The failure of the Policy Committee to curtail expansion and the rapidly rising costs of GM's expansion program had a profound impact on the ongoing debate over organizational structure. Between March and

---

25 Frederic Donner to Policy Committee, as quoted in Walter Carpenter to Policy Committee, February 25, 1946, Accession 542, Box 838. Donner's report also acknowledged that material and labor shortages presented "a problem" in getting the project into operation on a timely basis.
26 Walter Carpenter to Policy Committee, February 25, 1946, Accession 542, Box 838.
27 Other sources report that Alfred Sloan and GM's finance staff opposed the small car from the outset because it did not promise adequate returns. Nonetheless Sloan voted to continue the program and later wrote to Carpenter that "I was thoroughly convinced . . . , assuming that the program is within the financial capacity of the Corporation, that we ought to go right along the lines that we have been discussing right along including, I really think, the little car itself." Sloan's opposition seems to have developed later, after incidents surrounding the small car created a rift between the financial and operating sides of the organization. On Sloan's reported opposition to the small car, see Ludvigsen (1974, p. 16); Cray (1980, p. 323). The preceding quoted material is from Alfred P. Sloan, Jr., to Walter S. Carpenter, Jr., March 5, 1946, Accession 542, Box 838.
28 Marvin E. Coyle to Walter S. Carpenter, March 1, 1946, Accession 542, Box 838.

June 1946, owners redoubled their efforts to regain financial veto power by resurrecting the old Finance Committee. With the emergence of hard budget constraints, they insisted that GM's organization separate issues of operating policy from financial matters, leaving the latter in the hands of shareholders. As is shown later, owners' efforts paid off in the end. Sloan finally capitulated on the issue of financial control, later acknowledging that the increasing importance of financial issues played a key role in his decision.[29]

Problems of Succession and Shifting Coalitions

Debate over GM's postwar structure was also strongly influenced by Sloan's resolve to preserve participative decentralization and by the issues of succession and personnel that his planned retirement raised. Convinced that the Policy Committee had become too powerful in the prewar era, and hoping to avoid financial dictatorship from the top, Sloan had decided that the president and operating executives in Detroit needed to be put more firmly in charge of managing the business. In order to achieve this goal, Sloan traveled to Wilmington on February 26, 1946, to propose a new and somewhat peculiar redistribution of authority at the top of GM's hierarchy. The title of chief executive officer would pass to president Wilson. Donaldson Brown would take Sloan's place as chairman of the board, but he would lack line authority over the operating side of the business. Brown thus "would not exercise administrative function[s]" except over New York's finance staff, GMAC, and part of the public relations staff.[30] All other departments, including the legal offices in New York, would report to Wilson. Finally, Sloan would continue on as chairman of the all-powerful Policy Committee, which would continue to hold all powers of the board. Sloan would no longer serve on the various policy groups, though Brown might continue to do so.

Sloan's plan encountered opposition both from internal constituencies and from owners. Internal opposition was linked to a growing distrust between president Wilson and Donaldson Brown, heir apparent to succeed Sloan as chairman of the board. Conflicts between Brown and Wilson had emerged as Wilson gained power in the postwar era. The first indication of strain came in response to the UAW strike that began on November 21, 1945. Between 1937 and 1941, labor negotiations had

---

29 See Sloan (1964, p. 186). Sloan deposition. *U.S. v. Du Pont*, pp. 85–86 (71). Sloan, direct testimony. *U.S. v. Du Pont*, pp. 4364–4365 (2470).
30 Sloan's plan is summarized in Walter S. Carpenter, Jr., to Lammot du Pont, February 26, 1946. *U.S. v. Du Pont*, GTE #222.

been handled largely by Brown, vice-president of New York's legal staff John T. Smith, and then-president William Knudsen. As part of his desire to strengthen the operating side of the organization, however, Sloan decided to make Wilson GM's lead negotiator in the postwar era. When the strike began, the Policy Committee thus appointed a special committee headed by Wilson and composed of executives in Detroit to handle the situation.[31] Brown quickly began to question Wilson's handling of the strike, and on January 31, 1946, he wrote to Wilson and Sloan complaining about a press release issued by Wilson. Wilson's statement indicated that GM's offer of a 13.5-cent pay hike would be open for renegotiation little more than three months later. Objecting that there was "no contemplation" of such renegotiation, Brown argued that this announcement contradicted testimony given by GM executives to President Truman's fact-finding commission. Warning that the statement would "come to plague us in our future" negotiations, Brown excoriated Wilson for not clearing his actions through the Policy Committee.[32]

Brown's animosity toward Wilson deepened as a result of Sloan's plan to redefine the responsibilities of the president and chairman of the board. On February 4, 1946 – only three days after his memo to Wilson concerning the labor situation – Brown wrote a letter to the Policy Committee threatening to resign from the corporation.[33] While this document touched on his unhappiness with Wilson's handling of the strike, it focused primarily on dismay at an organization chart issued over Sloan's signature. Brown believed that the changes depicted in the chart violated the principles of decentralization. While the specifics of the chart are not known, Brown's objections probably centered on the decision to transfer the title of CEO to Wilson and to the presidency, a move that would strip the chairman of line authority over operations. Brown complained that as vice-chairman he should have been consulted concerning plans for reorganization, and he argued that the proposed changes should have been cleared through the Policy Committee rather than announced unilaterally by Sloan.

Whatever Brown's objections, Sloan had managed to quell them by early March. Following his February 26 visit to Wilmington, Sloan

---

31 See Donaldson Brown to Policy Committee, February 4, 1946, Accession 1334, Box 1.
32 Donaldson Brown to Charles E. Wilson, January 31, 1946, Accession 1334, Box 1.
33 Donaldson Brown to Policy Committee, February 4, 1946a, 1946b, Accession 1334, Box 1. There are two versions of this memo in archival files. Files contain no replies from Policy Committee members, making it unclear whether Brown actually sent the letter in the end. The letter also indicates that these events occurred while Sloan was away from New York; it is possible that Brown's objections softened after conversations with Sloan.

approached Brown about the possibility of serving as chairman of the board following Sloan's retirement. Despite his earlier objections, Brown showed none of the indignation that he had displayed only three weeks earlier. Instead, a "deeply gratified" Brown told Sloan that the decision to transfer the title of CEO to Wilson was "as I would want it in order that the responsibilities for . . . operations . . . be more clearly centered in Detroit."[34] This time, however, Wilson and operating executives balked. Irritated at Brown's interference in the strike, and convinced that he was a financial man who did not understand operating issues, a delegation of operating men led by Wilson privately implored Sloan to stay on as chairman of the board in order to prevent Brown from assuming the office.[35] The rift between Wilson and Brown raised difficulties for Sloan's postwar organization plan, and it eventually shattered the general office coalition that had run GM since 1937.

As the rift between Wilson and Brown became apparent, owners began to challenge Sloan's plan as well. Arguing that GM's existing structure had been built around the assumption that the chairman of the board would also serve as CEO and chairman of the Policy Committee, owners maintained that the new plan would create complex and conflicting lines of authority. The proposal to make the president the CEO, someone else chairman, and Sloan chair of the Policy Committee would lead to overlapping responsibilities at the top of the corporation and an unclear chain of command. Either the chairman of the Policy Committee "might feel . . . that it was part of his responsibility to follow the administration of matters . . . to a point where they might very easily conflict with the administration of the President," or "the President might feel . . . that he . . . should consult with the [chair of the Policy Committee] on matters which he should properly administer without such consultation."[36] Moreover, given the ongoing debate over postwar expansion and the small car, as well as the rift between Brown and Wilson, owners probably were not eager to cede more power to Wilson and Detroit. They believed that increases in participative decentralization had already given the operating side of the organization more influence in planning and resource allocation than was warranted.

Predictably, owners argued that GM should resurrect a more traditional M-form, converting the Policy Committee into a Finance Committee with no power over operations, while turning the Administration Committee into an Executive Committee reporting directly to the board of directors. This arrangement would provide for a clear separation of

---

34 Donaldson Brown to Alfred P. Sloan, Jr., March 4, 1946, Accession 1334, Box 1.
35 Cray (1980, pp. 333-334).
36 Walter S. Carpenter, Jr., to Alfred P. Sloan, Jr., April 8, 1946, Accession 542, Box 838.

authority and responsibility. The financial side of the corporation would be run by the chairman of the board and New York's finance staff; because the chairman would no longer serve as CEO, he would not need a deep knowledge of operations and would not need to get involved in policy formulation except at the financial level. The president and Detroit's general office staff would report directly to the board, making them responsible and accountable for operational issues and planning. Owners emphasized that members of the proposed Executive Committee should be free from divisional duties and should lack line authority, thereby eliminating partisan bargaining. Finally, owners also argued for the first time that a traditional M-form would make it "possible to abandon a number of the ... policy groups" and have the process of policy formulation carried out directly by the Executive Committee.[37] They undoubtedly hoped that this would help to identify clearly those individuals responsible for strategic planning so that they could be held accountable for the policies that they devised.

Faced with owner objections on one side and growing discord within management ranks on the other, Sloan struggled to find a compromise. In order to placate owners, he agreed in principle that it was acceptable to establish Finance and Executive Committees, each reporting directly to the board.[38] Yet he argued that such changes would involve more form than content; the organization would "work exactly the same whichever way the chart shows it."[39] The important point was to leave the task of running the business up to the Executive Committee or Administration Committee rather than the Policy Committee or Finance Committee. Sloan emphasized again that he wanted to give Detroit more responsibility for running the business and that he still intended to make Wilson the CEO. As in the past, Sloan's definition of "running the business" included many aspects of strategic planning, including virtually every aspect of decision-making regarding present and future operations in the automobile industry.[40] Moreover, the fact that Wilson would be CEO in the postwar era made it imperative that Wilson support future reorganization plans.

37 Walter S. Carpenter, Jr., to Alfred P. Sloan, Jr., April 8, 1946, Accession 542, Box 838.
38 Despite his professed willingness to compromise, Sloan remained clear that he preferred GM's existing form of organization. Noting the long-standing disagreements over organizational form, he commented wryly: "I do not think it makes any difference what you call the two Committees.... [W]e can call it Finance ... and Executive Committee because then I am quite certain the matter would be settled for some time to come." Alfred P. Sloan, Jr., to Walter S. Carpenter, Jr., April 9, 1946, Accession 542, Box 838.
39 Alfred P. Sloan, Jr., to Walter S. Carpenter, Jr., April 9, 1946, Accession 542, Box 838.
40 See the discussion that follows and the reference to proposed by-law definitions of the Administration Committee's duties.

Despite his willingness to compromise with owners on the responsibilities and powers of the top two committees, Sloan remained unwilling to yield on the issue of participative decentralization. He adamantly opposed an Executive Committee composed of general executives free from divisional responsibilities. Reiterating that owners did not understand how GM's organization worked in this regard, he argued that transforming the makeup of the existing Administration Committee would further exacerbate "conflicting personalities," creating more tension between New York and Detroit at a time "when the least amount of disturbance is highly desirable."[41] Indeed, Sloan was so committed to participative decentralization that he threatened to withhold his endorsement of the new organization if owners insisted on implementing a top committee composed of general executives free from operating responsibilities. Commenting that it would have to be "the responsibility of the executive who is going to run the re-organized set-up" to approve such a move, he concluded that "it is just impossible for me personally to have anything to do with it."[42] If owners thought it essential to transform the membership of the Administration Committee/Executive Committee, then a meeting could be called involving Sloan, Carpenter, Lammot du Pont, Wilson, and Albert Bradley to discuss the matter.[43] Sloan's commitment to participative decentralization was thus complete, for it remained the one feature of GM's organization that was not open to compromise.

Struggling to Preserve Participative Decentralization

Both owners and managers in GM had hoped to arrive at an acceptable postwar organization by the annual shareholders' meeting scheduled for early June 1946. As outlined earlier, however, by early April they had run up against the same set of issues that had been preventing agreement on a new structure since 1944. In the two months between April 10 and June 6, 1946, both sides struggled to find a solution. On the management side, Sloan began considering a number of alternative plans for reorganization that he hoped would preserve participative decentralization, increase Detroit's power, and avoid financial dictatorship. His efforts to convince owners to accept these plans were hindered by

---

41 Alfred P. Sloan, Jr., to Walter S. Carpenter, Jr., April 9, 1946, Accession 542, Box 838.
42 Alfred P. Sloan, Jr., to Walter S. Carpenter, Jr., April 9, 1946, Accession 542, Box 838.
43 Sloan's inclusion of Bradley rather than Brown probably indicates that he and Wilson were now thinking of making Bradley the next chairman of the board.

Donaldson Brown. Disappointed and perhaps resentful that he would not become chairman after all, Brown now joined owners in criticizing Sloan's proposals. Brown's support, along with GM's continuing postwar financial difficulties, ultimately tipped the balance of power. The eventual result was an uneasy compromise between owners and managers that produced another variant of the M-form.

Faced with Sloan's insistence on preserving participative decentralization, owners initially suggested that reorganization be delayed. Sympathetic to Sloan's claim that Wilson and others would have to approve the new organization, and recognizing that personality conflicts would escalate if Sloan failed to endorse it, Lammot du Pont commented that "it is clear to me that it would take a long time, if it ever could be done, to convert Alfred to our thinking on the matter of Administration and Policy Committees."[44] He therefore suggested that GM keep its current structure for another year. During that time, Sloan could continue to serve as chairman of the Policy Committee, and future organization plans could be worked out by the Policy Committee as a whole. Lammot emphasized that such a solution was acceptable only as long as Sloan continued to serve. The Policy Committee/Administration Committee setup required a top executive highly versed in operations who had the confidence of both owners and managers. Once Sloan departed, it would be extremely difficult to find somebody with these qualifications to replace him. If the Finance Committee/Executive Committee plan was put into place, on the other hand, the chairman would "be of a different type and not so difficult to find" – that is, he could be a financial man with less background in operations.

Despite owners' offer to delay reorganization, neither management nor owners really wished to do so. About to turn 71, Sloan was anxious to retire or at least reduce his responsibilities within GM, while Wilson undoubtedly looked forward to taking over as GM's top officer. Similarly, Lammot du Pont also sought to retire from active duty in both Du Pont and as a member of GM's governing committees. Moreover, given owners' dislike of the Policy Committee setup at GM, it is unlikely that they wanted to continue it any longer than was necessary. Consequently, both owners and managers continued to struggle with the issue of reorganization at GM. Sloan again took the initiative and began to work on a number of plans simultaneously. By late April, after consulting with "the more important and . . . interested" board members, he had begun to work out the details of his first choice, which he hoped would provide an adequate compromise between interested parties.[45]

44 Lammot du Pont to Walter S. Carpenter, Jr., April 10, 1946, Accession 542, Box 838.
45 Alfred P. Sloan, Jr., to Walter S. Carpenter, Jr., April 25, 1946, Accession 542, Box 838.

Sloan's "new" plan looked remarkably like the versions he had put forward earlier. As he often did, Sloan attempted to sell what was essentially the same plan by adopting a different ideology. The one area in which he clearly made concessions to owners concerned the legal delegation of authority from the board of directors to the top governing committees: both the Policy Committee and the Administration Committee would have their powers delegated directly from the board. The Administration Committee, headed by the president, would continue to include divisional executives and other operating men with line authority. It would have complete authority to run the business and formulate operating policy in all areas, including research, engineering policy, production schedules, distribution, and personnel.[46] In addition, it would make all decisions regarding maintenance and expansion of production in existing and potential markets. Finally, it would have the power to authorize expenditures up to a specified limit, with appropriations beyond that limit being approved by the Policy Committee. The Policy Committee, like the Finance Committee favored by the du Ponts, would retain all authority over "financial policies and procedures . . . , including accounting practices [and] capital expenditures."[47] Thus, its responsibilities appeared to be limited more narrowly to financial issues; significantly, the Policy Committee would have no direct authority over the president or operating side of the organization, except in terms of approving expenditures. The chief financial officer and New York's finance staff would report to the Policy Committee. Finally, following operating executives' request, Sloan agreed to stay on as chairman of the board under the new setup.

The plan to delegate power directly from the board to each of the governing committees was an attempt to address owners' criticism that the Policy Committee and Administration Committee had overlapping spheres of authority. Sloan argued that conferring power directly to the Administration Committee from the board rather than from the Policy Committee would eliminate "any feeling that might exist on the part of the President and . . . the Administration Committee that they can not

[46] This description of Administration Committee responsibilities comes from Sloan's proposed by-law revisions, attached to Alfred P. Sloan, Jr., to Walter S. Carpenter, Jr., April 25, 1946, Accession 542, Box 838. A month later, Sloan and vice-president of legal affairs John Smith laid out the responsibilities of the Administration Committee even more clearly, giving it "complete charge and control" over all "operating phases of the Corporation's business," including research, product design and styling, engineering, engineering policy, production, process, and product development, production schedules, product pricing, distribution, personnel, and public relations. See proposed by-laws defining duties of Administration Committee in Robert H. Richards to Alfred P. Sloan, Jr., May 24, 1946, Accession 542, Box 838.

[47] Policy Committee responsibilities are laid out in proposed by-law revisions, attached to Alfred P. Sloan, Jr., to Walter S. Carpenter, Jr., April 25, 1946, Accession 542, Box 838.

make decisions except as they may be reviewed by some higher authority."[48] The plan would also preserve participative decentralization, giving operating executives and division managers on the Administration Committee clear jurisdiction over planning and decision-making. Indeed, Sloan now claimed that this had been his intent all along. Even though he had previously insisted that the Policy Committee "should be the top Committee ... and not one having only equal power with the other Committees," Sloan now asserted that he had "never intended that everything ... the Administration Committee did ... be passed upon 'yes' or 'no' by the Policy Committee."[49] The latter situation had arisen only when his conception of the 1937 organization had been translated into by-laws designed to conform to laws of incorporation. In the new organization, Sloan claimed, operating men on the Administration Committee would be free to oversee planning and administration without having to worry about encroachment from above.

Sloan's new plan did not entirely eliminate overlapping spheres of authority, however, for Sloan was loath to give up the Policy Committee's veto power over the Administration Committee completely. Hidden away in his proposed by-law revisions was an attempt to preserve most of the Policy Committee's existing power. Rather than limiting the Policy Committee to financial veto power over prospective policies, as the du Ponts suggested, Sloan's proposed by-laws required the committee's approval of "all operating policies related" to such expenditures. That is, if a proposed program involved expenditures above a specified limit, the Policy Committee could veto or perhaps revise the policy itself, irrespective of whether it voted to provide the funds. Sloan's proposal thus eliminated duplication of responsibilities only up to a point. Despite his protestations to the contrary, Sloan wanted to retain a superordinate Policy Committee that could review and modify policies formulated below. Sloan's unwillingness to cede complete authority to the Administration Committee is indicative of the tension between control and consent. On the one hand, he really did seek to increase the power of the Administration Committee and the divisions over decision-making, both because he thought it would create better decisions and because it would produce consent. On the other, Sloan also sought to retain ultimate veto power over the Administration Committee for those presumably rare instances in which the corporation's top officers felt intervention was absolutely necessary. Sloan's notion of consent was not

48 Alfred P. Sloan, Jr., to Walter S. Carpenter, Jr., April 25, 1946, Accession 542, Box 838.
49 The first passage is from Alfred P. Sloan, Jr., to Lammot du Pont, April 13, 1942. *U.S. v. Du Pont*, GTE #203; the second is from Alfred P. Sloan, Jr., to Walter S. Carpenter, Jr., April 25, 1946, Accession 542, Box 838.

The Split between Finance and Operations

to be confused with democratic governance, but was a form of constrained participation in planning where top officers retained ultimate veto power.

Donaldson Brown was quick to point out that Sloan's proposal did not take adequate account of the distinction between policy approval and policy formulation. Over the years, Brown had played a key role in crafting GM's organization and convincing owners to accept it. Bitterly disappointed that he would not become chairman of the board after all, Brown now told the du Ponts that he intended to retire from GM and attacked Sloan's latest plan as an attempt "to throw to Detroit the complete responsibility of management beyond the limits that I would consider in the best interest of the business."[50] While his criticisms were almost certainly fueled by resentment at Wilson and the operating men who had rejected him as chairman, they nonetheless provide a clear picture of the issues at stake. Brown emphasized that the existing organization achieved consent by allowing the Administration Committee to approve or veto plans formulated in the policy groups. Division managers on the Administration Committee thus participated in policy approval, but they were excluded from policy formulation. If the Administration Committee's powers were delegated directly from the board, on the other hand, its members would be given the legal authority to formulate policy directly, especially in the arrangement favored by owners. In that case, Brown cautioned, it would no longer be appropriate to include division managers on the Administration Committee. Moreover, because "every operating division is directly represented on the present Administration Committee" and because that committee would be charged with "critical analysis of divisional operations" in Sloan's proposal, the existing Administration Committee "could not appropriately serve as a top governing committee."[51] Brown thus joined owners in opposing Sloan's plan, proposing a complicated alternative that involved a three-committee system similar to the arrangement that had existed in the mid-1920s.[52]

---

50 Donaldson Brown to Walter S. Carpenter, Jr., May 15, 1946. *U.S. v. Du Pont*, GTE #223.
51 Donaldson Brown to Alfred P. Sloan, Jr., April 30, 1946, Accession 542, Box 838. See also Donaldson Brown to Alfred P. Sloan, Jr., April 12, 1945, Accession 1334, Box 2.
52 Brown's plan called for retaining a superordinate Policy Committee with all the powers of the board, indicating his agreement with Sloan on this point. In addition, Brown proposed to convert one of the existing policy groups – the Policy Executive Group – into a sort of Executive Committee. This was the same policy group that Walter Carpenter earlier claimed had been informally carrying out the functions of an Executive Committee for several years. See Walter S. Carpenter, Jr., to Alfred P. Sloan, Jr., June 7, 1945. *U.S. v. Du Pont*, GE #161, which is summarized in Chapter 5. Brown's plan was so complicated and unorthodox that neither owners nor Sloan

Aware that Brown's criticisms would encourage further owner resistance, Sloan wrote to owners to oppose a three-committee system. His opposition was again predicated on issues of information and consent. In the three-committee system, the "real power" to make operating policy would lie with the Executive Committee, but Sloan argued that an Executive Committee composed of general executives would lack adequate information and knowledge of operating issues and would thus not be "as competent to make the operating decisions as those who are now on the Administration Committee."[53] He reiterated that divisional men with line authority should be in charge of planning "because the lower the executive level[,] the greater [the] knowledge ... of what is going on."[54] He also emphasized that the three-committee system proposed by Brown would wreak havoc with consent and cooperation within the firm. Arguing that an Executive Committee composed of "some people from Detroit and some from New York ... is highly detrimental to moral[e] and progress," he reiterated that preserving consent meant giving the operating side of the organization more control over and involvement in organizational decision-making:

> [T]he responsibility of the management of the business should be a direct responsibility located in Detroit under the President.... If we set up an Executive Committee that comprises people here as well as there we are going to continue what now exists; viz., the responsibility at Detroit and ... at New York.... To my mind, that would condemn the plan of itself.[55]

Although Sloan clearly did not favor the three-committee system, he gave owners the impression that such an organization might be adopted if nothing better could be devised by the time of the annual shareholder meeting little more than a month away. Indeed, Sloan outlined his own version of a three-committee system, which he sent to Du Pont representatives for comment.[56] Owners were not completely satisfied with this

---

seriously considered implementing it in the form outlined by Brown. But the more general idea of a three-committee system did prevail in the end, albeit in a somewhat different form.
53 Alfred P. Sloan, Jr., to Walter S. Carpenter, Jr., May 1, 1946, Accession 542, Box 838. Sloan compared the three-committee system to the organization that had existed in the mid-1920s, but he tacitly acknowledged that in the older organization, the Executive Committee had not held the "real power" in decision-making.
54 Alfred P. Sloan, Jr., to Walter S. Carpenter, Jr., May 1, 1946, Accession 542, Box 838.
55 Alfred P. Sloan, Jr., to Walter S. Carpenter, Jr., May 1, 1946, Accession 542, Box 838.
56 Sloan's version of the three-committee system, summarized in Walter S. Carpenter, Jr., to Donaldson Brown, May 16, 1946, Accession 542, Box 838, was virtually identical with the organization that was finally adopted in June 1946.

plan, probably because they believed that it still did not adequately delineate the responsibilities for the top committees. Nonetheless, they preferred it to GM's existing organization and were prepared to accept it, albeit grudgingly. Recognizing that too much interference would serve only to exacerbate tensions, Du Pont's Walter Carpenter wrote:

> Personally, I am inclined – under all the circumstances and considering the enormous problems now before General Motors and considering further that we have got to place such great responsibilities upon Wilson and his associates – to accept their decision on this. I reached this conclusion reluctantly[,] as I feel that we are further crystallizing an organization about which I am not very happy, but which, I must admit, has worked with tremendous success.[57]

Apparently believing that the three-committee plan outlined by Sloan had been agreed upon by all parties, owners wrote to Donaldson Brown, urging him to stay on at GM in the postwar era, rather than retiring, as Brown now planned to do.

Despite owners' apparent belief that the three-committee plan had been agreed upon, Sloan continued to work feverishly behind the scenes on an entirely different plan that would preserve participative decentralization. Still believing that divisional participation in planning was a top priority in the postwar era, Sloan and vice-president of legal affairs John T. Smith attempted to draft by-laws that would preserve a two-committee system in which divisional managers would participate directly in strategic planning and resource allocation through membership on the Administration Committee. They focused specifically on legal difficulties that would arise if the Administration Committee's power were delegated directly from the board rather than from the Policy Committee. The prevailing interpretation of Delaware laws of incorporation was that any subcommittee of the board of directors had to be composed entirely of board members. Under GM's existing organization, this law did not apply to the Administration Committee, since it was not legally a subcommittee of the board: its powers were delegated entirely from the Policy Committee, which retained all legal responsibility for governance. As a result, seven of the division managers serving on the Administration Committee in early 1946 were not board members. If the Administration Committee was to have its powers delegated directly from the board, prevailing legal opinion was that these men would have to become directors. But owners had long fought against making too many operating men directors, and they were not about to appoint over

---

57 Walter S. Carpenter, Jr., to Lammot du Pont, May 17, 1946, Accession 542, Box 838.

half a dozen divisional representatives to the board, especially if it helped to preserve a structure that they did not like. Sloan therefore sought to find a way of including divisional men on the Administration Committee without having them elected to the board. Smith obliged with an unorthodox interpretation of the law, claiming that only the chairman of the Administration Committee needed to be a board member in order to satisfy legal guidelines. Together, he and Sloan were in the process of working out by-laws that they believed would withstand legal scrutiny.

When owners learned of this plan, they immediately insisted that Smith and Sloan get an opinion from outside counsel. Noting that Du Pont's lawyers had always advised that all members of a board sub-committee had to be directors, they warned that the plan could leave both GM and individual directors, including the du Ponts, open to litigation. Moreover, if it was later learned that the organization was illegal, GM either would have to dismiss non–board members from the Administration Committee, which would be "very awkward," or would have to elect those men to the board, which would make the board "top-heavy" with management representatives, "thereafter complicat[ing] . . . the action of the Board on matters affecting officers and employees."[58] In a meeting that included legal representatives from Du Pont, Sloan and Smith reluctantly presented their proposed by-laws to Delaware counsel. Fearing that their plan would be overruled, Sloan also requested that counsel consider the legality of an Administration Committee in which only the majority of members were directors and all decisions by that body required an affirmative vote from a plurality of those members who were also directors.[59] When outside counsel found both proposals to be illegal, a clearly frustrated Sloan complained that the decision did "not make very much sense."[60] After all, between 1942 and 1946 members of GM's Administration Committee had not been required to be directors, yet that body had run the corporation. Indeed, Sloan and Smith argued that even if the plan was illegal, it was "hard . . . to see" how its implantation could create problems, since "the Board will always support what its committees and its executives do."[61] Nonetheless, they agreed that GM would have to abide by the decision.

The decision by outside counsel was the death knell of the two-

58 Walter S. Carpenter, Jr., to John T. Smith, May 17, 1946, Accession 542, Box 838.
59 Alfred P. Sloan, Jr., to Walter S. Carpenter, Jr., May 22, 1946, Accession 542, Box 838.
60 For the decision of outside counsel (the firm Richards, Layton, and Finger), see Robert H. Richards to Alfred P. Sloan, Jr., May 24, 1946, Accession 542, Box 838. Sloan's reaction can be found in Alfred P. Sloan, Jr., to Walter S. Carpenter, Jr., May 22, 1946, Accession 542, Box 838.
61 Alfred P. Sloan, Jr., to Walter S. Carpenter, Jr., May 22, 1946, Accession 542, Box 838.

The Split between Finance and Operations

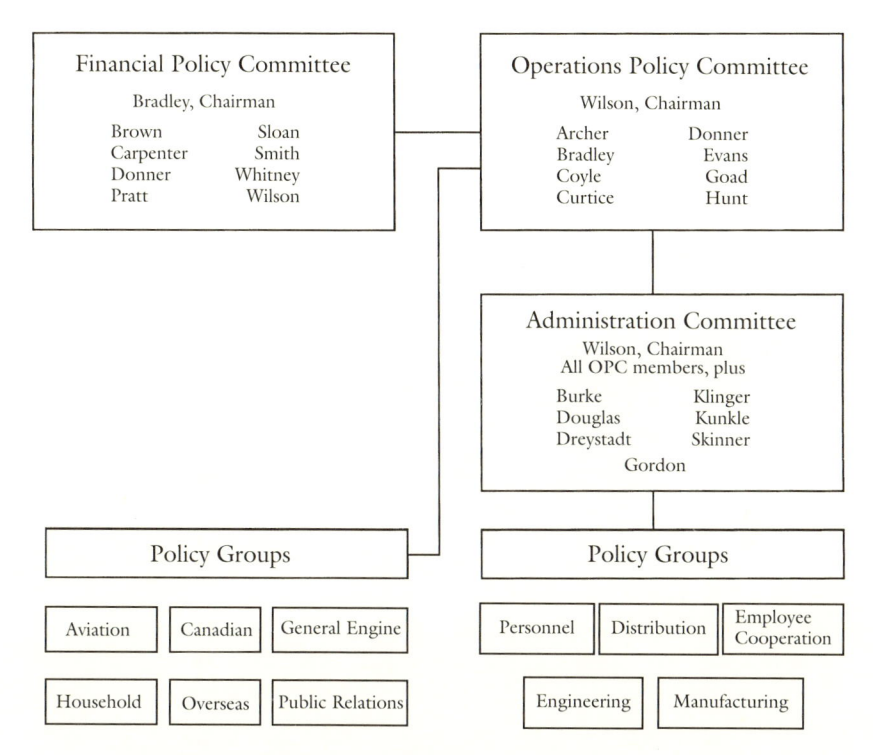

Financial Policy Committee	Operations Policy Committee
Bradley, Chairman	Wilson, Chairman
Brown Sloan	Archer Donner
Carpenter Smith	Bradley Evans
Donner Whitney	Coyle Goad
Pratt Wilson	Curtice Hunt

Administration Committee
Wilson, Chairman
All OPC members, plus
Burke   Klinger
Douglas   Kunkle
Dreystadt   Skinner
Gordon

Policy Groups: Aviation | Canadian | General Engine | Household | Overseas | Public Relations

Policy Groups: Personnel | Distribution | Employee Cooperation | Engineering | Manufacturing

Figure 5.1. General Motors' top governing committees, 1946

committee system, and it seemed to jeopardize Sloan's plans to preserve participative decentralization. With both owners and outside lawyers opposed to Sloan's plan for a two-committee organization, and with the shareholder meeting at which the new organization was to be approved scheduled to occur only ten days after counsel's decision, the only remaining alternative was the three-committee system that Sloan had put forward earlier.

Organization as Compromise: GM's 1946 Structure

The new organization, announced on June 3, 1946, adopted the three-committee setup as a compromise between owners and managers[62] (Figure 5.1, Tables 5.1 and 5.2). In the new structure, the duties of the

---

62 The new organization is depicted in General Motors Corporation, "Organization Chart, July 1, 1946." *U.S. v. Du Pont*, DTE #GM8.

Table 5.1. *Responsibilities and Powers of GM's Top Governing Committees, 1946*

	Powers	Membership
Financial Policy Committee	The FPC "shall have and may exercise the power of the board...in the determination of the financial policies of the corporation and in the management of the financial affairs of the corporation, including all accounting policies and procedures.... All capital expenditures of the corporation shall be approved by the financial policy committee, except that the financial policy committee may authorize the operations policy committee to approve capital expenditures to such extent and up to such amounts as the financial policy committee may establish. The financial and accounting officers,... the general counsel,... the secretary... and the transfer agent of the corporation and their respective staffs, shall be under the supervision of the financial policy committee."	Must be board members.
Operations Policy Committee	The OPC "shall have and may exercise the powers of the board of directors...in the management of the business and affairs of the corporation...."	Must be board members.
Administration Committee	"The administration committee shall make recommendations to the operations policy committee with respect to the manufacturing and selling activities of the corporation.... All action by the administration committee shall be reported to the operations policy committee and shall be subject to revision by the operations policy committee...."	"The members...with the exception of the chairman, need not be directors."

Source: General Motors Corporation, *By-laws,* as amended to June 1946.

Table 5.2. *Membership of Financial Policy, Operations Policy, and Administration Committees, June 1946*

Financial Policy Committee

Name	Position(s) in Corporation
Albert Bradley	Chairman, FPC; Executive Vice President
Donaldson Brown	Du Pont Representative
Walter Carpenter	Du Pont Representative
Frederic Donner	Vice President, Finance
John L. Pratt	Du Pont Representative
Alfred P. Sloan	Chairman of the Board
John Smith	Vice President, Legal
George Whitney	J.P. Morgan Representative
Charles Wilson	President, CEO; Chair, OPC; Chair, AC

Operations Policy Committee

Name	Position(s) in Corporation
Albert Bradley	Chairman, FPC; Executive Vice President
Frederic Donner	Vice President, Finance
Charles Wilson	President, CEO; Chair, OPC; Chair, AC
Thomas Archer	Group Executive, Body; Division Manager, Fisher
Marvin Coyle	Executive Vice President; Group Exec, Car & Truck
Harlow Curtice	Division Manager, Buick
Ronald Evans	Group Executive, Engine
Louis Goad	Group Executive, Assembly
Ormond Hunt	Executive Vice President

Administration Committee

Name	Position(s) in Corporation
Albert Bradley	Chairman, FPC; Executive Vice President
Frederic Donner	Vice President, Finance
Charles Wilson	President, CEO; Chair, OPC; Chair, AC
Thomas Archer	Group Executive, Body; Division Manager, Fisher
Marvin Coyle	Executive Vice President; Group Exec, Car & Truck
Harlow Curtice	Division Manager, Buick
Ronald Evans	Group Executive, Engine
Louis Goad	Group Executive, Assembly
Ormond Hunt	Executive Vice President
Francis Burke	Group Executive, Accessory
Morgan Douglas	Division Manager, Truck
Nicholas Dreystadt	Division Manager, Chevy
John Gordon	Division Manager, Cadillac
Harry Klingler	Division Manager, Pontiac
Bayard Kunkle	Group Executive, Overseas
Sherrod Skinner	Division Manager, Oldsmobile

Source: General Motors Corporation, "Organization Chart," July 1, 1946.

old Policy Committee were split in two. To satisfy owners' increasing demands for greater control over scarce capital, a Financial Policy Committee (FPC) was created to oversee financial matters. The FPC was given complete authority over capital expenditures and accounting policies; the finance, accounting, and legal staffs would report to the FPC rather than to the operating side of the organization. Since the FPC had to approve all major capital appropriations, this committee finally reestablished a group with financial veto power. Although owners did not constitute a majority on the FPC, their representation did increase. The nine-man FPC included four owners, including Donaldson Brown, who, after resigning from active duty in GM's management, had agreed to represent Du Pont on the board.[63] Three committee members, including FPC chairman Albert Bradley, were members of New York's financial or legal staff; president Charles Wilson was the sole representative of operations, giving Detroit little voice in financial affairs. Sloan served as an FPC member and continued on as chairman of the board, but because he no longer held line authority as CEO, his responsibilities were reduced significantly.[64] The FPC was clearly designed to provide owners with the financial veto power that they had long desired, as well as to create a clearer division of responsibilities between finance and operations. Yet Sloan cautioned owners that the FPC should be regarded "as a group of observers" whose responsibility was to "'balance' rather than 'control'" management.[65] Clearly, he did not intend to let owners have uncontested control of financial decisions.

On the operating side of the organization, the disagreements between owners and managers produced an uneasy compromise between a Du Pont–style Executive Committee and Sloan's brand of participative decentralization. At the top of the operating structure was a new Operations Policy Committee (OPC), chaired by president Wilson, who became chief executive officer. In accordance with owners' recommendations, the nine-man OPC was a legal subcommittee of the board holding all authority to carry out planning and oversee daily operations.

---

63 The other owner representatives were Walter S. Carpenter, Jr., former GM executive John L. Pratt, who had originally come to GM from Du Pont, and J. P. Morgan's George Whitney, who had long served on the Policy Committee. Lammot du Pont retired from active duty following the reorganization. See "General Motors Press Release," June 3, 1946, Accession 542, Box 838. On Brown's decision to represent Du Pont on the FPC, see Walter S. Carpenter, Jr., to Donaldson Brown, May 16, 1946, Accession 542, Box 838; Walter S. Carpenter, Jr., to Donaldson Brown, May 22, 1946. *U.S. v. Du Pont*, GTE #224.

64 Besides Bradley, Sloan, and Wilson, the other management members of the FPC were vice-president of finance Frederic Donner and vice-president of legal affairs John T. Smith.

65 Alfred P. Sloan, Jr., to Walter S. Carpenter, Jr., June 7, 1946, Accession 542, Box 838.

It could also approve appropriation requests below a specified limit; appropriations above that limit had to be approved by the FPC.[66] Two OPC members were division managers, two were group executives, and one member was an executive vice-president who also served as a group executive. The other members were general office executives, most of whom were members of Detroit's technical staffs rather than New York's finance staff.[67] In principle, the OPC held complete control over strategic planning. Excepting the limited presence of division managers and group executives, the OPC thus appeared to be very similar to the model that owners had advocated for years.

Despite the apparent dominance of the OPC, the 1946 organization also retained aspects of participative decentralization. First, the Administration Committee continued to exist as a third committee that reported to the OPC; Administration Committee members were not required to be on the board, clearing the way for division managers to sit on that committee. The Administration Committee was composed of sixteen members and included all OPC members, division managers of the car and truck groups, and a number of other operating executives. Equally important, the distinction between policy formulation and policy approval remained intact. Policies continued to be formulated in the various policy groups, each of which was chaired by a staff executive.[68] Once policy proposals were worked out in these groups, they went on to the Administration Committee, which voted to ratify or reject them.[69]

66 On the powers of the OPC and FPC, see General Motors Corporation, *By-laws*, 1946, Sections 36–37, pp. 7–8.
67 In addition to Wilson, Curtice, and Archer, the operating members of the OPC were as follows: executive vice-president Marvin Coyle; Ronald Evans, group executive in charge of the Engine Group; group executive in charge of the new Buick-Olds-Pontiac assembly group, Louis Goad; and executive vice-president Ormond Hunt. The two OPC members from the financial staff were executive vice-president and chair of the FPC Albert Bradley and vice-president of finance and FPC member Frederic Donner. While most of these men were free from allegiances to specific divisions, all but Donner (and possibly Bradley) held at least limited line authority over the divisions; since the changes made in the 1930s, even group executives held limited line authority. See Alfred P. Sloan, Jr., to Lammot du Pont, April 21, 1931. Longwood, 430 (22), First Series, v. 15, pp. 4549–4550. Donaldson Brown to Alfred P. Sloan, Jr., June 1, 1937, Accession 1334, Box 1.
68 Organization charts identify only the chairmen for the eleven groups existing in 1946. It is thus not possible to determine complete membership of the policy groups after this date.
69 The 1946 organization chart shows one set of policy groups reporting to the Administration Committee and a second set reporting directly to the OPC. The implication is that policies formulated in the latter policy groups were not reviewed or ratified by the Administration Committee. There is insufficient data as to whether this was actually the case. Even if it was, the situation was evidently short-lived: subsequent organization charts depict all groups reporting directly to the Administration Committee rather than to the OPC. See, for example, the organization chart depicted in General Motors Corporation (1948).

If proposals were passed by the Administration Committee, they were forwarded to the OPC in the form of recommendations for action.[70] This arrangement kept division managers formally and explicitly involved in the policy approval process, a distinct contrast to the arrangement that prevailed in the 1920s and 1930s. In this sense, at least, formal participative decentralization continued.

If the OPC was not the textbook M-form that owners supported, neither did the 1946 organization achieve the autonomy for the operating side of the organization that Sloan desired. The hope was that the OPC/Administration Committee setup would provide a mechanism to manufacture divisional consent while giving Wilson and Detroit more control of the corporation and its operating policies.[71] Yet because the OPC had to obtain FPC approval for expenditures, it did not have the freedom from "financial dictatorship" that Sloan sought. In addition, the Administration Committee's ability to produce divisional consent was problematic. The hope was that the Administration Committee would create consent by allowing division managers to retain veto power over prospective policies. Although the Administration Committee included division managers in the policy approval process, however, the OPC was in no way obligated to follow the recommendations of the Administration Committee. The OPC held all legal authority over operating policy, and it could reverse or modify policy recommendations at will. Indeed, by-laws specified that any actions taken by the Administration Committee were "subject to revision by the operations policy committee."[72] If this occurred, there was at least the possibility that divisional consent would be destroyed, as the OPC began to operate via fiat.

In the short run, the 1946 organization seemed to achieve owners' desire for financial control. As owners had hoped, the FPC gained financial veto power over the operating side of the organization, in large part because Alfred Sloan and New York's finance staff joined owners in voting down management-sponsored initiatives for expansion. Yet the exercise of financial veto also produced unintended consequences. The FPC's ascendance created an oppositional identity among operating management. Reacting to financial veto, top executives with line authority, led by Wilson, forged an alliance with division managers to resist FPC control. In the short run, their attempts were unsuccessful. Between mid-1946 and early 1948, operating management was able to implement prospective policies only by obtaining FPC sponsorship. The FPC's

---

70 General Motors Corporation, *By-laws*, 1946, Article 38, p. 8.
71 Alfred P. Sloan, Jr., to Walter S. Carpenter, Jr., June 7, 1946, Accession 542, Box 838.
72 General Motors Corporation, *By-laws*, Section 38, as amended to June 1946, p. 8.

victory served only to exacerbate tensions between finance and operations, however, creating deep resentments that would haunt GM in the years ahead.

Owners Exercise Financial Veto

The 1946 organization gave owners increased influence over the corporation's financial affairs, and they wasted little time in attempting to use it. On June 4, 1946 – the day after the reorganization – Du Pont executives began lobbying other FPC members to hold a special meeting of the FPC in order to discuss GM's financial situation. With costs still rising and output well below capacity, it was clear that GM needed to cut costs and find additional sources of capital. Owners sought to give these matters immediate attention, and within days had arranged for the FPC to meet on June 14.[73]

Owners' desire to act grew out of what they saw as a deepening financial crisis. Following the Policy Committee's March 1946 decision to continue the small-car program and maintain expansion at full scale, the corporation's financial condition had rapidly worsened. On March 19, 1946, the UAW strike that had shut down production lines for nearly five months came to an end, with workers agreeing to a wage increase of 18.5 cents per hour plus assorted fringe benefits.[74] Higher wages, along with the costs of the long shutdown, intensified owners' worries about controlling expenditures. Their concern was heightened by the fact that while costs for the expansion program continued to rise, both the reconversion process and GM's ability to produce automobiles remained woefully behind schedule. By the time reorganization occurred in June, it had become apparent that production for 1946 would not reach anything close to capacity. Although the expansion program had hardly begun, meaning that capacity was still relatively low, and although there was virtually unlimited demand for automobiles, GM simply could not manage to meet production schedules. Operating well below capacity, the corporation could not generate enough profit to cover costs, much less capital to fund the postwar program.

The primary reason for lack of output was a shortage of parts and materials that kept production lines idle. One report noted that Fisher Body's ability to produce bodies was limited by a shortage of cushion springs – a seemingly trivial supply – while other critical materials were

---

73 Frederic Donner to Walter S. Carpenter, Jr., June 7, 1946, Accession 542, Box 838.
74 Cray (1980, p. 341). See also General Motors Corporation, *Annual Report*, 1946, pp. 19–20.

available "only on a day to day basis."[75] While all manufacturers faced such difficulties, GM's reconversion process lagged behind those of other producers, and Chrysler, Ford, and the independents had all increased their market share relative to GM's prewar production. In June 1946 GM was forced to reduce its production schedules for the following four months by 750,000 cars and trucks, "because we knew we just could not produce them," and keeping them on the production schedule would lead to inventory imbalances.[76] While the expansion program was designed to create a capacity of 14,000 cars and 3,500 trucks per day, in June 1946 GM was not even able to reach an output of 3,500 cars and trucks combined.[77] Although these problems were short-run in nature, GM management acknowledged that the situation constituted "rather a pathetic picture" in comparison with the production levels they had expected to obtain.[78]

GM's difficulties led to a struggle over how to meet the corporation's financial needs. It was now apparent to everybody that GM would soon need new capital: as long as production was limited so severely, the corporation could hardly hope to earn enough money to cover its working-capital needs, let alone pay for the expansion program. As late as October 1946 GM continued to lose some $20 million a month in "excess overhead burden" alone, that is, overhead costs that had to be deducted from earnings due to low volume; conditions in the period between March and July were much worse, and losses during that period would have been significantly larger.[79] While nobody doubted that GM's production and profits would eventually improve, the corporation was facing a cash shortage that cost reductions alone could not meet; new capital was essential. Owners argued that new capital should come from the issue of new equity, for they believed that borrowing more money was simply too risky, given uncertainties such as material shortages, labor unrest, and price controls. GM's financial staff, on the other hand, argued that the best way to obtain additional capital was through short-term borrowing, especially since interest on debt could be deducted from taxes. The immediate issue to be addressed in the June 14 meeting of the FPC was thus what form of capital to obtain.

75 John C. Felli, assistant treasurer, to Donaldson Brown, August 14, 1946, Accession 542, Box 838. The following sentence in the text draws on information from the same source.
76 Alfred P. Sloan, Jr., to Walter S. Carpenter, Jr., June 18, 1946, Accession 542, Box 838.
77 John C. Felli to Donaldson Brown, August 14, 1946, Accession 542, Box 838.
78 Alfred P. Sloan, Jr., to Walter S. Carpenter, Jr., June 18, 1946, Accession 542, Box 838.
79 Walter S. Carpenter, Jr., "Notes of Conversation with Frederic G. Donner," October 17, 1946, Accession 542, Box 838.

The positions of owners and managers can be seen in the exchange of correspondence that occurred in conjunction with the FPC meeting. Du Pont's Walter Carpenter estimated that GM needed additional capital of $100 million to $300 million, figures that were based on a number of factors and contingencies. Inflation had caused projected expenditures on plant to climb from $500 million to $800 million. Working-capital requirements had also increased dramatically because of inflation, and expansion would increase cash requirements for the business still further. Moreover, GM's financial projections had been carried out on the assumption that the need to reinvest earnings "would be unusually low [once expansion was completed] due to the fact that so much of our plant would be new."[80] This provision, undoubtedly made in order to assure owners that healthy dividends would continue, was beginning to look quite dubious. Carpenter pointed out that once annual model changes began a few years down the road, "large segments of our investment" might be rendered "obsolete."[81] He further estimated that the strike had cost the corporation another $100 million, and he worried that with unions growing stronger, more such losses were in store. Carpenter argued that these factors, coupled with the uncertainties of the postwar era, had brought about "a complete reversal in our financial condition."[82] The surplus of $500 million that the corporation had developed during the war was nearly exhausted, and more capital was needed. Carpenter argued that the high level of environmental uncertainty made it wise to put aside money to cover unforeseen contingencies, rather than to incur debt; increases in capital should thus come in the form of new equity.

GM's vice-president of finance, Frederic Donner, acknowledged that the corporation had "a sizable deficiency" of capital, but he argued that the shortage could be met by borrowing funds.[83] Donner estimated that by the end of 1947 GM's deficit would be about $235 million, which could increase further if inflation continued to rise. Yet he found most of Carpenter's assumptions to be far too pessimistic. He did not worry about future labor unrest, for instance, because the 1945 strike had not cost GM anything like the $100 million that Carpenter estimated. Provisions of the tax code had allowed the corporation to write off most of the losses: even though the strike had cost GM $120 million before taxes, the after-tax cost was only $20 million.[84] Donner maintained that Carpenter also overstated the risk from other contingencies and failed to

80 Walter S. Carpenter, Jr., to Frederic Donner, June 4, 1946, Accession 542, Box 838.
81 Walter S. Carpenter, Jr., to Frederic Donner, June 4, 1946, Accession 542, Box 838.
82 Walter S. Carpenter, Jr., to Frederic Donner, July 30, 1946, Accession 542, Box 838.
83 Frederic Donner to Walter S. Carpenter, Jr., June 7, 1946, Accession 542, Box 838.
84 Frederic Donner to Walter S. Carpenter, Jr., June 7, 1946, Accession 542, Box 838.

make allowances for money that would become available through depreciation and tax refunds. If the FPC accepted Carpenter's analysis, Donner agreed, it would be necessary to enlarge the corporation's preferred stock by about $100 million, thereby increasing the capital base against which GM could borrow and reducing the necessity of large, scheduled repayments. But Donner argued that because many of the contingencies outlined by Carpenter could not yet be measured accurately, a permanent expansion of capital was unwarranted; the capital deficit should be met through additional borrowing.[85]

The special meeting of the FPC ended with a victory for management. Despite owners' arguments, the FPC agreed to proceed with efforts to borrow $125 million by selling twenty- and thirty-year notes paying 2.5 percent interest to a consortium of insurance companies.[86] Yet the proceeds from this bond issue would not cover GM's capital needs. Donner's financial report to the FPC estimated that even with these funds, there would be a deficit of some $300 million by mid-1947.[87] Incredibly, the report went on to recommend that this amount be covered by borrowing another $290 million, exhausting a large portion of GM's credit. Aghast at the magnitude of indebtedness recommended by New York's financial staff, owners redoubled their efforts to exert control over GM's finances. They not only continued their campaign to generate capital through equity issue but also once again sought to cut back expansion. This time, however, they sought to develop independent information so that they would not have to rely on the figures provided by GM's management.

Following the June 14 meeting, owners quickly attacked management's plan to incur further debt. They charged that the capital projections provided by GM's financial staff were "all on the rosey [sic] side" and that capital deficits would probably be far larger than projections indicated.[88] For instance, despite GM's continuing inability to produce at anything approaching capacity, Donner's estimates of capital needs were predicated on an inventory turnover of seven times per annum, nearly equal to the highest numbers achieved in record sales years like 1941 and 1929.[89] These estimates also assumed that the cost of short-term labor stoppages could be offset by inventory liquidation, while write-off for

---

85 Frederic Donner to Walter S. Carpenter, Jr., June 7, 1946, Accession 542, Box 838.
86 Sloan (1964, p. 208). The decision to go ahead with this plan was probably made at the special FPC meeting of June 14, though the deal was not completed until August 1.
87 Walter S. Carpenter, Jr., to Frederic Donner, July 30, 1946, Accession 542, Box 838.
88 Walter S. Carpenter, Jr., to Frederic Donner, July 30, 1946, Accession 542, Box 838.
89 See the Appendix for inventory turnover figures; the actual inventory turnover for 1946 was 3.57, half of Donner's estimate.

tools and depreciation of plant would recover over $300 million of funds. Owners found both of these assumptions unreasonable in the uncertain postwar atmosphere: a strike would cause cash reserves to be "gone with the wind," while depreciation and write-offs would provide income only "if we have no interruption of our operations during that period."[90] If the financial staff's assumptions proved to be false, GM's indebtedness would be far more than the projected $290 million. Owners again argued that it was essential that GM increase its capital through new equity.

Convinced that GM was headed for financial crisis, owners also renewed their efforts to curtail the scope of postwar expansion, arguing that it was foolish to continue with a program of such magnitude when GM was not even able to produce at its current capacity. The GM program called for increasing the corporation's peak production capacity to 14,000 cars and 2,500 trucks per day, or some 2,990,000 cars and 475,000 trucks per year.[91] Questioning the accuracy of the data and assumptions used by GM's financial and operating staffs, owners instructed staff members of Du Pont's Economics Office to carry out independent assessments of the postwar plan. The Du Pont–developed figures indicated that GM's expansion program was far too ambitious and "wildly optimistic."[92] GM projections indicated that in the three years from 1947 to 1949, the corporation's production would average some 3.5 million cars and trucks per year, a figure that was "almost 50 percent higher than any previous year's production" and did not even include the still-debated small car.[93] Du Pont analysts charged that it was also unlikely that GM would achieve anything like the 2.85 million units per year in sales that it projected over the longer run, once pent-up demand had been met.[94] The Du Pont report further charged that GM's figures overestimated long-range inflation and failed to make allowances for the effect that "unprecedented" automobile price increases would

---

90 Walter S. Carpenter, Jr., to Frederic Donner, July 30, 1946, Accession 542, Box 838.
91 Walter S. Carpenter, Jr., "Notes on telephone conversation with John Felli," August 2, 1946, Accession 542, Box 838. These numbers assumed industry-wide production of 6.2 to 6.5 million cars and 1.25 to 2.6 million trucks per year, with GM's capacity being set based on 45% of the market for automobiles and 42% of trucks.
92 Edmond E. Lincoln, E. I. du Pont de Nemours' Economics Office, to Walter S. Carpenter, Jr., August 2, 1946, Accession 542, Box 838. See also Edmond E. Lincoln to Alfred P. Sloan, Jr., July 23, 1946, Accession 542, Box 838, which outlines many of the same conclusions in much more circumspect language. GM did not sell 3.5 million cars annually until 1950. See General Motors Corporation, *Annual Report*, 1960, pp. 40–41.
93 Edmond E. Lincoln, E. I. du Pont de Nemours' Economics Office, to Walter S. Carpenter, Jr., August 2, 1946, Accession 542, Box 838.
94 In fact, GM did sell well over 2.8 million units per year in most of the years following 1950. See General Motors Corporation, *Annual Report*, 1960, pp. 40–41.

have on consumer demand. Finally, it indicated that GM's figures were based on an "assumption that there will be no re-investment of earnings," a position that "seems somewhat extreme."[95] Using this new information, owners continued to lobby for a reduction in the expansion program and for equity financing.

GM's financial management finally agreed to go along with owners when continuing material shortages and low production made it clear that the financial decline was continuing. On September 9, 1946, the FPC voted to scale back the postwar program, reducing peak capacity from 14,000 cars and 3,500 trucks per day to 10,000 cars and 2,500 trucks. Recognizing that GM "would not be able to secure materials sufficient to operate at a higher level," the FPC instructed "the operating management to adjust its plant enlargement program and also its organization to the basis of these new figures."[96] If materials did become available, production would be carried out through overtime and extra shifts. Charles Wilson protested that because construction had already begun on the expansion program, there was "no possibility" that reduction in capacity would "result in anything like the corresponding reduction in capital expenditures."[97] While owners agreed that reducing capacity would create only a slight reduction in fixed capital, they knew that it would result in a reduction in working-capital requirements. To cut fixed-capital commitments, the FPC also voted to defer all expenditures on the small-car program for ninety days, a move that Wilson also opposed. Finally, the committee agreed to issue $125 million in preferred stock, a plan that had been tentatively approved a month earlier.[98]

The developments of late summer and early fall 1946 seemed to mark a victory for owners and the rebirth of financial control under hard budget constraints. All of the major recommendations espoused by owners had finally been supported and approved by GM's top financial executives. Indeed, owners now began to talk of strengthening their control through bringing a wider range of decisions into the FPC's purview; Donaldson Brown, for instance, pointed out that inventory commitments were being made far in advance because of shortages and suggested that the FPC have final authority over such commitments, as

---

95 Edmond E. Lincoln, E. I. du Pont de Nemours' Economics Office, to Walter S. Carpenter, Jr., August 2, 1946, Accession 542, Box 838.
96 Walter S. Carpenter, Jr., to Donaldson Brown, September 10, 1946, Accession 1334, Box 1.
97 Donaldson Brown to Walter S. Carpenter, Jr., September 11, 1946, Accession 1334, Box 1. The quoted passage is Brown's summary of Wilson's position; both Brown and Carpenter basically agreed that Wilson's assertions were correct.
98 Because of sluggishness in the stock market, the preferred issue was later cut to $100 million, which was offered on November 27, 1946. See Sloan (1964, p. 208).

it had in 1921.⁹⁹ Over the next year, owners would strengthen their financial control and solidify their alliance with general office executives in New York. Ironically, however, their victory in 1946 had already created tensions between the financial and operating sides of General Motors' management. As owners attempted to strengthen their control, a new set of coalitions would emerge, with owners and financial executives on one side, and operating executives from the general office and the divisions on the other.

The Split between Finance and Operations

The FPC's decision to cut back the expansion program and delay the small-car project marked the beginning of a deep rift between the financial and operating sides of the business. In the short run, the FPC's actions helped to improve GM's profits. Sometime between December 1946 and May 1947, the FPC "held up the small car [program] rather definitely" in order to cut costs.¹⁰⁰ This, along with other reductions in the expansion program, such as delaying the construction of the new technical center, helped to lower the corporation's break-even point. Although material shortages kept production during this period well below the 2.5 to 3 million units that GM hoped to sell, by early 1947 the corporation was turning a healthy 30 percent return on net investment. This performance was achieved in part through extremely high sales of replacement parts and accessories, as well as through cost savings realized by delaying the introduction of annual model changes.¹⁰¹ Yet

---

99 Donaldson Brown to Walter S. Carpenter, Jr., September 11, 1946, Accession 1334, Box 1.
100 Alfred P. Sloan, Jr., to Walter S. Carpenter, Jr., June 10, 1947, Accession 542, Box 838. Sloan's letter puts this decision around the beginning of 1947, but memos by Carpenter (cited later) indicate that the issue of the small car came up again late in April 1947. It seems likely that the discussions referred to by Carpenter never materialized into a full-scale reconsideration of the issue by the FPC.
101 On the latter two points, see Frederic Donner to Walter S. Carpenter, Jr., April 10, 1947, Accession 542, Box 838. The reduction in capacity cut GM's "standard volume" – the anticipated "normal" sales volume required to realize a 30% return on net investment – to 1.8 million cars and trucks per annum. (See also Walter S. Carpenter, Jr., to Frederic Donner, April 3, 1947, Accession 542, Box 838.) During the course of the year, GM achieved sales very close to this standard volume (see General Motors Corporation, *Annual Report*, 1947, p. 11) and realized slightly over a 30% return on net investment (see Appendix). Yet GM's sales targets were well above the standard volume of 1.8 million units; with the postwar bulge in demand, they believed they should be able to sell at least 2.5 million cars and trucks, a level not realized until 1949. See Walter S. Carpenter, "Notes of conversation with John Felli," August 2, 1946, Accession 542, Box 838; Charles E. Wilson to Walter S. Carpenter, Jr., August 28, 1947, Accession 542, Box 838.

improved profits led to more struggles between finance and operations. This time the issue was how to allocate surplus. Owners favored increasing dividends and contingency allowances, while operating management pushed for a resumption of expansion, including a reinstatement of the small-car program. Representatives of New York's finance staff, including Sloan, vacillated between these goals, but when operating management began to resist openly, the finance staff allied with owners.

The primary catalyst of this struggle was again the small car. The decision to suspend the Cadet in 1947 had been based largely on the fact that GM remained unable to produce at its existing capacity, making it inadvisable to undertake production of an entirely new model. Moreover, the price of the Cadet remained only $100 to $150 lower than that of a full-sized Chevrolet, a considerably larger and more luxurious car.[102] At that price, the finance staff argued, it would not be able to achieve sufficient sales to generate a profit. Yet operating representatives continued to argue that the Cadet was necessary to protect Chevrolet's market share; led by president Charles Wilson, they sought to reinstate the program.[103] Aware that other FPC members opposed the small car, Wilson tried to obtain funds for the project via a roundabout political maneuver. At an FPC meeting on June 2, 1947, he argued that more money needed to be spent to increase the corporation's automobile manufacturing capacity. In conjunction with this argument, he made two remarkable claims. First, he asserted that GM had spent postwar expansion funds "in the wrong place" by increasing capacity too much for higher-priced lines above Chevrolet and not enough for Chevrolet.[104] Second, he maintained that despite expenditures of over $100 million in the postwar period, Chevrolet had not substantially increased its capacity. The result, Wilson maintained, was that GM now had excess capacity in the higher-price classes and a shortage of capacity in the low-priced field.

Wilson's remarks quickly helped to solidify the split between operations and finance. Owners were aghast at the suggestion that nearly $1

---

102 Walter S. Carpenter, Jr., to Henry Belin du Pont, Lammot du Pont, Lammot du Pont Copeland, and Angus B. Echols, April 30, 1947, Accession 542, Box 838.
103 Commenting on the possibility that some other manufacturer might seek to enter the price class below Chevrolet in order to compete, Walter Carpenter noted that he had "always been amazed with the lack of information which we seem to have regarding this" possibility. See Walter S. Carpenter, Jr., to Henry Belin du Pont, Lammot du Pont, Lammot du Pont Copeland, and Angus B. Echols, April 30, 1947, Accession 542, Box 838.
104 The first quote is from Alfred P. Sloan, Jr., to Walter S. Carpenter, Jr., June 10, 1947, Accession 542, Box 838. The second is from Albert Bradley to Charles E. Wilson, June 6, 1947, Accession 542, Box 838.

billion had been spent "in the wrong place." Sloan quickly reassured them that there was no basis for Wilson's statements. The claim that Chevrolet's capacity had not increased could "easily be disproved," while the assertion that too much money had been spent on higher-priced lines above Chevrolet involved "the exercise of business judgment."[105] Specifically, Wilson's argument drew on demand and sales figures from the relatively undifferentiated car market that had existed in the 1930s, when low-priced cars accounted for some 70 percent of the market. In the early 1940s and following the war, the market became more differentiated, as low-priced cars fell to around 50 percent of sales.[106] Thus, the postwar program correctly called for Chevrolet to produce about 50 percent of all GM cars, while Wilson's assertions rested on older data.[107] Wilson's claims, Sloan told owners, were little more than a political attempt to revive the small car. Pointing out that the charges concerning Chevrolet's capacity had not arisen in earlier discussions, Sloan commented, "I am inclined to think now that the front door has been closed against the small car, the purpose is to try to get it through the side door."[108] Irritated by Wilson's ploy, Sloan instructed FPC chair Albert Bradley and the finance staff to collect data on the matter and told owners that he would submit his own report to the FPC on the issue of capacity.

Sloan's resolve to submit his own report was the beginning of a new coalition between owners and finance, but it also led to surprising and often ironic differences of opinion between the two groups. During his years as CEO, Sloan had long maintained that financial policy should not act as a control over operations, an opinion he had reiterated during the reorganization of 1946. Yet he now took the initiative to put the FPC squarely in the middle of a debate over the corporation's capacity, an operational policy question developed and recommended by the Administration Committee and OPC. Even more surprising, although owners had struggled for years to resurrect financial control over operations, they now worried that Sloan's move would create resistance among operating personnel. In a "personal and confidential" memo to FPC chair Albert Bradley, Du Pont's Walter Carpenter suggested that any report on capacity should be issued by Bradley rather than Sloan and that it should be treated as a "routine matter" intended only as "background material" for discussion rather than as a policy recommendation in the wake

---

105 Alfred P. Sloan, Jr., to Walter S. Carpenter, Jr., June 10, 1947, Accession 542, Box 838.
106 Albert Bradley to Walter S. Carpenter, Jr., June 10, 1947, Accession 542, Box 838.
107 Albert Bradley to Walter S. Carpenter, Jr., June 6, 1947, Accession 542, Box 838.
108 Alfred P. Sloan, Jr., to Walter S. Carpenter, Jr., June 10, 1947, Accession 542, Box 838.

of Wilson's assertions.[109] The reason for this request, Carpenter made clear, was a fear that Sloan's report would cause a head-on clash between the FPC and the operating side of the organization:

> ... I am a little anxious about Mr. Sloan's statement that he will use ... material [provided by Bradley and the finance staff] as a basis of a further report on [capacity and the postwar program] to the [FPC]. ... I am a little fearful that written under such circumstances it may not foster that cooperative relationship between the operating end and the Financial Policy Committee which to me seems ... more necessary now than ever before. ... I fear that such a report on this subject, unless approached with the greatest care, may be subjected to the criticism that the writer is dealing with matters of operating management somewhat beyond the extent required or expected of Financial Policy Committee members. I rather hope that Alfred may abandon this idea and that a suggestion from you in that direction may be helpful.[110]

Carpenter's emphasis on the need for cooperation and his fears over confrontation between the operating and financial sides of the business were borne out in the ensuing months.

The debate over capacity and the small car quickly led to further confrontation. Following Wilson's remarks in the June 2 meeting, the FPC voted to postpone the discussion over capacity for several months, while information on the topic was compiled.[111] Since the plan to expand capacity to 10,000 cars and 2,500 trucks per day would be largely completed by the end of 1947, the FPC decided that future discussions would center around the need to increase capacity for 1948 and beyond.[112] It thus charged both finance and operating personnel with drawing up projected capital needs in the years following 1947. When the FPC meeting finally took place on August 1, 1947, owners were stunned by what occurred. Wilson presented appropriations requests and capital expenditure forecasts through 1949 that had been approved by the Administration Committee and OPC and evaluated by the New York financial staff. These requests for new plant, equipment and tools for the introduction of new models in 1948, engines and transmissions, and the last installment of appropriations for the postwar expansion program totaled

---

109 Walter S. Carpenter, Jr., to Albert Bradley, June 13, 1947, Accession 542, Box 838.
110 Walter S. Carpenter, Jr., to Albert Bradley, June 13, 1947, Accession 542, Box 838.
111 Walter S. Carpenter, Jr., to Charles E. Wilson, July 8, 1947, Accession 542, Box 838.
112 Sloan (1964, p. 209).

a "staggering" $600 million.[113] Depreciation reserves and amortization would cover only about half of this amount, leaving a capital deficit of $250 million to $300 million. As the largest expansion in GM's history drew to a close, operating executives were clamoring for additional funds and insisting that increased capacity was necessary.

Owners were especially shocked because the expansion proposed by management would cut deeply into anticipated dividends. The entire postwar plan had been predicated on the assumption that once facilities were in place, the need for continued investment would be minimal for a period of several years. GM management had given "repeated reassurance" the corporation would be able to use its profits to pay off debts, enlarge contingency funds and reserves, and increase dividends to shareholders once the postwar program was complete.[114] As a result, owners on the FPC had come to the meeting hoping to increase annual dividends from three dollars per share to four. Instead, they were presented with proposals for a new expansion plan that equaled the postwar program in scope and that would increase debt at the expense of dividends. The projections and requests put forward by the operating end of the business seemed to owners a complete betrayal of earlier promises:

> ... All of this presents a very sorry picture [that] presents to us, as members of the Financial Policy Committee and the Board of Directors, a very serious problem. Must we conclude that we have an operating management entirely oblivious of the responsibilities and importance of financial management?[115]

Charging that operating management was engaged in a "reckless spending spree" that threatened the "financial strength and integrity" of General Motors, owners refused to approve the appropriations.[116]

The FPC meeting led to open confrontation between financial and operating management. Although appropriations and capital projections had been developed by the divisions, submitted to the Administration Committee, and approved by the OPC, the job of preparing the final report that amalgamated and evaluated the various requests fell to New York's finance staff. When owners expressed their dismay at the scope

---

113 Walter S. Carpenter, Jr., to Charles E. Wilson, August 7, 1947, Accession 542, Box 838; Walter S. Carpenter, Jr., to Donaldson Brown, August 6, 1947, Accession 542, Box 838.
114 Walter S. Carpenter, Jr., to Donaldson Brown, August 6, 1947, Accession 542, Box 838.
115 Walter S. Carpenter, Jr., to Donaldson Brown, August 6, 1947, Accession 542, Box 838.
116 Walter S. Carpenter, Jr., to Donaldson Brown, August 6, 1947, Accession 542, Box 838.

of appropriations requested, operating representatives present at the FPC meeting responded by asserting that the figures provided by the finance staff "must be all wrong."[117] This resulted in a prolonged argument between the finance staff and operating men concerning the accuracy of the figures. Incredibly, Wilson claimed that as president of GM, he "had never had an opportunity to review" the figures presented by the finance staff, though an irate Walter Carpenter noted that "I gather that the appropriations requests had been signed by you."[118] Unable to reach any agreement on the matter, the FPC finally voted to defer most of the expenditures, approving only a few critical appropriations associated with ongoing operations. The bulk of the program would be reviewed by both finance staff and operating executives, and "more realistic" requests would then be presented to the FPC.[119] Having postponed the expenditures, owners spent the months following the meeting trying to determine how such a complete turnaround had occurred and how similar incidents could be avoided in the future.

The period of review did little to bridge differences of opinion. Owners charged that problems had arisen in part because there was a lack of "sufficient coordination between operating and financial management" in GM, and they questioned whether significant expansion was even necessary.[120] Lack of coordination had occurred because operating management, including Wilson, had been preoccupied with problems of reconversion and expansion and had devoted their time and energy to these issues. As a consequence, communications between operating management and the finance staff had suffered, and neither side had "been able to obtain a full appreciation of the effect of operating programs upon our financial position."[121] Owners admonished Wilson to ensure that operating management would not undertake capital commitments unless and until adequate capital to finance those commitments existed, and they emphasized that the postwar period entailed unprecedented economic and political uncertainties that made conservative financial practices essential. Owners clearly feared that the postwar boom might experience an abrupt downswing, leaving GM in a situation similar to that of 1921 – overcommitted and cash-poor. Yet owners also questioned

[117] Walter S. Carpenter, Jr., to Donaldson Brown, August 6, 1947, Accession 542, Box 838.
[118] Walter S. Carpenter, Jr., to Charles E. Wilson, August 7, 1947, Accession 542, Box 838.
[119] Walter S. Carpenter, Jr., to Charles E. Wilson, August 7, 1947, Accession 542, Box 838.
[120] Walter S. Carpenter, Jr., to Charles E. Wilson, August 7, 1947, Accession 542, Box 838.
[121] Walter S. Carpenter, Jr., to Charles E. Wilson, August 7, 1947, Accession 542, Box 838.

whether significant expansion of facilities was even necessary. Noting that GM's postwar standard volume was set on the basis of a two-shift, 180-day work year – a reduction of the 225-day year used prewar – they argued that increased production could be achieved by more efficient utilization of existing plant. The new figures meant that GM's plants would operate only about 30 percent of the hours available during a year. Insisting that "the thought of operating anything at 30% of capacity is ... shocking," owners suggested that GM was providing too much capacity for prevailing conditions, and they argued that output could be increased by adding more shifts, rather than by increasing fixed capital.[122]

Although Wilson and operating management responded cordially to owner suggestions, they gave little indication that they intended to introduce real change. In response to owners' charge that there was a lack of coordination between finance and operations, for instance, Wilson complained that he was the only operating executive who sat on the FPC.[123] Implicitly, he hinted that owners and financial executives failed to understand the problems facing operations, and he suggested that the solution was to increase the operating presence on the FPC, not increase financial control over operations. Wilson also promised that management would review its plans in order to achieve "a sound dividend policy" and a strong financial position, but he provided no details on how this would be achieved.[124] Perhaps most disturbing to owners, Wilson presented no evidence that management intended to cut back expansion plans. To the contrary, he insisted that profit goals were now being met, even though production remained below target because of short-term exigencies. If capacity and production could be increased, profits would be even better, surpassing the projections made by the finance staff.

Wilson's lack of concern fortified owners' belief that GM's president was intent on subverting financial oversight in order to increase his own power. Noting that Wilson often remarked that it was "damned difficult to serve two masters," Donaldson Brown asserted that Wilson had set out to undermine owner oversight while weakening financial control over the operating side of the organization in Detroit.[125] Since he had become president, Wilson had sought "to undermine opportunities for New York's influence upon basic policies" and to weaken "du Pont

---

[122] Walter S. Carpenter, Jr., to Charles E. Wilson, August 7, 1947, Accession 542, Box 838.
[123] Charles E. Wilson to Walter S. Carpenter, Jr., August 28, 1947, Accession 542, Box 838.
[124] Charles E. Wilson to Walter S. Carpenter, Jr., August 28, 1947, Accession 542, Box 838.
[125] Wilson, as quoted in Brown (1977).

Company influence and 'outside interference'" from owners.[126] Publicly ridiculing owners and financial staff for their "lack of understanding" concerning operating problems, Wilson had resurrected "the same kind of conflict... between Detroit and New York" that had existed in the early 1920s.[127] Brown argued that this trend had begun during the war years: at the time that the WAC ran the corporation, Sloan came to be "batted down... by C.E.'s endless arguing over matters of all kind" and allowed the operating side of the organization greater autonomy.[128] Yet Brown also acknowledged that a jealous finance staff helped exacerbate the split. As the operating side of the organization became stronger during the war, the power of Brown and others in New York waned, and they reacted "by often working through devious channels."[129]

Owners also worried about what they perceived as a shift in how agreements were reached under Wilson's reign. Donaldson Brown, in particular, warned that Wilson's style of leadership held the potential to disrupt cooperation within GM by relying too extensively on coercion rather than eliciting genuine agreement:

> You are very familiar with [Wilson's] argumentative quality and his unwillingness to give up an idea that he has, even though it has been formed without the benefit of complete understanding. He prides himself on his salesmanship [and] he has [often] made the remark that he did not care how large ... a central governing committee might be, [n]or [whether it was composed of] general managers of divisions or other executive officers.... He has put it that he "could handle a committee of any size and sell such committee on any course of action deemed to be desirable."[130]

While the emphasis on "selling" a committee derived from Sloan, Brown argued that there was a subtle difference between the two men. Sloan understood that "delay in the adoption of a ... policy or action is [often] justified until those depended upon for execution have come to a mental acceptance of [the] purpose and principles involved."[131] He was thus

---

126 Donaldson Brown to Walter S. Carpenter, Jr., August 9, 1947, Accession 542, Box 838.
127 Donaldson Brown to Walter S. Carpenter, Jr., August 9, 1947, Accession 542, Box 838.
128 Donaldson Brown to Walter S. Carpenter, Jr., August 9, 1947, Accession 542, Box 838.
129 Donaldson Brown to Walter S. Carpenter, Jr., August 9, 1947, Accession 542, Box 838.
130 Donaldson Brown to Walter S. Carpenter, Jr., August 9, 1947, Accession 542, Box 838.
131 Donaldson Brown to Walter S. Carpenter, Jr., August 9, 1947, Accession 542, Box 838.

careful not to insist that a policy be implemented unless and until he generated support among all actors involved. Wilson, on the other hand, was apt to force a plan through governing committees, obtaining only superficial endorsement from committee members. Ironically, although Brown worried that Wilson's style would eventually disrupt divisional consent by making decentralization a matter of form rather than substance, the more immediate problem was that the divisions were acting in concert with Wilson. In the short run, at least, the problem was not lack of divisional consent, but lack of genuine buy-in at the general office level, especially among the finance staff.

Their concerns over Wilson fortified owners' resolve to strengthen financial control further. Charging that Wilson's track record was "not consistent with ... first-class executive management," and that the "acknowledgment of ... mistakes is poor compensation for making them," owners sought to rein in the operating side of the corporation.[132] They believed that Wilson and the divisions were pushing for expansion out of resentment that Ford was threatening to displace Chevrolet in sales, not because economic conditions warranted expansion. The operating side of the organization sought to retain GM's position as the largest automobile manufacturer in the world, while Wilson strove to increase his own power in the organization. It was up to owners to exercise financial control.

Owners Control Finance

Owners were able to achieve financial control by establishing a majority on the FPC, thereby enabling them to dominate votes in the committee. Ironically, owner control over finances was resurrected by none other than Alfred Sloan, who had begun to agree with many owner criticisms of Wilson and the problems facing GM. Lacking line authority for the first time in his career, Sloan became frustrated with his relative powerlessness and began to agree that greater financial control over operations was necessary. Recognizing the political machinations used by Wilson as he attempted to keep the small car and the postwar expansion program alive, Sloan began to concur that Wilson was attempting to subvert financial oversight. Incredibly, Sloan now argued that Wilson's support for the pre-1946 organization with a single top Policy Committee – the structure that Sloan himself had invented and insisted upon – was evidence that Wilson wanted to escape financial control. Wilson favored the Policy Committee setup, Sloan argued, because it gave oper-

---

132 George Whitney to Walter S. Carpenter, Jr., September 5, 1947, Accession 542, Box 838.

ating executives greater strength in numbers, thereby diminishing financial oversight.[133]

Sloan's change of heart became clear in September 1947, when GM's John Smith passed away, creating a vacancy on the FPC. Fixing on Wilson's complaint that he was the only operating executive serving on the FPC, owners entertained the idea of putting executive vice-president Marvin Coyle on that body in order to create a "greater appreciation of the over-all financial problems of the Corporation by the Detroit organization."[134] They were dissuaded from this position by Sloan, who urged that a retired GM executive or another Du Pont representative be placed on the FPC instead. Although he had argued for years that a separation between finance and operations was "absurd" and that operating management should be included on top committees to avoid financial "dictatorship," Sloan now maintained that FPC membership should not be increased "by bringing in executives who are still active in the administration end of the business."[135] While he continued to believe that the OPC should be in charge of strategic planning and policy formulation, whereas the FPC "should be [an] auditing and general review group," Sloan now took the audit functions of the FPC much more seriously than he had when serving as CEO.[136] Insisting that there needed to be a rigid distinction between finance and operations, Sloan encouraged owners to fill Smith's position with a Du Pont representative.

Sloan's support ensured an end to the debate over expansion by creating a new majority on the FPC. Despite their consideration of Coyle for FPC membership, owners shared Sloan's concerns about increasing the number of operating men on that committee.[137] Following a meeting between Du Pont representatives Donaldson Brown, Walter Carpenter, Lammot du Pont, and Angus Echols, they therefore elected to take up Sloan's suggestion; on December 1, 1947, Echols was elected to the FPC to fill the position left by Smith's death.[138] With owners holding a majority on the FPC and Sloan beginning to agree with many of their criticisms, the fate of GM's expansion program was sealed. The FPC used its financial veto power to scale back operating requests and significantly

---

133 Alfred P. Sloan, Jr., to Walter S. Carpenter, Jr., October 13, 1947. Longwood, 438 (30), First Series, v. 31, pp. 9432–9433.
134 Walter S. Carpenter, Jr., to Alfred P. Sloan, Jr., October 7, 1947. Longwood, 438 (30), First Series, v. 31, pp. 9430–9431.
135 Alfred P. Sloan, Jr., to Walter S. Carpenter, Jr., September 30, 1947. *U.S. v. Du Pont*, GTE #228.
136 Alfred P. Sloan, Jr., to Walter S. Carpenter, Jr., October 13, 1947. Longwood, 438 (30), First Series, v. 31, pp. 9432–9433.
137 See Walter S. Carpenter's handwritten marginalia to Sloan's letter of September 30, which indicates explicit agreement on this point.
138 General Motors Corporation, "General Motors Corporation Financial Policy Committee." *U.S. v. Du Pont*, DTE #GM25.

curtail capital expenditures. Instead of allocating the $600 million requested by Wilson and the divisions, capital expenditures through 1949 were a "relatively modest" $273 million.[139] Management's "reckless spending spree" had been averted by the new coalition between owners and financial management.

Between the end of 1947 and the beginning of 1949, the coalition between Sloan and owners allowed the FPC to exercise effective financial veto power over both operating management and corporate policy. One of their earliest initiatives, for example, was to cut back GM's diversification into other industries, particularly the field of aviation. GM had acquired an interest in a number of aviation concerns during the 1930s, including both airlines and aircraft manufacturers.[140] By 1947 these holdings had been consolidated into a 30 percent interest in North American Aviation (NAA) and a 19 percent interest in Bendix Aviation. Although both companies had been highly profitable during the war – with combined sales of some $1.5 billion – by 1948 owners had concluded that GM should sell its holdings in both companies because of shortages of capital and managerial resources. As early as 1946, J. P. Morgan's George Whitney had complained that diversification had put GM in "too many unrelated businesses as to distribution and the type of markets."[141] Du Pont representatives initially disagreed with Whitney, arguing that GM's decentralized structure would allow it to handle the management of diverse businesses.[142] But following battles over expansion and management's continuing inability to get automobile production up to capacity, the du Ponts began to believe that these businesses employed capital that could better be used in the auto business and created "a certain distraction of management."[143]

Alfred Sloan and his associates in GM management agreed that NAA should be sold. During the war, when NAA's sales were at their highest, GM had decided that its postwar participation in the aviation industry should be minimal.[144] This decision rested on both economic and political considerations. While there was a potential for profit in the aviation

---

139 Sloan (1964, p. 209).
140 Sloan (1964, pp. 362–374). The 1930s acquisitions included the following: Allison, later to become a GM division producing aircraft engines and defense-related products; Fokker Aircraft, later absorbed into North American Aviation; Bendix Aviation; Eastern Airlines; and Trans World Airlines. Eastern and Trans World Airlines, both owned by NAA, were sold following passage of the Air Mail Act of 1934, which prohibited airplane manufacturers from owning stock in air carriers.
141 George Whitney to Walter S. Carpenter, Jr., December 13, 1946, Accession 542, Box 838.
142 Walter S. Carpenter, Jr., to George Whitney, January 23, 1947, Accession 542, Box 838.
143 Walter S. Carpenter, Jr., to Frederic Donner, May 11, 1948, Accession 542, Box 847.
144 Sloan (1964, pp. 372–373).

industry, competition would hinge on engineering innovation and development and, as in the early years of the automobile industry, demand would not be stable enough to undertake high-volume manufacture. Concluding that "sales and engineering [would be] of more importance than low costs" in the postwar aviation industry, GM decided that it should not continue to participate in the industry.[145] This was particularly true for NAA, which by the end of the war specialized in the manufacture of airframes, a component that could not be easily mass-produced in assembly-line fashion.[146] The decision to sell NAA was also motivated by antitrust considerations. While later analysts have criticized GM's decision to minimize participation in aviation and other markets as a "deep and myopic involvement in ... automobile[s]," Alfred Sloan later acknowledged:[147]

> I was against ... the expansion of [GM] into other industries. ... It is not a question [of] our ability to make a profit, or do a good job or contribute to technological advance in another area. It is a question whether it is desirable from the standpoint of political expediency. Maybe I am all wrong in looking at it that way. Maybe I sense changes that will never occur, but that is what I am thinking about just the same.[148]

With owners and managers in agreement, GM sold its holdings in NAA in 1948.

While owners and managers agreed that GM should dispose of NAA, they disagreed over what to do with Bendix. Although it was primarily an aviation concern, Bendix's products were largely accessories and electronic items that were more amenable to mass production. Even more important, since its acquisition in the 1930s, Bendix had become a significant supplier for the automobile industry, and it held a number of important patents on items such as brakes, starters, and carburetors.[149] Owners wanted GM to sell its holdings in Bendix, but management sought to buy Bendix outright, converting it into a wholly owned division. An internal report commissioned by Wilson acknowledged that Bendix's aviation products might not be desirable to GM, but it saw "a

---

145 W. F. Armstrong (vice-president of real estate) to Charles E. Wilson, "Untitled Study of Bendix Aviation Holdings," undated (circa March 1947). Longwood, 438 (30), First Series, v. 30, pp. 9061–9157. See also "Report to Financial Policy Committee, Secretary's #579: Earnings Position North American Aviation, Inc.," March 25, 1948, Longwood, 438 (30), First Series, v. 32, pp. 9505–9650.
146 Sloan (1964, p. 374).
147 Burton and Kuhn (1979, pp. 10–11), as quoted in Williamson (1985, p. 288).
148 Alfred P. Sloan, Jr., to Donaldson Brown, September 19, 1955, Accession 1334, Box 2.
149 Sloan (1964, p. 363).

great future" in Bendix's automobile and electronic lines.[150] A protracted disagreement was averted when government action forced management to back down. Executive vice-president Ormond Hunt warned Wilson and Bradley that if GM took over Bendix, the automaker would "almost certainly" invite antitrust scrutiny by the government "because of the dominant interest we might be alleged to have in some fields."[151] When the U.S. Department of Justice began to investigate the GM-Bendix relation, the FPC quickly passed a resolution expressing its intent to sell Bendix holdings.[152] Despite this resolution, GM held the shares for eight months, until the Department of Justice filed a complaint in December 1947 accusing GM and Bendix of monopolizing the hydraulic brake industry. GM sold its interest in Bendix the following month, denying that its decision was in any way influenced by government action.[153]

The FPC also used its financial veto power to impose restrictions on policies proposed by operating management and to force management to address financial concerns in its proposed policies. This became apparent when top executives opened discussions over whether GM should resume operating its Opel subsidiary following the end of the war. A committee appointed to look into the matter in mid-1945 could reach no conclusion: the condition of the property was unknown, as were the tax implications of resuming control. Sloan and owners believed that there was "no justification whatsoever" for GM to resume control of Opel, as the war had destroyed the market and any chance of Opel returning to profitability.[154] Yet operating management favored resuming control of German operations, and when the U.S. military government urged GM to take back Opel properties, Wilson began to push for a reassessment.[155] In November 1947, Wilson and the OPC recommended that GM resume its control of Opel; the FPC responded by

---

150   W. F. Armstrong (vice-president of real estate) to Charles E. Wilson, "Untitled Study of Bendix Aviation Holdings," undated (circa March 1947). Longwood, 438 (30), First Series, v. 30, p. 9157.
151   O. E. Hunt to Albert Bradley, February 10, 1947, included in cover letters to "Untitled Study of Bendix Aviation Holdings," undated (circa March 1947). Longwood, 438 (30), First Series, v. 30.
152   Financial Policy Committee minutes, April 17, 1947. Longwood, 438 (30), v. 31, p. 9312.
153   United States Congress (1956, p. 3660).
154   Alfred P. Sloan, Jr., to Edward Riley, general manager of GM's Overseas Division, March 1, 1946, as quoted in Sloan (1964, p. 331). The following account draws heavily on information presented in pp. 330–337 of the Sloan book.
155   GM was urged to reclaim the properties by General Lucius D. Clay, the U.S. military governor in Germany. In 1951 Clay became a member of GM's board, and on January 7, 1952, he became a member of the FPC. Clay would later serve on the special committee responsible for overseeing GM's 1958 reorganization, and he would chair the U.S. committee that recommended the adoption of nationwide interstate highways. On the latter, see Cray (1980, pp. 357–358).

calling for the appointment of a special committee to review the matter further. Wilson appointed a five-man group that issued its report on March 26, 1948.[156] The report cautioned that political and economic uncertainties meant that "the projection of any operating figures at this time is extremely hazardous and of little meaning."[157] Postwar conditions – including wage, price, and financial controls imposed by the military government, rampant inflation, and an Opel management gutted by the denazification program – meant that profits and sales would be small for at least several years. Nonetheless, the report advocated that GM resume control of Opel "before it becomes necessary for it to be turned over to a custodian under German state control."[158]

Despite the recommendations of the special committee, on April 5, 1948, the FPC again concluded that "the Corporation is not justified in resuming the responsibility for [Opel's] operation at this time."[159] While Wilson and special committee member Frederic Donner advocated resuming control of Opel, Sloan and owner representatives wanted assurances that GM would not use scarce investment capital generated from North American operations to shore up the German subsidiary. In addition, they sought to ensure that resumed ownership of Opel would not alter GM's U.S. tax obligations. Operating management could achieve its goal only with FPC sponsorship, and to gain this, it had to justify the program in a way that addressed the FPC's concerns. When Wilson complained that he was "surprised" to find that he and Donner were the only FPC members "willing to resume operations in Germany," Sloan responded that he had "been willing right along to resume operations," provided that operating management could furnish assurances that such a move would not affect financial and capital obligations in North America.[160] In the absence of such assurances, Sloan told Wilson, he was "forced, against my fundamental convictions," to vote against the pro-

---

156 The members of the group were chairman B. D. Kunkle, who served as group executive in charge of Canadian and overseas operations, Frederic Donner, vice-president of finance, Ronald Evans, group executive in charge of the Engine Group, Henry Hogan, general counsel, and E. S. Hoglund of the overseas division. See Sloan (1964, p. 332).
157 "Report to Financial Policy Committee by Special Committee Appointed by President on Examination of Desirability of Resuming Operations in Western Germany," March 26, 1948, Accession 1334, Box 3, p. 40.
158 "Report to Financial Policy Committee by Special Committee Appointed by President on Examination of Desirability of Resuming Operations in Western Germany," March 26, 1948, Accession 1334, Box 3, p. 40. The quote is from the summary page of this document, which is unnumbered.
159 Financial Policy Committee minutes, April 5, 1948, as quoted in Sloan (1964, p. 333).
160 The first quote is from Charles E. Wilson to Alfred P. Sloan, Jr., April 9, 1948; the second, as well as the quote in the following sentence, is from Alfred P. Sloan, Jr., to Charles E. Wilson, April 14, 1948. Both letters are quoted in Sloan (1964, p. 334).

posal. Telling Wilson that efforts to reverse the decision should be directed at other members of the FPC, Sloan went on to develop and submit his own report on the topic. Sloan's recommendations included explicit provisions that no additional capital would be risked in Opel and that resumption of ownership would occur only if it did not have an adverse effect on GM's U.S. income taxes. Once these factors were made an explicit part of the agreement, owners' representatives were willing to support it, and on May 3, 1948, the FPC voted to allow resumption of operations in Germany.

The debate over Opel and the issue of investment in the aviation industry show that after 1947, the FPC exercised effective financial veto, just as owners had hoped it would. In order to get proposals passed, operating management had to have sponsorship within the FPC, and they had to address the financial concerns raised by that committee. Yet the FPC's ability to exercise financial veto would prove remarkably short-lived. Despite owners' majority on the FPC and their coalition with Sloan and New York's finance staff, organizational and environmental factors would limit the FPC's ability to control operations after 1947. By 1948, executive vice-president Ormond Hunt would hint at operating management's unhappiness over financial control by complaining publicly to a congressional committee about "how little the board members know about the business."[161] As long as hard budget constraints existed, owners managed to keep this resentment in check, but as postwar affluence grew, their ability to exercise financial veto power would wane. After 1948, operating management gained increasing control of the corporation.

Summary

As World War II drew to a close, owners and top executives within GM continued to struggle over the form that GM's postwar organization would take. The disagreements that occurred during this period highlight three important points. First, owners' ability to implement an organization that increased owner financial control was a function of hardening budget constraints. Because GM's postwar expansion would require the corporation to borrow large sums for the first time in decades, owners were able to insist that a separate committee responsible for financial oversight be restored. Second, discussions of the postwar structure show that retaining participative decentralization and giving Detroit and the president more authority over operations were Alfred Sloan's top

---

161 United States Congress (1949, p. 570).

priorities in the postwar era. He felt so strongly about these issues that he threatened to withhold his endorsement of the new structure if owners insisted on a textbook M-form. Third, however, efforts to achieve participative decentralization were complicated by a number of factors. The personnel disagreements and shifting coalitions that emerged during this period thwarted Sloan's plans to implement the structure he wanted, as did continuing owner objection and legal problems raised by participative decentralization.

The postwar structure that was finally implemented in 1946 entailed a series of compromises between management and owners. On the financial side, the FPC implemented stronger financial control, and after GM's finance staff formed a coalition with owners, it reestablished owner veto over finances. As we will see in Chapter 6, that control was short-lived. On the operating side, the compromise between owners and managers created a Du Pont–style Executive Committee (the OPC) while simultaneously retaining Sloan's brand of participative decentralization (exemplified by the Administration Committee and the policy groups). This structure probably helped solidify the new coalition between top-line operating executives – the president, the executive vice-presidents, and the group executives – and the division managers. Although this group of operating executives was subordinate to the FPC during the period from 1946 to 1948, after that time they took control in the corporation. Finally, the disagreements and reorganizations of the postwar period solidified a nascent rift between the financial and operating sides of the organization. Although owners believed that their control of the FPC would allow them to repair this split, they soon learned that such would not be the case.

6

Consent as an Organizational Weapon: Coalition Politics and the Destruction of Cooperation, 1948–1958

The years from 1948 to 1955 were among the most profitable and successful in GM's history. Growing consumer income led to unprecedented demand for automobiles and enabled manufacturers to sell larger, more profitable cars. During much of this period, GM realized record-breaking return on investment. Yet in 1958, following nearly a decade of unparalleled success, GM implemented yet another reorganization – one that marked the beginning of the corporation's long decline. In this chapter, I examine both the postwar years of success and the factors behind GM's reorganization and decline. During the postwar era, the split between finance and operations that emerged following the war led to increased factionalism and political struggle within the corporation. In this context, consent became a weapon in Detroit's battle against New York, solidifying political alliances between the president and the divisions, who took on general office staff and owners. The result was paradoxical. At the same time that GM entered the most profitable period in its history, it was also very much a corporation at war with itself. The reorganization of 1958 occurred as owners and general office executives attempted to reassert their control in response to Detroit. Although the reorganization put New York's finance staff in charge of the corporation, it did so at a price: the textbook M-form implemented in 1958 smashed the mechanisms for producing divisional consent, leading to resistance from below and eventual economic decline.

Ironically, GM's success in the postwar era helped to loosen the oversight of owners and financial staff. Owners' control of the FPC and their insistence that GM keep capital expenditures low played an important role in creating exceptionally high return on investment in the postwar era. But as record profits accrued, GM had more than enough money to pay the highest dividends in its history while renewing its drive toward expansion. Surplus once again created slack capital, making it difficult to claim that funds for expansion were not available. The emergence of slack capital resources was exacerbated by three additional factors. First, continuing structural problems in GM's 1946 organization made it easier for the president and operating side of the corporation to circumvent financial oversight. Second, economic conditions caused a deterioration in the efficacy of financial control. Finally, owners' unwillingness to limit growth was reinforced by an antitrust suit that charged E. I. du Pont de Nemours with using its ownership of GM as a means of restraining trade. Faced with government investigation, Du Pont representatives on GM's board were hesitant to intervene too forcefully in GM's affairs after 1948.

As financial oversight loosened, the operating side of the business again pushed for rapid expansion, leading to a reemergence of hostilities between New York and Detroit. This time, however, even GM's financial staff would be unable to curb growth. These developments occurred only gradually. The first expansion wave, carried out between 1950 and 1953, entailed a minimum of conflict, even though it was larger in scale than the postwar growth that had taken place between 1946 and 1948. Still mindful of the confrontation that had occurred in 1947, management sought to finance the 1950–1953 program entirely out of retained earnings and depreciation reserves. With unprecedented profits available to them, they were able to do so while paying out dividends that ranked among the highest in the corporation's history. Yet as earnings continued at a high level, management pushed for even more growth. When a new president took office late in 1952, he quickly set out to increase divisional and operating participation in the strategic planning and resource allocation process, thereby intensifying the drive for expansion. In 1954, a two-year, $1-billion expansion plan was announced, which soon doubled in size. Owners were alarmed by this new plan, but like GM's own financial staff, they seemed powerless to stop it. Only when the new president began to invade the divisional domain, disrupting consent and undercutting the base of his own support, did owners and financial staff finally intervene.

In 1958, owners and top executives implemented a reorganization of General Motors' corporate structure. Intended to prevent another situation like the one that had developed between 1953 and 1958, the new organization marked a return to the textbook M-form. For the first time since 1921, GM would institute a strong separation between strategic and tactical planning, putting the general office in charge of the former, and leaving the latter up to the divisions. This new organization laid the groundwork for GM's subsequent failure by destroying the formal mechanisms for producing consent. It led not to cooperation and efficiency, but to contestation and decline. Over time, the evisceration of consent also led to increasing centralization, exacerbating governance problems even further. The reorganization of 1958 was thus the beginning of GM's long decline.

Decline of Financial Oversight

Although owners reestablished effective financial oversight when they gained a majority on the FPC late in 1947, their ability to exercise financial veto proved remarkably short-lived. The primary reason for the decline of financial oversight was the emergence of slack capital that occurred between 1948 and 1950, a development that is discussed in the next section of this chapter. Yet even before capital surplus emerged, difficulties in exercising financial control had surfaced. These problems were the results of three factors, each of which is discussed more fully later. First, although owners had regained control of the FPC, there were still structural problems with the 1946 organization that helped operating executives circumvent financial oversight and prevented owners and finance staff from exercising intelligent judgment. Second, the economic conditions that characterized the postwar era wreaked havoc with GM's financial controls, making it difficult for owners and financial executives to assess divisional performance. Finally, antitrust action by the U.S. government against GM and E. I. du Pont de Nemours challenged the legitimacy of owner intervention, making them hesitant to exercise their financial veto power. Each of these factors weakened financial control in the period from 1948 to 1950; when they combined with excess capital after 1949, financial oversight was seriously impaired.

Even before the emergence of slack capital resources, owners were concerned about structural shortcomings in the 1946 organization which they believed gave the president too much power over and independence from the financial side of the organization. More specifically, although president Charles Wilson was formally subject to orders issued by the FPC, conflicting lines of authority made it difficult for financial executives to enforce such orders. In the prewar structure, when Sloan served as chairman and CEO, the financial side of the organization was totally independent from the operating side; neither the president nor any operating officer, excepting Sloan, held line authority over the finance staff, which reported to vice-chairman of the board Donaldson Brown. On the surface, the 1946 organization seemed to replicate these independent reporting lines: Wilson served as president and CEO, while the finance staff reported to FPC chair Albert Bradley, and organization charts depicted Bradley as formally independent of Wilson's authority.[1] Yet Bradley held the title of executive vice-president, rather than serving as vice-chairman of the board. Despite his position as chair of the FPC, owners feared that Bradley's title of executive vice-president appeared to

---

1 See General Motors Corporation, "Organization Chart, July 1, 1946."

make him Wilson's subordinate, giving Wilson line authority – or at least influence – over the man who served as both head of the finance staff and chairman of the FPC.

In practice, the 1946 organization appears to have given the president more influence over the financial side of the organization. While the FPC could issue orders to Wilson, management executives on the FPC were unable or unwilling to make sure those orders were carried out. Because Bradley lacked the authority and autonomy to challenge Wilson directly, as did other financial executives on the FPC, he was hesitant to confront the president directly. Even Sloan, who continued to serve as chairman of the board, no longer held line authority over Wilson and thus could not issue orders to him. As a consequence, Sloan sought instead to use his personal influence to prevail on Wilson; when he was unable to do so, he accepted Wilson's decisions "as inevitable and something over which he has no control" and let Wilson have his way.[2] Sloan's reticence to confront Wilson was reinforced by his belief that continued financial opposition to Wilson would disrupt consent on the operating side of the business and lead to divisional resistance to policies approved by the OPC. The 1946 organization thus made it difficult for general office executives to rein in Wilson.

Increased representation on the FPC made it easier for owners to exercise financial veto power to strike down proposed operating policies, but it did nothing to resolve the ambiguous relationship between Wilson and the financial side of the organization. Despite owners' pleas that Bradley be relieved of his title as executive vice-president in order to provide "greater prestige [and] a greater degree of independence from matters which are more distinctly of an operating nature," no changes were made.[3] As a result, Wilson continued to have at least informal influence, if not outright authority, over both Bradley and New York's financial staff.[4] As the sole GM executive not under Wilson's authority, Sloan was the logical choice to push for a change in the relationship between Wilson and New York, but he evidently did not share owners' concerns on this point. Consequently, as we will see later, the president's influence over finance continued and grew more pronounced over time.

Structural factors also made it more difficult for owners and financial executives to oversee operations by exacerbating problems of impacted

---

[2] Donaldson Brown to Walter S. Carpenter, Jr., August 9, 1947, Accession 542, Box 838.
[3] Walter S. Carpenter, Jr., to Alfred P. Sloan, Jr., October 20, 1947. Longwood, 438 (30), First Series, v. 31, pp. 9434–9435. See also Donaldson Brown to Walter S. Carpenter, Jr., August 9, 1947, Accession 542, Box 838.
[4] Walter S. Carpenter, Jr., to Alfred P. Sloan, Jr., October 20, 1947. Longwood, 438 (30), First Series, v. 31, pp. 9434–9435. See also Donaldson Brown to Walter S. Carpenter, Jr., August 9, 1947, Accession 542, Box 838.

information. Although both owner and management members of the FPC had access to the information provided by GM's financial and statistical controls, such abstract data proved to be inadequate for evaluating proposed policies and weighing the claims made by the operating side of the organization. This lack of information was due primarily to the fact that the bulk of the work that went into the formulation of operating policy was carried out in the policy groups and the Administration Committee, where operating executives dominated. Owners had no representation in these groups, and on the financial side only Bradley and Donner, both subordinate to Wilson, continued to be included. As a result, little detailed information about proposed policies reached the FPC. The new organization made few provisions for regular contact between top operating and financial executives, and there was little opportunity for the former to sell their ideas to the latter through mutual discussion.

Imperfect information and a lack of knowledge about the business made it difficult for FPC members to evaluate proposed policies. The lack of knowledge was greatest for owners, who had become too removed from daily operations to have access to the sort of information that they had possessed during the 1920s and 1930s. J. P. Morgan's George Whitney commented that during his more than twenty years on GM's top committees, he "came to have an almost childlike trust in ... the accuracy" of GM's forecasts.[5] In the postwar era, however, that trust was "finally shattered as month after month we have been shown results which are a long way from what we have been previously led to expect."[6] Yet lacking knowledge of the business, Whitney felt powerless to rectify the situation. Ironically, the lack of financial oversight was so bad that even the old Policy Committee setup began to look desirable to owners. Indeed, GM's own finance staff now lacked a detailed knowledge of the business. The fact that Wilson and operating management could argue before the FPC that capital projections developed by the finance staff were "all wrong" shows how little information now reached New York. Even men like Sloan and Brown were no longer privy to such information, leaving planning almost entirely in the hands of operating executives.[7] As Walter Carpenter put it, "it is difficult for us on the [FPC] to know too much about the present and prospective needs of the operating end. We must ... depend upon the representations which we receive from the administrative [sic] committee."[8]

5 George Whitney to Walter S. Carpenter, Jr., August 9, 1947, Accession 542, Box 838.
6 George Whitney to Walter S. Carpenter, Jr., August 9, 1947, Accession 542, Box 838.
7 See Donaldson Brown to Walter S. Carpenter, Jr., August 9, 1947, Accession 542, Box 838; Alfred P. Sloan, Jr., to Charles E. Wilson, July 26, 1948, Accession 542, Box 847.
8 Walter S. Carpenter, Jr., to Donaldson Brown, August 6, 1947, Accession 542, Box 838.

Financial oversight was also diminished by postwar economic conditions that reduced the efficacy of financial controls. Postwar inflation and increasing consumer affluence made it much easier for GM and other manufacturers to pass increases in the cost of labor and materials along to consumers rather than taking them out of profits. Yet the entire "standard volume" concept of accounting that the corporation had developed in the 1920s assumed that such costs would remain stable over time.[9] If operating management could pass price increases on to consumers, these assumptions began to crumble. In such a situation, the divisions could achieve or even improve upon return-on-investment targets despite failing to control costs; inflated costs could be recovered through higher prices. This, in turn, made it difficult to identify and reward effective managers, for high return rates did not necessarily reflect efficient production. Moreover, inflated costs would eventually be incorporated into estimates of standard volume, leading to inflated prices. If and when consumers' willingness or ability to pay such prices began to decline, GM's entire accounting system would reflect grossly inflated costs and prices, making it difficult or impossible to continue making a reasonable profit at standard volume. Nobody understood these issues better than Donaldson Brown, who warned that he was "deeply concerned over the dangers of managerial inefficiencies creeping in due to the ease with which abnormalities in costs and expenses can be offset by price increases."[10]

The same economic conditions that degraded the effectiveness of financial controls also forced the FPC to give operating management greater control over pricing policy. For decades GM had determined its automobile prices by setting them to a level that would yield a 30 percent pre-tax return on net investment when producing at "standard volume," or 80 percent of rated normal capacity.[11] This process had long been

---

9 Sloan (1964, pp. 145, 147).
10 Donaldson Brown to Angus B. Echols, July 23, 1948, Accession 1334, Box 1. This statement occurs in a discussion of GM's bonus plan, with Brown arguing that the ability to pass on price increases makes it difficult to assume that divisional performance is linked to low-cost production. See also Donaldson Brown to Albert Bradley, July 14, 1948, Accession 542, Box 847.
11 For a detailed account of how this pricing policy worked, see Brown (1924), reprinted in Chandler (1979). Although GM's Albert Bradley testified in public hearings that prices were set to yield a return between 15 and 20 percent on net investment, internal documents clearly state that the target for net return had long been 30 percent, which would yield around a 20 percent return on gross investment. Actual performance data (see Appendix) show that the 30 percent return on net was met more often than not. Bradley's testimony is in United States Congress (1956, p. 3585). On the 30 percent figure, see, for example, Walter S. Carpenter, Jr., to Frederic Donner, July 13, 1948b, Accession 542, Box 847; Frederic Donner to Walter S. Carpenter, Jr., July 26, 1948, Accession 542, Box 847.

carried out by New York's finance staff, which, subject to the FPC, had final authority over all pricing decisions. In the postwar era, however, two factors combined to make this pricing method problematic. The first was the continuing shortage of cars that caused the demand for automobiles to outstrip supply as late as 1950. In the prewar era, such discrepancies between supply and demand did not lead to large fluctuations in automobile prices, primarily because of manufacturers' leverage over dealer franchises: if dealers attempted to cash in on shortages by selling automobiles above suggested retail price, their dealerships would be revoked by the manufacturer. In the postwar era, however, manufacturers feared that cancellation of contracts would lead to prosecution, in light of renewed antitrust enforcement.[12] As a result, dealers often charged prices well above list and pocketed the excess profits. This practice was exacerbated by rapidly increasing consumer income, which by 1948 was 85 percent higher than prewar.[13] Despite rampant inflation, more consumers than ever could afford to pay premium prices for cars. The result was a relatively inelastic demand curve for autos and continued price gouging on the part of dealers.

Postwar economic conditions led the FPC to give operating executives greater control over pricing decisions. FPC members feared that if operating management adhered to prices set by the general office, GM would be at a competitive disadvantage. Their reasoning was somewhat startling. GM's competitors had begun to raise list prices in order to capture higher profits during the period of shortages. If GM continued to set its prices at a level that obtained a 30 percent return on net investment, its cars would be priced well below competitors' products. But Alfred Sloan argued that it would be harmful for GM to sell its cars at lower prices than the competition. His concern was with the reputation effects GM would incur if its cars were less expensive than those of competitors. In an FPC meeting held July 12, 1948, Sloan argued that if GM cars were priced "substantially below" those of its competitors, "the public may be led to a false impression as to relative values inherent in the Corporation's products."[14] Moreover, if competitors raised their prices during the period of shortage and lowered them later, GM would be forced to match price reductions, even if it had never raised its list prices. While FPC members bemoaned the pricing practices of their competitors, they

---

12 See Marvin Coyle's testimony in United States Congress (1949, p. 564). On the general revival of antitrust efforts, see Fligstein (1990, pp. 167–190).

13 United States Congress (1949, p. 518).

14 This summary of Sloan's arguments is from Donaldson Brown to Albert Bradley, July 14, 1948, Accession 542, Box 847. Sloan's argument is a classic example of what Stiglitz (1987; see also Akerlof 1970) has termed the dependence of quality on price, a phenomenon that radically alters the neoclassical understanding of supply and demand.

believed that GM had to follow suit in order to preserve the reputation of its products. This meant giving the operating side of the organization greater discretion over pricing, and in July 1948 the FPC advised operating management on the OPC that the corporation's pricing policy "is not to be construed as prohibiting the pricing of products above standard prices determined by the prescribed formula."[15] Henceforth, it would be up to the OPC and the divisions to set prices; they responded by raising the prices of GM's models more than 8 percent in one month.[16]

Worried that giving additional discretion to the OPC would further undermine financial oversight, owners sought to find ways to increase their influence over Detroit. Little more than a week after the OPC was given discretion over pricing policy, Du Pont's Walter Carpenter recommended that the FPC "be informed before the fact" about any important policy decisions being contemplated by the operating side of the business, so that FPC members would "have an opportunity to familiarize themselves" with the issues and so that they could "express an opinion" on such matters to operating executives.[17] Clearly concerned about Detroit's growing power, owners sought to develop some sort of input into decision-making at the operational level. With Sloan's backing, owners convinced Wilson to try out an informal procedure wherein the FPC would be "informed before the fact... of consequential policy questions... from the point of view of information, better coordination, the avoidance of misunderstanding..., but not in any sense to impose their will [on] the exercise of [the OPC's] business judgment."[18] Owners hoped that this arrangement would give them better information about and influence over operating policy.

Owners' efforts to increase their influence over Detroit did little to help, for the new arrangement left power to call joint FPC/OPC meetings in the hands of GM management. Initially the plan had been that FPC chair Bradley, president Wilson, or Sloan would have the power to call a joint meeting. But Sloan quickly decided – perhaps at Wilson's urging – that he and other nonmanagement representatives on the FPC lacked the information and authority to convene such a meeting. Object-

---

15 The wording of the resolution is reproduced in Donaldson Brown to Albert Bradley, July 14, 1948, Accession 542, Box 847; modifications (reflected in the foregoing quote) are outlined in George Brooks (GM secretary) to Walter S. Carpenter, Jr., Accession 542, Box 847.
16 United States Congress (1949, pp. 530–531) shows the immediate price increases that occurred when GM adopted this policy. White (1971, pp. 121–125, especially p. 122) shows dramatically the price increases that occurred during this period for both GM and the industry as a whole.
17 Alfred P. Sloan to Charles E. Wilson, July 26, 1948a, Accession 542, Box 847.
18 Alfred P. Sloan to Charles E. Wilson, July 26, 1948a, Accession 542, Box 847.

ing that "I do not know what is going on [on the operating side of the business] except that I may be told about it by some one or accidentally hear about it," Sloan argued that only those with a knowledge of operating issues should have the power to call a joint meeting.[19] If non-management representatives insisted on calling such a meeting, it "could easily be construed by some as ... 'butting into' operating matters."[20] Fearing that this would lead to resistance on the part of operating management, Sloan argued that only Wilson or Bradley should have the power to call a joint FPC/OPC meeting. The new arrangement thus left the definition of "consequential policy questions" entirely up to management, doing little to help owners.

The failure of the new arrangement to strengthen owners' influence became apparent weeks later, when Wilson began to make a series of personnel and organizational changes. On August 2, 1948, Wilson appointed two additional group executives to the OPC.[21] In order to serve on the OPC, these men also had to be elected to the board of directors. Under Sloan's reign, the du Ponts had always been deeply involved in discussions surrounding such promotions and had closely guarded election to the board. But now, with active management holding a majority on the board and with little information passing to owners from Detroit, the appointments were made without the knowledge of key owner representatives. A month after the changes had been made, Walter Carpenter told Charles Wilson that he "did not learn of the inclusion of Messrs. Burke and Godfrey on the Operating Policy Committee and the Board of Directors until I received this new [organization] chart" on September 3.[22] While Carpenter noted that he was pleased with the appointments, he also questioned "whether the Board of Directors is not becoming too heavily weighted with organization men as distinguished from non-employee members."[23] Indeed, with the new appointments, active management held half of the seats on the board, strengthening its position even further.

19 Alfred P. Sloan to Charles E. Wilson, July 26, 1948a, Accession 542, Box 847.
20 Alfred P. Sloan to Charles E. Wilson, June 26, 1948b, Accession 542, Box 847.
21 The new members were Francis Burke, who headed the Accessories Group, and Edward Godfrey, head of the Household Appliances Group. These appointments followed the June 7 election of Bayard Kunkle, group executive in charge of the overseas and Canadian operations.
22 Walter S. Carpenter, Jr., to Charles E. Wilson, September 10, 1948. Longwood, 438 (30), First Series, v. 32, pp. 9585–9586. This claim should be viewed with a certain amount of caution, however, as it occurred little more than a month after the U.S. government filed an antitrust suit charging Du Pont with using its influence in GM to restrain trade (as discussed later). It is possible that Carpenter's letter was written with an eye on the upcoming antitrust trial.
23 Walter S. Carpenter, Jr., to Charles E. Wilson, September 10, 1948. Longwood, 438 (30), First Series, v. 32, pp. 9585–9586.

The changes instituted by Wilson also ignored owners' continuing request that FPC chairman Bradley be given a new title. Even though "there had been some discussion of Albert being listed merely as Chairman, Financial Policy Committee and dropping entirely his title as Executive Vice President," Wilson's new organization chart showed no change in Bradley's title nor in his relation to the president. While owners had made it clear that they favored changing Bradley's title in order to increase the financial staff's autonomy from Detroit, Wilson simply ignored their advice. When the board met on September 13, 1948, to discuss and ratify Wilson's proposed organization changes, those in attendance included seven outside owner representatives, fourteen active members of management, and four retired members of management. With these numbers, there was little chance that Wilson's plan would be overturned, and those in attendance adopted Wilson's proposals without modification.[24] Perhaps even more surprising, owners heard about the proposed changes only days before the board meeting, and with little time to organize, they remained unable to stop them.

Owners' unwillingness to put more direct pressure on operating management was partly the result of the U.S. Justice Department's ongoing investigation of relations between GM and Du Pont. Even before the war had ended, some executives within E. I. du Pont de Nemours had warned that the relationship between Du Pont and GM would become the focus of increasing legal scrutiny in the postwar era. In a memo written January 30, 1945, Du Pont's Angus Echols cautioned his colleagues that the financial reports which the chemical company received from General Motors could form the basis of prosecution and might be regarded as "evidence that the Du Pont Finance Committee controls the financial operations of the General Motors Corporation and dictates its policies."[25] An incredulous Walter Carpenter failed to heed Echols' warnings, writing in the margins of the memo, "Not true. Who thinks this way?" He soon found out. On August 20, 1948, following months of

24 See "Excerpt from Minutes of Meeting of Board of Directors of General Motors Corporation," September 13, 1948. Longwood, 438 (30), First Series, v. 32, pp. 9587–9588. The numbers given count Sloan as an active member of management, though this is debatable. Wilson's proposals also promoted Harlow Curtice to executive vice-president and named Ivan Wiles to succeed Curtice as general manager of Buick. In addition, John Cronin was named to head the Fisher Body Division, while W. F. Armstrong took over as general manager of Chevrolet, following the sudden death of Nicholas Dreystadt.
25 Angus B. Echols, "Monthly Statements of [General Motors] Consolidated Bank Balances to the [E. I. du Pont de Nemours] Finance Committee," January 30, 1945. Longwood, 437 (29), Second Series, v. 10, pp. 3103–3105. Echols' statements referred primarily to reports concerning GM's bank balances.

investigation, the U.S. Department of Justice served Du Pont and General Motors with subpoenas, an action that marked the beginning of antitrust prosecution charging that the relationship between the two companies had resulted in restraint of trade. Because one of the issues at stake was whether or to what extent E. I. du Pont de Nemours influenced GM's internal operating policies, owners became much more hesitant to interfere with management decision-making.

The antitrust suit accelerated the decline in owner control that was already under way. On June 6, 1949, three weeks before the government filed formal charges in the antitrust suit, Carpenter resigned from GM's FPC, citing health reasons.[26] Although Carpenter stayed on as a member of the board and was replaced on the FPC by Lammot du Pont Copeland, the move was probably made to eliminate the appearance that Du Pont's highest-ranking officer – Carpenter served as chairman of Du Pont's board and its Finance Committee – held undue influence over GM's decision-making process.[27] Writing to owners to discuss the government suit, Alfred Sloan tacitly acknowledged that the antitrust charges made it more difficult for shareholders – especially Du Pont – to exercise financial control over management. Perhaps anticipating the eventual ouster of Du Pont, Sloan advised that "the last contribution" he and the du Ponts could make to GM was to determine how "to strengthen the Corporation's position at the policy level" over the long term.[28]

By 1948, financial oversight had already been weakened by a combination of three factors – structural problems in the 1946 organization, postwar economic conditions that weakened financial controls and led operations to increase its control over decision-making, and the government antitrust suit that challenged the legitimacy of owner intervention in GM's internal affairs. Yet these developments were only the beginning. By 1950, these factors had combined with excess capital, leaving owners, the FPC, and GM's own financial staff almost powerless to exercise meaningful financial oversight. Under a new president, GM pursued unprecedented expansion.

---

26 On the date of the formal charges, see General Motors Corporation, *Annual Report*, 1949, p. 29. On Carpenter's resignation, see General Motors Corporation, "General Motors Corporation Financial Policy Committee." *U.S. v. Du Pont*, DTE #GM25, and undated resolution of the FPC accepting Carpenter's resignation for health reasons, attached to Alfred P. Sloan, Jr., to Walter S. Carpenter, Jr., November 5, 1954, Accession 542, Box 856D.
27 Carpenter returned to GM's FPC late in 1954, immediately after the federal district court ruled in favor of Du Pont and GM in the antitrust suit. See note 69 to this chapter.
28 Alfred P. Sloan, Jr., to Walter S. Carpenter, Jr., May 12, 1949, Accession 542, Box 847.

Slack Capital Resources and the Return to Expansion

Between 1948 and 1950, GM's profits skyrocketed, creating enormous surplus and slack resources that played a key role in eviscerating the FPC's control over operations. Return on investment increased for two reasons. The first, ironically enough, was owners' success in curtailing expansion at the end of 1947. With fixed investment remaining relatively stable, the corporation's fixed-capital turnover improved dramatically. The second factor behind rising returns was the new pricing policy, which substantially increased profits per unit without adversely affecting demand. Together these factors led to dramatic improvement. In mid-1948 GM was still operating below capacity, producing fewer cars per day than it had in 1937, largely because of steel shortages.[29] Moreover, its share of the North American market was around 40 percent during this period, well below its prewar share of 46.7 percent.[30] Yet because of reduced capital expenditures, higher prices, and high sales of replacement parts, return on net investment increased to 38.3 percent in 1948, up substantially from 1947's return of 31.0 percent.[31] In 1949, as shortages of supplies finally eased, return on investment surpassed the record levels of 1941, climbing to 49.5 percent. Finally, in 1950, return on net investment skyrocketed to an unprecedented 69.5 percent. During this period, after-tax profits rose from around $288 million to just over $834 million, providing GM with enormous surplus that enabled the corporation to increase dividend levels on common stock from $1.50 per share in 1947 to $6.00 in 1950.[32] Yet even after a 400 percent increase in dividends, significant surplus remained, fueling a new drive toward rapid expansion. In December 1949, GM paid off the remaining balance on the $125 million bond debt that it had taken out in 1946,[33] and in November 1950 management began to formulate new plans for expansion.[34]

The expansion drive that began in 1950 was shaped by the declaration of a national emergency on December 16, 1950, following the out-

---

29 Frederic Donner to Walter S. Carpenter, Jr., July 26, 1948, Accession 542, Box 847.
30 See United States Congress (1949, p. 526).
31 Frederic Donner to Walter S. Carpenter, Jr., July 26, 1948, Accession 542, Box 874; Sloan (1964, p. 209); United States Congress (1949, p. 514).
32 General Motors Corporation, *Annual Report*, 1950, p. 49. These figures have been adjusted to reflect the two-for-one stock split that occurred in November 1950.
33 The two series of debenture issues were scheduled to mature in 1966 and 1976, and GM paid a penalty for retiring them early. See General Motors Corporation, *Annual Report*, 1946, pp. 32–33. United States Congress (1949, p. 563).
34 Sloan (1964, pp. 208–210).

break of war in Korea, and by GM's strategic response to that event. The war created a need for additional facilities to handle defense production. In addition, the experience of World War II led GM's management to believe that there would be a "backlog of unsatisfied demand" when the Korean war ended.[35] As a result, GM executives decided on a new strategy for pursuing growth – one that was diametrically opposed to the strategy utilized between 1942 and 1946. During World War II, GM sought to maximize its return on investment by increasing fixed-capital turnover, a strategy carried out in large part by using government-owned facilities and plant. This tactic improved capital turnover figures dramatically, but it also necessitated a lengthy reconversion period at the end of the war, when GM had to build new plant and switch back to automobile production. Management believed that this reconversion process was directly responsible for the fact that GM had never recovered its prewar level of market share; because it had taken so long to bring new plant on line, GM had lost sales to competitors.

In order to avoid lost sales due to postwar reconversion of plant, GM executives vowed to adopt a new strategy during the Korean War. The corporation would pay for defense plant with its own funds in order to build dual-purpose factories that could easily be used for additional automobile production when the war ended. At the same time, even though the war would reduce demand for automobiles in the short run, GM would also expand its automobile capacity in order to be ready for the postwar boom. Management realized that both strategies would decrease short-run profits below the record levels of 1950. In the case of defense work, the U.S. government had again limited total profits to 10 percent of defense sales. In order to realize a healthy return on investment for such work, GM would have to achieve high capital turnover figures. Yet by purchasing its own plant, rather than letting the government bear the cost, it would effectively lower fixed-capital turnover, leading to lower return on investment. In the case of civilian plant, return would be reduced because GM would carry excess capacity during the war in order to maximize sales after the war. The corporation thus decided that it would trade lower short-term profits for higher profits and market share in the long run:

> ... the economic consequences of having too little capacity as measured by loss in competitive position, prestige and reduced profits, is entirely out of relation to the cost of carrying surplus capacity....
>
> We should use corporation funds for ... new plants needed

---

35 Sloan (1964, p. 209).

for armament if that gives us better control over same from the long-term position.... Accelerated depreciation and high taxes make the use of corporation funds all the more feasible. We should avoid conversion. The policy should be, expansion.[36]

Although the expansion program was expected to push return on investment below the record levels of 1950, GM would continue to earn healthy profits. Because automobiles were selling at prices well above the standard 30 percent return level, the civilian side of the business would bring in enough profit to compensate for the cost of carrying overcapacity. On the defense side, special tax laws allowing rapid depreciation of defense plant would help recoup part of the cost of expansion. In February and March 1951, the FPC thus approved an expansion program that was larger than the one undertaken following World War II: GM would spend some $750 million to increase automobile capacity by 24 percent, while simultaneously building new factories to handle defense contracts. Unlike the expansion of 1946–1947, however, this growth would be paid for entirely out of reinvested earnings and depreciation reserves. By reducing dividends on common stock from 1950's $6.00 per share to $4.00 per share – still the second highest dividend ever – management was able to fund growth without going to the capital markets.[37]

The expansion program of the Korean War period resulted in a marked decline in return on investment. Like its World War II counterpart, the program ran significantly over budget. In the four years from 1950 to 1953, GM spent $1.279 billion on new plant.[38] Of this amount, some $400 million to $425 million was used to construct defense-related plant, with the remainder going to facilities for civilian production.[39] In addition, GM advanced another $78 million to steel producers during this period as a means of inducing them to expand their facilities in order to avoid steel shortages after the war.[40] GM's fixed costs thus increased enormously during the war years. On the automotive side, increases in investment and capacity were accompanied by a decline in sales volume.

---

36 Alfred P. Sloan, Jr., to Financial Policy Committee, November 17, 1950, as quoted in Sloan (1964, pp. 386, 210).
37 General Motors Corporation, *Annual Report*, 1953, pp. 38, 51.
38 General Motors Corporation, *Annual Report*, 1953, p. 38.
39 These estimates can be made by comparing the figures from General Motors Corporation, *Annual Report*, 1953, p. 40, and those presented in Sloan (1964, p. 210); the latter (higher) are probably more accurate.
40 See General Motors Corporation, *Annual Report*, 1952, p. 34. In exchange for these advances, GM was guaranteed a certain percentage of the steel producers' new capacity. See United States Congress (1958, p. 2598).

In 1952, North American unit sales were some 36 percent below 1950 sales.[41] Government regulations implemented in 1951 effectively prevented GM from increasing its market share, making additional capacity unnecessary, while price controls prevented automakers from raising prices further to compensate for lost sales.[42] The decline in automobile sales was more than offset by increased sales to the government, but because defense contracts were limited to a 10 percent return on net sales, and because GM owned most of the plant in which defense production took place, this work realized a lower return on investment than did automotive production.[43] The expansion program thus increased fixed costs at a time when automobile sales were falling and defense work could realize only limited returns.

The difficulties created by this strategy are illustrated by the case of New Departure, a GM division that manufactured ball bearings and other parts. In 1952, New Departure – which for years was one of the most profitable operations in GM's lucrative accessories group – saw its return plummet to practically a break-even basis.[44] With auto sales declining, New Departure's income on civilian sales fell while fixed costs remained high. Moreover, the division failed to make a profit on its $20 million worth of defense sales: in "one important type of defense business, miniature bearings, New Departure ... actually lost money in meeting competitive prices."[45] While this case was hardly typical, it highlights the strains created by GM's decision to pay for defense plant while simultaneously expanding civilian facilities: rising fixed costs and overcapacity caused the corporation's return on investment to fall, primarily because of decreased turnover of fixed capital.

Even though return on net investment decreased, however, it remained above 50 percent for every year between 1950 and 1953, a level that would have been unthinkable prior to 1947. High returns were largely the result of a marked increase in working-capital turnover that helped offset the decline in fixed-capital turnover. This improvement, shown in Table 6.1, was an indirect effect of owners' efforts to prevent finance of the expansion by going to the capital markets. Mindful that owners' earlier intervention had occurred when expansion was paid for by

---

41 General Motors Corporation, *Annual Report*, 1952, p. 48.
42 General Motors Corporation, *Annual Report*, 1953, p. 11. White (1971, p. 13).
43 See General Motors Corporation, *Annual Report*, 1951, p. 7. Because no information is available concerning the breakdown of GM's investment in civilian and defense plant, it is impossible to verify this statement with certainty. It is at least possible that return on investment for defense work was higher than that for civilian production, with profits in the former sector offset by overcapacity in the latter. The evidence that is available suggests that such a scenario is unlikely.
44 Walter S. Carpenter, Jr., to Albert Bradley, January 5, 1953, Accession 542, Box 856D.
45 Albert Bradley to Walter S. Carpenter, Jr., January 7, 1953, Accession 542, Box 856D.

Table 6.1. *Turnover of Real Estate and Plant, Working-Capital Turnover, and Return on Investment, 1942–1945 versus 1950–1953*

Year	1. Net REP Turnover[a]	2. Net Working Cap. Turnover[b]	3. Net Total Turnover[c]	4. Net Income/ Net Sales	5. Net ROIC (3*4)
1950	9.39100	4.99987	2.88804	24.06%	69.49%
1951	7.92654	5.12477	2.65176	19.94%	52.88%
1952	5.97775	6.33732	2.52744	19.90%	50.29%
1953	6.52723	8.11238	3.11304	16.48%	51.30%
Avg.	7.17011	6.04291	2.80056	19.82%	55.50%
1942	6.05828	3.45004	1.77487	11.59%	20.56%
1943	11.60077	4.57783	2.73831	10.50%	28.76%
1944	14.27651	4.71796	3.00891	10.22%	30.74%
1945	8.94210	4.03485	2.29465	6.79%	15.59%
Avg.	9.97493	4.25189	2.47274	9.73%	24.06%

[a] Net real estate and plant (REP) turnover is defined as the value of net sales divided by the value of net real estate and plant (i.e., real estate and plant after subtracting depreciation reserves).
[b] Working-capital turnover is defined as the value of net sales divided by the value of net working capital (gross working capital minus current liabilities).
[c] Total net turnover is defined as the value of net sales divided by the value of net working capital (cash; securities and tax notes; accounts receivable; inventories) plus net fixed capital (investments in other companies; other investments; miscellaneous assets; capital stock in treasury; prepaid expenses and deferred charges; net real estate, plant, and equipment).
Source: All figures calculated from General Motors' annual reports.

outside funds, management financed the expansion of 1950–1953 entirely out of earnings and depreciation. In order to pay for this program, the corporation liquidated hundreds of millions of dollars worth of short-term government securities that were held to pay taxes and meet unforeseen contingencies. In effect, management elected to operate on narrower working-capital margins in order to appease owners. They did this by drastically reducing holdings in cash and highly liquid securities. While this may have put a strain on the corporation, it also led to more efficient use of working capital. As long as more efficient use of working capital could offset declining efficiency in the use of fixed capital, GM had little reason to worry about overcapacity. While it is undoubtedly true that the corporation's returns during this period would have been significantly higher if it had not undertaken the huge expansion that was carried out during these years, management was banking on a postwar boom. Unwilling to risk losing market share during a period of reconversion, GM chose to carry the cost of overcapacity.

The expansion program of the 1950s suggests a compromise between financial and operating interests. Expansion itself was promoted by the operating side of the organization, still eager to push its market share back to pre–World War II levels. The slack resources made it difficult for the FPC to veto the program. With both profits and dividends at record levels, it would be hard to claim that the money for expansion was unavailable. Moreover, given the government's antitrust suit, owners were probably particularly hesitant to intervene in GM's internal affairs, even though the expansion program would cut into their future dividends.[46] Yet the 1950 program was not the "reckless spending spree" that owners had feared in 1947. Still mindful of owners' objections to earlier expansion plans, operating management made sure that the 1950 program would be financed entirely by retained earnings. Although this decision may have put a severe strain on working capital, it foreclosed one of the owners' most powerful objections. Slack resources thus led to expansion, but at least in 1950, management was nonetheless careful to address potential FPC objections.

Consent as an Organizational Weapon

Although the expansion that occurred between 1950 and 1953 was undertaken in order to create adequate capacity for anticipated postwar markets, it simply fueled the hunger for further growth. In a parallel to the post–World War II situation, the expenditure of $1.279 billion that took place during the Korean War was followed by calls for even more massive expansion. This time, however, both owners and financial executives would be unable or unwilling to rein in operating management. The "reckless spending spree" that had threatened in 1947 reemerged on an even more massive scale in 1954.

Postwar expansion occurred under the leadership of a new president. On December 1, 1952, Charles Wilson left GM's presidency to serve as secretary of defense in the Eisenhower administration. His position was taken by Harlow H. Curtice, former division manager of Buick, who, since September 1948, had served as executive vice-president in charge of Detroit's operating staff. As president, Curtice also acquired the title of CEO and took over as chairman of both the OPC and the Administration Committee.[47] From the outset, Curtice strove to increase GM's

---

46 There is a conspicuous absence of archival documents from owners concerning the 1950 expansion program, in part because key players like Carpenter withdrew from GM's FPC.
47 The dates of Curtice's appointments are shown in General Motors Corporation, *Annual Report*, 1952, pp. 2–3.

overall market share by producing and selling more cars and trucks. Despite GM's enormous growth following World War II, the corporation had never recaptured the 47 percent share of the North American automobile market that it had held in 1941. Even the record sales of 1950 had resulted in only a 45.4 percent market share, and the production limits that went into effect following the outbreak of the Korean War had caused this figure to slip to 41.7 percent by the end of 1952.[48] Thus, only months after taking over as president, Curtice announced that "our first objective will be to regain our prewar percentage of the market on cars and obtain as high a percentage on trucks."[49] To achieve this goal, Curtice would push for further expansion beyond the program that he inherited from Wilson.

The unprecedented expansion that took place during Curtice's reign relied on both an increase in and a redefinition of participative decentralization. Popular accounts of Curtice's administration have emphasized his "leaning toward centralization" and his use of coercion.[50] And indeed, Curtice did attempt to increase his own power. Following his appointment to the presidency, he failed to fill the post that he had previously occupied – executive vice-president in charge of the operating staff – opting instead to have Detroit's technical staff report directly to him as president, thus giving him more direct control over the staff side of the organization.[51] At the same time, Curtice modified reporting lines so that all nonautomotive operating groups (including truck operations) reported directly to him rather than to an executive vice-president.[52] Informally, Curtice often bypassed group executives and executive vice-presidents to deal directly with division managers.[53] Yet existing accounts have failed to note that this increase in Curtice's power was initially achieved through increasing divisional participation in strategic planning and resource allocation. Curtice used consent as an organizational weapon, building consensus in the divisions and the operating side of the organization in order to increase his own power to oppose and subvert financial oversight. He thus completed the transformation that had begun under Wilson, making divisional participation in planning a vehicle for political coalition-building rather than a means of achieving cooperation among all levels of the organization.

48 See Wolf (1962, pp. 479–480).
49 Harlow Curtice, as quoted in *Business Week* (1953, p. 93).
50 *Fortune* (1956, p. 19); Sheehan (1965, p. 52).
51 *Fortune* (1956, pp. 18–19); Bradley, Fisher, and Paulson (1959, pp. 24–28).
52 See United States Congress [1956, pp. 3496 (organization chart), 3563–3564]. These formal changes were in effect after 1954, excluding 1956, when Ivan Wiles served as executive vice-president in charge of the technical staff. See General Motors Corporation, *Annual Report*, 1955–1958.
53 *Fortune* (1956, p. 18).

Curtice first sought to increase participative decentralization by placing divisional representatives directly on the OPC, just as Sloan and Wilson had done before him. Early in 1954, he sought to expand OPC membership to include the general managers of Buick, Chevrolet, and Allison. He was only partially successful. Alarmed by Curtice's actions, owners made the same arguments that they had presented to Sloan for decades – division managers did not have the time to serve on the OPC, nor were they sufficiently objective to evaluate corporate performance and formulate policies. Arguing that the practice "of again including divisional heads on [the OPC] appear[s]... to be a move in the direction of that system which was tried out for a number of years and which [was] found unsatisfactory," owners opposed Curtice's proposed appointments.[54] Despite this resistance, Curtice was able to have the general managers of Buick and Chevrolet appointed to the OPC, probably because the ongoing antitrust trial made Du Pont representatives hesitant to intervene too forcefully. Nonetheless, they did persuade Curtice to withdraw the nomination of Allison's general manager and replace it with the appointment of a group executive in charge of the Dayton, Household Appliance, and GMC Truck Group.[55] This was as far as divisional representation on the OPC would go, however. Following owners' initial victory in the antitrust suit at the end of 1954, further divisional nominations were sure to encounter increased resistance. When the two divisional representatives on the OPC were promoted to positions at corporate headquarters in 1956, the OPC was again composed solely of general office representatives.

Unable to increase divisional representation on the OPC, Curtice turned more responsibility for planning and resource allocation over to the Administration Committee, where all of the car and truck divisions were already represented. It was the Administration Committee's responsibility to discuss and approve policy proposals originating in the various policy groups.[56] Moreover, appropriation requests were worked up in the divisions, then modified and approved in the Administration Committee, where division managers were full participants.[57] Even though all

---

54 Walter S. Carpenter, Jr., to Harlow Curtice, May 5, 1954, Accession 542, Box 856D. Carpenter wrote this letter after discussions with Du Pont members of the FPC who were evidently uncomfortable with the proposed changes, but who had less familiarity with the issues involved because of their recent appointments to the FPC.
55 The new appointments were Thomas Keating, general manager of Chevrolet, his counterpart at Buick, Ivan Wiles, and Roger Kyes, group executive of GMC truck, Dayton, and household appliance activities. See General Motors Corporation, *Annual Report*, 1954, pp. 2–3, 56.
56 I have been unable to locate data on whether division managers served on the policy groups during this period.
57 On the former point, see Gerstenberg (1954, p. 42).

Table 6.2. *Membership of Operations Policy Committee and Administration Committee, January 1955*

Operations Policy Committee		Administration Committee	
Name	Position(s) in Corporation	Name	Position(s) in Corporation
Harlow H. Curtice	President, CEO	Harlow H. Curtice	President, CEO
Albert Bradley	Exec VP, Finance; Chair, FPC	Albert Bradley	Exec VP, Finance; Chair, FPC
Frederic Donner	Vice President, Finance	Frederic Donner	Vice President, Finance
Louis C. Goad	Executive Vice President	Louis C. Goad	Executive Vice President
Edward R. Godfrey	Vice President, Special Assignments	Edward R. Godfrey	Vice President, Special Assignments
John F. Gordon	Group Executive, Body	John F. Gordon	Group Executive, Body
Thomas H. Keating	Division Manager, Chevy	Thomas H. Keating	Division Manager, Chevy
Carl H. Kindl	Group Executive, Overseas	Carl H. Kindl	Group Executive, Overseas
Roger M. Kyes	Group Executive, Dayton, Household, Assembly	Roger M. Kyes	Group Executive, Dayton, Household, Assembly
Cyrus R. Osborn	Group Executive, Engine	Cyrus R. Osborn	Group Executive, Engine
Sherrod E. Skinner	Group Executive, Accessory	Sherrod E. Skinner	Group Executive, Accessory
Ivan L. Wiles	Division Manager, Buick	Ivan L. Wiles	Division Manager, Buick
		Don E. Ahrens	Division Manager, Cadillac
		Robert M. Critchfield	Division Manager, Pontiac
		James E. Goodman	Division Manager, Fisher
		Philip J. Monaghan	Division Manager, GM Truck
		Edward B. Newill	Division Manager, Allison
		Edward Riley	Division Manager, Overseas
		Jack F. Wolfram	Division Manager, Olds

OPC members sat on the Administration Committee, allowing general office executives to take part in Administration Committee deliberations and decisions, Administration Committee membership was evenly divided between divisional representatives and general executives. Moreover, members of Detroit's technical staff were not represented on either committee, while financial representatives were vastly outnumbered by operating men on both committees. Under Curtice, the OPC consisted primarily of group executives from the operating side of the organization, while the Administration Committee was made up of division managers (Table 6.2). This arrangement made it difficult for the financial and technical staffs to exercise audit or control over the divisions. When disagreements arose within the Administration Committee, Curtice could pit the division managers against general office executives in order to minimize the influence of headquarters.

In order to further weaken New York's ability to exercise financial control, Curtice also altered the way the OPC functioned. In theory, the OPC served as a check on the Administration Committee, since any policies approved by the Administration Committee went on to the OPC for further discussion and approval. Under Curtice, however, the OPC did not engage in extensive discussions where all members participated freely and equally. Instead, Curtice severely limited the input of OPC members, allowing them to address proposed policies only in terms of each member's area of administrative responsibility. As a result, the OPC came to function as "a rubber stamp" in which general office representatives "were rendered voiceless outside the scope of [their] immediate administrative jurisdiction."[58] Its decisions became "more or less perfunctory," and it simply approved "appointments of personnel and ... appropriations which have been already reviewed by the Administration Committee."[59] In this situation, real power lay with Curtice and the Administration Committee. By the end of Curtice's reign, owners and top executives were shocked to learn that the OPC had become entirely *pro forma*, leaving the Administration Committee firmly in control of planning and resource allocation. Walter Carpenter commented in disbelief:

> I am amazed to find how inactive and ineffective [the OPC] is. In fact, I believe it was said by one [OPC member] that if that Committee disappeared from sight overnight, no difference would be noted in the management of the Corporation.
>
> I called to the attention of these men that in accordance with the by-laws of the Corporation that the Operating Policy Committee has complete responsibility for the management of the business of the Corporation.... This seemed a little surprising [to them].[60]

Participative decentralization thus became an organizational weapon, used to increase the power of Curtice and the operating side of the organization *against* New York's financial staff. Whereas Sloan's version of participative decentralization attempted to find a workable compromise acceptable to all factions, Curtice's style of governance deepened the existing rift between finance and operations, exacerbating power struggles between these coalitions.

With support and assistance from divisional men in the Administration Committee, Curtice drew up a two-year expansion plan that was almost as large as the entire Korean War program. The plan, announced

---

58 Donaldson Brown to Alfred P. Sloan, Jr., November 9, 1957, Accession 542, Box 849.
59 Walter S. Carpenter, Jr., to Alfred P. Sloan, Jr., October 9, 1957, Accession 542, Box 849.
60 Walter S. Carpenter, Jr., to Alfred P. Sloan, Jr., October 9, 1957, Accession 542, Box 849.

in January 1954, called for an expenditure of $1 billion over a two-year period in order to increase GM's North American capacity to an output of 16,000 cars and trucks per day.[61] Much of this money would go to build up working capital. The remaining funds would be allocated to fixed capital, largely to increase capacity for accessories and components such as air-conditioning, "automatic transmissions, power steering, power brakes, and V-8 engines."[62] With consumer purchasing power at an all-time high, such features – previously unavailable or regarded as unnecessary luxuries – were selling well, adding significantly to profit margins per car.[63] Despite the record earnings of the war years, GM could not finance this unprecedented growth out of retained earnings alone. In part this was because plans called for expansion to be accompanied by higher dividends, probably to help forestall owner objections. But the shortage was also due to the magnitude and duration of the program, which entailed larger expenditures in two years than were made during the entire post–World War II period of growth. In order to pay for the new program, GM turned again to the capital markets, and in January 1954 issued $300 million in debenture notes.[64] After the most successful and profitable years in its history, GM was acquiring its largest debt.

Owners were alarmed and shocked by burgeoning expansion, but despite holding a majority of seats on the FPC, they remained unwilling to intervene too forcefully.[65] Following the announcement that GM would borrow $300 million, one former Du Pont executive wrote his colleagues to caution that the expansion program was a sign of "imprudent and probably wasteful management" – GM was expanding

---

61 General Motors Corporation, *Annual Report*, 1953, p. 38; Walter S. Carpenter, Jr., to Frederic Donner, July 27, 1954, Accession 542, Box 856D.
62 Sloan (1964, p. 210).   63 Cray (1980, pp. 346–348, 376).
64 General Motors Corporation, *Annual Report*, 1953, p. 38. Sloan (1964, pp. 210–211).
65 The membership of the FPC had undergone considerable change following Walter Carpenter's resignation and the appointment of Du Pont's Angus Echols to replace him in 1948. In 1949 another Du Pont representative had been added – Lammot du Pont Copeland. In 1950 Henry Alexander was added as a second representative of J. P. Morgan, and early in 1951 Harlow Curtice, then executive vice-president, joined the FPC. In 1952, Du Pont's John L. Pratt resigned from the committee and was replaced by the first "outside" (non-GM, non–Du Pont, non-Morgan) director to sit on the FPC, General Lucius Clay. In 1953, Charles Wilson left the committee, and in 1954, following a Du Pont-GM victory in the initial round of the government's antitrust suit, Angus Echols resigned and was replaced by Walter S. Carpenter, Jr., chairman of the board of E. I. du Pont de Nemours. Thus, in 1954 and 1955, when the expansion program was being carried out, the FPC was a ten-member body consisting of four GM men (Bradley, Curtice, Donner, Sloan), five major-shareholder representatives (Brown, Carpenter, and Copeland of Du Pont; Alexander and Whitney of Morgan), and one "outside" director (Clay).

capacity too rapidly, was too optimistic in its forecasts of future sales, and was attempting to increase market share "regardless of consequences."[66] Du Pont's top executives agreed with this evaluation, but they were reluctant to challenge Curtice too directly. Owners warned GM's top financial executives that the growing expansion program was creating problems similar to those that had existed in 1947, and they cautioned that "these programs sometimes are furthered by the mere force of momentum... once considered."[67] In addition, the FPC whittled away at the proposals put forth by the operating side of the corporation. The initial program put forward by Curtice late in 1953 called for expanding GM's capacity to 18,000 cars and trucks per day.[68] After some debate, the FPC scaled the plan back to 16,000 units per day, thereby shaving hundreds of millions of dollars off the program's cost. Yet, as had happened in 1947, Curtice and the divisions began to lobby for additional expansion almost immediately. In November 1954, their requests went to the FPC for approval. Unwilling to challenge Curtice's authority, financial management reluctantly supported the plan; still under antitrust scrutiny, owners supported it as well.

By late December 1954, when a federal court ruled in Du Pont's favor in the antitrust suit, it was too late.[69] The court ruling was handed down one month after the FPC approved additional expansion. Only days after the verdict, Du Pont's chairman of the board, Walter Carpenter, Jr., rejoined the FPC. But by this time, the decision to spend over $300 million to expand capacity further had already been ratified, and Curtice's emphasis on capturing market share had led the already-huge program to balloon to more than twice its original size. All owners could do at this point was haggle over how the expansion should be funded. While management sought to pay for the program through issuing more debt, owners insisted that GM should issue new common stock in order to raise capital "from sources other than future earnings."[70] In February 1955 GM raised $325 million through the offer of over 4.3 million shares of new common – the first sale of new GM

66 Edmond E. Lincoln to Walter S. Carpenter, Jr., Lammot du Pont Copeland, Henry Belin du Pont, Pierre S. du Pont, Angus B. Echols, and C. H. Greenwalt, December 12, 1953, Accession 542, Box 856D.
67 Walter S. Carpenter, Jr., to Frederic Donner, July 27, 1954, Accession 542, Box 856D.
68 Walter S. Carpenter, Jr., to Frederic Donner, July 27, 1954, Accession 542, Box 856D.
69 The decision was handed down on December 3, 1954, by Judge Walter La Buy; three days later, Walter Carpenter returned to the FPC, attending his first meeting in six years. The decision was reversed by the U.S. Supreme Court in 1957 (353 U.S. 586, 1957). On the timing of the decision, see General Motors Corporation, *Annual Report*, 1954, pp. 17–18; on Carpenter's reappointment, see Walter S. Carpenter, Jr., "Memorandum for File," December 7, 1954, Accession 542, Box 856D.
70 Walter S. Carpenter, Jr., "Memorandum for File," December 7, 1954, Accession 542, Box 856D.

common in decades.[71] The $1-billion program had grown to $1.5 billion, and before it was completed it would become a three-year endeavor costing over $2 billion.[72]

The scope of expansion increased even while the drive for market share was reducing profit margins. In an attempt to increase sales on 1954 Buick and Oldsmobile models, for instance, Curtice urged Fisher Body to introduce unscheduled, last-minute styling changes; in 1955 he urged similar changes for Chevrolet in an attempt to quash Ford's challenge to Chevy's sales leadership.[73] Because such changes occurred well into the tooling runs for these models, they were enormously expensive, requiring last-minute retooling at overtime rates. In order to be able to make such unscheduled modifications, GM "substantially increased" expenditures on tool-and-die capacity, thus reducing its reliance on outside toolmakers.[74] Moreover, such late changes meant that new models often got into production later than anticipated. Divisions then had to produce "way above the normal operating capacity [at] a considerable additional expense in overtime" in order to build up stock for the new model year.[75] During the Korean War, this tendency was exacerbated by government controls that effectively delayed the introduction of new models, making for even more last-minute production at overtime rates.[76] Nor were such practices limited to the period prior to the introduction of new models: production schedules were already so high under Curtice's reign that in July 1953 they had to be reduced by some 300,000 units in order to bring production in line with demand. The result was a reduction in profit due to "higher fixed costs" and increased expenditures for material, labor, and design.[77]

The expansion carried out under Curtice increased GM's market share, but only at the expense of further decreasing turnover and return on investment. Between 1952 and 1954, GM's share of the North American car market jumped from 41.7 percent to 50.7 percent, and it remained above the 50 percent level in every year of the expansion program.[78] Yet this increase in sales was accompanied by a continuing decline in turnover of fixed capital. Table 6.3 shows that as new fixed plant was brought on-line between 1954 and 1956, fixed-capital

---

71 General Motors Corporation, *Annual Report*, 1954, p. 39.
72 Sloan (1964, pp. 210–211).   73 *Fortune* (1956, pp. 6–7, 12–13).
74 General Motors Corporation, *Annual Report*, 1954, p. 39. White (1971, p. 201).
75 Alfred P. Sloan, Jr., to Donaldson Brown, January 11, 1954, Accession 1334, Box 2.
76 Alfred P. Sloan, Jr., to Donaldson Brown, January 11, 1954, Accession 1334, Box 2; White (1971, p. 201).
77 Alfred P. Sloan, Jr., to Donaldson Brown, January 11, 1954, Accession 1334, Box 2.
78 Wolf (1962, p. 480); White (1971, pp. 292–295).

Table 6.3. *Turnover of Real Estate and Plant, Working-Capital Turnover, and Return on Investment, 1948–1956*

Year	1. Net REP Turnover[a]	2. Net Working Cap. Turnover[b]	3. Net Total Turnover[c]	4. Net Income/ Net Sales	5. Net ROIC (3*4)
1948	6.06611	4.32673	2.24714	17.05%	38.30%
1949	7.33270	4.50333	2.50636	19.73%	49.45%
1950	9.39100	4.99987	2.88804	24.06%	69.49%
1951	7.92654	5.12477	2.65176	19.94%	52.88%
1952	5.97775	6.33732	2.52744	19.90%	50.29%
1953	6.52723	8.11238	3.11304	16.48%	51.30%
1954	6.05828	7.27366	2.46098	16.75%	41.21%
1955	5.28819	6.04554	2.51531	20.44%	51.40%
1956	3.63785	6.18362	2.04114	16.75%	32.92%

[a] Net real estate and plant (REP) turnover is defined as the value of net sales divided by the value of net real estate and plant (i.e., real estate and plant after subtracting depreciation reserves).
[b] Working-capital turnover is defined as the value of net sales divided by the value of net working capital (gross working capital minus current liabilities).
[c] Total net turnover is defined as the value of net sales divided by the value of net working capital (cash; securities and tax notes; accounts receivable; inventories) plus net fixed capital (investments in other companies; other investments; miscellaneous assets; capital stock in treasury; prepaid expenses and deferred charges; net real estate, plant, and equipment).
Source: All figures calculated from General Motors' annual reports.

turnover rates continued the decline that had begun with the 1950–1953 expansion program; even in the record sales year of 1955, net fixed-capital turnover was lower than it had been in any year since 1946. During the years between 1950 and 1953, decreasing fixed-capital turnover had been offset by higher turnover in working capital. But with the addition of hundreds of millions of dollars to working-capital funds in the 1954–1956 period, these turnover rates declined as well. While return on investment declined along with turnover, it could hardly be called bad. In 1956, when GM experienced its poorest performance since 1947, return on net investment remained above the 30 percent target dictated by standard-volume accounting. Yet even the record sales of 1955 – which produced an after-tax profit of over $1 billion, a first for any corporation in the world – were achieved in the face of declining efficiency. Increasingly, GM's profits were a function of selling more expensive cars with optional accessories, rather than technical efficiency. Moreover, return on investment had been steadily declining since 1950; after the expansion program was completed in 1956, it would tumble still further.

Autocratic Centralization in a Changing Political Environment

Buoyed by his success in pushing through the expansion program, Curtice began to centralize more power in his own hands. Eventually his autocratic form of centralization would go so far as to disrupt divisional consent, but initially it was less severe. Yet even this milder form of centralization came at an inopportune moment, for it occurred in the context of a changing political environment. The renewed emphasis on antitrust regulation by the U.S. government following World War II was in full swing by early 1953, when Curtice took over GM's presidency.[79] This new political climate meant increasing government scrutiny of and intervention into GM's affairs, for the sheer size and scope of the corporation's activities made it one of the most visible actors in the U.S. and world economies. Alfred Sloan understood instinctively that in this new climate, GM's growing visibility would create political problems. Although he insisted that GM's size was simply a by-product of its attempts "to do an intelligent, imaginative job," he also cautioned that "we should be most careful in everything we do, to act with equity and a certain amount of humility, rather than to act from the standpoint of force or power."[80] Failure to do so would result in resentment, government intervention, and negative public reaction. Yet Sloan's warnings went unheeded by Curtice, hurtling GM headlong into a series of legislative and public relations disasters. Curtice's poor performance on such issues eventually led Sloan and owners to become increasingly dissatisfied with his presidency, as well as with GM's organizational structure.

The earliest and most important incident solidifying owner unhappiness with Curtice was an uprising of automobile dealers that led to congressional hearings late in 1955. The dealer hearings were tied directly to Curtice's drive for increased market share. For years dealers had been able to sell their stock above list price and garner high profits because of the shortage of automobiles that followed World War II. But as the shortage of autos ended, GM's drive to expand market share, along with continuing battles between Chevrolet and Ford to achieve sales leadership in the low-price class, soon drove dealer profits down to low levels.[81] There were two factors behind falling dealer profits. The first was the practice of "forcing," in which a manufacturer tried to stimulate sales

---

79 See Fligstein (1990, Chapters 5–6).
80 Alfred P. Sloan, Jr., to Donaldson Brown, September 19, 1955, Accession 1334, Box 2.
81 White (1971, pp. 152–155).

by forcing too many cars and/or parts on dealers: manufacturers might cancel dealership franchises that failed to meet implicit sales quotas; factory shipments of popular models could be delayed until a dealer agreed to order a number of less popular models as well; or a manufacturer could approve new franchises in high-volume areas to stimulate sales wars.[82] The second major factor behind dealer dissatisfaction and falling profits was "bootlegging," in which used-car dealers obtained new cars and resold them below retail. Usually this occurred when a high-volume franchise dealer sold surplus cars to a used-car dealer in another state at only a slight markup above dealer cost. The used-car dealer would then sell the auto as a "used" vehicle, charging well below suggested list price. In this way, "the original dealer was able to preserve part of his local monopoly [and meet factory-imposed sales quotas], while dealers in other geographical areas found themselves faced by still more selling competition."[83]

The problems of forcing, bootlegging, and declining dealer profits led to state intervention. Acting through their trade association – the National Automobile Dealers Association – dealers lobbied for congressional action to redress their grievances. In November 1955, the U.S. Senate's Judiciary Committee began hearings on the topic. GM representatives initially claimed that there was little the corporation could do to improve the situation. While they "never denied their use of forcing practices," GM maintained that the targets they set for dealers were fair and explicit, and they asserted that failure to utilize such targets would result in lost sales and revenue.[84] They maintained that the vast majority of franchise cancellations were voluntary, at the request of dealers, and that bootlegging was itself an outcome of the Sherman Act, which had made it impossible for manufacturers to enforce territorial security provisions in dealer contracts.[85]

---

82 White (1971, pp. 157–158). United States Congress (1956, especially pp. 3707–3844). Cray (1980, pp. 366, 400–401).
83 White (1971, p. 159); see also Cray (1980, p. 400). The phenomenon of bootlegging was particularly significant in the western states, where manufacturers' retail prices were higher due to "phantom freight" charges. That is, the cost of automobiles included a surcharge for shipping assembled automobiles from Detroit to point of sale, even though most cars were shipped as unassembled parts that were put together in regional assembly plants, with the joint cost of shipping and assembly being below the cost of shipping fully assembled cars. The higher prices in outlying areas like the western states thus created an incentive for bootlegging. One California dealer estimated that around 20 percent of the cars sold in that state had been bootlegged. See White (1971, p. 160).
84 White (1971, p. 150). United States Congress (1956, pp. 3683–3702).
85 Prior to 1949, GM had prevented any dealer from selling cars for the purpose of resale, and dealers who sold outside the areas in which they were authorized to do business were subject to financial penalty, with compensation being paid to the dealer in whose territory they sold. In November 1949 GM removed both provisions from

GM's tactic of arguing that it was powerless to change the dealer situation, whatever its merits, was a political and public relations disaster. GM's performance in the hearings led the company to look like a "giant corporation . . . trampling the small businessman underfoot."[86] This perception was exacerbated when GM did a sudden about-face. Sensing that public and political sentiments were running against the corporation, and fearful that the hearings would lead to government intervention in the form of regulation, GM suddenly announced a plan to improve the position of its dealers. During his opening testimony on December 5, 1955, Harlow Curtice announced that GM was extending all its dealer franchise contracts from a one-year term to a five-year term in order to allay dealer concerns over franchise termination for failure to meet quotas. In the ensuing months, GM also introduced a number of other provisions to reduce bootlegging and meet other dealer complaints.[87] While these changes left the manufacturer firmly in control of franchise agreements, they also reduced dealer complaints, belying GM's earlier position that it was powerless to change the situation.

The dealer hearings and Curtice's response to them increased dissatisfaction with Curtice's presidency among owners and financial executives. Their unhappiness was due in part to Curtice's failure to understand the political implications of his actions. Sloan and other top executives, who had long been sensitive to such public relations issues, believed that Curtice had created an impression of arrogance that should "be stamped out from the public mind."[88] Yet they worried that Curtice remained oblivious to the impression that his actions had created, and they feared that his insensitivity, along with GM's ongoing expansion, would lead only to further government intervention and negative public opinion. Indeed, when Sloan and others on the FPC made suggestions about how Curtice could repair GM's reputation, Curtice responded only by giving "what he thought was an excellent reason" for not heeding their advice.[89] As a result, both owners and financial executives grew increasingly dissatisfied with Curtice's administration.

its dealer contracts after its legal staff warned that they might be seen as violations of the Sherman Act. Indeed, in an effort to avoid bootlegging, GM had drafted proposed revisions to dealer contracts in the early 1950s, which the corporation had then submitted to the Department of Justice for consideration. When government attorneys would not give assurances that the proposed revisions would not lead to antitrust prosecution, GM decided not to implement the changes. See United States Congress (1956, pp. 3635–3636, 4381). White (1971, p. 298). Sloan (1964, pp. 298–299).

86 White (1971, p. 160).
87 White (1971, pp. 160–161). Sloan (1964, pp. 300–301).
88 Donaldson Brown to Alfred P. Sloan, Jr., December 14, 1955, Accession 542, Box 856D.
89 Alfred P. Sloan, Jr., to Donaldson Brown, December 15, 1955, Accession 1334, Box 2.

Even more important than Curtice's failure to understand the public relations angle was his increasingly autocratic style and his poor business judgment. Curtice had made the decision to extend dealer contracts unilaterally, failing to clear it through either the FPC or the OPC. Donaldson Brown emphasized that this demonstrated the lack of general office and financial control over Curtice and operations, and he later argued that the FPC should be given power over decisions regarding dealer contracts.[90] While Brown and others worried that the five-year contract would "come to plague" GM by making it more difficult to terminate franchises, they were even more concerned that it did little to remedy dealer complaints over the long run.[91] Top executives took it for granted that competition for sales and market share "inevitably" led to "over-forcing cars on dealers at times," yet they believed that such tactics hinged on "degree and . . . proper timing" and had to be used sparingly.[92] The extent of dealer unhappiness manifest in the hearings made it clear to these executives that such tactics had been grossly abused. Alfred Sloan, who had played a key role in fostering dealer relations between 1923 and 1950, was appalled by the events that had occurred under Curtice. Admitting that he was "flabbergasted" by the dealers' attitude toward GM, Sloan nonetheless admitted that such "a volume of resentment, dissatisfaction and unhappiness could not arise [unless there was] something behind it."[93] Like Brown, he believed that Curtice's extension of dealer contracts would do nothing to remedy the situation, and he worried that continuing dealer unhappiness would hurt GM's sales. Even more disturbing, Curtice still did not seem to have "any true appreciation" of the events that had occurred.[94] Arguing that the problem with dealers should have been anticipated and dealt with before it blew up, Sloan concluded that Curtice had grossly mismanaged the situation.

Despite their dissatisfaction with Curtice and a general feeling that GM would be subject to even closer government scrutiny and investigation in the future, general office executives in New York conceded that

---

90 Donaldson Brown to Alfred P. Sloan, Jr., December 14, 1955, Accession 542, Box 856D. See also Donaldson Brown to Walter S. Carpenter, Jr., February 19, 1957, Accession 542, Box 849.
91 Donaldson Brown to Alfred P. Sloan, Jr., December 14, 1955, Accession 542, Box 856D. See also Donaldson Brown to Walter S. Carpenter, Jr., February 19, 1957, Accession 542, Box 849.
92 Donaldson Brown to Alfred P. Sloan, Jr., December 14, 1955, Accession 542, Box 856D.
93 Alfred P. Sloan, Jr., to Donaldson Brown, December 15, 1955, Accession 1334, Box 2.
94 Alfred P. Sloan, Jr., to Donaldson Brown, December 15, 1955, Accession 1334, Box 2.

there was little they could do to change the situation. Cut off from information concerning the operating side of the business, they acknowledged that they were "not in [a] position to judge" many of the issues involved.[95] Even when they did have adequate information, Curtice's position as chief executive officer meant that he was "running the business, and that's that."[96] Indeed, because Curtice's regime had been successful in increasing market share while keeping return above the standard-volume target, they reluctantly concluded that intervention was not warranted. As a result, Curtice and operating management continued to ignore the growing public relations problems brought about by expansion. Between 1950 and 1956, for instance, GM expanded its production of buses, raising its North American market share from 51 to 85 percent.[97] This led the U.S. government to file suit against GM on July 6, 1956, charging the corporation with "monopolizing the manufacture and sale of both transit and intercity buses... by successively driving twenty manufacturers out of business through unfair competition."[98] GM's growing share of the car market also led to further antitrust investigations by the U.S. Senate Judiciary Committee,[99] while the corporation's 1953 acquisition of the Euclid Road Machinery Company, a manufacturer of heavy-duty construction equipment, eventually led the U.S. Justice Department to file yet another antitrust suit, charging GM with violation of the Clayton Act and restraint of trade in this market as well.[100]

The congressional inquiries and antitrust actions of the 1950s demonstrate that Curtice not only weakened the FPC's financial control, but evaded New York's oversight on public relations issues as well. In earlier eras, New York's finance, legal, and public relations staffs had played a key role in crafting GM's public image and advising the corporation's CEO. Curtice acted unilaterally, however, with little oversight on such matters from either the FPC or New York. Increasingly, Curtice centralized more power into his own hands. But even during this period, he was careful to cultivate divisional support and assistance through the Administration Committee. Only after Curtice's autocratic tendencies began to disrupt divisional consent and performance began to deterio-

---

95   Donaldson Brown to Alfred P. Sloan, Jr., December 14, 1955, Accession 542, Box 856D; Donaldson Brown to Walter S. Carpenter, Jr., February 19, 1957, Accession 542, Box 849.
96   Alfred P. Sloan, Jr., to Donaldson Brown, December 15, 1955, Accession 1334, Box 2.
97   Wolf (1962, p. 487).   98   Cray (1980, p. 390).
99   See United States Congress (1958).
100 On the purchase of Euclid, see General Motors Corporation, *Annual Report*, 1953, p. 16. For a brief description of the antitrust suit related to Euclid, see Cray (1980), pp. 391–392).

rate did New York executives and owners mount a challenge to the coalition between Curtice and Detroit.

Declining Performance and the Disruption of Consent

The coalition between Curtice and the operating side of the organization finally began to falter in 1956. There were two factors behind its decay and eventual demise. The first was a rapid decline in performance that occurred between 1956 and 1958. Second, and related, was the fact that Curtice's autocratic centralization finally disrupted divisional consent when Curtice began to intrude more directly into the jurisdiction of division managers. These two factors operated around the same time, beginning in mid-1956. In response to these developments, owners and top executives – especially Sloan – finally intervened in corporate affairs. Stunned at what they learned, they eventually struggled to reorganize GM one last time. It is important to note that general office executives did not play a significant role in this intervention. By this time they were thoroughly subordinate to Curtice and, as events revealed, unwilling to challenge his power. Intervention came almost exclusively from owners and from Alfred Sloan, who by this time had retired from his position as chairman of the board.

GM's performance faltered and declined dramatically between 1956 and 1958. The corporation's return on investment had declined steadily in almost every year since 1950, as investment and fixed costs rose. Yet this decline was not overly alarming, since postwar returns continued to be well above prewar levels. GM's goal was to meet its target of 30 percent return on net investment over the long run, and in 1955 returns were still over 50 percent on net investment. The decline in performance that occurred between 1956 and 1958, on the other hand, was unexpected and precipitous. Return on net investment for 1956 was 32.9 percent – still slightly above standard-volume targets, but a huge decline from 1955's return of 51.5 percent, and the worst performance by far since 1947. In 1957, GM's return on investment dropped still further, sinking slightly below the 30 percent target. This decline was due primarily to a sudden drop in GM's market share, traditionally a strong point under Curtice. Between 1956 and 1957, GM's share of the North American car market fell from 50.8 percent to 44.9 percent. Leading the decline were divisions catering to the lucrative mid-price market, especially Buick.[101] While the drop in returns between 1955 and 1956 could

---

101 Wolf (1962, p. 480).

be attributed to decreased demand, the automobile market grew slightly between 1956 and 1957, making the decline during that period particularly alarming. As headquarters and owners would soon learn, it occurred primarily because Curtice had taken centralization too far, invading the divisional domain and disrupting consent.

GM's faltering performance occurred in conjunction with a number of events that further heightened concerns over the Curtice regime, especially among owner representatives from Du Pont. The first occurred on April 2, 1956, when eighty-year-old Alfred P. Sloan, Jr., retired from his position as chairman of the board following the death of his wife Irene.[102] After more than thirty years as the corporation's top executive, Sloan and GM seemed unable to part company: the board gave him the title of "honorary chairman," and he remained on the FPC. Albert Bradley became chairman of the board, while Frederic Donner took over Bradley's previous post as executive president and chair of the FPC. While Sloan's resignation and the associated personnel changes could hardly have been a surprise, they probably served to exacerbate owners' worries about the Curtice administration. By September 1956, the combination of declining profits and the government's antitrust charges concerning the bus industry had owners actively worrying about "the situation at GM."[103] Concern turned to alarm on June 3, 1957, when the U.S. Supreme Court stunned owners by reversing their earlier victory in the 1949 antitrust suit. Ruling that Du Pont's controlling interest in GM had led to restraint of trade, the court recommended that E. I. du Pont de Nemours be required to divest itself of GM stock and remove its representatives from GM's board and governing committees. Although these actions were to be carried out only after consideration by the U.S. district court, it was clear that the coalition of owners and executives who had overseen GM for decades was about to be shattered.[104]

The combination of declining performance, imminent divestment, and Sloan's retirement finally spurred owners into action. In mid-1957, at the urging of Sloan and Du Pont representatives, the board of directors appointed a "special committee" to investigate GM's organization and governance.[105] Knowing that Curtice would retire in August 1958, the

---

102 General Motors Corporation, *Annual Report*, 1956, p. 8. Cray (1980, pp. 368–369).
103 Donaldson Brown to Walter S. Carpenter, Jr., September 24, 1956, Accession 542, Box 849.
104 Sheehan (1965, pp. 51–53). For the Supreme Court decision, see 353 U.S. 586, 1957; General Motors Corporation, *Annual Report*, 1957, p. 20. Du Pont executives considered arguing that the corporation should be allowed to keep its GM stock for "investment" purposes, with no exercise of control over GM, but they knew this was not likely to happen. See Alfred P. Sloan, Jr., to Donaldson Brown, September 11, 1957, Accession 1334, Box 2.
105 The exact date of the committee's appointment is not known. The first mention of

committee was charged with making recommendations for Curtice's successor and for GM's future organization. Its recommendations would be the last gasp of GM's old guard. Headed by Sloan and known within GM as the Sloan committee, the group included GM chairman Albert Bradley, Walter S. Carpenter, Jr., chairman of the board of E. I. du Pont de Nemours, "outside" GM director General Lucius Clay, and Curtice. Yet the most active participants were Sloan, Carpenter, and Donaldson Brown, who was not even a committee member. Curtice himself was sometimes kept in the dark concerning the group's activities, probably because the committee in effect set out to investigate Curtice's administration.[106] Through interviewing members of operating management it sought to discover what lay behind the corporation's declining performance. Using this information, Sloan and the committee would attempt to modify GM's structure to provide for effective governance in the post-Sloan era.

The members of the special committee were shocked by what their investigation uncovered. For the first time, they realized the extent to which Curtice had subverted general office oversight. They learned that no substantive discussions of corporate problems took place in the OPC; instead, the committee simply authorized decisions made by the Administration Committee, in order to legalize them.[107] As a result, the OPC had paid little attention to GM's declining profits and performance. The most striking example of the OPC's inactivity concerned the performance of Buick, which had been declining in sales, profits, market share, and quality since late 1955. Between 1955 and 1957, Buick's market share fell from 10.3 to 6.6 percent of the North American market.[108] Members of the Sloan committee were astounded to learn that although the situation had reached critical proportions, "the plight of the Buick Division ... had never been mentioned in any of the [OPC's] meetings."[109] Even more shocking was the reason for Buick's decline and the OPC's failure to investigate it. Beginning in 1956, Curtice had taken direct control of Buick, operating

---

the body in available documents can be found in Donaldson Brown to Walter S. Carpenter, July 9, 1957, Accession 542, Box 849 – just over a month after the Supreme Court decision.

106 See, for instance, Alfred P. Sloan, Jr., to Albert Bradley, Walter S. Carpenter, Jr., and Lucius Clay, September 25, 1957, Accession 542, Box 849, which accompanies Sloan's initial set of recommendations for GM's future organization. The proposals for reorganization were evidently not even sent to Curtice.
107 Alfred P. Sloan, Jr., to Walter S. Carpenter, Jr., October 16, 1957, Accession 542, Box 849.
108 Wolf (1962, p. 480).
109 Walter S. Carpenter, Jr., to Alfred P. Sloan, Jr., October 9, 1957, Accession 542, Box 849.

the division on his weekend trips to his home in Flint, where the division was located.[110] OPC members were afraid to challenge Curtice's action and the subsequent decline in Buick's position because they were afraid to oppose Curtice, who controlled their salaries, bonuses, and promotion prospects.[111] This centralization had occurred even though the OPC was composed entirely of the corporation's top officers and group executives and even though the president was, in theory, subordinate to the OPC as a whole.

The Buick case also demonstrates that over time, the relationship between Curtice and the divisions gradually moved from one of consent and cooperation to one of coercion. In the early years of his presidency, the participation of division managers in policy-making and resource allocation produced support for corporate policies among the divisions. This was especially true during the period from 1954 to 1956, during the drive to increase capacity and expand market share. Expansion during this period was carried out with strong divisional input, it increased divisional resources, and it convinced division managers that Curtice was "as strong a product man as GM has ever known."[112] Yet over time, Curtice began to rely increasingly on fiat in his interactions with the divisions, destroying consent and initiative at the divisional level. In the Buick case, he relieved the division manager, chief engineer, and head sales representative of their responsibilities in order to take complete control of the division's operations.[113] He then changed the division's place in the pricing pyramid by pushing it into the low-priced field to compete with Chevrolet.[114] In making these moves, he destroyed the participation in planning that served as the basis of consent. With Curtice taking control of such decisions, Buick's manager had little real authority over the division's operations, and his input into corporate policies was unlikely to conflict with Curtice's position. As a result, morale within Buick plummeted, and with it went performance, quality, and sales.

Realizing that Curtice's presidency manifest "extreme faults of dictatorship," the Sloan committee sought to reestablish effective

---

110 Alfred P. Sloan, Jr., to Walter S. Carpenter, Jr., October 16, 1957, Accession 542, Box 849.
111 Alfred P. Sloan, Jr., to Walter S. Carpenter, Jr., October 16, 1957, Accession 542, Box 849.
112 Wright (1979, p. 41); see also pages 206–207, where it is indicated that while division representatives supported Curtice, general office and financial representatives did not.
113 Alfred P. Sloan, Jr., to Walter S. Carpenter, Jr., October 16, 1957, Accession 542, Box 849.
114 See Walter S. Carpenter, Jr., to Frederic Donner, October 2, 1959, Accession 542, Box 856D.

governance.[115] In the short run, they attempted to remedy the problems in Buick by working within the existing organizational framework. Operating through the FPC, Sloan and owner representatives pressured Curtice to review the Buick situation and make concrete suggestions for improvement. Yet even this was no simple matter: faced with pressure from above, Curtice indicated that he would appoint his own committee to review personnel changes in Buick and to evaluate the qualifications and performance of the division's personnel. Following the report of this committee, Curtice would make a report to the FPC. Yet a committee chosen by Curtice was unlikely to place the blame where it belonged. Moreover, FPC members were not content to have Curtice issue a report, since "the Operating Policy Committee has a responsibility under the By-Laws and we have a right to expect action from them as a Committee."[116] Sloan thus insisted that the FPC pass a resolution that would "tie the responsibility... to the Operations Policy Committee through the President."[117] In doing so, FPC members hoped to reestablish the OPC's authority over Curtice and over operating decisions.

The Sloan committee also recommended increased FPC review and control of corporate policies. There was a general feeling that GM's "distressing situation" was due in part to the failure of chairman of the board Albert Bradley and FPC chair Frederic Donner to maintain adequate financial oversight.[118] Under Curtice's rule, the task of monitoring and evaluating divisional performance had been carried out almost exclusively by the *pro forma* OPC, and the FPC had virtually abrogated "its responsibilities relating to financial results from divisional operations" and its role in assuring effective divisional performance.[119] Chairman Albert Bradley pointed out that in order to strengthen financial oversight, the FPC would need "more... information on the economic position of each of the major divisions."[120] Incredibly, the FPC did not currently have full access to such data. To avoid future changes to the pricing pyramid such as those Curtice had made at Buick, for instance, the FPC would receive more information on divisional pricing proposals, and corporate by-laws would be modified to give the FPC more

---

115 Donaldson Brown to Alfred P. Sloan, Jr., November 9, 1957, Accession 542, Box 849. See also Alfred P. Sloan to Walter S. Carpenter, Jr., October 16, 1957, Accession 542, Box 849.
116 Alfred P. Sloan, Jr., to Donaldson Brown, March 27, 1958, Accession 542, Box 849.
117 Alfred P. Sloan, Jr., to George Brooks (GM secretary), March 28, 1958, Accession 542, Box 849.
118 Donaldson Brown to Alfred P. Sloan, Jr., November 9, 1957, Accession 542, Box 849.
119 Donaldson Brown to Frederic Donner, March 29, 1958, Accession 542, Box 849.
120 Albert Bradley to Alfred P. Sloan, Jr., June 5, 1958, Accession 542, Box 849.

control over prices. While the OPC would still have responsibility for "the formulation of the pricing policy and procedure," that policy would be subject to explicit review and veto by the FPC.[121] At the same time, rules governing appropriation requests were modified in an attempt to make the OPC more accountable for investment projects and to increase the FPC's review of such projects.[122]

Although these changes sought to alleviate the worst excesses of the Curtice regime, they were little more than short-term fixes. Rebuilding corporate governance would require permanent structural modifications. The special committee thus turned to the task of rebuilding GM's organization.

The Traditional M-form Resurrected

The first task in rebuilding the M-form was to strengthen financial oversight. With the exception of Curtice, members of the Sloan committee agreed that there was "a crying need for restoring the kind of relationship that used to exist ... between 'New York' and 'Detroit'."[123] The failure of financial control was seen as an outcome of the structural changes that had been made in 1946 – transferring the title of CEO from the chairman to the president, and giving the president power over the finance staff by naming the chair of the FPC to the post of executive vice-president. Thus, excepting Curtice, the committee quickly came to the tentative agreement that the title of CEO should revert to the chairman of the board, while the autonomy of the finance staff should be strengthened. By restoring the title of CEO to the chairman, the committee sought to ensure that the chairman "would have the power to act" when he thought it necessary, for since the changes made in 1946 the chairman had possessed no line authority, and as a result, "nobody pays any attention to him."[124] By ensuring that the FPC chair did not have the title of executive vice-president, the committee sought to eliminate any

---

121 See "Proposed Revision of [GM by-law] Article 36" (OPC) and "Proposed Revision of [GM by-law] Article 37" (FPC), both attached to Alfred P. Sloan, Jr., to Walter S. Carpenter, Jr., July 25, 1958, Accession 542, Box 849. See also Walter S. Carpenter, Jr., to Albert Bradley, June 17, 1958, Accession 542, Box 849.
122 Perhaps in reference to the Euclid antitrust case, these provisions included a clause explicitly specifying that "any capital expenditure that involves the Corporation entering a new line of business shall be submitted to the Financial Policy Committee for approval." See "Proposed Revision of [GM by-law] Article 37" (FPC).
123 Donaldson Brown to Alfred P. Sloan, Jr., November 9, 1957, Accession 542, Box 849.
124 Alfred P. Sloan, Jr., to Donaldson Brown, September 11, 1957, Accession 1334, Box 2.

hint that New York's financial staff was subordinate to the president. All of these changes would be made easier by the fact that Curtice's 1958 retirement would coincide with the retirement of current chairman Albert Bradley.

Despite general agreement that GM's new chairman should serve as CEO, there was active debate over who the new chairman should be. Sloan believed that there were no suitable candidates for the chairmanship within GM, making it necessary to bring in somebody from outside the corporation. Yet the two unnamed men he had in mind for the job were not available, leaving Sloan in a quandary. Du Pont's Walter Carpenter, on the other hand, believed that it would be a mistake to bring in a chairman from outside. Such a move would create morale problems and would lead to the appointment of a top officer with no previous experience in the automotive industry. He therefore suggested that no recommendation for the chairmanship be made until after the committee had talked to officers within GM.[125] From the start, Carpenter favored FPC chair Frederic Donner for the position of chairman, yet he found little support for this position among GM executives. One retired group executive summed up the GM viewpoint when he told Carpenter that Donner was "more in the nature of a financial specialist than a general executive" and that he was "too much a detail man and perhaps lacked the necessary stature of leadership" to be chairman.[126] Even John L. Pratt, who had served in GM and as a Du Pont representative on the FPC, agreed that there was no one in GM suitable for the chairman's job.[127] Like Sloan, Pratt suggested that one of GM's "outside" board members would be the best candidate for the position.

The question of who would be chairman had a significant impact on the shape of GM's future structure, all but ruling out a return to the old type of organization with a single, superordinate Policy Committee.

---

125 See Walter S. Carpenter, Jr., to Alfred P. Sloan, Jr., September 25, 1957, Accession 542, Box 849. Documents suggest that Sloan's candidates were outside members of the board, possibly J. P. Morgan's Henry Alexander or Gulf Oil's William K. Whiteford.

126 Walter S. Carpenter, "Memo of call from E. F. Johnson," January 3, 1958, Accession 542, Box 849. Prior to his retirement, Johnson had served as a group executive in charge of GM's Eastern and Dayton aircraft groups. Johnson told Carpenter that at one time he would have favored long-time executive vice-president Louis Goad – whom many in management regarded as heir apparent to the presidency – for chairman, but that Goad "had lost a good deal of his drive and enthusiasm and aggressive leadership" in recent years. Instead, Johnson favored General Lucius Clay, Henry Alexander, or William K. Whiteford, all outside directors. For president, his choices were Cyrus Osborn, group executive in charge of the Engine Group, John Gordon, Body and Assembly Group executive, or Accessories Group executive Sherrod Skinner.

127 John L. Pratt to Walter S. Carpenter, Jr., December 28, 1957, Accession 547, Box 849.

Sloan initially asked the special committee to consider three different plans of formal organization: the existing structure, with an FPC, an OPC, and an Administration Committee; the same organization, but with the chairman serving as CEO rather than the president; and the 1937–1945 M-form, with a superordinate Policy Committee headed by the chairman.[128] Retaining the existing structure was never seriously considered, and it was probably included as an alternative only to appease Curtice, who continued to oppose making the chairman CEO. Sloan may have hoped to resurrect the old Policy Committee setup, but any thoughts of doing so were quickly extinguished. Donaldson Brown pointed out that such an organization required a chairman who was extremely knowledgeable and influential in both the operating and financial spheres. Yet in an age of increasing specialization, it was almost impossible to find men like Sloan, who had an ownership stake in the firm as well as a deep knowledge of both operating and financial issues.[129] Without such candidates for the chairmanship, a structure that gave the chairman direct control over both financial and operating decisions was not viable. Brown's remarks, along with the du Ponts' long-standing dislike of the 1937 organization, ruled out the idea of a superordinate Policy Committee run by the chairman. By December 1957 the committee had reached a tentative agreement that GM's new organization would continue to have dual committees atop the hierarchy, with the chairman of the board serving as CEO.[130]

Despite agreement over the general outlines of GM's future organization, the role of the chairman continued to be cause for concern. There were at least three issues at stake. First, Curtice's record made committee members hesitant to vest too much power in any single officer; they hoped to achieve some division of authority that would prevent centralization of power in any one person or group. Second, Sloan and Brown still believed that the president should have primary authority over the operating side of the business, although they held different views of what the scope of the president's powers should be. Finally, Sloan emphasized that a chairman who held line authority over the president but who lacked detailed knowledge of the business should not be allowed to exer-

---

128 Alfred P. Sloan, Jr., to Albert Bradley, Walter S. Carpenter, Jr., and Lucius Clay, October 25, 1957, Accession 542, Box 849.
129 Donaldson Brown to Alfred P. Sloan, Jr., June 22, 1958, Accession 542, Box 849.
130 See Walter S. Carpenter, Jr., to John L. Pratt, December 20, 1957, Accession 542, Box 849. The long debate over what to call the committees continued, with Carpenter referring to them as the Finance and Executive Committees and Sloan retaining the FPC/OPC nomenclature. In addition, Carpenter indicated that one committee member – almost certainly Curtice – continued to oppose the idea that the chairman would be CEO. See Walter S. Carpenter, Jr., to Alfred P. Sloan, Jr., January 3, 1958, Accession 542, Box 849.

cise too much control over corporate operating policies, even if he was CEO. Uncertainty over who would be the next chairman exacerbated concern over these issues. Indeed, Sloan indicated that he would be especially concerned about the chairman's influence over operations if Donner were to become chairman.[131]

These issues created differing opinions over the exact definition of the chairman's role. Sloan believed that the new chairman should function as "an auditor [with only] indirect charge of finances [and] operations."[132] He did not think the chairman should head either the FPC or the OPC: the former would be chaired by a vice-chairman of the board, while the latter would be chaired by the president. His hope was that this arrangement would allow the chairman to serve as CEO, but would temper that person's ability to take direct charge of corporate affairs. Walter Carpenter agreed that the chairman should "not become too definitely involved" in operating issues, but because owners saw the FPC as a vehicle for exercising financial veto power over operations, Carpenter believed the chairman should serve as head of the FPC.[133] Brown proposed a more complicated arrangement with completely independent lines of authority and co-equal spheres of jurisdiction: the chairman would have line authority over finance and public relations, while the president would have direct control of operations, subject only to the FPC as a whole.[134] Sloan effectively vetoed this idea, arguing that independent and co-equal lines of authority would lead to continued deadlock and contestation.[135] Yet he continued to worry about the power the chairman would have in the new organization. Unable to agree on the details of reorganization, the special committee postponed its report to the board from April to June, and later to August 1958.[136]

By June 1958 the committee had moved closer to agreement on the outline of the new organization. The corporation would continue to have three committees – the FPC, the OPC, and the Administration Committee – with the chairman of the board serving as chief executive officer. The president would serve as the chief operating officer, with line author-

---

131 Alfred P. Sloan, Jr., to Walter S. Carpenter, Jr., May 1, 1958, Accession 542, Box 849.
132 Alfred P. Sloan, Jr., to Donaldson Brown, September 11, 1957, Accession 1334, Box 2.
133 Walter S. Carpenter, Jr., to John L. Pratt, December 20, 1957, Accession 542, Box 849.
134 Donaldson Brown to Walter S. Carpenter, Jr., June 17, 1958, Accession 542, Box 849. Donaldson Brown to Alfred P. Sloan, Jr., June 22, 1958, Accession 542, Box 849.
135 Alfred P. Sloan, Jr., to Donaldson Brown, June 19, 1958, Accession 542, Box 849.
136 Alfred P. Sloan, Jr., to Albert Bradley, Walter S. Carpenter, Jr., Harlow Curtice, and Lucius D. Clay, March 26, 1958, Accession 542, Box 849.

ity over operations, yet he would report to the chairman rather than to the FPC or OPC, thus giving the chairman ultimate authority over operations.[137] In order to ensure its independence, the finance staff would report to a vice-chairman of the board, who would chair the FPC and report directly to the board of directors rather than to the chairman of the board. In theory, this would prevent a single individual from controlling both the operating and financial sides of the corporation. The FPC itself would be enlarged in order to include more operating executives, thereby increasing overlap and coordination between the FPC and the OPC.

Despite this progress, important differences remained. The most important disagreements centered on the constitution of the OPC. When the Sloan committee first began its investigation, owner representatives argued that the OPC's failure to control Curtice sprang from the fact that many of its members were group executives whose time was devoted to overseeing operations. As a consequence, Walter Carpenter argued that the OPC should be composed only of general executives above the group level.[138] As he had in the past, Sloan insisted that group executives had no "direct responsibility whatsoever in our operations," since such responsibility belonged to division managers.[139] Brown concurred that group executives should be included on the OPC, since they were "intended to function in an advisory capacity and not in a dict[at]orial capacity" over the divisions.[140] Faced with disagreement from both Sloan and Brown, Carpenter dropped the matter, not mentioning it in the ensuing eight months. But in mid-June 1958, when the committee appeared to be reaching a final agreement, Carpenter suddenly revived the issue, arguing that the OPC should exclude group executives.[141] In addition, Carpenter continued to emphasize the chairman's ultimate authority over the operating side of the business, while Sloan sought to give the president and Detroit some degree of autonomy from financial control. Despite his frustrations with Detroit in the postwar era, Sloan continued to worry about the imposition of "financial dictatorship" from

---

[137] Walter S. Carpenter, Jr., to Alfred P. Sloan, Jr., June 19, 1958a, Accession 542, Box 849.
[138] Walter S. Carpenter, Jr., to Alfred P. Sloan, Jr., October 9, 1957, Accession 542, Box 849. Walter S. Carpenter, Jr., to Alfred P. Sloan, Jr., September 25, 1957, Accession 542, Box 849.
[139] Alfred P. Sloan, Jr., to Walter S. Carpenter, Jr., October 16, 1957, Accession 542, Box 849.
[140] Donaldson Brown to Alfred P. Sloan, Jr., November 9, 1957, Accession 542, Box 849.
[141] Walter S. Carpenter, Jr., to Alfred P. Sloan, Jr., June 19, 1958b, Accession 542, Box 849.

Consent as an Organizational Weapon 263

owners and New York. Finally, aware that Du Pont would soon have to divest its holdings in GM, Sloan's proposals for GM's future organization omitted Du Pont representatives from the FPC. Carpenter acknowledged that it was "just a question of time" before these three men would be forced to resign, but he requested that they be kept on the FPC for the time being.[142]

Between June 20 and August 14, 1958, the special committee's recommendations changed substantially. While virtually all of the changes that took place during this period were championed by Carpenter, there are few available records that indicate how he convinced other committee members to support them.[143] Possibly disagreements over the OPC caused the committee to rethink the entire structure, or perhaps final personnel decisions altered the shape of the organization. It is even possible that the changes were made partly at the suggestion of the men chosen to serve as president and chairman of the board. Whatever their source, the modifications that were introduced during this period altered the proposed governance structure significantly. There were three main changes. First, at Carpenter's suggestion, the FPC and OPC were renamed the Finance and Executive Committees, as the du Ponts had urged for decades.[144] Second, the chairman of the board was made chair of the Finance Committee, giving him direct authority over financial matters. There would be no vice-chairman of the board, as Sloan had urged, and thus no independence of the finance staff from the chairman. Instead, the head of finance would retain the title of executive vice-president, but would report directly to the chairman rather than to the president or the board. The president would serve as "chief operating officer" and would chair the Executive Committee, but that body would report to the chairman of the board, who would hold line authority over the president and operations. In effect, the president would be subordinate to the chairman. Despite Sloan's earlier reservations concerning such an arrangement, the chairman would effectively control both the financial and operating sides of the business. In accordance with this plan, the public relations staff would now report directly to the chairman, rather than to the president as it had under Curtice.

---

142   Walter S. Carpenter, Jr., to Alfred P. Sloan, Jr., June 19, 1958b, Accession 542, Box 849.
143   During this period Carpenter and Bradley exchanged a few "personal and confidential" memos on the subject of reorganization, perhaps indicating that Carpenter was doing some lobbying behind the scenes. See Walter S. Carpenter, Jr., to Albert Bradley, July 1, 1958, Accession 542, Box 849; Albert Bradley to Walter S. Carpenter, Jr., June 13, 1958, Accession 542, Box 849.
144   Walter S. Carpenter, Jr., to Albert Bradley, July 1, 1958, Accession 542, Box 849.

Perhaps the most important change in the new organization concerned the Administration Committee, which had barely been mentioned in earlier discussions. In order to "enhance the responsibility and activities of the Executive Committee," the Administration Committee was relieved of any authority over policy formulation, policy approval, or resource allocation.[145] The policy groups would report and make proposals directly to the Executive Committee in the new structure, rather than to the Administration Committee as they had in the past. Instead of serving as the arena of policy formulation and approval, the Administration Committee would be appointed "by the President rather than by the Board and will in effect serve as a Presidential Cabinet," offering advice to the president on operating matters.[146] These changes meant that the Administration Committee was "below the President," and the discussions that took place there would not be regarded as in any way binding on the president or the corporation.[147] The new arrangement entirely removed the Administration Committee from the formal policy formulation and approval process and at long last eliminated divisional representation in strategic planning and resource allocation.

Final decisions on personnel for the new organization were made between mid-June and August 1958. The new chairman of the board would be Frederic Donner, as Carpenter had urged from the beginning. John F. Gordon, previously the group executive in charge of body operations, would become the corporation's new president, much to the surprise of outside observers and GM's own operating management, who regarded executive Louis Goad as the heir apparent.[148] Sloan's committee was careful to announce that the choices were made by the special committee rather than by Curtice, for they did not want the new officers to "feel a sense of gratitude" to Curtice, especially given the antipathy that Sloan and Du Pont representatives felt toward Curtice – sentiments that would make it "just that much more objectionable" if the new men believed that Curtice had urged their appointments.[149]

---

145 Walter S. Carpenter, Jr., to Emile F. du Pont, undated, but circa August 14, 1958, Accession 542, Box 849.
146 Walter S. Carpenter, Jr., to Emile F. du Pont, undated, but circa August 14, 1958, Accession 542, Box 849.
147 Walter S. Carpenter, Jr., to Alfred P. Sloan, Jr., August 14, 1958, Accession 542, Box 849.
148 See Sheehan (1965, p. 54); Wright (1979, p. 41). Walter Carpenter suggested that before the appointments were announced, Sloan should "talk with the only individual who may feel that he will have been bypassed in the selections" – almost certainly a reference to Goad. See Walter S. Carpenter, Jr., to Alfred P. Sloan, Jr., July 22, 1958, Accession 542, Box 849.
149 Alfred P. Sloan, Jr., to Walter S. Carpenter, Jr., July 23, 1958, Accession 542, Box

Gordon and executive vice-president Louis Goad were added to the Finance Committee in order to increase operating representation on that body and to create greater overlap with the Executive Committee.[150] Despite Carpenter's admonitions, the ten-man Executive Committee would initially be composed of six group executives and only four general executives, though over the years the former would decline in number, while the latter would grow.[151]

The new organization marked a return to the textbook M-form (Figure 6.1). After more than thirty years of careening back and forth between "corrupted" versions of the multidivisional structure, GM would reestablish a strong distinction between strategic and tactical planning. Although Alfred Sloan had long attempted to preserve some form of divisional participation in policy formulation, and although he warned of the dangers associated with giving too much power to a chairman of the board who had little experience in operations, he seems to have accepted the 1958 plan as a reasonable compromise.[152] Perhaps the excesses of Curtice's presidency tempered Sloan's enthusiasm for participative decentralization. Or perhaps he had become more conscious of and concerned with his place in business history. When the government antitrust suit against Du Pont and GM led to the publication of internal GM documents in the popular press, Sloan realized that trial documents would serve as the basis of books about the company he had done so much to build.[153] Unhappy with this prospect, Sloan resolved – against the advice of Du Pont legal counsel – to write his own history of GM. In the process, he became determined to demonstrate that "the idea of [GM's] organi-

---

849. See also Walter S. Carpenter, Jr., to Alfred P. Sloan, Jr., July 22, 1958, Accession 542, Box 849.
150 General Motors Corporation, *Annual Report*, 1958, p. 3. Sloan 1964, p. 186.
151 General Motors Corporation, *Annual Report*, 1958, p. 3. The Executive Committee contained only one new member when compared with the old OPC: James E. ("Bud") Goodman, who took over Gordon's old post as group executive in charge of body and assembly units. In addition, Harlow Curtice and Albert Bradley retired from the Executive Committee, though both remained on the Finance Committee and the board. In 1959 two of the group executives on the Executive Committee, Cyrus Osborn of the Engine Group and Sherrod Skinner of the Accessories Group, were promoted to new positions as executive vice-presidents, making the Executive Committee a ten-man group with six general executives and four group executives. The creation of two new executive vice-president positions probably occurred to buttress general office authority, ensuring that Curtice's tactic of having both staff and divisions report to him could not be replicated. On the creation of the new positions, see General Motors Corporation, *Annual Report*, 1959, p. 14.
152 See Alfred P. Sloan, Jr., to Walter S. Carpenter, Jr., September 4, 1958, Accession 542, Box 849. Alfred P. Sloan, Jr., to Walter S. Carpenter, Jr., September 10, 1958, Accession 542, Box 849.
153 Alfred P. Sloan, Jr., to Walter S. Carpenter, Jr., April 23, 1953, Accession 542, Box 852. For an example of the type of articles spawned by the suit, see *Business Week* (1953, pp. 77–91).

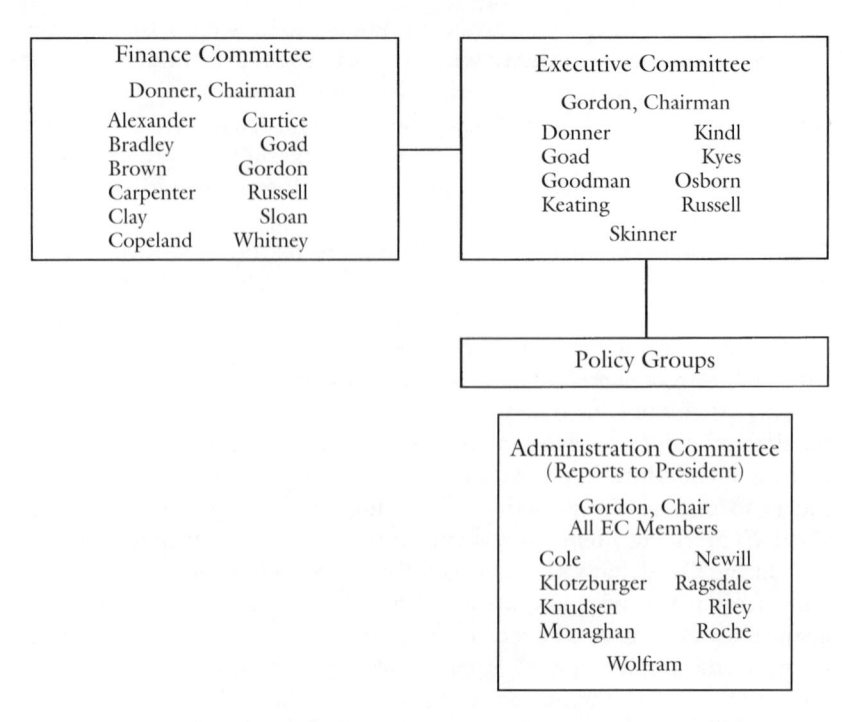

```
┌─────────────────────────────────┐        ┌─────────────────────────────────┐
│       Finance Committee         │        │      Executive Committee        │
│       Donner, Chairman          │        │       Gordon, Chairman          │
│   Alexander      Curtice        │────────│    Donner         Kindl         │
│   Bradley        Goad           │        │    Goad           Kyes          │
│   Brown          Gordon         │        │    Goodman        Osborn        │
│   Carpenter      Russell        │        │    Keating        Russell       │
│   Clay           Sloan          │        │           Skinner               │
│   Copeland       Whitney        │        │                                 │
└─────────────────────────────────┘        └─────────────────────────────────┘
                                                          │
                                                ┌─────────────────┐
                                                │  Policy Groups  │
                                                └─────────────────┘

                                        ┌─────────────────────────────────┐
                                        │    Administration Committee     │
                                        │      (Reports to President)     │
                                        │       Gordon, Chair             │
                                        │       All EC Members            │
                                        │   Cole            Newill        │
                                        │   Klotzburger     Ragsdale      │
                                        │   Knudsen         Riley         │
                                        │   Monaghan        Roche         │
                                        │           Wolfram               │
                                        └─────────────────────────────────┘
```

Figure 6.1. General Motors' top governing committees, 1958

zation was mine" rather than the du Ponts' and that it had changed little over the years.[154] When Sloan's book was finally published, it presented the 1958 structure as a logical evolution of the organization that he devised in the 1920s.[155]

Owners were even more enthusiastic about the new structure, since they saw it as a return to financial control from above in a form that closely paralleled the organization of E. I. du Pont de Nemours. Donaldson Brown wrote that the new structure would "prove highly constructive," restoring "the relations formerly existing... between New York and Detroit."[156] In addition, Brown believed, the changes made to the Administration Committee would allow that body to manufacture divisional consent by providing "wide and free discussions of the why's and wherefores of basic policy considerations," while leaving the actual

---

154 Alfred P. Sloan, Jr., to Donaldson Brown, July 13, 1956, Accession 1334, Box 1.
155 Sloan (1964, pp. 186–188, 429–435).
156 Donaldson Brown to Frederic Donner, August 27, 1958, Accession 542, Box 849.

power to approve policy in the hands of the Executive Committee. Owners believed that at long last they had succeeded in implementing the organizational form best suited to effective governance of General Motors.

Summary

Between 1948 and 1958 GM went through a number of complex and tumultuous changes, as both the external environment and internal political coalitions shifted. Although owners' ability to engage in financial veto had reemerged following the war, this power proved short-lived. Even though owners held a slim majority on the FPC, they were unwilling to intervene in operating affairs too forcefully. The reemergence of slack capital resources after 1948 made it difficult for them to claim that funds for expansion were not available, while the government's continuing antitrust suit made owners hesitant to exercise the full weight of their legal powers. Yet owner pressure continued to shape events during this period in two ways. First, mindful of owners' intervention in 1947, management was careful to finance the 1950 expansion program out of retained earnings. To do so, they had to reduce working-capital margins significantly. Thus, GM's profitability during this period was due in large part to the threat of owner intervention. By 1954, however, operating management was relatively unconcerned about owner intervention. To finance the 1954 expansion program, GM took on the largest indebtedness in its history, despite emerging from its most profitable period ever. The second way in which owner pressure shaped postwar events was to deepen the rift between finance and operations. The FPC and New York's finance staff became increasingly identified with owners and Sloan. For this reason, the corporation's top officer – first Wilson, then Curtice – sought to subordinate the finance staff to the presidency. Equally important, both Wilson and Curtice forged an alliance with operating men in Detroit, pitting division managers and group executives alike against the finance staff. Owners' insistence on exercising financial veto in 1947 thus exacerbated tensions between different factions within GM, leading to a prolonged power struggle.

Operating management's ability to subvert owner oversight derived from coalition politics that utilized consent as an organizational weapon. The formation of political coalitions rested on the subtle changes that had occurred on the operating side of the organization following the war. The postwar organization created a three-tier system for policy formulation and approval. The policy groups formulated prospective policies for the corporation. The Administration Committee, consisting of division managers and group executives, then discussed and modified policy proposals originating in the policy groups. After Administration Committee approval, policies then went on to the OPC, composed of group executives, top officers, and sometimes a few division managers. There are several things to note about this organization. First, headquarters technical staff no longer participated in Administration Committee or OPC discussions, as they had before the war; their involvement in the policy-making process was now limited to the policy groups. As a result, although technical staff were theoretically responsible for monitoring and auditing operations while ensuring objective policy, they no longer participated in final policy approval. This was an outcome of Sloan's insistence that the line should replace staff in GM's policy-making committees. Second, few representatives of the finance staff participated in the policy formulation and approval process, and those who did were subordinate to the corporation's president, weakening their ability to challenge the operating side of the organization. Third, Wilson and Curtice gave increasing responsibility for decision-making to the Administration Committee, where all of the car and truck divisions were represented. Although the OPC held legal authority to oversee operating policy, by Curtice's tenure it was little more than a rubber stamp.[157] By informally altering the nature of Administration Committee and OPC activities and relationships, Wilson and Curtice were able to forge an alliance among operating personnel in order to challenge and then subvert financial oversight. These overtly political machinations occurred during what is widely regarded as GM's golden era; the levels of return on investment achieved between 1948 and 1955 remain unmatched throughout GM's history. Taken together, these events suggest that the general office is far from the monolithic "monitoring and control" apparatus depicted by efficiency theory. Different actors in corporate headquarters – financial staff, technical staff, group executives, and the corporation's president – had different interests that changed over time. As alliances between these actors shifted, so too did the balance of power inside the organization.

Efforts to subvert financial oversight and owner control faltered only when Curtice's invasion into the operating sphere led to a decline in the firm's performance. By taking over what had once been divisional prerogatives, Curtice disrupted divisional consent and support for operating policies. As he took increasingly unilateral control over both policy

---

157 It is also possible that the group executives who constituted the OPC developed particularistic interests under Wilson and Curtice. Certainly it is unlikely that these men would have opposed expansion.

and operating decisions, morale in the divisions and among group executives plummeted, and performance became more perfunctory. Existing treatments of the M-form implicitly suggest that power within the organization is a zero-sum phenomenon – as headquarters' power grows, that of the divisions diminishes. GM's long era of participative decentralization suggests that this zero sum view is misleading. The power of the CEO – from Sloan to Curtice – derived in large part from the political support they were able to generate among constituencies within the corporation, including especially operating personnel in the divisions. By trading sovereignty for support, they actually enhanced their own power. Under Curtice, however, support crumbled as consent gave way to co-optation. By giving the Administration Committee increased responsibility for policy approval, Curtice ensured divisional consent and support, thus enhancing his own power. But over time, he began to act more unilaterally, making both policy and operating decisions without consulting these committees. Like many organization theorists, he assumed that formal inclusion and participation in the Administration Committee and other decision-making mechanisms was sufficient to co-opt divisional resistance, leaving him free to do as he pleased. He was mistaken. As Curtice's reign became increasingly unilateral, co-optation replaced consent, and divisional support for his leadership began to crumble. By attempting to seize additional power, Curtice thus undermined his bases of support, leading to perfunctory performance and organizational decline.

The rapid decline in GM's performance that occurred between 1956 and 1958 finally led owners and Alfred Sloan to intervene in an effort to resurrect financial control from above. Ironically, owners' willingness to intervene derived in large part from the fact that they had little left to lose. The Supreme Court's June 1957 decision in the antitrust case made it clear that Du Pont's holdings in GM were likely to be liquidated at some point in the near future. Knowing that little could be done to reverse the Supreme Court decision, owners put aside their reticence to become involved in GM's internal affairs. Their efforts to remake GM into a textbook M-form were renewed, as owners played a more active role in discussions over organization than they had since their debates with Sloan in 1945. Even more ironically, the excesses of the Curtice administration finally helped owners convince Alfred Sloan to give up his support for the form of participative decentralization that he had nurtured at GM throughout most of his career. The 1958 organization finally implemented the textbook M-form that owners had long urged, reestablishing financial control in New York and depriving the divisions of input into and decision-making power over policy formulation.

Owners also got their wish in naming Frederic Donner as GM's new chairman of the board and CEO; few in GM's organization, including Sloan, viewed Donner as their first choice. As their last act at GM, Du Pont representatives finally insisted on the form of organization they had long supported. Their choice would prove to be the downfall of General Motors.

7

Consent Destroyed: The Decline and Fall of General Motors, 1958–1980

The textbook M-form led not to rejuvenation and success, but to decline and eventual failure. Ironically, Du Pont representatives would have little opportunity to oversee the organization that they helped put into place. In November 1959, little more than a year after the reorganization, Donaldson Brown, Walter S. Carpenter, Jr., Lammot du Pont Copeland, Emile F. du Pont, and Henry B. du Pont resigned from GM's board as part of the final judgment in the U.S. antitrust suit.[1] With the sale of Du Pont's holdings of GM stock completed, ownership of the corporation was atomized. Financial control at GM would henceforth be carried out almost entirely by GM's own finance staff, with minimal oversight by shareholders. On the operating side of the organization, the new structure disrupted divisional consent rather than producing it. Because the Administration Committee no longer had any formal authority in the planning process, division managers were unable to participate in strategic planning, leaving them subject to legislation without representation. This led to what Fligstein has termed a finance conception of control: with operating men cut out of the planning and resource allocation process, top executives paid little attention to advice offered from the divisions. Instead, the decision-making process was dominated by men with little or no operating experience, and, just as Sloan had feared, operating issues were increasingly subordinated to financial criteria. Over time, even the Executive Committee became almost completely dominated by financial men, as group executives on that committee were replaced by financial men who were even further removed from divisional information and concerns.

Although the 1958 organization was designed as a textbook M-form, it set in motion a deflationary spiral that quickly led to administrative centralization. The primary factor behind this development was the destruction of consent. The reorganization of 1958 put the general office

[1] General Motors Corporation, *Annual Report*, 1959, p. 8. Walter S. Carpenter to General Motors Board of Directors, November 18, 1959, Accession 549, Box 856D. Donaldson Brown to Frederic Donner, November 24, 1959, Accession 1334, Box 2.

in charge of strategic planning, but it also destroyed the formal mechanisms for gaining divisional support for those strategies. Deprived of representation in the planning process, the divisions began to dismiss policies formulated by the general office as irrational and uninformed – an assessment that was undoubtedly exacerbated by Donner's lack of operating experience. As resistance grew, the divisions increasingly sought to circumvent general office oversight. The Donner administration responded to this resistance with fiat and centralization, taking over what had once been divisional prerogatives in an attempt to force Detroit to obey. Yet the deployment of even greater force served only to reinforce the divisions' belief that top management knew nothing about operations, leading to further opposition, and causing top executives to distrust operating management even more. As conflict heightened, the various players became increasingly rigid in their positions, and even high-ranking general office executives and headquarters technical staff became reluctant "to tell Donner anything other than what they thought he want[ed]...to hear."[2] General office and divisions soon became "openly critical of one another," leading to pervasive contestation and an inability to cooperate.[3] This, more than any other factor, was the source of GM's long decline.[4]

Initial Moves toward Centralization

Soon after Donner took office, the textbook M-form of 1958 became more centralized. Many analysts have noted this centralization and have pointed to it as a major factor in GM's downfall.[5] Yet they have tended to attribute this development to Donner's autocratic personality and his desire for control, overlooking the organizational factors behind this shift. In this section I argue that the centralization that occurred under Donner was due primarily to the destruction of mechanisms for creating divisional consent. The Donner administration set out to run GM with a textbook M-form in which top executives would make policy and

---

2 Cordtz (1966, p. 206).   3 Wright (1979, p. 219).
4 It is important to emphasize again that the evidence presented in this chapter should be considered suggestive at best. Although there is widespread agreement among existing analysts that the post-1958 period was marked by political factionalism and internal dissension at GM, there is little primary evidence available to substantiate these claims, especially after 1965. Nonetheless, the information that is available from internal documents, interviews, and memoirs seems to support this view. Moreover, the timing and form of GM's difficulties strongly suggest that they were linked to the organizational changes made in 1958.
5 See Kuhn (1986, Chapter 15). Cray (1980, Chapters 15–16). Wright (1979, Chapters 3 and 14). Keller (1989, Chapter 2).

allocate resources. Centralization quickly emerged, however, when lack of consent led divisions to resist policies handed down from above. Divisional resistance was partly rooted in the fact that the Donner-led Executive Committee implemented questionable policies that were ill-suited to the organization's competitive environment. These policies were themselves partially the result of an organization that cut off divisional input and feedback on proposed policies. Yet as Alfred Sloan had recognized in the early 1920s, the issue at stake in effective governance "lay not only in the question of whether [a proposed policy] was sound, but in how to get it carried out where it had to be carried out, namely, in the divisions."[6] With no formal mechanisms in place for creating consent, the Donner administration did little to solicit advice from the divisions or to sell operating management on proposed policies. Divisional management thus began to resist almost all of the policies formulated by headquarters, even those that were perfectly reasonable from a strategic point of view. Donner reacted by attempting to rely even more extensively on force, setting into motion a downward spiral of increasing centralization and fiat on the part of headquarters, and increasing resistance on the part of divisions. The 1958 organization, more than Donner's personality, created this rupture within the organization.

The move toward centralization began shortly after the reorganization of 1958, as the Donner administration attempted to deal with problems inherited from Curtice. One of the earliest and most important policy decisions made by Donner's administration concerned the pricing pyramid that differentiated GM's car divisions by price, creating "a car for every purse and purpose."[7] Under Curtice, the pricing pyramid had been modified somewhat – sometimes unilaterally, and sometimes at the suggestion of the finance staff, then headed by Donner. When Curtice took over Buick in 1956, for example, he attempted to increase the division's sales by pushing its cars into lower-price classes. The tactic failed miserably, as Buick's U.S. sales sank from 737,879 units in 1955 to 263,981 in 1958.[8] Even more important, beginning around 1955, Chevrolet began to crowd up into the medium-price groups, taking sales away from Pontiac, Buick, and Oldsmobile.[9] This decision had been recommended by headquarters' finance staff, acting in response to competitive pressures from other auto manufacturers.[10] By 1958 these mod-

6   Sloan (1964, pp. 75–76).   7   Sloan (1964, p. 441).
8   White (1971, pp. 292–294).   9   Sloan (1964, p. 439).
10 See Frederic Donner to Walter S. Carpenter, Jr., July 28, 1958, Accession 542, Box 856D. Chevrolet management presumably welcomed these changes, since they allowed Chevy to increase sales by entering the lucrative mid-priced market. Walter Carpenter would later argue that the Chevrolet move provided evidence that GM was too decentralized, since it showed that the divisions were ignoring pricing guidelines. Donner rebuffed this interpretation, clearly indicating that the 1955 Chevy decision

ifications had led to three related problems. First, by moving up into the medium-priced groups, Chevrolet (along with Ford and Plymouth) had essentially ceased to compete in the low-priced field, leaving it open to foreign competitors like Volkswagen who were willing to take the smaller profits per car that compact automobiles returned.[11] As the U.S. economy went into a recession in the latter half of 1957, sales of imports grew rapidly from about 58,000 units in 1955 to some 379,000 units, or 8.1 percent of the U.S. market, by 1958.[12] Imports captured 10.2 percent of the market in 1959, and in conjunction with American Motors' Nash and Studebaker's Lark, small cars accounted for some 18.4 percent of sales. In abandoning the low-priced field, Chevrolet thus gave both foreign and domestic competitors an opportunity to increase their market share. Even more important, the strategy put Chevrolet into direct competition with other GM lines, leading to declining sales and profits at Pontiac, Buick, and Oldsmobile. As Sloan put it, "we built up the status of the Chevrolet car to the point that it represents everything that is needed and, unfortunately, I fear not much more is desired."[13] Finally, declining sales of Buick, Olds, and Pontiac also hurt dealer profits, causing dealers for these lines to complain bitterly about direct competition from Chevrolet.

Donner and the Executive Committee responded to these problems by making even more radical changes. Although Donner admitted that "it may have been a mistake" for makers of low-priced cars like Chevrolet, Ford, and Plymouth "to 'upgrade' their product to the degree they have," he did nothing to alter Chevy's encroachment into the higher-price groups.[14] Instead, working through the Executive Committee, he instructed Chevrolet to go ahead with plans to develop a new model that would compete with the imports in the small-car market. Although the new car would sell for only slightly less than full-size Chevrolets, the Executive Committee hoped that "there will be a sales appeal not only in the somewhat lower price but ... in the smaller size itself and its greater economy of operation."[15] Because Buick, Olds, and Pontiac dealers continued to complain about lost sales to Chevrolet, the Executive Committee further decided that dealers for these medium-price cars

was carried out at the urging of Donner and the financial staff. A summary of Carpenter's argument can be found in Donaldson Brown to Walter S. Carpenter, Jr., July 22, 1958, Accession 542, Box 856D.

11 See Walter S. Carpenter, Jr., memorandum for file, September 15, 1958, Accession 542, Box 856D; Sloan (1964, p. 442).
12 White (1971, pp. 182–183). The following figures are from the same source.
13 Alfred P. Sloan, Jr., to Walter S. Carpenter, Jr., December 31, 1958, Accession 542, Box 856D.
14 Frederic Donner to Walter S. Carpenter, Jr., July 28, 1958, Accession 542, Box 856D.
15 Walter S. Carpenter, Jr., memorandum for file, September 15, 1958, Accession 542, Box 856D.

should be given lower-priced models to sell in order to recoup some of their losses. The Executive Committee thus made plans to expand the small-car program to include all the car divisions except Cadillac. In effect, the Donner administration chose to have four divisions producing both low- and medium-priced cars, thus increasing divisional interdependence and reducing the extent to which each division served a separate market. Sloan, Carpenter, and other longtime executives were aghast at the decision, complaining that it would "make a complete shambles" of the old pricing pyramid and would create "a situation among our distributing groups that will plague us for many years to come."[16] Despite these doubts, they ultimately acquiesced; late in 1958, Sloan and owner representatives voted with other Finance Committee members to ratify the new plan.

The destruction of the pricing pyramid raised thorny financial issues that led Donner's general office to become increasingly involved in what had once been divisional engineering decisions. On one side was the problem of having four divisions in the small-car field. GM's past experience had shown that such autos returned lower profits per unit than larger vehicles, making it difficult to obtain the corporation's targeted 30 percent return on net investment. If four divisions were to design and produce separate small-car lines, it would put an enormous squeeze on returns. Here, the Executive Committee created economies of scale by mandating that the four divisions share what was essentially a single small-car program. Chevrolet would design a new small car from the ground up, with an aim of keeping costs as low as possible. Once the new design was in production at Chevrolet, other divisions would adopt superficially different versions of the same car, creating economies of scale by sharing design and production costs. The situation was even more complicated in the medium-price groups, where Chevrolet's incur-

[16] Walter S. Carpenter, Jr., to Alfred P. Sloan, Jr., December 30, 1958, Accession 542, Box 856D. Sloan agreed that the changes had "destroyed our concept of the pyramid of demand." Alfred P. Sloan, Jr., to Walter S. Carpenter, Jr., December 31, 1958, Accession 542, Box 856D. In a letter to Frederic Donner, Carpenter also warned that "we may ... find that we have played into the arms of the antitrust division" by putting each division into a number of markets. As long as each division produced for a separate price class, it would be much more difficult to break the corporation up into separate entities, since all of the divisions were needed to cover the market as a whole. But if four of the divisions were to compete in a number of markets, they would be seen as redundant entities ripe for dismemberment; each could be spun off as a separate company. Walter S. Carpenter, Jr., to Frederic Donner, October 2, 1959, Accession 542, Box 856D. The latter memo, written only weeks before Du Pont's final divestiture and Carpenter's resignation from the board, was never sent. On the history of changes to the pricing policy and the Finance Committee's ratification of these modifications, see also Donaldson Brown to Walter S. Carpenter, Jr., July 22, 1958, Accession 542, Box 856D; Walter S. Carpenter, Jr., to Alfred P. Sloan, Jr., December 30, 1958, Accession 542, Box 856D; Frederic Donner to Walter S. Carpenter, Jr., July 28, 1958, Accession 542, Box 856D.

sion had taken sales away from other divisions, thereby reducing their profits. The question here was how Buick, Olds, and Pontiac could achieve profit targets given that Chevrolet would continue to compete in the mid-priced market. Donner and the Executive Committee decided that they would do so by cutting costs, primarily through reengineering their products. The medium-priced lines of Buick, Olds, and Pontiac would continue to sell at higher prices than Chevrolet, but their cars would be redesigned to bring in higher profits per unit. In effect, the Executive Committee decided to cut quality in order to increase profits for these lines.

Neither of these policies was completely novel. Car programs had been shared across divisions in the past, especially during the depression of the 1930s. Similarly, the notion that cost reductions should be obtained through engineering changes rather than through a reduction of profits had long been a cornerstone of GM's pricing policy.[17] But Donner implemented both policies in a completely different competitive and organizational context than had his predecessors. His administration pursued the strategy of sharing car designs and parts across divisions with a zeal unheard of in previous years, surpassing even Sloan's efforts in the 1930s. Moreover, Sloan had implemented such programs in the face of an undifferentiated and depressed market, and at a time when four of GM's car divisions were producing similar cars in a single price class. Donner's administration carried out similar policies in the face of a differentiated and affluent market, across highly differentiated divisions serving a diversity of price groups. The organizational context of Donner's programs was even more problematic. Prior to 1958, the engineering changes used to achieve cost reductions were often left to divisional discretion. Even when they were promulgated by headquarters, discussion and approval usually occurred in committees with divisional representation, especially when they involved changes across a number of divisions serving distinct markets. Furthermore, under Sloan, Wilson, and Curtice, GM's CEO possessed an engineering background and an intimate knowledge of GM's operations; when disagreements arose over proposed engineering changes, the CEO thus had at least some understanding of the trade-offs at stake. Under Donner, engineering changes were promulgated exclusively by headquarters, and the divisions provided little input or feedback. Even if they managed to register objections to proposed policies, operating management could not vote on such matters. Instead, Donner and the financial side of the organization would have the final word.

17 Albert Bradley to Alfred P. Sloan, Jr., June 5, 1958, Accession 542, Box 849. This document relates the policy explicitly to GM's 1958 situation.

Consent Destroyed: The Decline of GM

The problems created by Donner's strategy were most apparent in GM's medium-priced line of cars, where the Executive Committee pursued cost-cutting through a program in which the divisions were ordered to share a growing number of standardized parts and components. Initially standardization focused primarily on bodies and chassis, leading to increased centralization in the design phase of new products. In 1959, all the full-sized cars manufactured by Buick, Chevrolet, Oldsmobile, and Pontiac were instructed to share a single basic body shell, rather than the three shells they had shared in past years.[18] In 1961, a similar reduction was made for smaller cars, forcing the Buick Skylark, Oldsmobile F-85, and Pontiac Tempest to share a single body shell.[19] In addition, under Donner's regime body shells were also given longer runs to reduce costs, staying in production for six years instead of the usual three to four years.[20] In conjunction with this reduction in body shells, Donner and the Executive Committee "progressively trimmed the authority of the automotive divisions to design their own cars, insisting instead that preliminary design work be done at the corporate level and that the divisions share as many parts as possible."[21] The move toward centralization in styling was simply an acceleration of a trend that had begun decades earlier, but because Donner implemented his policy "with an abrupt and heavy hand," the divisions rebelled.[22] Having been neither consulted on the policy nor given input into its implementation, division management sought to sabotage it, "fighting futile, petty rear-guard actions as long as they could, even denying [GM president John] Gordon a key to their separate styling studios."[23] The new policies thus aggravated differences between financial and operating management that had been brewing for years.

The drive to standardize parts and increase interdependence intensified enormously in 1965, when Donner created the General Motors Assembly Division (GMAD). GMAD was an extension of the philosophy that had created the Buick-Olds-Pontiac Assembly Division (BOP) following World War II. Under the BOP plan, final vehicle assembly in outlying areas of the country was carried out not by the manufacturing divisions, but by a separate assembly operation that put together a number of different makes. While BOP had been motivated by a desire to reduce shipping costs to outlying areas of the country, GMAD was

18 White (1971, pp. 205, 333, fn. 17).   19 Yates (1983, p. 192).
20 Stout (1992, pp. 98–99). This should not be taken to mean that the bodies were "unchanged." Rather, the basic shell remained the same, but was subject to "facelifts" that altered its appearance from year to year.
21 Cray (1980, p. 406).
22 Kuhn (1986, p. 342); the quoted material is slightly out of context. On earlier centralization of design and styling, see Sloan (1964, p. 430, Chapter 15).
23 Cray (1980, p. 406).

widely regarded as an attempt to thwart U.S. Department of Justice threats to break up GM via an antitrust action: if the divisions were no longer self-contained units, it would be much more difficult to separate them.[24] Moreover, GMAD operations were to be far more extensive than those of BOP; the new division would take over virtually all final assembly for the entire corporation. The manufacturing divisions strongly objected to the creation of GMAD, in large part because removing assembly from their jurisdiction also had the effect of diminishing their ability to control quality; this concern was heightened by the fact that GMAD did not have the divisions' power to reject substandard components supplied by parts and accessories divisions.[25] Nonetheless, "ignoring the objections from the automotive divisions, Donner transferred six paired Fisher Body and Chevrolet factories, eight Buick-Oldsmobile-Pontiac facilities, and a new '4-in-1' plant in Oakland, California, into a single assembly division."[26]

The creation of GMAD was accompanied by an even more extensive program of parts standardization. The idea behind the standardization was to reduce costs by pooling them across a number of car models and to increase assembly efficiency by making it easier to assemble different models on a single GMAD assembly line.[27] Division managers again resisted the program, arguing that it would degrade performance and erode differences between the various makes. Indeed, despite the aim of lowering tooling costs, such expenses actually increased after the standardization program was introduced.[28] This occurred primarily because the program required divisions producing cars in different price and weight groups to share common parts. As a consequence, costs rose at Chevrolet because the division was forced to use a variety of parts engineered for bigger, bulkier cars: "By 1969 the manufacturing cost difference between [a Chevrolet] Impala and an Oldsmobile Delta 88 was only $70, where it had once been several times that."[29] Since the Chevrolet models continued to sell at lower prices than the cars from other divisions, Chevy's returns, which traditionally accounted for about half of GM's profits, fell dramatically. Between 1964 and 1969 the division's return on investment reportedly fell from 55.4 to 10.3 percent. Chevrolet management responded by trying to cut corners in other areas, causing a decline in product quality and appearance. Indeed, the standardization program led to a general decline in quality, as divisions

---

24 Rothschild (1973, p. 113); Cray (1980, p. 448); Yates (1983, p. 57); Keller (1989, p. 50).
25 Wright (1979, pp. 121–122, 211).   26 Cray (1980, p. 448).
27 Wright (1979, p. 130); Cray (1980, p. 449).   28 White (1971, p. 204).
29 Wright (1979, p. 130). Information on Chevrolet's return on investment is from page 100 of the same source.

Consent Destroyed: The Decline of GM

attempted to meet general office cost targets by "push[ing] out inferior parts."[30] Independent analysts judged GM's 1965 model year as "about the worst" in a decade "so far as sloppiness in production goes," while consumers ranked GM's quality "below that of Volkswagen, Chrysler, Ford, and American Motors."[31]

The 1965 program further eroded the styling and engineering differences that had once distinguished the products of the different divisions. With initial design and styling carried out by the general office, assembly in the hands of GMAD, and an increasing number of shared parts, bodies, and components, mid-sized automobiles from GM's various divisions began to resemble one another more closely than they had in the past, both in appearance and engineering. The creation of corporate "look-alikes" minimized the differences between the divisional products, further eroding the distinct identities that had served as the basis of the pricing pyramid.[32] The divisions responded to homogenization with attempts to reassert their separate identities, utilizing what little discretion they had left to introduce some semblance of product differentiation. Aided by new computer inventory techniques, divisional management attempted to differentiate their products by offering a wide choice of optional equipment and accessory combinations. In doing so, they introduced an "almost senseless proliferation of car models, parts and optional equipment" leading to an astronomical number of assembly combinations.[33] By 1969, Chevrolet alone offered "179 different engine combinations for cars and 299 for trucks"; comparable numbers of alternatives existed for axles, suspensions, accessories, paint, and trim.[34] The end result was paradoxical: while GM cars shared more parts and looked increasingly alike, they were undergoing an explosion of variability in ancillary equipment and parts combinations in an attempt to retain some semblance of individuality. Again the result was increased costs: Chevrolet management, for instance, later realized that "67 percent of all engine combinations went into only 1 percent of the cars we built," creating needless inventory expense.[35]

Divisional resistance to the Donner administration's policies was rooted primarily in the destruction of mechanisms for engendering consent, especially the elimination of meaningful divisional participation in strategic planning and resource allocation. Operating policy decisions

---

30 Wright (1979, p. 211); on Chevrolet's attempts to cut corners, see pages 129–130.
31 Kuhn (1986, p. 336); the first passage is Kuhn quoting *Consumer Reports*.
32 Cray (1980, p. 449).
33 Wright (1979, p. 121). See also Sloan (1964, pp. 441–442); White (1971, pp. 202–204); Cray (1980, pp. 428–429). Stout (1992) explains how standardized body shells were superficially altered to increase diversification, but his contention that this strategy resulted in distinct cars appears to be very much in the minority.
34 Wright (1979, p. 104).   35 Wright (1979, p. 121).

– the modification of the pricing pyramid, the creation of GMAD, the program to standardize parts – were formulated by general office executives in the policy groups, then discussed and approved by top executives on the Executive Committee. Nowhere in this process did the divisions have formal input into the policy proposals, nor the right to vote on or approve the plans, nor the ability to modify proposals put forth by the general office. Division managers did participate in Administration Committee discussions of proposed policies, but that body had no authority to approve, reject, or alter proposed polices. Even when division managers expressed their concerns or criticisms within the Administration Committee, they were not heeded. In the case of the 1965 decision to implement extensive standardization, for instance, the "divisions rebelled at various stages of the ... program," but their "cries were unanswered."[36] Absent both formal authority and informal influence to intervene in policy matters, Administration Committee meetings became increasingly perfunctory and autocratic. Division managers did not attempt to engage top executives in debate, because they believed that their objections would not be heard. Operating management complained that the lack of formal representation in the policy formulation and approval process made it "impossible" for them "to raise meaningful constructive dissent" to proposed policies.[37] Stripped of meaningful representation in the planning process, and noting that a growing number of general office executives were financial men with little or no experience in operations, division managers came to believe that executives at headquarters manifest "a fundamental ignorance of our business and our company," and they concluded that the policies handed down from above were suboptimal or altogether wrong.[38]

Convinced that they were powerless to exert influence over policy, the divisions began to resist general office directives. Donner's administration responded by relying even more heavily on fiat, doing more than any of its predecessors "to constrain the divisions' decision-making freedom" by encroaching ever deeper into divisional affairs.[39] In the mid-1960s, for instance, Pontiac management began experimenting with the idea of putting large eight-cylinder engines into relatively lightweight, mid-sized cars. After building and testing prototypes, Pontiac's division manager and chief engineer decided to proceed with production of the vehicles without first clearing the project through the general office. They later acknowledged that the engineering policy group "technically should have been consulted" about the plan, but they "were afraid they would

36 Wright (1979, p. 211).
37 Wright (1979, p. 215). For a characterization of Administration Committee meetings under Donner, see page 39 of the same source.
38 Wright (1979, pp. 215, 219–220).   39 Kuhn (1986, p. 342).

turn us down or take so long to give their approval that we wouldn't get the car into production" in time for the new model year.[40] The Pontiac GTO was thus introduced in fall 1963 without having been approved by corporate headquarters. Angered by Pontiac's malfeasance, general office executives responded by becoming more deeply involved in engineering decisions, demanding that decisions once made in the divisions now be subject to headquarters' approval. By the time the GMAD program of standardization had been implemented in 1965, the engineering policy group had taken over decisions regarding "the size and design of bumpers for individual car lines or carburetor configurations or the tone of the seat belt buzzer," and virtually "every operational product decision, no matter how small" had to be cleared through this committee.[41] The destruction of consent thus touched off a downward spiral, wherein the divisions resisted general office rule, causing headquarters to invoke even greater force in a vain effort to stem divisional discretion.

The downward spiral of struggle and centralization, along with Donner's relative lack of experience in the operating end of the business, also contributed to a decline in the quality of strategic planning. The small-car program provides a good example of how these elements interacted. The 1958 plan called for the divisions to share a small-car design based on Chevrolet's Corvair, a revolutionary model that had been under development since spring 1957.[42] Designed to reduce production costs and meet return-on-investment targets, the Corvair included a number of innovations: it utilized a relatively lightweight, air-cooled engine that would cut down on the cost and weight of associated chassis, frame, axles, and cooling equipment; the engine would be mounted in the rear of the car in order to maximize room in the passenger compartment; and the car would use a new, low-cost "swing-axle" suspension in which each rear wheel was mounted on an independent control arm that pivoted near the center of the car. Unfortunately, the design also suffered critical safety problems, especially a tendency to oversteer and flip that resulted from the interaction of the car's rear-engine placement and swing-axle suspension.[43] This problem was well known before the car went into production, and headquarters' engineering staff recommended that stabilizer

---

40 Wright (1979, p. 92).   41 Wright (1979, pp. 93, 97).
42 Nader (1972, p. 19) reports that the project was approved in spring 1957 by both the engineering policy group and the Executive Committee. The latter body did not exist until 1958, however; approval undoubtedly came from the Executive Committee's predecessor, the OPC. Additional information presented later is drawn from Nader (1972); Cray (1980, pp. 408–414).
43 The Corvair's air-cooled engine also combined with the car's heating system to allow deadly carbon monoxide to leech into the vehicle's passenger compartment. See Nader (1972, pp. lxvi–lxix).

bars be added to the car's suspension and that wider tires be introduced to reduce handling problems. Chevrolet engineers disagreed with this analysis, however, and division manager Edward Cole argued that there was no need for modification. Lacking a detailed knowledge of the engineering issues at stake, Donner made the decision on financial grounds: even though "attachment points" for the stabilizer bar "were already built into the vehicle frame" when the Corvair was introduced in 1960, his administration rejected both the stabilizer and the wider tires as too expensive.[44] The decision eventually led to an avalanche of lawsuits, and the car's poor safety record, along with GM's attempts to discredit Corvair critic Ralph Nader, created a public relations disaster that contributed to increasing government intervention in the area of auto safety.[45]

The Corvair decision did not begin as a dispute between general office and divisions, but it soon exacerbated the growing rift between New York and Detroit. The decision to omit the stabilizer quickly created a "massive internal fight," as managers at Buick, Oldsmobile, and Pontiac scrambled to keep the Corvair out of their divisions.[46] The struggle spread to Chevrolet when Donner named Edward Cole vice-president of the car and truck group in 1961; Cole's successor at Chevy, Semon Knudsen, reportedly threatened to resign as division manager if the stabilizer bar was not included in subsequent production runs. Such disputes derailed plans to introduce the Corvair design in other divisions during the 1961 and 1962 model years. Even though prototypes for the Buick, Oldsmobile, and Pontiac versions of the Corvair had already been built, the original plan was scrapped and a backup program adopted.[47] The three divisions introduced front-engine compact cars for the 1961 model year, all of which were variations on a conventional design developed jointly by Buick and Oldsmobile.[48] While free from the Corvair's safety defects, the new compact suffered problems of its own: Pontiac's version of the car was dismissed by one automotive magazine as "probably the worst riding, worst all-around handling car available to the American public."[49] More important, the clash over the small car increased distrust and animosity between headquarters and divisions. The Executive Committee's decision to omit the stabilizer bar on finan-

---

44 Nader (1972, p. lxiv); Cray (1980, p. 410).
45 Kuhn (1986, p. 325); Cray (1980, pp. 411–429).
46 Wright (1979, pp. 54–56); Cray (1980, p. 410). Information on Chevrolet and Knudsen is from the same sources.
47 See *Collectible Automobile Magazine* (1987).
48 The cars were the Buick Special, the Oldsmobile F-85, and the Pontiac Tempest. See General Motors Corporation, *Annual Report*, 1960, p. 9; Cray (1980, p. 585, fn. 410); *Collectible Automobile Magazine* (1987).
49 *Road Test*, as quoted in Cray (1980, p. 585, fn. 410).

cial grounds contributed to division management's belief that the new administration lacked an understanding of operating issues. Divisional efforts to replace the Corvair with another design strengthened headquarters' belief that the divisions were attempting to subvert general office policies in order to further their own agenda.

The distrust that grew out of these disputes helped to weaken the efficacy of strategic planning. Despite the problems with both the Corvair and GM's conventional compact cars, the programs were initially successful. Between 1959 and 1962, imports fell from 10.1 percent of the U.S. market to 4.9 percent, with Volkswagen the only foreign competitor continuing to gain ground.[50] But as import sales fell and the Corvair debacle unfolded, Donner's administration retreated from smaller cars, turning again to larger vehicles loaded with profitable options. GM's compacts began to grow larger and heavier, inching up into the "intermediate" group. These cars made higher profits per unit, yet they again left the bottom end of the market open to competitors: after 1963, import sales began to rise again, reaching 10.5 percent of the market by 1968. GM's failure to develop and stick with a viable small car is widely viewed as a crucial strategic error.[51] Yet top management was apprised of the need for a smaller car a number of times during the course of the Donner administration. In 1959, before the Corvair even went on the market, Alfred Sloan warned that GM needed to develop an even smaller model in preparation for the coming world market. Complaining that although GM was the largest automobile manufacturer in the world, it was "not in the low-price field at all," Sloan argued that "it would be a smart thing" for GM to develop a subcompact car; even if such a car was never marketed, GM would "learn from it" and "be prepared" for future changes in the market.[52] Throughout the 1960s, Sloan's warnings were reportedly echoed by the car divisions, which proposed a number of programs to develop small cars or downsize existing models.[53] In each case, general office executives on the Executive Committee or the engineering policy group turned the proposals down for cost-related reasons, aruging that the small cars would not generate adequate returns. Because operating management was "not allowed" into Executive Committee and policy group meetings where their proposals were discussed, they were unable to convince headquarters to accept them.[54] Divisional initiatives to upgrade quality in the face of changing government regulations were vetoed for similar reasons.[55] Viewing the divisions as

50 White (1971, p. 185).
51 Cray (1980, Chapter 18); Yates (1983, Chapter 3); Keller (1989, pp. 52–53).
52 Alfred P. Sloan, Jr., to Donaldson Brown, June 18, 1959, Accession 542, Box 856D.
53 Wright (1979, p. 182). 54 Wright (1979, pp. 7–8, 38, 159, 178–183).
55 Wright (1979, pp. 215–216).

self-interested actors, and lacking the experience that would allow them to evaluate proposals originating from below, general office management rejected them.

Increasing centralization and antagonism did not lead immediately to economic decline. Indeed, in financial terms, the Donner administration was successful. Following the recession year of 1958, Donner's focus on cutting costs pushed return on net investment up near the 30 percent target for 1959 and 1960. Although return fell well below this level in the recession of 1961, between 1962 and 1965 growing consumer income pushed return on net investment up to the 40 percent level. While these figures were considerably lower than those achieved in the period from 1949 and 1955, they were still quite high. Like Curtice before him, Donner achieved this success by concentrating on medium- and high-priced cars loaded with options.[56] Early efforts to achieve standardization probably helped by cutting costs on GM's most profitable mid-sized models. Following the creation of GMAD and the more pervasive standardization program of 1965, however, return on net investment fell significantly, hovering near the 30 percent target until Donner's retirement in November 1967.[57] Finally, GM's market share increased during Donner's chairmanship, growing from 46.4 percent in 1958 to 49.6 percent in 1967.

Donner's short-term financial success came at a price. As outlined earlier, GM's profits during this period were achieved at the expense of product quality and differentiation. Moreover, the emphasis on mid-sized cars hurt performance at Chevrolet, long the mainstay of GM's profit base. Chevy's market share, and reportedly its returns, fell under Donner's leadership, even though GM's overall market share increased.[58] The corporation's financial success thus occurred even as the performance of its most important division declined. Most important, the rupture of consent, the move toward centralization, and the decline of strategic planning silently destroyed GM's ability to adapt to a changing environment.[59] Under Donner, planning was carried out in the Executive Committee and the policy groups, with little or no divisional input. As long as markets remained relatively stable, especially in the lucrative medium-price field, this arrangement sufficed; GM could make profits

---

56 White (1971, pp. 182–188); Wright (1979, p. 219); Cray (1980, pp. 435–437); Kuhn (1986, p. 321); Keller (1989, pp. 52–53).
57 On Donner's retirement date, see General Motors Corporation, *Annual Report*, 1967.
58 Chevrolet's decline in market share, from 26.5 percent in 1958 to 23.7 percent in 1967, was nearly as large as GM's overall gain in market share. See White (1971, Appendix); on Chevy's return figures, see Wright (1979, p. 100).
59 Kuhn (1986, p. 341) makes a similar point, though he does not recognize that these problems were created by the organizational changes of 1958.

by doing what it had always done.⁶⁰ But as the environment changed rapidly in the late 1960s and early 1970s, GM could not keep pace. Rapid adaptation to changing conditions required that the general office elicit cooperation, information, and expertise from the divisions. Yet the organizational changes of 1958, along with the break between divisions and headquarters that occurred under Donner, virtually ensured that such adaptation would not be forthcoming.

A Corporation without Consent

The centralization that began under Donner was carried further by his successors, resulting in almost open warfare between headquarters and divisions. When Donner resigned in November 1967, James Roche, who had served as president of the corporation since 1965, took over as chairman of the board and chief executive officer. Unlike Donner, Roche had not come up through the financial side of the organization, leading to further adjustments at the top of the organizational hierarchy: during Roche's brief tenure, the powerful Finance Committee would be chaired by George Russell, who would serve in a newly created position as vice-chairman of the board. Roche, rather than new president Edward Cole, would chair the Executive Committee in charge of operating policy, diminishing the power of the presidency and giving the chairman of the board even more authority over planning. Perhaps even more important, by the time Roche took office, the membership of the Executive Committee had been transformed. When Donner had become chairman in 1958, the Executive Committee consisted of six group executives and four top officers of the corporation. During his tenure, the Executive Committee's composition slowly became weighted more toward general executives, with fewer and fewer group executives and operating men represented. When Roche took over in 1967, the Executive Committee was composed of seven top officers and contained no group executives; by 1970, at the end of Roche's short tenure, the committee was a five-man group of top officers, with more financial than operating men.⁶¹ The

60 Keller (1989, p. 19).
61 In 1967, Executive Committee members were as follows: Roche (chairman of the board, CEO, and Executive Committee chair); Edward Cole (president); Richard Gerstenberg (executive vice-president, finance); Roger Kyes (executive vice-president, car, truck, body, assembly and components groups); Edward Rollert (executive vice-president, overseas, nonautomotive, and defense groups); George Russell (vice-chairman of the board); and Harold Warner (executive vice-president in charge of operating staff). See General Motors Corporation, *Annual Report*, 1967, pp. 3, 40. In 1970 the Executive Committee consisted of Roche, Cole, Gerstenberg (vice-chairman of the board), Oscar Lundin (executive vice-president, finance), and Warner (executive vice-

committee in charge of strategic planning thus became even smaller and more removed from operations, giving Detroit even less input into policy.

These adjustments further exacerbated the split between headquarters and divisions. Although president Cole was formally the chief operating officer, he was now under two New York executives and had no control over the main committee in charge of strategic planning. His power was further curtailed in March 1970, when new vice-chairman of the board Richard Gerstenberg was given authority over all overseas operations, leaving the president in charge of only the North American portion of GM's automobile business.[62] These changes reportedly led to open confrontation at the top of GM's organization, with the corporation's president and top financial executives publicly trading barbs. Cole complained about the financial staff's "meddling in product decisions about which they knew nothing," while financial executives retorted that Cole was merely GM's "chief engineer," with no real power in the organization.[63] Such open animosity probably made division management even more likely to resist policies handed from above. Moreover, the absence of operating men on the corporation's top planning committees made it more difficult for New York to audit the operating side of the business; lacking experience in and knowledge of operations, these men found themselves unable to evaluate divisional proposals using anything except financial criteria. With headquarters unable to "evaluate [operating] programs on any basis except the numbers," divisional management "learned how to make the numbers 'come out right'" by manipulating the plans they submitted to the general office.[64]

The changes that occurred after 1967 destroyed GM's ability to adapt to sweeping environmental changes that were beginning to jolt the automobile market. Perhaps the best example of this failure was the Roche administration's attempt to react to the growing threat of imported compact cars in the late 1960s and early 1970s. When Roche took office in 1967, foreign auto manufacturers had recaptured almost 10 percent of the U.S. market, and their sales were climbing, especially in the small-car field that domestic producers had begun to abandon around 1963. Accordingly, in October 1968 Roche announced that in 1970 Chevrolet would introduce a new subcompact designed to compete directly with the imports. Known as the XP-887 during its development phase, the

president, operating staff). General Motors Corporation, *Annual Report*, 1970, pp. 2–3, 18.
62 General Motors Corporation, *Annual Report*, 1970, p. 18. This change was part of a larger redefinition of GM's various "groups."
63 Edward Cole and Richard Terrell (executive vice-president, finance), as quoted in Wright (1979, pp. 21–22). The exchange reportedly occurred in 1972.
64 Keller (1989, p. 28).

new car was to weigh less than 2,000 pounds and have a retail price of around $1,800, which would put it in direct competition with Volkswagen. Perhaps the most revolutionary aspect of the new car, however, was that both the initial design and the subsequent development of the car were to be the responsibility of the general office staff. The XP-887 was to be the first car ever to be initiated, designed, and developed by corporate headquarters. Like the copper-cooled engine that Charles Kettering had tried to push on the divisions some 45 years earlier, the new car would lead to open hostilities between the general office and divisions, and its failure would inflict further damage on the reputations of both Chevrolet and General Motors.

Disagreements over the car were present almost from its inception. In choosing the design for the XP-887, Roche and the Executive Committee rejected proposals outlined by Chevrolet and Pontiac in favor of one put forward by president Edward Cole, the man who had designed the Corvair.[65] Cole's design had been worked out with engineering and technical staff from the general office rather than with divisional assistance. Moreover, it included an untested engine design that utilized a lightweight, aluminum block rather than a standard cast-iron one. Chevrolet engineers worried about the heat-distortion problems associated with aluminum designs and feared that the engine would not hold up over continuous operation. Moreover, they argued that the engine should adopt a newer "short-stroke" design to improve its performance and reduce its size, while Cole's team insisted that the older "long-stroke" design be retained to reduce emissions. As a result of the general office's insistence on its own design and its rejection of divisional suggestions, divisional resistance to the car was pervasive, with Chevrolet engineers criticizing its technical aspects, its performance, and its styling. Even the name of the car became a source of friction, with Chevrolet and headquarters producing competing market research studies to support their different choices.[66] Not surprisingly, the general office's preferred name won out: the car would be known as the Chevy Vega.

Headquarters' reliance on fiat and its failure to allow divisional input into the project led to resistance and perfunctory performance at Chevrolet. Convinced that the design of the car was mediocre and its performance poor, engineers in the division took no interest or initiative in improving the car or adapting it to mass production. As Chevrolet's general manager would later put it, "Chevy engineers were almost totally disinterested in the car [and its] engineering staff was disgruntled because

65 Information in this paragraph is drawn from Wright (1979, Chapter 10); Cray (1980, pp. 470–478).
66 Wright (1979, p. 165). My summary draws heavily from the account presented in this source.

it felt it had proposed a much better car.... This was not their car, so they did not want to work on it."[67] Such perfunctory response was particularly problematic because the Vega was beset with problems before it began production. The general office technical staff had badly miscalculated the weight and cost of the car. For instance, their plans failed to include side-door crash beams, even though federal safety regulations made them mandatory equipment. Similarly, the front end of the first prototype fell off, after being driven only eight miles, because of an inadequate support structure. In fixing these problems, Chevrolet's engineers, just like those who had worked on Kettering's copper-cooled half a century earlier, seemed to deliberately sabotage the car. The changes that they made added to the Vega's weight and cost, causing Chevy's marketing staff to recommend that the new vehicle be sold as a larger, more upscale, and more expensive compact. Although the suggestion was turned down by the general office, the division engineers had their way: by the time the Vega went on the market in 1971, it was "382 pounds heavier and a foot longer than the Volkswagen," and it cost over $300 more than that car.[68] Its "lightweight" aluminum engine weighed more than the conventional engine in Ford's rival Pinto. Designed by men who lacked information about the markets, and modified for mass production by engineers who were unenthusiastic about the car from the start, the Vega was far from the promised import-fighter that Roche had described three years earlier.

The Vega's heritage of poor planning and perfunctory implementation led to an extremely poor quality automobile beset by mechanical problems. In 1972 alone, the Vega was recalled three times for defects involving as many as 95 percent of the cars produced at that time. The first recall involved a "combination of deficiencies in the carburetor and the muffler that could cause fires in the ... gas tank"; the second related to a design defect that caused the accelerator pedal to jam while the car was in gear; the third involved "a rear axle that was 'a fraction of an inch' too short," causing the rear wheel to fall off.[69] But these were hardly the only problems with the car. As feared, the aluminum engine block sometimes overheated and warped, damaging or destroying the engine.[70] Reviews of the car noted its tendency to skid violently in sudden stops, a problem that Chevrolet engineers were aware of but did little to correct; in addition, the electrical system was prone to failure, the gearshift lever "sometimes fell off," and in some cases the brakes failed completely.[71] The final blow to the Vega came in October 1971, when Roche's brief reign as chairman of the board came to an end and his

67 Wright (1979, pp. 161, 163).   68 Keller (1989, p. 54).
69 Rothschild (1973, p. 86).   70 Cray (1980, p. 473).
71 Rothschild (1973, pp. 85–89); Cray (1980, p. 473).

position was taken by the financial staff's Richard Gerstenberg. In a continuation of Donner's centralization program, Gerstenberg turned Chevrolet's remaining assembly plants over to GMAD, including the Lordstown plant where the Vega was built. GMAD then fired some 700 workers from the plant, leading to a bitter and highly publicized strike. During the course of the strike, workers charged that Lordstown's automated assembly line and robotic welders suffered from an egregious lack of quality control and that they were "forced to push cars along the line that were little more than 'pieces of junk'."[72] In making these claims, they singled out the Vega, since its assembly was the most heavily automated. The resulting publicity, coupled with recalls and consumer complaints about defects, meant that by "the time the strike was settled, the Vega's reputation was unsalvageable."[73]

GM lost money on the Vega in 1971, selling only 245,000 of the cars rather than the projected 400,000.[74] It fared little better in 1972 following the Lordstown strike. In an attempt to salvage the car's profitability, management returned to its old strategy of adding more options, which increased the car's cost and weight, along with its profits.[75] The strategy was successful enough to put the Vega into a profit position by 1973, and in 1974 the car sold almost as many units as its primary American competitor, the Ford Pinto. Yet in achieving this position, the Vega gave up any pretext of competing with subcompacts like the Volkswagen. Larger, heavier, and more expensive than its foreign competition, the Vega could not achieve the gas mileage or economy in operation offered by such cars, much less the reliability or price. Moreover, its checkered history only reinforced the belief that GM made poor small cars. This legacy would prove to be far more important than any direct impact the Vega would have on GM's profits. The organization structure put into effect in 1958 had crippled the corporation's ability to adapt to a changing market, and the Vega's poor record had made that failure manifest. GM's continuing inability to build a successful small car would soon prove to be devastating.

The oil embargo announced in October 1973 by the Organization of Petroleum Exporting Countries (OPEC) created a sudden and dramatic shift in demand for small, fuel-efficient cars. With the largest cars and the worst fuel efficiency of any American producer, GM was hit hard by this change. Between 1973 and 1974, its unit sales fell by over 30 percent, and sales of large cars declined even more; with profitable, mid-sized cars doing poorly, GM's net income fell 63

---

72 The quote is from Wright (1979, p. 169). On Lordstown and the strike, see Rothschild (1973, Chapter 4).
73 Keller (1989, p. 55). 74 Wright (1979, pp. 166–167).
75 Rothschild (1973, p. 81).

percent.[76] Chairman Richard Gerstenberg responded by announcing an immediate "downsizing" program designed to reduce the size and weight of all GM cars. In the short run, Gerstenberg's program simply meant cutting the size and weight of existing models by reducing their wheelbases, substituting lighter parts, and trying to improve fuel efficiency. In addition, as many assembly plants as possible would be converted to production of compact cars. Finally, Chevrolet would undertake a crash program to introduce a new subcompact called the Chevette by 1975; adopted from existing designs developed by Opel and other foreign subsidiaries, the idea was finally to produce a car to compete directly with the imports. These short-run measures did not fare well. In 1974, only about 25 percent of the cars produced by GM were compacts, though by 1975 production was up to 40 percent of GM's output. Yet because Gerstenberg and the Executive Committee decided that GM's small cars should be loaded with options in order to increase their profitability, the prices on these vehicles were often as high as those for larger cars. Moreover, in the recession year of 1974, GM raised retail prices four times, creating a 20 percent increase over 1973 prices that further damaged sales. Finally, GM's small cars still suffered from both real and perceived poor quality compared with their foreign competition. When the Chevette was introduced in 1975, for instance, its base price was below that of many imports, but it performed and sold poorly in comparison. Some analysts reported that GM was actually losing money on every Chevette it sold. Despite efforts to downsize, therefore, return on net investment plummeted, falling from 32.1 percent in 1973 to just below 12 percent in 1974, and improving only to 15.6 percent in 1975. If GM was to compete successfully in the small-car market, longer-run measures would have to be taken.

To achieve more permanent changes, Gerstenberg advocated the development of a new line of front-wheel-drive compacts that came to be known as GM's "X-cars." This program would suffer from many of the same problems that had plagued the Vega. First, even in the midst of crisis the Executive Committee – still without a single division manager or group executive as a member – opposed the plan to implement a new line of small cars.[77] The initiative to downsize and convert GM's models came from Gerstenberg and an "outside" director, while most of the Executive Committee "fought like hell" to oppose the idea.[78] As a result,

76 General Motors Corporation, *Annual Report*, 1974, pp. 4, 22. Information in the remainder of this paragraph is from Cray (1980, pp. 486–502).
77 Executive Committee members in late 1973 were as follows: president Edward Cole; chairman of the Executive Committee; Gerstenberg; vice-chairman of the board Thomas Murphy; and executive vice-presidents Elliott Estes, Oscar Lundin, and Richard Terrell. See General Motors Corporation, *Annual Report*, 1973, p. 46.
78 Yates (1983, pp. 137–138). See also Wright (1979, p. 218).

the Executive Committee did not give the X-car project final approval until February 1976, over two years after the oil crisis. It would take another three years beyond that for the cars to actually reach the market. When the program was approved, its development was once again turned over to the general office rather than the divisions. New "project centers" were created within the technical staff to oversee design and development of the X-cars, giving the general office complete authority over engineering, manufacturing, and styling decisions.[79] Four divisions, some under orders from the Executive Committee, would sell some version of the X-car, yet all models would be essentially the same car with only minor variations in styling to distinguish cars marketed by different divisions. The X-car program was thus a continuation and extension of the Donner-Roche strategy. The car divisions had little or no input into or influence over product planning, while the general office had virtually taken over operating decisions. "The five car divisions had become isolated from the creation of the vehicles they would ultimately sell. With key decisions now made... by central engineering and manufacturing staffs, GM seemed blind to the market."[80]

The results of the X-car program paralleled those of the Vega. Between 1976 and 1978, while the X-cars were being developed, gasoline shortages eased, and consumers returned to large-car purchases, allowing GM to again achieve target levels for return on investment and market share to reach record highs. This recovery would be short-lived; in February 1979, the turmoil surrounding the fall of the shah of Iran produced rising fuel prices and a second gasoline shortage. Scheduled to go on sale in April 1979, the X-cars seemed perfectly poised to take advantage of the new crisis, and initial sales were brisk. Yet problems again surfaced quickly. The X-cars were recalled seven times during their first year of production, with "serious problems" in brakes, steering system, "manual transmissions and clutch, electrical system, fuel system, and paint."[81] Even the six-cylinder engine – a variation on a 25-year-old design – experienced difficulties.[82] Such problems continued well beyond the first year of production, damaging sales and reinforcing the belief the GM made poor-quality cars. Sales also suffered from the destruction of the pricing pyramid and the fact that X-cars sold by the four different divisions looked alike. By the time the new cars were introduced, four of GM's five divisions were selling cars in almost every price class, and models from different divisions looked virtually identical. As a result, divisional differentiation was minimal, and consumers were less willing to pay more for a Buick compact than a Chevrolet compact, since there

79 Hampton and Norman (1987, p. 106).   80 Hampton and Norman (1987, p. 106).
81 *Consumer Reports*, as quoted in Kuhn (1986, p. 308). See also Yates (1983, p. 47).
82 Keller (1989, p. 70). Kuhn (1986, pp. 338–339).

appeared to be (and was) little difference between them. Finally, the entire conversion to front-wheel drive required heavy capital expenditures that even brisk initial sales could not recoup. In 1979 GM's return on net investment fell almost one-third, to 22.7 percent. As the energy crisis worsened and quality problems with the new cars surfaced, sales and profits deteriorated.

The problems associated with the X-car program were not atypical. By the late 1970s, similar difficulties plagued most of GM's products. In 1977, for instance, an Oldsmobile owner sued GM for fraud when he learned that his car contained a Chevrolet engine. While such swapping was hardly new, it shocked consumers and led to a settlement costing GM as much as $40 million. Even more disturbing, component interdependence now extended beyond intended design tolerances. In 1979, the Center for Auto Safety disclosed that transmissions designed for the 2,100-pound Chevrolet Chevette had been used in a number of different GM models, including the 3,765-pound Chevrolet Caprice.[83] Many of the transmissions in the larger cars failed because they were not designed to handle the heavier weight of those vehicles. Top executives seemed unable to recognize or acknowledge the problems, and repeatedly made the same kinds of mistakes. When the corporation sought to introduce a new line of subcompact J-cars in the early 1980s, general office staff in charge of development simply borrowed components from the poor-quality X-cars, including a four-cylinder version of the 25-year-old engine.[84] Even more similar in appearance across models than their predecessors, the J-cars were offered by all five automobile divisions. Because these cars were once again heavier, more expensive, and inferior in performance and appearance when compared with foreign competition, none sold well. Plagued by internal confusion and contestation, GM seemed unable to adapt to the new market. In 1980, the corporation reported a loss for the first time in almost sixty years. Over the next decade, the decline would continue, as GM suffered losses in profits and market share. After being regarded for over half a century as the most efficient corporation in the world, General Motors' long reign had come to an end.

Summary

The textbook M-form put into place in 1958 led quickly to administrative centralization in which corporate headquarters, especially the CEO

---

83 The information on both the "Chevymobile" and the Chevette transmission can be found in Cray (1980, pp. 506–509).
84 Keller (1989, pp. 69–71); Yates (1983, Chapters 1 and 3).

and New York's finance staff, took control of policy decisions and encroached ever more deeply into operating affairs. Just as Sloan had done in the 1930s, Donner increased interdependence between the operating divisions in order to justify increased general office intervention. But Sloan's centralization had occurred in the context of a depressed market characterized by little market differentiation, while Donner's occurred in a relatively affluent period in which demand for automobiles was much less homogeneous and more differentiated. Even more important, Donner made virtually no effort to include the divisions in deliberations over these proposed policy changes, nor to persuade them to accept policies promulgated by headquarters. The result was a destruction of consent and the outbreak of open animosity between New York and Detroit. The destruction of consent was central to GM's decline. Absent either formal or informal participation in the planning process, division managers were predisposed to view Donner's moves as unwarranted incursions into the operating domain. Regardless of whether headquarters' proposals made economic or business sense, operating management resisted them. I have argued that the result was a downward spiral of distrust and dissension: when the divisions resisted general office initiatives through perfunctory performance and deceit, headquarters responded by intruding ever more deeply into operations.

The GM case is broadly consistent with Fligstein's argument that a "finance conception of control" emerged among U.S. corporations in the 1960s and 1970s.[85] Most of the secondary studies cited in this chapter criticize Donner's emphasis on narrowly financial criteria in decision-making, and divisional resistance to corporate policy was clearly exacerbated by Donner's lack of experience on the operating side of the organization. Yet the GM case underscores the fact that this shift had important organizational underpinnings: it occurred only after the reorganization of 1958 demolished structural mechanisms that would force those at the top to take the operating point of view seriously. Had the divisions been able to participate in planning and resource allocation or to exercise veto power over prospective policies, as they had throughout most of GM's history, it would have proved much more difficult for a finance conception of control to triumph. Instead, the trend was in the opposite direction. In the years following Donner's chairmanship, strategic planning and resource allocation became even more centralized in New York's financial staff, and decision-making came to rest even more exclusively on financial criteria. By the 1970s, group executives had been removed from the Executive Committee, leaving strategic planning completely in the hands of the chairman, the president, and a handful of

---

85 See Fligstein (1990).

executive vice-presidents. None of these men were in close contact with daily operations, and most had little or no experience on the operating side of the business. Far from increasing efficiency and improving governance, the textbook M-form led to GM's long decline.

8

Conclusion

The General Motors case raises important questions concerning the governance of the modern corporation. Clearly, the modifications to the M-form that were in place through most of GM's history did not arise out of ignorance or error, nor did they necessarily lead to suboptimal performance. Instead, such changes were introduced as a way of creating and maintaining cooperation and order within the firm. This chapter examines the implications of the GM case for organizational analysis and the theory of the firm. I begin by addressing the changing role of owners in the modern corporation. I argue that the M-form was originally created as a means of ensuring continuing owner control in the face of the ongoing growth and differentiation between the functions of ownership and management. Yet its efficacy as an instrument of owner control was predicated on assumptions that became increasingly problematic over time. Using the Du Pont–GM relationship as a starting point, I seek to understand the conditions under which shareholders can exert effective control over corporate governance. In the second half of the chapter I turn to the relation between general office and divisions in the M-form, contrasting efficiency accounts with an approach emphasizing the role of consent in corporate governance. I argue that these two types of explanations invoke very different understandings of cooperative action that raise important theoretical and practical questions concerning the relationships among consent, information, order, and efficiency in corporate governance.

The Limits of Owner Control

The first question raised by the GM case concerns the role of owners in the modern corporation. I have argued that owners at GM constrained top management's capacity to create consent by limiting headquarters' ability to introduce participative decentralization and administrative centralization. In effect, owners set the rules and limits within which headquarters had to operate when attempting to manufacture consent. But this formulation raises a number of questions. Why is it that owners at GM sometimes succeeded in constraining management, while at other times they seemed powerless? More fundamentally, why did they favor the textbook M-form to begin with, and why were they so vehemently opposed to Sloan's modifications to that structure? The answers to these questions lie in the fact that the M-form itself was initially created to reestablish and ensure owner control over the modern corporation. Yet its ability to do so was predicated on a number of assumptions that became increasingly problematic over time. In effect, owners' image of the M-form was grounded in a historically specific conception of governance – one that was beginning to crumble even as the M-form was put into place at General Motors.

Owners' conception of the M-form as a governance structure that would reestablish and solidify owner control over the modern corporation was implicitly built on four assumptions. First, it presupposed that hard budget constraints would remain in effect, making investment capital a scarce resource and thereby ensuring that shareholders would have considerable influence over strategic planning by virtue of their control over access to external investment funds. Despite the growing importance of professional management, owners would thus retain the ability to oversee corporate governance. Second, owners assumed that their oversight would continue to be accepted as legitimate and justified, both by the state and by managers inside GM. Believing that there was "just one central motive in industrial management, ... the permanent welfare of the owners of the business," Du Pont representatives assumed that their exercise of financial veto and their intervention into management affairs would be accepted by internal and external constituencies.[1] Third, owners believed that information from financial control mechanisms would provide them the knowledge and information necessary for evaluating competing investment claims, thereby allowing them to exercise intelligent veto over proposed policies. Finally, they implicitly assumed that the informal ties and relationships that they had relied on to run their own family business would, when combined with situational sanctions and financial veto, be sufficient for extracting compliance from professional managers at GM. Yet each of these assumptions was grounded in a historically specific image of the firm that looked back to an earlier era when owners also managed. As GM grew, these assumptions would become increasingly problematic, limiting owners' ability to constrain management and insist on a textbook M-form.

1 Brown (1927, p. 5), as reprinted in Chandler (1979).

Conclusion

I have argued that three factors were primarily responsible for weakening shareholder control and limiting owners' ability to implement a textbook M-form. The first was the existence of slack capital resources created by long periods of extensive surplus. As GM developed a substantial, continuing surplus, investment funds were no longer a scarce resource, and the cost of capital declined dramatically.[2] This weakened owners' ability to exercise financial veto over management by changing the way that prospective policies were evaluated. Owners found it increasingly difficult to claim that capital for funding proposed projects did not exist, and the criteria for justifying financial decisions came to focus more on an assessment of the consequences and trade-offs involved in particular policies and projects, rather than simply on whether funds were available and at what cost. Owners' difficulty in assessing prospective policies resulted from a second factor – their lack of knowledge of and direct involvement in the automobile business. Although the decomposition between strategic and tactical planning gave owners access to information concerning internal performance, it did not ensure that they would be capable of making sound judgments based on this information. The abstract statistical data provided from financial controls was by itself rarely adequate to make informed decisions about future investments and often was not even adequate for purposes of audit. For such information to be evaluated in depth, it needed to be combined with a "personal knowledge" of the business, its markets, and the trade-offs that various concrete decisions would entail.[3] For early owner representatives such personal knowledge was easier to come by – they had participated in the growth and management of the business, and following decentralization many continued to sit in on meetings of strategic planning committees. But over time, owners became more removed from the management side of the business and increasingly lost the ability to eval-

---

[2] The Hungarian economist János Kornai (1980; 1990) has emphasized that, over time, slack capital resources may also increase the demand for investment by creating soft budget constraints. When this occurs, the "strict relationship between expenditure and earnings" is relaxed, since actors remain confident that sufficient capital exists to cover proposed expenditures (1990, p. 21). Kornai contends that significant and continuing surplus has a profound impact on subjective expectations; under hard budget constraints "a deficit causes fear, because it may lead to extremely serious consequences," but under soft constraints there is a "relaxation of financial discipline, [and a] weakening of the feeling that spending, survival, [and] expansion depend on earning capability" (1990, p. 27). Although Kornai explicitly rejects the idea that the concept of soft budget constraints can be meaningfully applied to a single firm, the events in GM following World War II suggest that slack capital resources there may have had a similar psychological effect, increasing demands for capital at both the divisional level and general office level.

[3] Chandler (1990, p. 623; 1992, pp. 277–278) makes this point with reference to general office executives in the 1970s and 1980s, but it is equally applicable to owners at an earlier stage of historical development.

uate the information provided to them. As this happened, owners became dependent on management to interpret as well as provide information, and to that degree lost their autonomy from and control over the general office.[4] This was particularly true in later years, when owners lacked representation on committees dealing with the more detailed aspects of operating policy and thus had to rely extensively on management for information about these areas.

Slack capital resources and owners' relative lack of knowledge combined to effectively decrease shareholders' ability to exercise financial veto over policy decisions. While owner-controlled committees still held the formal authority to exercise financial veto, attempts to actually utilize this power in the face of soft budget constraints were likely to be viewed by management as unjustified and would give rise to resistance. Because capital was readily available, and because owners lacked both the information and expertise required for making broader policy evaluations, their veto was likely to be seen as irrational, arbitrary, or self-serving – a redistribution of surplus to shareholders rather than to "legitimate" needs of the corporation. Top operating executives in GM chafed at owner attempts to institute financial control, complaining publicly about "how little the board members know about the business"; even Alfred Sloan believed that under conditions of capital surplus, the Du Pont–dominated Finance Committee constituted a "financial dictatorship."[5] Thus, while owners continued to hold legitimate legal authority to exercise financial veto whenever they wanted, they were much less likely to do so in the face of soft budget constraints. Fearing that the exercise of such authority might well lead to resistance, owners hesitated to strike down management proposals that involved significant expenditures, even when they opposed those plans.[6]

The third factor inhibiting owners' ability to exercise financial veto was state regulation and the question of whether owner intervention would be perceived as legitimate by actors outside the firm. Antitrust laws in the United States have long reflected a suspicion both of large business and of corporations that use their holdings in other industrial enterprises to exercise operating control over those firms. Moreover, U.S. courts have often distinguished between investment for financial purposes and investment for the purpose of achieving oper-

---

4 Chandler (1962, p. 313).
5 The first quote is from GM executive vice-president Ormond Hunt, as quoted in United States Congress (1949, p. 570). The Sloan quote is from Alfred P. Sloan, Jr., to Walter S. Carpenter, April 11, 1942a, Accession 542, Box 837.
6 Note that this situation is directly related to the separation of ownership and management functions. If ownership and management functions continue to be fused, soft budget constraints allow owners more discretion, rather than less. Henry Ford provides a well-known example.

ating control.[7] Du Pont's concern over antitrust issues played a key role in owners' decision to create a distinction between financial and operating policy, and to eventually withdraw from the operating end of GM's affairs.[8] Du Pont's 1933 decision to end owner representation on GM's Executive Committee derived primarily from a fear that owner involvement in operations would increase owners' vulnerability to antitrust action. Similarly, owners' unhappiness with the Policy Committee stemmed at least in part from their fear that the committee's involvement in operating issues would leave owners open to lawsuits from both the state and shareholders. These fears were clearly warranted. The U.S. government's 1948 antitrust suit charged Du Pont and GM with restraint of trade and sought to show that E. I. du Pont de Nemours had used its shareholdings of GM to exercise undue influence over the policies and operations of the automaker. Following the 1948 suit, owners became hesitant to exercise even purely financial veto power. Even in the purely financial realm, soft budget constraints thus undermined the legitimacy of owner intervention. Since GM was one of the most successful corporations in the world, owner veto of management proposals risked being interpreted by outsiders as uninformed meddling in the affairs of a highly competent management team.

Finally, owners' hesitance to exercise financial veto was shaped at least in part by a fourth factor – their confidence and trust in Alfred Sloan. Although owners had long-standing and sometimes heated disagreements with Sloan and his methods, they had great respect for his managerial abilities and the record of success that GM had achieved under his leadership. It is unlikely that owners would have agreed to some of the organizational changes implemented by Sloan had they been promulgated by a less successful chief executive, especially since those changes often effectively reduced owner power and gave increased financial control to management. Pleased and impressed by GM's record of success and profitability, owners gave Sloan considerable latitude in running General Motors in the later years of his tenure. To a certain degree, then, their hesitance to exercise financial veto was embedded in personal and professional relations of trust. But it is important to remember that even though owners did not have the same confidence in Sloan's successors, they still found themselves unable to use their formal authority and control of financial resources to rein in management during the

---

7 On the more general antitrust climate in the United States, see Fligstein (1990); Roe (1994); Roy (1997). On the distinction between investment for financial and operating purposes, see *Gottesman et al. v. General Motors.* 279 F. Supp. 361, 1967, pp. 383–384.
8 In addition to the historical evidence cited in preceding chapters, see Dirlam and Stelzer (1958).

postwar era. By that time, soft budget constraints, lack of information, and issues of legitimacy had combined to paralyze owners' attempts at intervention.

This understanding has important implications for existing debates over corporate governance. Beginning with Berle and Means, the literature on the separation of ownership and control has focused on the question of whether owners or managers control the modern corporation. Although a number of scholars have accepted the Berle and Means conclusion that owners no longer exercise effective control over the corporation, a diverse set of observers, including agency theorists and Marxists alike, have focused on formal and informal governance mechanisms that, in their view, can allow owners to retain such command.[9] The GM case suggests that we might better ask under what conditions such mechanisms are effective, and under what conditions they begin to fail. The GM case supports the contention of Chandler and others that financial controls alone are not sufficient to provide owners with effective control over the corporation, primarily because the abstract information provided by such mechanisms is rarely sufficient to allow owners to evaluate prospective policies. This being the case, owners in the modern corporation often remain "captives of the professional entrepreneurs," despite the fact that they hold the power to hire and fire management and veto management proposals.[10] Less recognized, however, is the enormous importance of institutional factors in determining the efficacy of mechanisms designed to ensure owner control over the corporation. Although a number of scholars recognize that antitrust law has played an important role in shaping organizational form and managerial strategies of expansion, there has been less attention paid to the fact that state intervention has also influenced owners' willingness to exercise control over existing corporate assets.[11] The literature on property rights and agency theory takes it as a given that owners have a relatively unencumbered right to exercise control over financial assets, property, and management initiatives. Yet the GM case suggests that actual and potential state interventions often present a challenge to such rights, making owners hesitant to exercise their legal prerogatives.

9 The literature on ownership and control issues is vast. For an extremely abbreviated sampling, see the following: Marris (1964); Domhoff (1967); Bunting and Barbour (1971); Zeitlin (1974; 1989); Fama (1980); Mizruchi (1982; 1983); Fama and Jensen (1983); Jensen (1983); Mintz and Schwartz (1985); Jensen and Meckling (1986); Demsetz (1988); Easterbrook and Fischel (1991); Roy (1997). In addition to these sources, see the symposium published in the *Journal of Law and Economics*, 26:301–326, 1983, for an overview of agency-theory debates on the issue.
10 Chandler (1962, p. 313).
11 For a partial exception, see Roe (1994); on the importance of antitrust law in shaping corporate form and strategy in the United States more generally, see Fligstein (1990).

Perhaps the most important implication of the GM case in this regard, however, is that technical factors like profitability can have significant, unanticipated consequences for the perceived legitimacy of owner control. Few internal or external observers would have disputed that E. I. du Pont de Nemours was legally empowered to intervene in GM's internal affairs, and in most instances, both state and federal courts would have readily upheld this power. But, as I have argued, sustained surplus made the effective exercise of such rights problematic within the firm by making it difficult for owners to claim that funds for proposed policies were not available, thereby creating a subtle shift in the way policies were evaluated. Under these conditions, owners' exercise of their "legitimate" property rights ran the risk of engendering overt or covert resistance from top management. Recognizing that top executives were likely to resist intervention under these conditions, Du Pont representatives reluctantly ceded much of their power to management. Some readers may object that this is neither surprising nor alarming. There is no need for owners to intervene when a firm is profitable, they might contend, for profitability is a sign of efficient management. When returns are threatened, on the other hand, owners can and do take corrective action. Yet the GM case suggests that there is considerable cause for skepticism of this view. First, as was outlined earlier, owners remained dependent on management both for information and for its interpretation, making it difficult for them to intervene in an independent and informed way. Second, and more problematic, even when owners insisted on exercising their legal right to intervene, the outcome was often extensive managerial resistance. In the years immediately after the war, for instance, owners intervened in GM's affairs when management continued to pursue expansion in the face of a capital shortage. The split between finance and operations that emerged in the ensuing years was a direct outcome of owner intervention. Finally, we should keep in mind that the du Ponts were relatively strong owners. They owned nearly one-quarter of GM's voting stock, they had at least some knowledge of the automobile business, and they had a long history of formal and informal relationships with top executives at General Motors. All of these factors put them in a much better position to exercise control than their successors would have, yet their success in constraining GM management is debatable at best.

Taken together, the findings outlined here suggest that it is erroneous to think of ownership as simply a set of formal legal and property rights that can be invoked at will. The effective exercise of these rights depends crucially on both technical and institutional conditions, both of which can affect the perceived legitimacy of owner intervention. When owners insist on exercising their "legitimate" rights in the face of unfavorable conditions, the result is likely to be a disruption of corporate governance and extensive conflict between owners and managers.

Ownership, Authority, and Embeddedness

While the nature of budget constraints facing the firm may explain owners' ability to coerce management, this still does not tell us why owners at GM favored the textbook M-form in the first place. The reasons behind their desire for a superordinate Finance Committee are clear enough: such a body was the primary mechanism for ensuring owner oversight and control. But why were they so adamantly opposed to participative decentralization and administrative centralization? I have argued that the du Ponts' enthusiasm for the textbook M-form arose out of their experience as owner-managers of E. I. du Pont de Nemours. The textbook M-form had succeeded admirably there, and the du Ponts were convinced that GM would benefit from its adoption. Moreover, success at Du Pont had occurred despite owners' seeming lack of concern with issues of consent in corporate governance there. Like today's efficiency theorists, they believed that order could be achieved through the application of fiat in the context of a firm distinction between strategic and tactical planning. In the case of their own company, at least, they seemed to be correct. Why did this philosophy fail at GM while succeeding at Du Pont?

Evidence suggests that the textbook M-form succeeded at Du Pont in large part because the extensive division of labor characteristic of the modern corporation had not progressed as far there as it had at General Motors. This was true at two levels. First, Du Pont was a firm in which owners also managed and possessed a knowledge of the business. In order to become top executives and members of the Finance or Executive Committee, they worked their way up through operations, gaining considerable experience in the business. This experience allowed them to retain much more effective financial control, for it meant that they were better able to evaluate prospective policies. Owners at Du Pont were thus less dependent on managers for information – or they were managers as well as owners – and they thereby retained substantive financial veto. They were not limited simply to approving or denying funds for prospective policies, but could actually evaluate and revise the substance of operating policies. This was true even when excess earnings created soft budget constraints at Du Pont. The relative fusion of ownership and management roles at Du Pont, in conjunction with owners' greater knowledge of the business, meant that there was less interdependence and thus less room for managerial discretion.

The textbook M-form also succeeded at Du Pont because the chemical company's smaller size and its relative fusion of ownership and management made it easier to produce consent through informal practices rather than requiring formal organizational mechanisms. There were two primary reasons for this. First, authority relations at Du Pont were deeply embedded in personal and family ties. There was a recognition that "no one gets into the top management of this company... unless he's married to one of them [i.e., a du Pont]," a practice that continued well into the 1950s.[12] As a consequence, authority relations at Du Pont had a much more patrimonial tinge than those at GM. Second, the relative fusion of roles, along with Du Pont's smaller size, allowed for close, daily contact among owners, corporate headquarters, and the divisions. Although Du Pont was a more diversified firm than GM, and thus presumably more complex in that it operated in many distinct markets, it was nonetheless considerably smaller in size, with far fewer divisions.[13] Smaller size meant that in Du Pont "everything is closely tied in together and... there is a continual crossover between departments."[14] Donaldson Brown, who served as a top executive in both corporations, emphasized that in Du Pont "you are all together in Wilmington. Views are exchanged on corporate matters in the normal course," and policy issues could be worked out through formal action in the Executive Committee or "by way of informal discussion" among owners, executives, and managers in Wilmington.[15] This daily informal contact, coupled with the du Ponts' substantive knowledge of the business, worked to create consent. Because owners, top executives, and division managers could discuss policy issues face-to-face on a daily basis, agreement on policy issues could be reached outside of top committee meetings, and there was less of a sense that policies were handed down from on high. The relative fusion of ownership and management, owners' knowledge of the business, geographic proximity, and the embeddedness of communication and authority in personal, patrimonial relationships all worked together to make the production of consent less problematic at Du Pont.

At General Motors, geographical separation and a more extensive division of labor disrupted informal social networks and created a need for formal mechanisms to produce consent. Brown insisted that "the problems of General Motors" were "entirely different" from those

---

12 Drucker (1978, p. 265), paraphrasing an observation made by Donaldson Brown.
13 For information on Du Pont's divisions in the 1920s and 1930s, see Chandler (1991b, p. 45). Compare this to the number of divisions at General Motors by examining General Motors Corporation, "Organization Chart," 1924, 1937.
14 Alfred P. Sloan, Jr., to Lammot du Pont, April 13, 1942. *U.S. v. Du Pont*, GE #150.
15 Donaldson Brown to Walter S. Carpenter, Jr., September 8, 1938, Accession 542, Box 821. Note that for most of the period under consideration, there was often little distinction between "owners" and "top executives" at Du Pont.

at Du Pont, making the textbook M-form inappropriate at the former.[16] More specifically, at GM "the chief operating executive is located in New York – 800 miles distant from the President of the Company and the principal operating executives." This geographic distance was probably partly responsible for the long history of divisional independence that arose under Durant and continued into the Du Pont era. In addition, GM was larger and more complex and had more operating divisions than Du Pont, despite the chemical company's greater diversification. Finally, owners at GM had a much more limited knowledge of the automobile business and were thus less competent to evaluate policy proposals and less capable of exercising financial control. The lack of regular, face-to-face contact among top executives, managers, and owners meant that at GM, informal networks and discussions were not sufficient to produce agreement among the various actors in the firm. Instead, growth, the division of labor, geographic distance, and the diminishing importance of personal and family ties combined to make achievement of consent less automatic and more problematic.[17] In order to create cooperation between different levels of management, formal mechanisms had to be devised. Ironically, the move to rationalize decision-making and to base planning on "facts" rather than on formal and personal authority that occurred under Sloan and Pierre du Pont probably helped to further undermine the binding power of informal ties at GM, thereby increasing the need for formal mechanisms to produce consent. Finally, because the dynamics of consent were largely invisible and taken for granted at Du Pont, representatives of the chemical company were baffled by Sloan's

16 Donaldson Brown to Walter S. Carpenter, Jr., September 8, 1938, Accession 542, Box 821. The following quote is from the same source.
17 As Du Pont grew, it faced many of the same issues that Sloan and GM had wrestled with decades earlier. Following World War II, the number and size of operating divisions within Du Pont increased significantly. As this occurred, the rigid separation between strategic and tactical planning became a liability, and long-range planning devolved to the divisional level. "Close working contact between members of the Executive Committee at headquarters and the senior division managers disintegrated. The [Executive] Committee now did little more than approve of divisional plans and review actual performance by relating it to the plans." Executive management at Du Pont, raised on an ideology of the textbook M-form, took much longer to adapt to these new conditions. In the 1960s and 1970s, corporate headquarters sought to reclaim its authority by exercising more control over resource allocation and becoming more involved in strategic planning. These efforts were largely unsuccessful and led to conflict. In 1991, a radical reorganization was effected which eliminated both the Executive Committee and the divisions, redefining the latter along functional lines. The new body in charge of strategic planning – the 24-member Operating Group – included both top executives as well as managers allied with particular operations. It is too early to tell what the outcome of this change will be, but it is important to note that Du Pont, like GM, eventually found it necessary to include operating management in the planning process as the division of labor progressed. See Chandler (1991b, pp. 45–48).

continual attention to the issue at GM. The du Ponts saw little need to create formal mechanisms for producing cooperation either between owners and managers or between different levels of management. Unaware of the social bases of consent in their own firm, the du Ponts assumed that problems of cooperation and authority either would work themselves out naturally or could be addressed entirely through the crafting of economic incentives.

The GM case suggests that the textbook M-form is most appropriate as a mechanism for owner control when the division of labor among owners, top executives, and line managers is moderate but not extensive. It is thus not surprising that the decentralized structure first arose in large firms that were either directly managed or closely controlled by a group of dominant owners. These businesses were the first to feel the strains of differentiation, and when crises developed, owners reacted by creating the M-form as a means of retaining their control over the firm. Yet the textbook M-form that they created was predicated on short-lived historical conditions. With continued growth, the assumptions behind the owner-dominated version of the M-form became increasingly problematic: excess capital created soft budget constraints; owners became more removed from the management of the business and were thus less able to adjudicate competing claims; and informal patrimonial ties became less effective in regulating behavior, as social relationships were increasingly rationalized by specialization within the firm. As these developments occurred, the textbook M-form became less able to maintain social order, and owners were less able to exercise active and intelligent financial control over the firm. Even before Du Pont was forced to divest its holdings in GM, owner representation on top committees declined over the years, thereby diminishing owners' ability to exercise even formal financial veto. Following the atomization of ownership that occurred after 1958, top committees were dominated by management representatives, and there was much less formal or informal contact between management and owner representatives. In this situation, it is not hard to imagine that the mechanisms of governance originally designed to allow owners to retain control of the modern corporation were even less effective.

More generally, the brief GM–Du Pont comparison outlined here raises important questions regarding the embedded nature of consent and corporate order.[18] As I pointed out in Chapter 1, much of the industrial sociology of the 1950s tended to dismiss formal structure as largely irrelevant to issues of consent and cooperation, arguing that order within

---

18 I am indebted to Mark Granovetter for emphasizing many of the issues highlighted in this paragraph and the following. He would undoubtedly disagree with many of my conclusions.

the firm derived primarily from informal networks and social relations. Not surprisingly, the GM–Du Pont comparison suggests that this image of order as completely and overtly embedded in personal ties may be more appropriate to the smaller, family-owned firm. When ownership and management are fused and specialization is minimal, authority rests heavily on patrimonial ties and daily social relations inside and outside of the corporation. In this context, consent may indeed rely more overtly on informal organization, and its production may seem both invisible and automatic. But in the Western world, at least, the ongoing development of the modern corporation disrupts the effectiveness of such informal sources of cooperation in a number of ways. As ownership holdings are fragmented and as owners become "outsiders" to the businesses they oversee, both patrimonially tinged authority and the ability to make informed judgments about the business decline. As corporations become larger and scattered over a wider geographic area, informal ties – between owners and managers and within management ranks – become more difficult to develop and sustain. And as specialization increases, the tension between formal authority and expertise is heightened, making subordinates less likely to accept orders or advice from above – be they from owners or higher-level managers. For all of these reasons, the rationalization and development of the modern corporation may problematize or undermine the informal bases of cooperation, making it necessary to supplement them with more formal mechanisms for creating and maintaining order.

To say that formal mechanisms for producing consent have become more important should not be taken to mean that informal ones have disappeared or become irrelevant, however. Even in the modern corporation, cooperation continues to be embedded in personal relations in complex and subtle ways. As the historical evidence makes clear, the du Ponts allowed Alfred Sloan to implement and preserve an organization about which they had grave reservations. I have argued that they did so at least in part because their continued association with Sloan created trust and confidence in both his business judgment and his good intentions. It is extremely unlikely that they would have given such leeway to a CEO they knew less well. Indeed, when Sloan was replaced by Wilson and later Curtice, relations between owners and managers also changed. Although I have argued that this change was due primarily to the structural, technical, and institutional factors that I have described in the preceding chapters, some of it was undoubtedly due to the changes in informal relations wrought by the introduction of new players and personalities. The GM structure may thus have functioned or failed at least in part because of the identities of key actors and the nature of their personal history and relationships. Had owners insisted on enforcing their prerogatives more strictly during Sloan's era, it is quite possible that organization and cooperation would have taken on a very different tone at General Motors. Similar dynamics probably played a role in the relationships between GM headquarters and divisions. Sloan's ability to create consent undoubtedly rested to no small degree on his long association with others in top management, his almost hallowed reputation as a gifted CEO, and his willingness to compromise when necessary. Conversely, it is quite clear that the conflicts between finance and operations that emerged after World War II were due at least in some degree to longstanding rivalry and jealousy between Donaldson Brown and Charles Wilson.

Throughout this book, I have argued that the shifts that took place at GM, as well as the need for consent itself, were systematically related to technical and institutional factors. I have further argued that as the modern corporation has developed, formal mechanisms have become more important as sources for creating order within the firm. But this does not mean that informal relations are therefore unimportant. Rather, future research on consent and cooperation needs to focus on the agenda set by Chester Barnard over half a century ago – to examine the ways in which formal organization and informal organization constrain and reinforce one another, and the ways in which they work against one another, creating tensions and contradictions.

Management and Authority in the M-form

I have argued that the distinction between divisions and general office does not resolve the problem of order in the modern corporation so much as it re-creates it within management ranks. Divisionalization is a form of specialization that arises to enhance technical efficiency. As the firm enters separate markets, it creates unique units dedicated to addressing uncertainty in each. But this division of labor, while technically efficient, has unanticipated social consequences; it creates a problem of social order. Problems of cooperation arise primarily from two sources. First, issues of resource dependence mean that as divisions become more specialized, they come to control unique resources and information to which headquarters needs access in order to carry out strategic planning. The interdependence created by specialization and resource dependence means that no single actor controls all of the resources and information necessary for governing through fiat, a fact that has been emphasized by resource-dependence accounts.[19] Second, and less recognized, specialization gives rise to normative expectations that divisional knowledge will be utilized in the planning process. By constructing and institutionalizing divisional spheres of expertise, the M-form defines a system in which failure to utilize specialized knowledge controlled by the divisions will be seen as irrational and unjustified. Competing logics of order and efficiency thus build contradiction into the heart of the M-form, for the very practices that maximize efficiency and rationalize information processing are also likely to disrupt order within the firm. In this view, the distinction between strategic and tactical planning that reduces opportunism and bounded rationality also engenders divisional resistance to policies handed down from above, precisely because it excludes the divisions from planning and resource allocation.

The idea that the M-form involved trade-offs between efficiency and cooperation was central to Alfred Sloan's concept of governance. In his view, it was centralization that created efficiency and cost reduction, while decentralization led to "initiative, responsibility [and] all the qualities necessary for an organization to adapt to new conditions."[20] Since Sloan believed that it was impossible to maximize both simultaneously, he relied on a form of satisficing in which efforts to create consent led him to temper the emphasis on efficiency. Yet the need for consent was itself not a constant, but varied with the extent to which divisions served separate markets. That is, when divisions operated in unique and distinct markets, each developed different areas of expertise, and the need for consent was high. When they competed in the same market, their knowledge was redundant, and the need for consent was lower. As a result, the balance between coercion and consent changed with the extent of divisional involvement in different market segments, resulting in shifts between participative decentralization and administrative centralization at the top of GM's governance structure.

Periods of administrative centralization arose first and foremost as an effort to increase efficiency by reducing costs, and they implemented a form of order that relied more on fiat than consent. The centralization of the 1930s, for instance, arose during a period of market stability, reduced product innovation, and lack of demand differentiation created by the depression. Competition in the automobile market during this period centered more on cost than quality, for product variety was low, and technological innovation resulted in little or no competitive advantage. Stability and the reduced need for innovation meant that top exec-

---

19 For similar views, see the following: Dalton (1950; 1959); Cyert and March (1963); Crozier (1964); Hickson et al. (1971); Hinings et al. (1974); Pfeffer and Salancik (1978); Pfeffer (1980); Perrow (1981; 1986); Eccles (1985); Eccles and White (1988).
20 Sloan (1964, p. 429).

utives in headquarters effectively possessed better information, since there was relatively little market uncertainty to which the corporation had to adapt. In this context, financial controls provided information sufficient for loss prevention, while value creation required little in the way of technical innovation. Equally important, however, the stable technical environment allowed Sloan to introduce internal structural changes that reduced the need for consent. When market differentiation declined in the 1930s, GM did not simply reduce its internal differentiation to match the changes occurring in the external environment. Rather, the corporation retained internal differentiation between the divisions, forcing them to compete with one another in the market for low-priced cars. This tactic reduced the need for divisional consent, for it meant that a division could no longer claim to possess a unique sphere of jurisdiction or expertise. The combination of better information at the top and reduced autonomy in the divisions allowed administrative centralization to be relatively successful, for in this environment headquarters could rely more extensively on sanctions and fiat. Moreover, the forms of uncertainty that did exist during this period – labor unrest, increasing state intervention, and new forms of legal regulation – encouraged centralization, for these uncertainties in the institutional environment called for a uniform corporate response across operating divisions.

The GM case also suggests that relying too extensively on fiat and sanctions may be inadvisable, even when markets are extremely stable and undifferentiated. During the 1930s, Sloan was careful to combine centralization with changes that undermined divisional claims to autonomy and redefined managerial expectations, thereby attenuating the need for consent. Yet even during this period, Sloan and other top executives at GM attempted to keep division managers "in the loop" by explaining their decisions, soliciting objections, and trying to work out differences. Despite these efforts, however, the changes made in the 1930s created divisional resistance to corporate policies, and GM was outperformed by Chrysler throughout this period. When headquarters failed to take such steps in the period after 1958, centralization created much more severe and prolonged resistance from below. During this period, the internal control and incentive mechanisms designed to constrain divisional discretion were inadequate to forestall continuing divisional rebellion. The resistance that occurred during this period did not show up immediately on the balance sheets. Centralization reduced costs in the 1960s, just as it had in the 1930s. Indeed, the centralization of the 1960s was far more effective than that of the 1930s in terms of short-run profitability. But cost reduction came at the expense of adaptability and product quality. Absent cooperation with the divisions, the general office could not respond effectively to changes in the marketplace that required innovation and adaptation. Consequently, as the stable markets of the 1950s gave way to the more competitive world of the 1970s, the destruction of consent extracted its toll.

GM's lengthy periods of participative decentralization implemented a form of cooperation that relied less on fiat and more on consent. When divisions served highly differentiated markets, headquarters' access to the information necessary for value creation and its ability to force compliance from the divisions were both limited. Differentiation also created expectations that divisional expertise would be incorporated into the planning process – expectations that persisted even when the information residing in the divisions was known and understood at higher levels. In response to these factors, Sloan implemented participative decentralization as a way of creating adaptability, cooperation, and consummate performance at the divisional level. His basic insight was that if divisional managers took part in formulating policies, they would be more likely to accept those policies and more committed to carrying them out in consummate fashion. Yet in attempting to create consent, Sloan faced a dilemma. On the one hand, he was constrained by owners, who were opposed to participative decentralization. More important in the present context, he did not wish simply to turn strategic decision-making over to the divisions, nor was he attempting to create an industrial democracy in which all actors were equal. To the contrary, Sloan sought to devise a system that retained general office hegemony over strategic planning, despite the inclusion of divisional management in that process.

Sloan and his colleagues used a number of different strategies over time in their attempts to create consent while retaining general office hegemony. In the 1920s, with strong pressure from owners to maintain a textbook M-form, divisional participation in planning occurred informally, making it difficult for operating men to dominate the strategic planning process. In the years after 1942, divisions were formally represented on committees responsible for strategic planning and resource allocation, giving them more influence in these processes. Yet during this period, the distinction between policy formulation and policy approval meant that the general office could often retain control of the general parameters of planning and the premises of decision-making. Policies were formulated in the functionally defined policy groups, where top executives and general office staff dominated. Proposed policies were then discussed, amended, ratified, or rejected in the Administration Committee, where divisional representatives participated. During the period from 1942 to 1946, further safeguards were provided by the fact that the superordinate Policy Committee could review, modify, or overturn

Administration Committee decisions if it so desired. Similarly, the Operating Policy Committee that existed from 1946 until 1958 could, at least in theory, overturn Administration Committee recommendations.

Despite these safeguards, divisional participation in planning was more than a form of symbolic or ritualistic co-optation that left real power in the hands of top executives. Participative decentralization gave the divisions substantive, if limited, power in the strategic planning process. Through their representation on bodies such as the Administration and Operating Policy Committees, divisional representatives could and did exert influence over long-range planning and resource allocation. Sometimes this influence extended to the pursuit of self-interested policies and decisions. Despite safeguards designed to ensure general office hegemony over planning, Sloan was reluctant to invoke fiat as a means of maintaining order, even when he knew or suspected such opportunism was at work. Because he believed that "issuing an order ... antagonized [subordinates] and [undermined] cooperation" at the divisional level, Sloan rarely used fiat to overturn divisional recommendations passed in the Administration Committee.[21] To be sure, the general office used available information to monitor the divisions, and top executives utilized pressure and coercion in their attempts to constrain opportunism. But when proposed policies encountered "antagonism," headquarters would "back out of the proposition and do some selling" in order to convince divisions that the policy was desirable. If the general office could not obtain the outcomes it wanted through this combination of persuasion and coercion, it often let operating management have its way, rather than using force to obtain compliance. Indeed, when the financial side of the organization did invoke fiat in the post–World War II era, the result was a protracted struggle between the financial and operating sides of the organization. Just as Sloan had feared, reliance on fiat led not to order and consummate performance, but to contestation and political infighting.

This view can be usefully contrasted with theories of the firm that understand internal organization primarily or exclusively in efficiency terms. Transaction cost economics (TCE) resurrects the problem of order in organizational analysis by raising dual issues of imperfect information and opportunism. But it then reduces the latter to the former, arguing that the way to motivate actors and constrain opportunism is through obtaining better information. In this formulation, both simple compliance and consummate performance are the outcomes of reward and punishment mechanisms that use improved information to reduce oppor-

---

21 Sloan (1969).

tunism and reward obedience. The GM case proves problematic for this view, because it suggests that order within the firm cannot be reduced to issues of information and fiat. Once efficiency and order are conceptualized as analytically independent factors, the neat symmetry involving information, compliance, and consummate performance is burst, and the trade-offs between these issues are often much more pronounced than indicated by TCE. In this world, order rests on voluntary acceptance as well as coercion, and reliance on fiat may lead to resistance and contestation rather than cooperation. These two approaches thus offer different images of order within the firm and different understandings of the trade-offs between consent and cost reduction.

The image of order as fiat developed by TCE and other efficiency theories of the firm is more appropriate for describing governance during periods of administrative centralization. Ironically, although Williamson expresses puzzlement that the temptation to centralize "is evidently difficult to resist" for top executives, TCE's theoretical framework is well suited to explaining this phenomenon.[22] An approach that sees fiat as the source of order, and information as the basis of effective fiat, will logically conclude that when the general office has access to adequate information, it will be able to make informed operating decisions, control opportunism, and extract compliance from subordinates, even as it usurps their prerogatives. This formulation is implicit in TCE's assertion that the "appropriate" degree of general office involvement in operating decisions varies with the extent to which information gives corporate headquarters the capacity to make such decisions.[23] Yet this conceptualization overlooks the fact that order based in fiat is very likely to erode both adaptability and motivation over the longer run. In a dynamic world of market uncertainty and complex interdependence, this image of order will not be viable, and new methods of organizing cooperation within the firm will have to be found.

TCE encounters much greater difficulties when it attempts to explain participative decentralization, for such efforts invariably violate the assumptions underlying efficiency theory. Proponents of TCE generally attempt to explain participative decentralization in one of two ways. The first and less satisfactory is to argue that participation in planning occurs as a means of extracting information from divisional management when internal monitoring mechanisms are incapable of providing such knowledge.[24] This explanation preserves TCE's emphasis on the importance of information in governance, but it assumes away problems of opportunism. Williamson is quite clear that "the concentration of strategic

22 Williamson (1975, p. 149).
23 Williamson (1975, pp. 151, 147, n. 13). See also Allen (1970).
24 See Shanley (1996).

decisions and controls in the general office is precisely what the M-form
... is designed to accomplish."[25] But if this is the case, divisional involvement in planning should lead to opportunism no matter what information it may introduce. Arrangements that allow the divisions to participate in strategic planning because monitoring mechanisms are imperfect will surely allow operating management to engage in costly, self-interested behavior. Such arrangements would thus be no more efficient than a centralized organization or market contracting, for any information gains created by participation would quickly be dissipated through opportunism. An approach that sees participative decentralization solely in information-processing terms thus violates the logic of TCE's theory in one of two ways: either it drops the assumption of opportunism, or it forgoes the claim that transactions within the M-form are less costly than those in the centralized structure.[26]

Cognizant of these difficulties, a second reformulation argues that participative decentralization arises precisely because the M-form's financial controls and sanctions prove adequate for maintaining order within the firm, making it unnecessary to maintain a rigid distinction between planning and operations. In this view, internal control mechanisms provide information sufficient to curtail opportunism. Once these monitoring mechanisms are in place, divisional participation in planning can occur as a means of co-opting divisional resistance and transmitting more detailed knowledge to headquarters. Should subgoal pursuit be detected, the general office can step in and remedy the situation by ordering the offending parties to change their behavior. This approach is more compelling, for it preserves the logic of TCE while allowing some room for the dynamics of consent. Moreover, such an explanation seems consistent with the fact that participative decentralization at GM was often accompanied by safeguards that attempted to ensure headquarters' hegemony over the planning process. Such safeguards would appear to indicate that top executives at GM retained the ability to intervene and overturn divisional recommendations when opportunism was detected. Yet this view, while more consistent with TCE's underlying assumptions, remains problematic.

---

25 Williamson (1983, pp. 355–356).
26 It may be plausible to argue that participative decentralization is used as a means of extracting information under temporary conditions of extreme uncertainty like those caused by GM's conversion to wartime production. Here, the need for knowledge essential to adaptation might outweigh the temporary prospects for and costs of opportunism. Once again, however, continuing participation over the longer run would not be expected, according to TCE, for it would result in costly opportunism, thus dissipating whatever informational gains were initially present. Participative decentralization at GM lasted for decades, making it difficult to view it as a temporary means of obtaining information.

The notion that participation in planning occurs when monitoring mechanisms are sufficient to control divisional indiscretion encounters two related difficulties. First, TCE has repeatedly warned that situational sanctions and informal influence by themselves cannot constrain opportunism once division managers are formally included in the planning and resource allocation process.[27] As Williamson has put it, if the divisions gain representation on the committees responsible for planning and resource allocation, "partisan political input [is] reintroduced" and "the organizational integrity of the M-form [is] fundamentally compromised."[28] The GM case strongly suggests that this view is correct. Division managers on GM's governing committees engaged in a variety of self-interested behaviors: trading votes over appropriations and salaries; pursuing "reckless" expansion against the advice of financial overseers; voting, against the recommendations of finance staff, to enter new businesses; and doctoring financial projections to preserve pet projects. This evidence suggests that participative decentralization was implemented at GM even though it increased opportunism and thereby raised the cost of governance. Even more problematic for efficiency accounts is the fact that Sloan and other top executives often chose not to curb such behavior, even when they knew it was present. Sloan attempted to overcome divisional indiscretion through a process of "selling" that combined persuasion and coercion. In some cases, his efforts at selling or persuading the divisions lasted for years – hardly an image of the efficient use of fiat for resolving disputes. Moreover, when resistance could not be quelled through persuasion and coercion, Sloan only rarely reverted to the alternative of issuing a direct order. Rather, he let the divisions have their way – he opted to live with divisional indiscretion in order to preserve cooperation. This approach is incomprehensible from the perspective of a theory that assumes boundedly rational managers who curb opportunism and align incentives based on the best information available.

The problems that TCE encounters in attempting to explain the variations at GM are deeply rooted in the theoretical logic of efficiency accounts. In the following section I return to a discussion of theoretical logic, arguing that overcoming these difficulties requires a revolution in organization theory. Once we introduce issues of consent and consummate performance, the assumptions underlying economic theories of the firm begin to crumble. To grasp the limits of hierarchy – indeed, to understand efficiency itself – we must acknowledge the social and nonrational dimensions of human behavior, and we must systematically incorporate these elements into the theory of the firm.

27 See, for instance, Williamson (1983, pp. 355–356; 1985, pp. 283–284).
28 Williamson (1983, pp. 355–356).

Order, Efficiency, and Rationality in Organization Theory

The idea that overreliance on fiat can produce disorder rather than cooperation is not new. Indeed, Oliver Williamson clearly acknowledges that this is the case, and he goes on to advise that we must focus on issues of whether authority is excessive or commands general respect.[29] For this reason, some commentators have expressed puzzlement and even indignation at the claim that economic theories of the firm are poorly equipped to understand the GM case.[30] Efficiency theories, they assert, have taken note of and accounted for such problems. It is my contention, however, that economic theories of the firm are incapable of making a meaningful distinction between "excessive" fiat and "respected" authority. To understand why this is the case, we must return to a discussion of theoretical logic. In this section, I make two related arguments. First, I show that the problems that TCE encounters in attempting to explain the variations at GM are deeply rooted in the theoretical logic of efficiency accounts. When we introduce issues of consent and consummate performance, the core assumptions underlying economic theories of the firm begin to unravel, creating intractable problems. Second, I argue that a theory that fails to systematically incorporate these elements into its framework will remain incapable of conceptualizing or operationalizing either bureaucratic dysfunction or efficiency with adequate specificity.

The economic theory of the firm constitutes what is commonly referred to in the social sciences as a rational-choice theory.[31] Such theories assume, among other things, that actors inside the firm (1) are motivated by self-interest and (2) use the most expedient means available to realize that interest. In these accounts, actions "are chosen not for themselves, but as more or less efficient means to a further end."[32] Rational-choice theories do not maintain that people *always* behave rationally; they acknowledge that norms and nonrational value commitments sometimes influence what people do.[33] But their models have little to say about such nonrational action. More technically, rationality is the only positively stated normative orientation within these models; such theories assume that action,

---

29 Williamson (1985, p. 239).
30 See the exchange between Shanley (1996) and Freeland (1996).
31 For a good overview and introduction to elementary rational-choice theory, see Elster (1989). The best critique of such theories, in my view, is still to be found in Parsons (1968, Chapters 1–3).
32 Elster (1989, p. 22).
33 Even a cursory glance at the current social-science literature in economics, political science, and sociology shows that the domain of admittedly nonrational behavior seems to be shrinking, however. These days, activities as diverse as voting, marriage, and friendship have all been modeled as rational exchange relationships.

whatever its actual motivation, can be modeled "as if" it were rational.[34] These assumptions lead the economic theory of the firm to conceptualize order (and thus efficiency) as an outcome of self-interest: order is realized by aligning the interest of the individual with the goals of the firm through the use of reward and punishment mechanisms. The failure of cooperation is also attributed to self-interest. Opportunistic actors couple self-interested behavior with deception, exploiting lacunae in reward and punishment mechanisms to pursue their own agendas at the expense of the corporation. The assertion that both order and disorder are to be understood as the rational pursuit of self-interest is what, at bottom, creates such difficulty for the economic theory of the firm when it attempts to explain the variations at GM.[35] The GM case suggests that both bureaucratic resistance and consummate performance are rooted to a substantial degree in nonrational commitments. But rational-choice theories cannot conceptualize or operationalize such commitments without violating their core assumptions or falling into tautology. Such theories thus encounter intractable difficulties once they attempt to grapple with the nonrational dimensions of corporate governance.

These problems are easiest to see when we examine the limits of hierarchy and fiat. As outlined earlier, resistance to fiat is often seen as rationally motivated: people defy and subvert orders because they are attempting to pursue their own interests.[36] But organizational analysts also recognize that normative commitments are primary sources of such behavior. That is, they acknowledge that resistance to fiat is sometimes based not in self-interested calculation but in normative commitments.

34 A few examples may be helpful. Economists often acknowledge that people do not always carefully weigh and calculate alternatives before making a decision, but they argue that people's behavior can be accurately modeled in terms of such rational cost–benefit analysis. Similarly, as Michael Weinstein used to point out to me, it is undoubtedly the case that Willie Mays – who is reputed never to have dropped a fly ball – did not perform complex vector analysis when playing baseball. Nevertheless, the actions he undertook in fielding fly balls can be modeled "as if" he performed such analyses.

35 These assumptions are not unique to economic accounts; rather, they are simply expressed more clearly and systematically in such theories. Rational-choice presuppositions pervade most of the organizational literature. Approaches that emphasize the political dimensions of corporate governance and the need for coalition-building among constituencies, for instance, tend to assume rational actors who pursue individual or collective interests via the most expedient means available. One well-known example can be found in the work of Cyert and March (1963), which is more explicit about behavioral assumptions than most political models. But other accounts that emphasize power and resource dependence also tend to assume rational actors, albeit less formally and systematically. For this reason, the criticisms that I make of economic theories of the firm apply, with some modifications, to a much wider range of research.

36 This formulation characterizes not only economic theories of the firm but also many "political" models that treat governance as a compromise between a number of actors pursuing different interests. See, for example, Cyert and March (1963).

When this is the case, people resist authority not because they will benefit from doing so – indeed, they may be punished if their actions are detected – but because they believe that resistance is the "right" thing to do, regardless of the outcomes it engenders. In this vein, Oliver Williamson's recent work clearly indicates that excessive reliance on monitoring and fiat can have negative, unintended outcomes that lead to inefficiency: when managers rely too heavily on fiat and monitor subordinates too closely, subordinates may react by resisting or defying orders.[37] Williamson acknowledges that these reactions are sometimes based in nonrational commitments: resistance to authority occurs when fiat is exercised "arbitrarily," internal norms are violated, or "quasi-moral" commitments are breached.[38] That is, actors inside the organization resist authority when they view the exercise of fiat as unjustified because it transgresses proper limits. To grasp the limits of hierarchy, Williamson concedes, we must determine whether fiat is excessive or whether it commands general respect. The problem from the theoretical point of view is that efficiency theories cannot make a meaningful distinction between "excessive" fiat and "respected" authority. As a result, they are incapable of predicting when the dysfunctional consequences of fiat will arise, and they are of little use in telling us how to avoid such pitfalls.

TCE's difficulties in understanding the limits of hierarchy stem from its underlying assumption that action can be explained as rational choice under constraint. Efficiency theories of the firm assume boundedly rational actors who evaluate transactions solely in cost–benefit terms.[39] Such actors follow orders from above because it is in their self-interest to do so – compliance allows them to realize rewards and avoid punishments. From this point of view, resistance to fiat is "quite perverse" (i.e., irrational) because it results in "neither immediate nor long-term gains."[40] But when instances are observed in which the exercise of fiat or the

---

37 Williamson (1996, pp. 226–227).
38 For examples, see Williamson (1975, pp. 37–39, Chapter 7; 1985, Chapter 6; 1996, Chapters 9–10). See also the exchange between Williamson and Ouchi (1981) and Perrow (1981), as well as the exchange between Freeland (1996) and Shanley (1996). Economic approaches often attempt to salvage the theory by treating nonrational beliefs as new preferences: actors maximize nonrational preferences rather than monetary payoffs. Such explanations inevitably lead to tautology (Fireman and Gamson 1979; Gould 1990). Since preferences cannot be specified in advance, all action can be reinterpreted as rational maximization of some preference. The theory is preserved, but it is devoid of predictive specificity.
39 Such theories occasionally make gestures toward relaxing this assumption by stating that action is "primarily" but not exclusively rational. This is little more than a dodge, however. Rationality remains the sole positively stated norm in the formal theory. Other (nonrational) orientations are simply residual categories that are invoked *ex post*. See Parsons (1968, Chapters 1–3).
40 Williamson (1996, p. 99). I am quoting slightly out of context, but not in a way that alters the meaning of the passage.

manipulation of incentives disrupts cooperation, the theory backtracks. Sometimes, it seems, people are perverse: they resist orders even though doing so does not result in gain and may result in punishment. As outlined earlier, TCE acknowledges that this perversity derives from nonrational commitments or beliefs: resistance to fiat occurs when implicit, normative standards regarding the proper limits of authority within the firm are breached. The problem, of course, is that these are simply residual categories that are invoked *ex post* to account for unexpected deviations from the theory. Because TCE begins with the fundamental assumption of rational actors, it is incapable of specifying *a priori* when nonrational beliefs will be important, the form that such beliefs will take, or the mechanisms that support those beliefs.[41] The theory "recognizes" the importance of nonrational commitments only insofar as action inside the firm fails to conform to the prediction that actors will behave rationally. Having encountered behavior that does not fit its predictions, TCE proceeds to "explain" this action by making *ad hoc* arguments that are inconsistent with its underlying theoretical assumptions. An adequate explanation would require a reformulation of the theory in a way that would allow us to specify *ex ante* when action would be rational and when it would be based in normative commitments. This, in turn, would require an abandonment of the fundamental assumption that all action is intendedly rational.

Less obvious is the fact that introducing issues of consent creates similar problems for the concept of efficiency. Some critics have charged that the idea that consent leads to consummate performance may itself be construed as an efficiency argument – a different way of saying that initiative and commitment lower costs.[42] I agree that this is sometimes so: consent and cooperation often lead to efficient outcomes.[43] Yet even

41 Williamson (1985, p. 44, fn. 3) has admitted as much, noting that his attempts to incorporate "dignitarian values" into his framework have been unsuccessful.
42 See Shanley (1996).
43 Consent does not always lead to efficiency. As Selznick (1948; 1949) long ago pointed out, specific organizational practices and beliefs sometimes become institutionalized as valued "ends in themselves" that are impervious to change, even when technical conditions demand such change. Economic theories of the firm avoid contemplation of such a scenario by assuming that competition will, over the long run, favor efficient firms, thereby weeding out those that value inefficient practices. But once we loosen that assumption by acknowledging that economic selection is imperfect, and once we concede that people do not always behave as self-interested maximizers, we must admit the possibility that actors may pursue one goal (consent) at the expense of another (cost reduction). We can thus no longer assume that efficiency (or cost reduction, or profitability) will be ensured by market selection. If that sounds unlikely, consider GM in the postwar period. Because this was the most profitable era in GM's history, it has widely been viewed as the zenith of GM's efficiency and good governance. Yet clearly, the organization's success during this period had much to do with the fact that the war had destroyed any credible form of foreign competition. Moreover, GM's success vis-à-vis Ford and Chrysler may have had more to do with pro-

if we limit our attention to cases in which consent creates efficiency, the theoretical assumptions underlying the economic theory of the firm are stretched to the breaking point. The problem again lies in the fact that such theories conceptualize order (and thus efficiency) as an outcome of self-interest: order is realized by aligning the interest of the individual with the goals of the firm. But if order is based purely in sanctions, rational actors will do no more than is necessary to collect rewards and avoid punishments. They will not take initiative nor exercise judgment, because they will not be rewarded (and may be punished) for doing so. To get beyond perfunctory performance, therefore, requires an appeal to nonrational commitments; it requires actors to work toward the goals of the firm even when there is no clear reward or punishment for doing so. Economic theories of the firm are incapable of conceptualizing or operationalizing such an image of efficiency. These approaches begin with the assumption of boundedly rational actors. Faced with a world in which order and consummate performance rest on nonrational commitments, the best they can do is to again introduce *ex post* qualifications that violate the core assumptions of their theory: consummate performance requires that employees work in an "undistorted" (i.e., nonrational) way that goes beyond the specifications of the employment contract.[44] But once again, efficiency theory cannot tell us what produces and sustains such behavior, for the core assumption is that actors will behave in a distorted (rational) way, weighing actions only in terms of self-interest. If efficiency derives from consummate rather than perfunctory performance, and if consummate performance depends on nonrational commitment and identification, we can no longer conceptualize efficiency as an outcome of rational choice under constraint. Instead, efficiency itself

> duction economies of scale, reputation, and the ability to pass costs on to consumers than with efficient governance practices. Indeed, as I have outlined, there is considerable evidence that GM's governance practices were not particularly efficient during this period. It is thus conceivable that GM's commitment to participative decentralization in the postwar period reflected an image of the organization as an end in itself – a practice kept in place even though it was ill-fitted to the environmental conditions. Unfortunately, it is difficult to determine whether this is the case, for in practice it has proved nearly impossible to create measures or obtain data that would allow us to compare the distinct contributions that production and governance factors make to corporate performance.
>
> 44 Williamson (1975, p. 69). See also Williamson's (1985, p. 263) discussion of worker discretion, where he cautions that employers who demand strict adherence to the employment contract do so only at the risk of generating perfunctory performance. This kind of formulation is typical of Williamson's work. On the one hand, he often acknowledges that the nonrational dimensions of governance play a crucially important role in the empirical world. For this he is to be heartily commended, for unlike most economists he does not simply assume away such problems, but acknowledges that they pose real dilemmas. On the other hand, he does not seem to recognize that the qualifications that he introduces often blatantly contradict his core assumptions, leading to severe difficulties with the theoretical logic of his arguments.

is socially constructed, and its conceptualization requires a systematic formulation of the nonrational factors underlying consummate performance.

With this background, we can see more clearly why the image of efficiency provided by TCE is based in perfunctory compliance rather than consummate performance. TCE argues that top executives in the M-form create control mechanisms to gather more accurate information about subordinates' performance and that they use this information to reward and punish those employees, thereby eliciting cooperative behavior. But as outlined earlier, if order is based purely in sanctions, rational actors have no incentive to go beyond perfunctory adherence to the rules. They will not take initiative nor exercise judgment, because they will not be rewarded for doing so. Order based in fiat and rational self-interest is thus the domain of Max Weber's specialists without spirit – subordinates who act not out of any commitment to their work, but only to further their own interests and remuneration.[45] Such an order lacks zeal and initiative on the part of subordinates, but as Weber recognized, it may well be efficient in some circumstances. The GM case suggests that order based primarily in fiat and perfunctory compliance may be efficient in static markets where price competition is prevalent and little innovation is necessary.[46] In such an environment, strategic planning focuses primarily on loss prevention – the *ex post* evaluation of divisional performance and adjustment of product lines in light of such evaluation. Here, financial control mechanisms often prove adequate to ensure success, for competitive strategy relies primarily on lowering costs within the context of existing technology, making individual initiative and consummate performance less crucial to organizational success. Yet, as I argued in Chapter 7, the GM case suggests that extensive reliance on such sanctions also promotes a "finance conception of control" that emphasizes short-term financial performance over long-run investment and competitive strategy.[47] As a result of the emphasis on short-term financial results and perfunctory compliance, a management strategy that relies on fiat promotes allocative rather than dynamic efficiency, making it poorly suited to a world of innovation and change.[48] Ironically, TCE's image of efficiency is thus most appropriate to a world in which the

---

45 The phrase is from Weber (1958).
46 See Goold and Campbell (1987); Chandler (1991b; 1992); Lazonick (1991); Langlois and Robertson (1995).
47 Fligstein (1990).
48 See Langlois and Robertson (1995). Lazonick (1991) argues that Williamson's image of the M-form favors a static notion of allocative efficiency over the more dynamic image of efficiency found in Chandler. Odagiri (1994) points out that Japanese corporations have been slow to adopt the M-form extensively precisely because it relies too heavily on stability and allocative efficiency.

"gales of creative destruction" characteristic of capitalism have been weakened.[49]

Because TCE is incapable of conceptualizing the social and nonrational dimensions of governance, it is incapable of recognizing efficiency that goes beyond bureaucratic compliance. It is in dynamic and rapidly changing environments that nonrational commitments and identification with the firm become particularly important as sources of initiative and efficiency. Classic contingency theory has emphasized one reason for this.[50] That is, in uncertain and complex environments, rapidly changing conditions make it difficult to measure performance, to tie outcomes to activities, or even to know what activities ought to be pursued and rewarded. For this reason, it is inadvisable for firms operating in such environments to adhere to hierarchical controls in a mechanistic way, for it is unlikely that such controls will recognize and reward appropriate behavior. Fiat is thus poorly suited to complex and uncertain environments, for it emphasizes predictability and accountability over flexibility and innovation. More recent work supports this view, emphasizing that in such environments, competitive advantage focuses less on cost reduction and more on value creation, or the identification of long-term competitive strategies and the allocation of resources to implement those strategies. Yet within the M-form, the abstract information conveyed by financial controls is not sufficient to identify promising competitive strategies, particularly when those strategies couple the need for substantial fixed investment and technological innovation with non-price forms of competition.[51] Like contingency theory, this work emphasizes that hierarchical control systems constitute inadequate sources of control in complex and uncertain environments. Less recognized by these approaches is that under such conditions, nonrational commitments become particularly important as a way of encouraging subordinates to go beyond perfunctory compliance to hierarchical rules.[52] Fiat and rule-based behaviors are poorly suited to encouraging innovation and consummate performance under any conditions. It is in complex and uncertain environments that this deficiency becomes particularly apparent. Dynamic environments thus favor more extensive divisional participation in planning as a means of generating the initiative and

49 The phrase is from Schumpeter (1962).
50 See, for example, Burns and Stalker (1961); Thompson (1967); Lawrence and Lorsch (1967); Lorsch and Lawrence (1970); Woodward (1980); Perrow (1986); Stinchcombe (1990).
51 See Best (1990); Lazonick (1991).
52 Ouchi (1980) emphasizes a similar view, though he sees the norms that support flexibility as originating outside the organization. Perhaps more important, Ouchi tends to posit a radical disjuncture between normative control and control via sanctions, ignoring the ways in which these two modes of motivation reinforce or contradict one another.

commitment that are needed to adapt to changing conditions. Reliance on fiat is especially likely to undermine cooperation in such circumstances, particularly when divisions are autonomous entities serving highly differentiated markets.

Executives at General Motors were particularly fortunate in dealing with the tensions between consent and cost reduction. The fact that GM was primarily a single-industry producer, rather than a diversified firm competing in highly dissimilar markets, meant that it had more options available to it than most multidivisional businesses attempting to reconcile these competing logics. Because the bulk of GM's production was for a single industry, its markets were defined almost exclusively by price and quality, rather than by product *per se*. This artificial construction of market segments probably made it more difficult to articulate a fixed boundary between strategic and operating decisions, since shifts in demand could bring the car-producing divisions into some degree of competition, making it necessary for the general office to attempt coordination.[53] Yet the fact that GM produced primarily for a single market also made both administrative centralization and participative decentralization more viable than they would have been in a diversified firm. With far fewer markets to attend to, executives at corporate headquarters could potentially possess a more detailed knowledge of operations than their counterparts in more diversified businesses. During periods of centralization, this knowledge allowed them to make intelligent operating decisions while manipulating divisional interdependences in order to reduce the need for consent. Despite perfunctory performance from below, this knowledge helped to ensure that GM would continue to be run effectively. During periods of participative decentralization, top executives' knowledge provided the basis of the informal persuasion and influence that executives used in their attempts to constrain opportunism.

Executives in highly diversified firms lack the options that were available to GM's management, for trade-offs between consent and cost reduction become more pronounced as diversification increases. As businesses expand into a wider range of markets, divisions gain more autonomy and expertise, while top executives find it increasingly difficult to have an extensive knowledge of the various businesses within the corporation. In a highly diversified firm operating in a number of distinct markets, corporate headquarters will find it extremely difficult to identify, evaluate, and implement long-range competitive strategies without the direct participation and initiative of divisional management. It is in

---

53 The importance of this point was initially brought to my attention by Alfred Chandler. For a similar point regarding decentralization at General Electric, see Greenwood (1974).

this context that the image of the M-form as a vehicle for hierarchical control becomes most dangerous, for if executives in such firms adhere to this textbook image of an M-form that relies extensively on fiat and financial control mechanisms, they will substitute bureaucratic or perfunctory compliance for consummate performance, and short-term profits for long-term competitive advantage. By overlooking the social and nonrational bases of corporate governance, this mythical M-form offers a prescription for economic decline.

Appendix: General Motors' Financial Performance, 1921–1987

This Appendix provides data on General Motors' financial performance between 1921 and 1987. Both organizational theorists and GM's own managers have argued that return on invested capital (ROIC) is a key indicator of financial performance. Surprisingly, however, neither GM's own public testimony on matters of profit nor scholarly analyses have attempted to calculate GM's return on investment using the methodology that the corporation developed in the mid-1920s. Published testimony and analyses usually measure "return on investment" by giving a ratio of net earnings or net profits to either gross or net assets. Such measures fail to take capital turnover into account and thus are of little use in providing a meaningful assessment of return on investment. The figures in this Appendix endeavor to adhere as closely as possible to the methodology for determining return on investment outlined by GM's Donaldson Brown.

All figures in Tables A.1 and A.2 are from General Motors' annual reports. In some cases, changes in accounting standards would cause GM to retroactively revise previously published data. In this Appendix, I have attempted to use data from the original annual report in which it was published, and usually I have not adopted subsequent revisions to those data.

From 1921 into the 1960s, the data and accounting methodology are extremely comparable. Beginning in 1962, accounts for real estate and plant began to report "unamortized special tools" as a separate entry. This had the effect of slightly lowering gross real estate and plant entries, while raising net values. In keeping with GM's accounting methodology, the figures in this Appendix include the value of "unamortized special tools" in the net-working-capital category. As GM's performance declined in the 1970s, changes in accounting methodology became much more common. In 1975, reported figures began to be rounded to the nearest million dollars. More significant, in 1971 the corporation began to define "prepaid expenses and deferred charges" as working capital, whereas in earlier years these expenses were listed as separate assets. The change occurred in order to take advantage of new tax laws that allowed some of these expenses to be deducted. Concurrent with this change in accounting, the total amount of these expenses jumped enormously, climbing from $257,123,779 in 1970 to $478,797,038 in 1971. The combined effect of redefining these expenses as working capital while they were undergoing exponential expansion was to greatly increase reported gross-working-capital values, thus lowering gross-working-capital turnover figures.

In order to make data definitions comparable over time, this Appendix continues to exclude prepaid expenses and deferred charges from working-capital figures, reporting them instead as a separate entry. This methodology ensures that gross-working-capital figures are uniform, but it also raises difficulties concerning the comparability of net-working-capital data. Net working capital is defined as the difference between gross working capital and total liabilities. As GM's gross working capital rapidly increased because of the inclusion of prepaid expenses and deferred charges, so too did the total level of liabilities it reported. When the higher liabilities are subtracted from a gross-working-capital figure that does not include prepaid expenses and deferred charges, working-capital levels are understated. This problem reaches absurd levels in the early 1980s, when net working capital is sometimes reported in this Appendix as a negative figure.

The bottom line is that the figures presented in this Appendix for net working capital and net-working-capital turnover in years after 1971 are not comparable with those reported for years prior to 1971. Interested readers can easily reaggregate the data to match the net-working-capital figures reported in GM's annual reports, though doing so will make gross-working-capital figures noncomparable. In either case, gross and net return-on-investment figures will remain unaffected. These issues demonstrate the extent to which the component parts of financial data are malleable and subject to arbitrary accounting definitions. This particular change was instituted to take advantage of tax laws, and after it took effect, charges in these categories grew exponentially. It would be naive to think that either method of reporting working capital necessarily gave a "true" definition of GM's working-capital situation.

Similar but more drastic problems make it difficult if not impossible to compare GM's post-1987 financial data with those reported in prior years. Beginning in 1988, General Motors' financial statements began to consolidate earnings and debt from the General Motors Acceptance Corporation, which had previously been reported in the corporation's consolidated financial reports on a single line. With the accounting methodology adopted in 1988, GMAC's assets, debts, working capital, fixed capital, etc., were included in GM's financial statement on an equity basis, rather than being reported on a single line. Because GMAC is essentially in the business of finance capital, rather than manufacturing, its debt–equity ratios and its balance sheet look very different from those of its parent company. For instance, GMAC's accounts included some $85 billion worth of "finance receivables" – primarily money owed to GMAC by consumers who financed their automobiles through that company. Under consolidated accounting, this entire figure was included in GM's reported gross working capital, seriously distorting figures for working-capital turnover and the like. Because of the drastic changes in accounting practices that occurred after 1987, and because this book does not deal with these more recent years, post-1987 figures are not included in this Appendix.

Table A.1. *Financial Data, GM 1921–1987 (cols. A–E)*

Year	A. Net Sales	B. Net income before Taxes (Incl. Other)	C. Net income after Taxes (Profits)	D. Income/ Sales (B/A)	E. Profit/ Sales (C/A)	Dividends (Common Only)
1921	$304,487,243	($38,680,770)	($38,680,770)	-12.70%	-12.70%	$20,468,276
1922	$463,706,733	$60,724,493	$54,474,793	13.10%	11.75%	$10,177,117
1923	$698,038,947	$80,143,955	$72,008,955	11.48%	10.32%	$24,772,026
1924	$568,007,459	$57,350,490	$51,623,490	10.10%	9.09%	$25,030,632
1925	$734,592,592	$129,928,277	$116,016,277	17.69%	15.79%	$61,935,221
1926	$1,058,153,338	$212,066,121	$186,231,182	20.04%	17.60%	$103,930,993
1927	$1,269,519,673	$269,573,585	$235,104,826	21.23%	18.52%	$134,836,081
1928	$1,459,762,906	$309,817,468	$276,468,108	21.22%	18.94%	$165,300,002
1929	$1,504,404,472	$276,403,176	$248,282,268	18.37%	16.50%	$156,600,007
1930	$983,375,137	$167,227,693	$151,098,992	17.01%	15.37%	$130,500,002
1931	$808,840,723	$111,219,791	$96,877,107	13.75%	11.98%	$130,500,001
1932	$432,311,868	$449,690	$164,979	0.10%	0.04%	$53,993,330
1933	$569,010,542	$95,431,456	$83,213,676	16.77%	14.62%	$53,826,355
1934	$862,672,670	$110,181,088	$94,769,131	12.77%	10.99%	$64,443,490
1935	$1,155,641,511	$196,692,407	$167,226,510	17.02%	14.47%	$96,476,748
1936	$1,439,289,940	$282,090,052	$238,482,425	19.60%	16.57%	$192,903,299
1937	$1,606,789,841	$245,543,733	$196,436,598	15.28%	12.23%	$160,549,861
1938	$1,066,973,000	$130,190,341	$102,190,007	12.20%	9.58%	$64,386,421
1939	$1,376,828,337	$228,142,412	$183,290,222	16.57%	13.31%	$150,319,682
1940	$1,794,936,642	$320,649,462	$195,621,721	17.86%	10.90%	$161,864,924
1941	$2,436,800,977	$489,644,851	$201,652,508	20.09%	8.28%	$162,608,296
1942	$2,250,548,859	$260,727,633	$163,651,588	11.59%	7.27%	$86,992,295
1943	$3,796,115,800	$398,700,782	$149,780,088	10.50%	3.95%	$87,106,758
1944	$4,262,249,472	$435,409,021	$170,995,865	10.22%	4.01%	$132,063,371

Table A.1. (cols. A–E cont.)

Year	A. Net Sales	B. Net income before Taxes (Incl. Other)	C. Net income after Taxes (Profits)	D. Income/ Sales (B/A)	E. Profit/ Sales (C/A)	Dividends (Common Only)
1945	$3,127,934,888	$212,535,893	$188,268,115	6.79%	6.02%	$132,066,520
1946	$1,962,502,289	$43,300,083	$87,526,311	2.21%	4.46%	$99,158,674
1947	$3,815,159,163	$554,005,405	$287,991,373	14.52%	7.55%	$132,167,487
1948	$4,701,770,340	$801,417,975	$440,447,724	17.05%	9.37%	$197,845,688
1949	$5,700,835,141	$1,124,834,936	$656,434,232	19.73%	11.51%	$351,380,264
1950	$7,531,086,846	$1,811,660,763	$834,044,039	24.06%	11.07%	$526,111,783
1951	$7,465,554,851	$1,488,717,641	$506,199,560	19.94%	6.78%	$350,249,851
1952	$7,549,154,419	$1,502,178,604	$558,721,179	19.90%	7.40%	$349,041,039
1953	$10,027,985,482	$1,652,647,924	$598,119,478	16.48%	5.96%	$348,760,514
1954	$9,823,526,291	$1,644,959,366	$805,973,897	16.75%	8.20%	$436,507,196
1955	$12,443,277,420	$2,542,827,439	$1,189,477,082	20.44%	9.56%	$592,245,497
1956	$10,796,442,575	$1,741,414,610	$847,396,102	16.13%	7.85%	$552,853,282
1957	$10,989,813,178	$1,648,712,588	$843,592,435	15.00%	7.68%	$555,453,812
1958	$9,521,965,629	$1,115,428,076	$633,628,076	11.71%	6.65%	$558,940,800
1959	$11,233,057,200	$1,792,200,149	$873,100,149	15.95%	7.77%	$561,838,126
1960	$12,735,999,681	$2,037,542,489	$959,042,489	16.00%	7.53%	$564,190,599
1961	$11,395,916,826	$1,768,021,444	$892,821,444	15.51%	7.83%	$707,383,013
1962	$14,640,240,799	$2,934,477,450	$1,459,077,450	20.04%	9.97%	$850,465,125
1963	$16,494,818,184	$3,353,923,058	$1,591,823,058	20.33%	9.65%	$1,135,809,405
1964	$16,997,044,468	$3,283,681,555	$1,734,781,555	19.32%	10.21%	$1,266,306,261
1965	$20,733,982,295	$4,091,606,440	$2,125,606,440	19.73%	10.25%	$1,496,812,657
1966	$20,208,505,041	$3,270,791,691	$1,793,391,691	16.19%	8.87%	$1,298,106,848
1967	$20,026,252,468	$3,013,376,076	$1,627,276,076	15.05%	8.13%	$1,084,355,349

1968	$22,755,402,947	$3,524,814,777	$1,731,914,777	15.49%	7.61%	$1,227,446,007
1969	$24,295,141,357	$3,202,377,450	$1,710,695,164	13.18%	7.04%	$1,227,429,173
1970	$18,752,353,515	$794,186,848	$609,086,848	4.24%	3.25%	$971,027,351
1971	$28,263,918,443	$3,719,809,493	$1,935,709,493	13.16%	6.85%	$972,443,676
1972	$30,435,231,414	$4,222,606,765	$2,162,806,765	13.87%	7.11%	$1,273,066,301
1973	$35,798,289,281	$4,513,103,408	$2,398,103,408	12.61%	6.70%	$1,501,311,797
1974	$31,549,546,126	$1,677,169,363	$950,069,363	5.32%	3.01%	$973,300,000
1975	$35,724,911,215	$2,371,291,965	$1,253,091,965	6.64%	3.51%	$688,400,000
1976	$47,181,000,000	$5,470,600,000	$2,902,800,000	11.59%	6.15%	$1,590,500,000
1977	$55,251,500,000	$6,271,700,000	$3,337,500,000	11.35%	6.04%	$1,944,800,000
1978	$63,221,100,000	$6,596,500,000	$3,508,000,000	10.43%	5.55%	$1,712,600,000
1979	$66,311,200,000	$5,076,100,000	$2,892,700,000	7.65%	4.36%	$1,520,300,000
1980	$57,728,500,000	($1,147,800,000)	($762,500,000)	-1.99%	-1.32%	$861,200,000
1981	$62,698,500,000	$210,300,000	$333,400,000	0.34%	0.53%	$717,600,000
1982	$60,025,600,000	$710,500,000	$962,700,000	1.18%	1.60%	$737,300,000
1983	$74,581,600,000	$5,954,000,000	$3,730,200,000	7.98%	5.00%	$879,300,000
1984	$83,889,900,000	$6,321,600,000	$4,516,500,000	7.54%	5.38%	$2,096,700,000
1985	$96,371,700,000	$4,621,300,000	$2,991,000,000	4.80%	3.10%	$2,165,000,000
1986	$102,813,700,000	$2,644,400,000	$2,944,700,000	2.57%	2.86%	$1,588,500,000
1987	$101,781,900,000	$3,491,000,000	$3,550,900,000	3.43%	3.49%	$1,579,600,000

Table A.1. *(cols. F–K)*

Year	F. Gross Real Estate & Plant (REP)	G. Net Real Estate & Plant	H. Gross Working Capital (WC)	I. Net Working Capital	J. Deferred Expenses	K. Investment in Other Companies
1921	$248,593,752		$178,135,545		$4,609,678	$56,377,032
1922	$255,207,971	$204,380,064	$180,239,160	$126,476,237	$3,947,794	$57,293,865
1923	$276,576,056	$213,327,252	$219,891,469	$140,750,582	$8,363,208	$60,805,853
1924	$288,940,449	$212,039,423	$298,179,254	$161,105,281	$6,522,849	$61,513,126
1925	$287,268,286	$195,642,857	$290,869,088	$181,826,881	$5,119,838	$86,183,747
1926	$434,373,903	$310,481,563	$336,338,213	$192,005,617	$7,404,422	$79,715,823
1927	$480,473,508	$338,600,568	$432,280,123	$272,923,976	$12,436,188	$98,262,014
1928	$542,987,155	$380,307,042	$468,809,287	$292,205,072	$19,552,635	$117,819,124
1929	$609,880,375	$415,785,412	$368,960,945	$247,575,207	$18,168,100	$207,270,443
1930	$614,030,329	$395,374,308	$364,817,496	$277,815,894	$22,246,234	$207,750,253
1931	$604,100,810	$362,628,116	$358,502,579	$269,896,499	$21,788,939	$211,548,200
1932	$499,982,231	$328,273,745	$283,258,874	$222,156,284	$17,433,418	$211,030,901
1933	$512,703,982	$303,764,839	$320,015,607	$241,332,117	$15,053,982	$228,893,524
1934	$541,507,042	$305,678,291	$365,844,370	$273,174,677	$14,213,654	$238,283,722
1935	$592,150,300	$319,177,619	$465,028,108	$319,961,219	$4,017,587	$245,641,384
1936	$690,190,826	$388,211,431	$513,986,449	$339,686,551	$4,687,377	$228,733,566
1937	$747,817,794	$408,466,262	$492,898,837	$347,216,116	$5,049,865	$245,563,031
1938	$758,830,738	$396,342,218	$520,327,783	$387,253,513	$8,098,056	$242,477,567
1939	$769,417,418	$385,859,609	$617,468,025	$434,172,831	$7,878,315	$246,434,121
1940	$814,219,268	$402,618,488	$824,346,367	$477,940,113	$7,887,118	$242,200,056
1941	$851,707,066	$409,874,456	$997,616,031	$500,023,010	$13,800,132	$267,883,156
1942	$872,924,635	$371,483,082	$1,313,850,010	$652,326,139	$28,261,330	$214,261,517
1943	$899,204,062	$327,229,678	$1,643,956,484	$829,238,238	$12,894,300	$212,310,219

Year						
1944		$298,549,884				$195,109,472
1945		$349,798,721			$14,235,963	$223,006,181
1946		$608,028,866			$9,405,725	$202,130,255
1947		$722,996,002			$12,468,302	$180,245,767
1948	$1,678,496,156	$775,088,502			$9,668,042	$212,078,714
1949	$1,776,103,965	$777,454,109			$10,682,678	$206,585,203
1950	$1,909,429,470	$801,947,256			$14,258,079	$249,790,664
1951	$2,162,918,601	$941,843,219			$20,692,426	$307,399,252
1952	$2,607,945,848	$1,262,876,314	$1,606,261,904	$903,409,918	$70,251,206	$342,031,166
1953	$3,053,445,869	$1,536,331,075	$1,162,756,377	$775,229,420	$138,806,989	$334,320,833
1954	$3,920,745,428	$2,161,121,210	$1,096,293,952	$768,730,888	$54,286,452	$363,102,997
1955	$4,354,352,101	$2,353,031,643	$1,490,512,139	$865,373,105	$48,065,902	$421,740,334
1956	$5,271,815,966	$2,967,812,359	$1,553,001,759	$1,086,680,131	$29,917,113	$442,289,247
1957	$5,765,331,004	$3,118,270,760	$1,752,228,323	$1,265,916,125	$44,041,648	$478,726,800
1958	$5,954,031,842	$2,963,100,035	$2,249,800,490	$1,506,256,144	$60,574,967	$494,538,428
1959	$6,185,599,942	$2,837,544,603	$2,142,426,536	$1,456,758,140	$58,623,756	$503,585,141
1960	$6,666,634,695	$3,010,422,087	$2,357,113,845	$1,191,221,891	$57,951,525	$551,427,910
1961	$7,004,849,133	$3,028,866,377	$2,425,499,582	$1,236,134,209	$65,404,592	$529,872,845
1962	$7,187,072,501	$3,207,146,269	$3,392,574,949	$1,350,561,015	$72,727,439	$548,265,319
1963	$7,657,753,841	$3,335,970,255	$2,962,523,024	$2,058,257,831	$82,045,521	$682,590,264
1964	$8,394,340,992	$3,899,685,840	$3,017,601,147	$1,745,974,246	$81,480,016	$659,558,453
1965	$9,526,463,680	$4,616,604,903	$3,238,233,125	$1,861,363,078	$88,605,350	$640,651,379
1966	$10,526,847,101	$5,129,783,091	$3,704,835,854	$2,098,705,137	$101,645,834	$745,248,725
1967	$11,234,257,247	$5,332,998,670	$4,057,019,269	$2,566,157,275	$117,909,865	$754,756,228
1968	$11,882,241,727	$5,438,055,964	$4,483,487,686	$2,799,315,560	$125,982,310	$860,354,536
1969	$12,700,178,000	$5,644,777,053	$5,158,853,722	$3,058,577,064	$167,194,840	$1,040,921,453
1970	$13,545,894,076	$6,395,839,663	$5,362,559,841	$3,528,029,982	$228,986,270	$1,113,123,934
1971	$14,242,155,542	$6,203,770,826	$5,455,508,083	$3,727,408,166	$257,123,779	$1,371,199,126
1972	$14,748,057,536	$6,198,524,579	$5,912,471,481	$3,651,041,721	$478,797,038	$1,234,792,852
1973	$15,615,898,926	$6,251,235,416	$6,711,761,034	$3,684,854,671	$585,214,833	$1,465,557,541
1974	$16,808,456,667	$7,033,348,245	$6,846,488,781	$3,605,988,574	$861,001,813	$1,551,561,945
			$7,335,435,143	$4,006,404,554	$306,328,780	
			$7,697,608,562	$4,230,273,858		
			$6,491,948,795	$4,352,044,501		
			$10,032,769,205	$3,010,467,194		
			$9,953,306,940	$4,051,590,259		
			$11,305,503,171	$4,979,560,099		
			$10,743,877,425	$5,335,849,362		
				$5,235,599,743		

331

Table A.1. *(cols. F-K cont.)*

Year	F. Gross Real Estate & Plant (REP)	G. Net Real Estate & Plant	H. Gross Working Capital (WC)	I. Net Working Capital	J. Deferred Expenses	K. Investment in Other Companies
1975	$17,503,583,496	$7,085,880,293	$12,416,407,062	$5,970,936,486	$423,086,553	$1,624,213,403
1976	$18,192,100,000	$6,961,100,000	$14,911,800,000	$6,995,800,000	$560,800,000	$1,872,200,000
1977	$19,860,900,000	$8,202,900,000	$15,096,800,000	$6,769,900,000	$860,400,000	$2,351,700,000
1978	$22,052,000,000	$9,605,600,000	$17,270,200,000	$7,219,600,000	$729,300,000	$2,812,100,000
1979	$24,879,400,000	$11,638,200,000	$16,093,100,000	$6,224,800,000	$463,400,000	$3,828,200,000
1980	$29,269,400,000	$14,986,800,000	$14,714,800,000	$4,846,500,000	$706,500,000	$4,047,100,000
1981	$34,811,500,000	$20,040,700,000	$12,186,700,000	($368,300,000)	$1,527,100,000	$5,153,000,000
1982	$37,687,200,000	$21,538,400,000	$12,174,900,000	($210,100,000)	$1,868,200,000	$5,781,100,000
1983	$37,777,800,000	$19,165,100,000	$19,802,600,000	$4,893,600,000	$997,200,000	$5,672,000,000
1984	$39,354,100,000	$19,401,500,000	$23,285,000,000	$5,848,400,000	$428,300,000	$6,947,400,000
1985	$47,267,100,000	$24,653,000,000	$22,119,900,000	($178,600,000)	$2,136,100,000	$8,788,300,000
1986	$55,240,700,000	$30,376,400,000	$24,148,800,000	$1,300,700,000	$2,619,600,000	$9,540,700,000
1987	$59,809,400,000	$32,040,400,000	$36,596,200,000	$11,068,000,000	$3,175,300,000	$10,423,600,000

Table A.1. *(cols. L–O)*

Year	L. Common Stock Held	M. Inventories (Included in Gross WC)	N. Gross Investment (F + H + J + K + L)	O. Net Investment (G + I + J + K + L)
1921	$3,889,800	$108,762,625	$491,605,807	$64,876,510
1922	$3,275,433	$117,417,823	$499,964,223	$395,373,393
1923	$5,046,323	$138,678,131	$570,682,909	$428,293,218
1924	$5,000,924	$97,201,686	$660,156,602	$446,181,603
1925	$11,963,578	$112,091,659	$681,404,537	$480,736,901
1926	$19,491,739	$156,203,663	$877,324,100	$609,099,164
1927	$31,338,034	$172,647,716	$1,054,789,867	$753,560,780
1928	$50,053,193	$196,692,868	$1,199,221,394	$859,937,066
1929	$69,929,476	$188,472,999	$1,274,209,339	$958,728,638
1930	$12,019,632	$136,298,891	$1,220,863,944	$915,206,321
1931	$12,512,537	$106,471,332	$1,208,453,065	$878,374,291
1932	$11,808,781	$75,478,612	$1,023,514,205	$790,703,129
1933	$16,644,233	$115,584,600	$1,093,311,328	$805,688,695
1934	$20,160,161	$138,598,157	$1,180,008,949	$851,510,505
1935	$23,549,722	$196,325,118	$1,330,387,101	$912,347,531
1936	$19,774,562	$225,644,813	$1,457,372,780	$981,093,487
1937	$25,021,584	$279,146,383	$1,516,351,111	$1,031,316,858
1938	$17,955,399	$175,609,306	$1,547,689,543	$1,052,116,753
1939	$15,419,632	$233,764,789	$1,656,617,511	$1,089,764,508
1940	$8,541,816	$265,000,682	$1,897,194,625	$1,139,187,591
1941	$4,486,510	$332,826,774	$2,135,492,895	$1,196,067,264
1942	$1,678,625	$466,265,585	$2,430,976,117	$1,268,010,693
1943	$4,627,661	$564,411,464	$2,772,992,726	$1,386,300,096

Table A.1. *(cols. L–O cont.)*

Year	L. Common Stock Held	M. Inventories (Included in Gross WC)	N. Gross Investment (F + H + J + K + L)	O. Net Investment (G + I + J + K + L)
1944	$5,237,951	$498,728,376	$2,751,047,572	$1,416,543,188
1945	$5,704,225	$348,080,639	$2,449,467,733	$1,363,144,272
1946	$556,429	$549,352,274	$2,656,264,747	$1,591,914,740
1947	$6,332,958	$692,889,191	$3,223,269,669	$1,784,615,874
1948	$7,805,924	$786,576,707	$3,462,065,231	$2,092,335,949
1949	$10,334,173	$721,525,796	$3,759,509,743	$2,274,547,689
1950	$28,997,709	$888,594,400	$4,488,463,845	$2,607,684,199
1951	$39,074,078	$1,140,906,659	$4,829,443,627	$2,815,325,895
1952	$51,939,373	$1,296,668,633	$5,283,149,912	$2,986,875,733
1953	$60,208,507	$1,446,677,578	$5,859,375,506	$3,221,281,076
1954	$68,861,438	$1,325,866,402	$6,826,275,347	$3,991,712,562
1955	$84,065,656	$1,601,654,593	$8,282,650,153	$4,947,012,577
1956	$89,291,992	$1,719,592,723	$8,809,961,877	$5,289,409,492
1957	$87,172,671	$1,730,785,080	$9,409,406,589	$5,606,108,276
1958	$72,916,570	$1,529,512,998	$9,818,343,721	$5,687,883,926
1959	$79,048,438	$1,799,807,607	$10,531,020,900	$6,044,286,982
1960	$89,949,671	$1,810,997,290	$11,430,436,137	$6,516,519,820
1961	$94,199,367	$1,800,142,041	$12,185,136,470	$6,784,243,092
1962	$109,300,319	$2,006,492,551	$13,083,537,382	$7,474,787,410
1963	$115,122,517	$2,221,203,868	$13,899,506,479	$7,942,571,218
1964	$126,028,336	$2,677,847,621	$14,724,041,214	$8,424,919,700
1965	$143,730,527	$2,986,541,397	$16,324,962,901	$9,187,487,314
1966	$148,174,333	$3,103,286,127	$18,249,941,058	$9,747,104,588

Year			
1967	$149,414,069		$10,369,555,831
1968	$145,692,193		$10,841,571,391
1969	$144,358,725		$11,411,088,002
1970	$116,349,156		$10,892,903,726
1971	$104,609,873		$12,209,967,122
1972	$129,540,350		$13,127,632,713
1973	$137,407,501		$14,051,051,633
1974	$86,698,431		$14,213,537,144
1975	$62,641,489		$15,166,758,224
1976	$99,600,000		$16,489,500,000
1977	$146,500,000		$18,331,400,000
1978	$181,100,000	$3,210,408,568	$19,110,898,635
1979	$192,900,000	$3,423,340,337	$20,390,918,439
1980	$125,800,000	$3,760,525,690	$21,812,053,010
1981	$71,500,000	$4,115,060,497	$21,524,439,740
1982	$35,200,000	$3,991,569,173	$26,229,530,784
1983	$56,300,000	$4,200,163,355	$26,650,912,511
1984	$144,200,000	$5,176,896,457	$29,385,368,952
1985	$190,200,000	$6,404,702,228	$29,496,923,248
1986	$190,300,000	$5,690,892,746	$32,029,932,003
1987	$0	$6,327,800,000	$35,636,500,000
		$7,175,700,000	$38,316,300,000
		$7,576,700,000	$43,044,700,000
		$8,076,300,000	$45,457,000,000
		$7,231,200,000	$48,863,600,000
		$7,222,700,000	$53,749,800,000
		$6,184,200,000	$57,546,600,000
		$6,621,500,000	$64,305,900,000
		$7,359,700,000	$70,159,000,000
		$8,269,700,000	$80,501,600,000
		$7,235,100,000	$91,740,100,000
		$7,939,700,000	$110,004,500,000

Table A.1. *(cols. R–W)*

Year	R. Gross REP Turnover (A/F)	S. Net WC Turnover (A/I)	T. Net REP Turnover (A/G)	U. Inventory Turnover (A/M)	V. Gross Turnover (A/N)	W. Net Turnover (A/O)	Gross ROIC (D × V)	Net ROIC (D × W)
1921	1.22484				0.61937	4.69334	−7.87%	−59.62%
1922	1.81698	3.66635	2.26885	2.79956	0.92748	1.17283	12.15%	15.36%
1923	2.52386	4.95940	3.27215	3.94920	1.22316	1.62982	14.04%	18.71%
1924	1.96583	3.52569	2.67878	5.03352	0.86041	1.27304	8.69%	12.85%
1925	2.55717	4.04007	3.75476	5.84360	1.07806	1.52806	19.07%	27.03%
1926	2.43604	5.51105	3.40810	6.55350	1.20611	1.73724	24.17%	34.82%
1927	2.64223	4.65155	3.74931	6.77419	1.20358	1.68469	25.56%	35.77%
1928	2.68839	4.99568	3.83838	7.35324	1.21726	1.69752	25.83%	36.03%
1929	2.46672	6.07656	3.61822	7.42153	1.18066	1.56917	21.69%	28.83%
1930	1.60151	3.53966	2.48720	7.98207	0.80547	1.07448	13.70%	18.27%
1931	1.33892	2.99686	2.23050	7.21484	0.66932	0.92084	9.20%	12.66%
1932	0.86465	1.94598	1.31692	7.59679	0.42238	0.54674	0.04%	0.06%
1933	1.10982	2.35779	1.87319	5.72761	0.52045	0.70624	8.73%	11.84%
1934	1.59310	3.15795	2.82216	4.92289	0.73107	1.01311	9.34%	12.94%
1935	1.95160	3.61182	3.62068	6.22427	0.86865	1.26667	14.78%	21.56%
1936	2.08535	4.23711	3.70749	5.88637	0.98759	1.46703	19.36%	28.75%
1937	2.14864	4.62764	3.93371	6.37856	1.05964	1.55800	16.19%	23.81%
1938	1.40608	2.75530	2.69205	5.75608	0.68940	1.01412	8.41%	12.37%
1939	1.78944	3.17115	3.56821	6.07583	0.83111	1.26342	13.77%	20.94%
1940	2.20449	3.75557	4.45816	5.88980	0.94610	1.57563	16.90%	28.15%
1941	2.86106	4.87338	5.94524	6.77333	1.14110	2.03734	22.93%	40.94%
1942	2.57817	3.45004	6.05828	7.32153	0.92578	1.77487	10.73%	20.56%
				4.82675				

1943	4.22164	4.57783	11.60077	6.72579	1.36896	2.73831	14.38%	28.76%
1944	4.58207	4.71796	14.27651	8.54623	1.54932	3.00891	15.83%	30.74%
1945	2.98298	4.03485	8.94210	8.98624	1.27699	2.29465	8.68%	15.59%
1946	1.45931	2.55291	3.22765	3.57239	0.73882	1.23279	1.63%	2.72%
1947	2.48300	4.40869	5.27687	5.50616	1.18363	2.13780	17.19%	31.04%
1948	2.80118	4.32673	6.06611	5.97751	1.35808	2.24714	23.15%	38.30%
1949	3.20974	4.50333	7.33270	7.90108	1.51818	2.50636	29.92%	49.45%
1950	3.94416	4.99987	9.39100	8.47528	1.67788	2.88804	40.36%	69.47%
1951	3.45161	5.12477	7.92654	6.54353	1.54584	2.65176	30.83%	52.88%
1952	2.89467	6.33732	5.97775	5.82196	1.42891	2.52744	28.43%	50.29%
1953	3.28415	8.11238	6.52723	6.93173	1.71144	3.11304	28.21%	51.30%
1954	2.50553	7.27366	4.54557	7.40914	1.43908	2.46098	24.10%	41.21%
1955	2.85766	6.04554	5.28819	7.76901	1.50233	2.51531	30.70%	51.40%
1956	2.04796	6.18362	3.63785	6.27849	1.22548	2.04114	19.77%	32.92%
1957	1.90619	5.90417	3.52433	6.34961	1.16796	1.96033	17.52%	29.41%
1958	1.59925	4.53707	3.21351	6.22549	0.96981	1.67408	11.36%	19.61%
1959	1.81600	4.37738	3.95872	6.24125	1.06666	1.85846	17.02%	29.65%
1960	1.91041	4.54968	4.23064	7.03259	1.11422	1.95442	17.83%	31.27%
1961	1.62686	3.72589	3.76244	6.33057	0.93523	1.67976	14.51%	26.06%
1962	2.03702	4.14969	4.56488	7.29643	1.11881	1.95862	22.43%	39.26%
1963	2.15400	4.42528	4.94453	7.42607	1.18672	2.07676	24.13%	42.23%
1964	2.02482	4.65540	4.35857	6.34728	1.15437	2.01747	22.30%	38.98%
1965	2.17646	5.62681	4.49118	6.94247	1.27008	2.25676	25.06%	44.53%
1966	1.91971	5.60415	3.93945	6.51197	1.10732	2.07328	17.92%	33.56%
1967	1.78261	4.99856	3.75516	6.23791	1.04790	1.93125	15.77%	29.06%
1968	1.91508	5.37918	4.18447	6.64713	1.11596	2.09890	17.29%	32.51%
1969	1.91298	5.58247	4.30400	6.46057	1.11384	2.12908	14.68%	28.06%

337

Table A.1. *(cols. R–W cont.)*

Year	R. Gross REP Turnover (A/F)	S. Net WC Turnover (A/I)	T. Net REP Turnover (A/G)	U. Inventory Turnover (A/M)	V. Gross Turnover (A/N)	W. Net Turnover (A/O)	Gross ROIC (D × V)	Net ROIC (D × W)
1970	1.38436	6.22905	2.93196	4.55701	0.87121	1.72152	3.69%	7.29%
1971	1.98453	6.97601	4.55593	7.08090	1.07756	2.31482	14.18%	30.47%
1972	2.06368	6.11203	4.91008	7.24620	1.14200	2.31841	15.84%	32.17%
1973	2.29243	6.70901	5.72659	6.91501	1.21824	2.54773	15.36%	32.12%
1974	1.87700	6.02597	4.48571	4.92600	1.06959	2.21968	5.69%	11.80%
1975	2.04101	5.98313	5.04170	6.27756	1.11536	2.35547	7.40%	15.63%
1976	2.59349	6.74419	6.77781	7.45615	1.32395	2.86128	15.35%	33.18%
1977	2.78192	8.16135	6.73561	7.69981	1.44198	3.01404	16.37%	34.21%
1978	2.86691	8.75687	6.58169	8.34415	1.46873	3.07680	15.32%	32.10%
1979	2.66531	10.65274	5.69772	8.21059	1.45877	2.96728	11.17%	22.71%
1980	1.97232	11.91138	3.85196	7.98325	1.18142	2.33599	−2.35%	−4.64%
1981	1.80109	na	3.12856	8.68076	1.16649	2.37279	0.39%	0.80%
1982	1.59273	na	2.78691	9.70628	1.04308	2.06894	1.23%	2.45%
1983	1.97422	15.24064	3.89153	11.26355	1.15979	2.42272	9.26%	19.34%
1984	2.13167	14.34408	4.32389	11.39855	1.19571	2.55998	9.01%	19.29%
1985	2.03887	na	3.90913	11.65359	1.19714	2.70791	5.74%	12.99%
1986	1.86119	79.04490	3.38466	14.21040	1.12071	2.33520	2.88%	6.01%
1987	1.70177	9.19605	3.35069	12.81936	0.92525	1.84912	3.17%	6.34%

338

Table A.2. Period Averages for Selected Data

	1924–29	1934–41	1942–45	1947–57	1958–63	1964–72	1973–80	1981–87
Net income/net sales	19.03%	17.06%	9.73%	18.18%	17.10%	14.38%	7.85%	4.11%
Net profit/net sales	16.89%	11.75%	5.01%	8.33%	8.43%	7.62%	4.20%	3.27%
Inventory turnover	7.14217	6.35651	7.15683	6.80395	6.80703	6.43393	7.31951	11.45255
Gross WC turnover	3.00370	2.44709	2.34630	3.54545	2.92336	3.04750	3.48963	3.87298
Gross REP turnover	2.49419	2.03612	3.58227	2.66899	1.86989	1.89576	2.39226	1.86622
Gross total turnover	1.14744	0.92287	1.29145	1.41429	1.07149	1.09432	1.29956	1.10257
Net WC turnover	4.89332	3.81239	4.25189	5.81424	4.27614	5.69174	8.08177	26.04325
Net REP turnover	3.55907	3.89226	9.97493	5.21533	4.13544	4.14383	5.47294	3.51651
Net total turnover	1.60517	1.42244	2.47274	2.41499	1.87939	2.10439	2.69276	2.29514
Gross return on investment	21.84%	16.40%	12.57%	25.71%	18.33%	15.74%	10.20%	4.54%
Net return on investment	30.55%	25.57%	24.06%	43.90%	32.14%	30.27%	21.14%	9.44%

References

Primary Sources

The basic sources for the primary historical documents used in this study have been the collections of more than 1 million documents housed in the Hagley Museum and Library outside of Wilmington, Delaware. The most important collections used in this study have been the papers of Walter S. Carpenter, Jr., a top executive within E. I. du Pont de Nemours; the papers of F. Donaldson Brown, who developed financial controls at Du Pont and General Motors and served as a top officer in both corporations; the collection of documents relating to the U.S. government's antitrust suit against E. I. du Pont de Nemours and General Motors; and the business papers of Pierre S. du Pont and John J. Raskob. The Carpenter papers are maintained at Hagley as Accession 542 and are cited accordingly. The papers of F. Donaldson Brown are maintained and cited as Accession 1334. The business papers of Pierre S. du Pont are in the Longwood manuscripts, Group 10, Series A. Because all of the material cited herein is from File 624 of this collection, it is referred to simply as Accession 624, though this is something of a misnomer. In addition, there are occasional references in this study to the papers of John J. Raskob, cited as Accession 473. Material from the Walter S. Carpenter papers and the Pierre S. du Pont papers is quoted courtesy of Hagley Museum and Library; material from the Donaldson Brown papers is quoted courtesy of the Trustees of the Donaldson Brown Trust. My thanks to both for their permission to quote from these sources.

The situation of the antitrust material is more complicated. Hagley keeps a complete trial transcript of the antitrust suit that includes all depositions and exhibits used as evidence in the original trial. This material is cited herein as *U.S. v. Du Pont*. Note, however, that the transcribed version of the trial found at Hagley and a few libraries around the country uses different pagination than that found in the original court transcript. In addition, Hagley's manuscript collection has material relating to the antitrust suit that is not part of the official record. This material includes documents that were "produced" for trial but never used, as well as in-house documents prepared by GM and Du Pont legal counsel. Most of that material was uncatalogued at the time I carried out the research for this study. It was in the process of being transferred to the Pierre S. du Pont papers described earlier. This material is cited initially as "Longwood," indicating that it is part of the Longwood manuscript collection. That designation is followed by two "box numbers," the second in parentheses. The first (in the 400 range) indicates the number that a box had been assigned in the Pierre S. du Pont papers; the second number (in parentheses, in the 1–40 range) indicates the number of the box within the antitrust material. Finally, citations of this material also include the phrase "First Series" or "Second Series." This designation indicates whether a document was part of the first or second "wave" of document production in the antitrust trial.

Secondary Sources

Abernathy, William J. *The Productivity Dilemma: Roadblock to Innovation in the Automobile Industry.* Baltimore: Johns Hopkins University Press, 1978.

Adams, Scott. *Dogbert's Top Secret Management Handbook.* New York: Harper Business, 1996.

Akerlof, George. "The Market for 'Lemons.' Qualitative Uncertainty and the Market Mechanism." *Quarterly Journal of Economics* 84:488–500, 1970.

Alchian, Armen, and Harold Demsetz. "Production, Information Costs, and Economic Organization." *American Economic Review* 62:777–95, 1972. Reprinted in Harold Demsetz, *Ownership, Control, and the Firm. Volume I: The Organization of Economic Activity.* Oxford: Basil Blackwell, 1988.

Allen, Stephen. "Corporate-Divisional Relationships in Highly Diversified Firms," pp. 16–35 in Jay Lorsch and Paul Lawrence (eds.), *Studies in Organization Design.* Homewood, IL: Richard D. Irwin, 1970.

Ansoff, H. I. *Strategic Management.* New York: Wiley, 1979.

Aoki, Masahiko, Bo Gustaffson, and Oliver Williamson. *The Firm as a Nexus of Treaties.* New York: Sage, 1990.

Ayres, Edward. *What's Good for GM.* Nashville, TN: Aurora, 1970.

Barnard, Chester I. *The Functions of the Executive*, thirtieth anniversary edition. Cambridge, MA: Harvard University Press, 1975.

Beasley, Norman. *Knudsen: A Biography.* New York: McGraw-Hill, 1947.

Bennis, Warren, G. Berkowitz, M. Affinito, and M. Malone. "Authority, Power, and the Ability to Influence." *Human Relations* 11:143–56, 1958.

Berle, Adolf A., and Gardiner C. Means. *The Modern Corporation and Private Property*, revised edition. New York: Macmillan, 1965.

Best, Michael. *The New Competition: Institutions of Industrial Restructuring.* Cambridge, MA: Harvard University Press, 1990.

Blau, Peter. *The Dynamics of Bureaucracy.* University of Chicago Press, 1955.

– *Exchange and Power in Social Life.* New York: Wiley, 1964.

– and Marshall Meyer. *Bureaucracy in Modern Society.* New York: Random House, 1971.

Bolton, Patrick, and David S. Scharfstein. "Corporate Finance, the Theory of the Firm, and Organizations." *Journal of Economic Perspectives* 12(4):95–114, 1998.

Bower, Joseph L. *Managing the Resource Allocation Process: A Study of Corporate Planning and Investment.* Boston: Harvard University Graduate School of Business Administration, 1970.

Bowles, Samuel. "The Production Process in a Competitive Economy: Walrasian, Neo-Hobbesian, and Marxian Models." *American Economic Review* 75:16–36, 1985.
– and Herbert Gintis. "Contested Exchange: Political Economy and Modern Economic Theory." *American Economic Review* 78(2):145–50, 1989.
Bradley, Albert. "Setting Up a Forecasting Program." American Management Association, annual convention series #41, March 1926a.
– "Forecasting Stabilizes Operations: Program of General Motors Corporation Aids Formulation of Fundamental Policies." *Iron Age* 117:691–3, 1926b.
– "General Motors Prepared to Vary Production Every Ten Days." *Automotive Industries* 54:488–90, 1926c.
– "How General Motors Copes with the Seasonal Problem." *Printer's Ink* 134:156ff., 1926d.
– "Financial Control Policies of General Motors and Their Relationship to Cost Accounting." *NACA Bulletin* 7:412–33, 1927.
Bradley, John, Bernard Fisher, and Lynden Paulson. *A Critical Analysis of Organization Planning at General Motors*. Unpublished manuscript, San Fernando State College, CA, 1959.
Braverman, Harry. *Labor and Monopoly Capital: The Degradation of Work in the Twentieth Century*. New York: Monthly Review, 1974.
Brown, F. Donaldson. "Pricing Policy in Relation to Financial Control: Tuning Up General Motors, Parts 2–4." *Management and Administration* 7(2):195–8; 7(3):283–6; 7(4):417–22; 1924.
– "Centralized Control with Decentralized Responsibilities." American Management Association, annual convention series 57:3–24, 1927.
– "Forecasting and Planning." *Survey* 68:34–5, 1929a.
– "Forecasting and Planning as a Factor in Stabilizing Industry, Parts 1 & 2." *Sales Management and Advertisers' Weekly* 17:181–3, 258–9, 1929b.
– "Industrial Management as a National Resource." *Conference Board Management Record* 5:142–8, 1943.
– *Some Reminiscences of an Industrialist*. Easton, PA: Hive, 1977.
Bunting, David, and Jeffrey Barbour. "Interlocking Directorates in Large American Corporations, 1896–1964." *Business History Review* 65:315–35, 1971.
Burawoy, Michael. *Manufacturing Consent: Changes in the Labor Process under Monopoly Capitalism*. University of Chicago Press, 1979.
– *The Politics of Production: Factory Regimes under Capitalism and Socialism*. London: Verso, 1985.
Burgelman, Robert A. *Inside Corporate Innovation: Strategy, Structure, and Managerial Skills*. New York: Free Press, 1986.
Burk, Robert. *The Corporate State and the Broker State: The Du Ponts and American National Politics, 1925–1940*. Cambridge, MA: Harvard University Press, 1990.
Burns, Tom, and G. M. Stalker. *The Management of Innovation*. London: Tavistock, 1961.
Burton, Richard, and Arthur Kuhn. "Strategy Follows Structure: The Missing

Link of Their Intertwined Relation." Working paper #260, Fuqua School of Business, 1979.
Business Week. "Du Pont and GM as the Family Saw Them." *Business Week* March 21, 1953, pp. 77–91.
- "General Motors' New Boss: The Idea Is Competition." *Business Week* March 21, 1953, p. 93.
Carew, Anthony. *Walter Reuther.* Manchester University Press, 1993.
Carter, Martin, Charles Ray, and Walter Weintraub (eds.). *Management: Challenge and Response.* New York: Holt, Rinehart & Winston, 1965.
Chandler, Alfred D., Jr. *Strategy and Structure: Chapters in the History of the American Industrial Enterprise.* Cambridge, MA: MIT Press, 1962.
- *The Visible Hand: The Managerial Revolution in American Business.* Cambridge, MA: Belknap Press of Harvard University, 1977.
- (ed.). *Managerial Innovation at General Motors.* New York: Arno Press, 1979.
- with Takashi Kikino. *Scale and Scope: The Dynamics of Industrial Change.* Cambridge, MA: Belknap Press of Harvard University, 1990.
- "History and Organizational Sociology." *Contemporary Sociology* 20(3):340–2, 1991a.
- "The Functions of the HQ Unit in the Multibusiness Firm." *Strategic Management Journal* 12:31–50, 1991b.
- "Corporate Strategy, Structure, and Control Methods in the United States during the Twentieth Century." *Industrial and Corporate Change* 1(2):263–84, 1992.
- and Herman Daems (eds.). *Managerial Hierarchies: Comparative Perspectives on the Rise of the Modern Industrial Enterprise.* Cambridge, MA: Harvard University Press, 1980.
- and Stephen Salsbury, with Adeline Cook Strange. *Pierre S. du Pont and the Making of the Modern Corporation.* New York: Harper & Row, 1971.
Chrysler, Walter P. *Life of an American Workman.* New York: Dodd, Mead, 1950.
Coase, Ronald. "The Nature of the Firm." *Economica* 4:386–405, 1937.
- "The Acquisition of Fisher Body by General Motors." *Journal of Law and Economics* (in press).
Collectible Automobile Magazine, February 1987.
Cordtz, Dan. "The Face in the Mirror at General Motors." *Fortune* 74(3):117ff., 1966.
Cray, Ed. *Chrome Colossus: General Motors and Its Times.* New York: McGraw-Hill, 1980.
Crozier, Michel. *The Bureaucratic Phenomenon.* University of Chicago Press, 1964.
Cyert, Richard, and James March. *A Behavioral Theory of the Firm.* Englewood Cliffs, NJ: Prentice-Hall, 1963.
Dale, Ernest. *Planning and Developing the Company Organization Structure.* Research report #20. New York: American Management Association, 1952.
- "Contributions to Administration by Alfred P. Sloan, Jr. and GM." *Administrative Science Quarterly* 1:30–61, 1956.

Dalton, Melville. "Conflicts between Staff and Line Managerial Officers." *American Sociological Review* 15:342–51, 1950.
– *Men Who Manage*. New York: Wiley, 1959.
Davis, Gerald, Kristina Diekmann, and Catherine Tinsley. "The Decline and Fall of the Conglomerate Firm in the 1980s: The Deinstitutionalization of an Organizational Form." *American Sociological Review* 59:540–70, 1994.
Demsetz, Harold. *Ownership, Control, and the Firm. Volume I: The Organization of Economic Activity*. Oxford: Basil Blackwell, 1988.
DiMaggio, Paul J., and Walter W. Powell. "The Iron Cage Revisited: Institutional Isomorphism and Collective Rationality in Organizational Fields." *American Sociological Review* 48:147–60, 1983. Reprinted in Walter W. Powell and Paul J. DiMaggio (eds.), *The New Institutionalism in Organizational Analysis*, pp. 63–82. University of Chicago Press, 1991.
Dirlam, Joel B., and Irwin M. Stelzer. "The Du Pont–General Motors Decision: In the Antitrust Grain." *Columbia Law Review* 58(1):24–43, 1958.
Dobbin, Frank R. *Forging Industrial Policy: The United States, Britain, and France in the Railway Age*. Cambridge University Press, 1994.
Domhoff, G. William. *Who Rules America?* Englewood Cliffs, NJ: Prentice-Hall, 1967.
Donner, Frederic G. *The World-wide Industrial Enterprise*. New York: McGraw-Hill, 1967.
Drucker, Peter F. *The Concept of the Corporation*, rev. ed. New York: John Day, 1972.
– *Adventures of a Bystander*. New York: Harper & Row, 1978.
Durkheim, Emile. *The Division of Labor in Society*, trans. H. D. Halls. New York: Free Press, 1984.
Easterbrook, Frank H., and Daniel R. Fischel. *The Economic Structure of Corporate Law*. Cambridge, MA: Harvard University Press, 1991.
Eccles, Robert. *The Transfer-Pricing Problem: A Theory for Practice*. Lexington, MA: Lexington Books, 1985.
– and Harrison C. White. "Price and Authority in Inter-Profit Center Transactions." *American Journal of Sociology (Suppl.)* 94:17–51, 1988.
Edelman, Lauren. "Legal Environments and Organizational Governance: The Expansion of Due Process in the American Workplace." *American Journal of Sociology* 95:1401–40, 1990.
Elster, Jon. *Nuts and Bolts for the Social Sciences*. Cambridge University Press, 1989.
Etzioni, Amitai. *A Comparative Analysis of Complex Organizations*. Glencoe, IL: Free Press, 1961.
Fama, Eugene. "Agency Problems and the Theory of the Firm." *Journal of Political Economy* 88:288–307, 1980. Reprinted in abridged form in Louis Putterman, *The Economic Nature of the Firm: A Reader*, pp. 196–208. Cambridge University Press, 1986.
– and Michael Jensen. "Separation of Ownership and Control." *Journal of Law and Economics* 26:301–26, 1983.
Fireman, Bruce, and William Gamson. "Utilitarian Logic in the Resource Mobilization Perspective." In: Mayer Zald and J. D. McCarthy (eds.), *The*

Dynamics of Social Movements: Resource Mobilization, Social Control and Tactics, pp. 8–44. Cambridge: Winthrop, 1979.

Fligstein, Neil. "The Spread of the Multidivisional Form." *American Sociological Review* 50:377–91, 1985.

– "The Intraorganizational Power Struggle: The Rise of Finance Presidents in Large Corporations, 1919–1979." *American Sociological Review* 52:44–58, 1987.

– *The Transformation of Corporate Control*. Cambridge, MA: Harvard University Press, 1990.

Fordham, Thomas B., and Edward H. Tingley. "Applying the Budget to Industrial Operations – Control Through Organization and Budget." *Management and Administration* 7:57–62, 205–98, 291, 1924.

Fortune. "Alfred P. Sloan, Jr.: Chairman." *Fortune* 17:72–7ff., 1938.

– "General Motors, Part I of a Study in Bigness." *Fortune* 18:40–7ff., 1938.

– "General Motors II: Chevrolet." *Fortune*. 19:36–46ff., 1939.

– "G.M. III: How to Sell Automobiles." *Fortune* 19:70–8ff., 1939.

– "General Motors IV: A Unit in Society." *Fortune* 19:44–52ff., 1939.

– "How Harlow Curtice Earns His $750,000." In: Editors of Fortune, *The Art of Success*, pp. 3–20. Philadelphia: Lippincott, 1956.

Fox, Frederick, and Barry Staw. "The Trapped Administrator: Effects of Job Insecurity and Policy Resistance on Commitment to a Course of Action." *Administrative Science Quarterly* 24:449–71, 1979.

Freeland, Robert F. "Theoretical Logic and Predictive Specificity: A Reply to Shanley." *American Journal of Sociology* 102(2):483–526, 1996.

– "Creating Hold-Up through Vertical Integration: Fisher Body Revisited." *Journal of Law and Economics* (in press).

Fuller, Lon L. *The Morality of Law*. New Haven, CT: Yale University Press, 1964.

General Motors Corporation. *Annual Reports*. Detroit: General Motors Corporation, 1915–1990.

– *By-laws* (unpublished documents). Detroit: General Motors Corporation, 1921–1958.

– *The Dynamics of Automobile Demand*. New York: General Motors Corporation, 1939.

– "Report to War Department Price Adjustment Board: Summary of War Operations of General Motors for the Year 1943" (unpublished document), September 30, 1943.

– *The College Graduate and General Motors*. Detroit: General Motors Corporation, 1948.

– *Job Opportunities in General Motors*. Detroit: General Motors Corporation, circa 1955.

– *The Automobile Industry: A Case Study of Competition*. Detroit: General Motors Corporation, 1968.

Gerstenberg, Richard. "Control Through Policing Performance." In: *Meeting and Beating Competition*, contributed papers, fifth annual Michigan Cost Conference, April 10, 1954. Ann Arbor, MI: University of Michigan, School of Business Administration, 1954.

Goold, Michael, and Andrew Campbell. *Strategies and Styles: The Role of the*

Centre in Managing Diversified Corporations. Oxford: Basil Blackwell, 1987.
Gottesman et al. v. General Motors. U.S. Civil 121–251, 279 F. Supp. 361, S.D. New York, 1967.
Gould, Mark. *Revolution in the Development of Capitalism: The Coming of the English Revolution.* Berkeley, CA: University of California Press, 1987.
– "The Problem of Order in Perfect and Imperfect Information Theories." Paper presented at the annual meeting of the American Economic Association, Washington, DC, 1990.
– "Parsons' Economic Sociology: A Failure of Will." *Sociological Inquiry* 61:89–101, 1991.
– "Legitimation and Justification: The Logic of Moral and Contractual Solidarity in Weber and Durkheim." *Current Perspectives in Social Theory* 13:205–25, 1993.
– and Michael Weinstein. "Class in a Neoclassical Theory of Competitive Markets." Unpublished manuscript, Haverford College, 1989.
Gouldner, Alvin. *Patterns of Industrial Bureaucracy.* Glencoe, IL: Free Press, 1954.
– "The Norm of Reciprocity." *American Sociological Review* 25:161–79, 1961.
Granovetter, Mark. "Economic Action and Social Structure: The Problem of Embeddedness." *American Journal of Sociology* 91:481–510, 1985.
– "Problems of Explanation in Economic Sociology." In: Nitin Nohria and Robert G. Eccles (eds.), *Networks and Organizations: Structure, Form, and Action,* pp. 25–56. Boston: Harvard Business School Press, 1992.
Greenwood, Ronald. *Managerial Decentralization: A Study of the General Electric Philosophy.* Lexington, MA: Lexington Books, 1974.
Gustin, Lawrence. *Billy Durant: Creator of General Motors.* Grand Rapids, MI: William B. Eerdmans, 1973.
Halaby, Charles. "Worker Attachment and Workplace Authority." *American Sociological Review* 51:634–49, 1986.
Hampton, William, and James Norman. "General Motors: What Went Wrong." *Business Week* March 16, 1987, pp. 102–9.
Hart, Oliver. *Firms, Contracts, and Financial Structure.* Oxford: Clarendon Press, 1995.
Hayford, Leslie. "Production Control and Planning in General Motors." Unpublished manuscript, General Motors Corporation, February 1955.
Hickerson, J. M. *Ernie Breech.* New York: Meredith, 1968.
Hickson, D. J., C. R. Hinings, C. A. Lee, R. E. Schneck, and J. M. Pennings. "A Strategic Contingencies Theory of Intraorganizational Power." *Administrative Science Quarterly* 16:216–29, 1971.
Hinings, C. R., D. J. Hickson, J. M. Pennings, and R. E. Schneck. "Structural Conditions of Intraorganizational Power." *Administrative Science Quarterly* 19:22–44, 1974.
Jensen, Michael. "Organization Theory and Methodology." *Accounting Review* 50:319–39, 1983.
– and William Meckling. "Theory of the Firm: Managerial Behavior, Agency

Costs, and Capital Structure." *Journal of Financial Economics* 3:305–60, 1976. Reprinted in abridged form in Louis Putterman (ed.), *The Economic Nature of the Firm: A Reader*, pp. 209–29. Cambridge University Press, 1986.

Johnson, H. Thomas. *System and Profits: Early Management Accounting at Du Pont and General Motors.* New York: Arno, 1980.

– and Robert S. Kaplan. *Relevance Lost: The Rise and Fall of Management Accounting.* Boston: Harvard Business School Press, 1987.

Keller, Maryann. *Rude Awakening: The Rise, Fall, and Struggle for Recovery of General Motors.* New York: Morrow, 1989.

Klein, Benjamin. "Vertical Integration as Organizational Ownership: The Fisher Body–General Motors Relationship Revisited." *Journal of Law, Economics, and Organization* 4(1):199–213, 1988.

– "Contracts and Incentives: The Role of Contract Terms in Assuring Performance." In: Lars Werin and Hans Wijkander (eds.), *Contract Economics*, pp. 149–72. Oxford: Basil Blackwell, 1992.

– Robert Crawford, and Armen Alchian. "Vertical Integration, Appropriable Rents, and the Competitive Contracting Process." *Journal of Law and Economics* 21(2):297–326, 1978.

Kornai, János. *Economics of Shortage, Volume B.* Amsterdam: North Holland, 1980.

– *Vision and Reality, Market and State: Contradictions and Dilemmas Revisited.* New York: Routledge, 1990.

Kuhn, Arthur. *GM Passes Ford, 1918–1938: Designing the General Motors Performance-Control System.* University Park, PA: Pennsylvania State University Press, 1986.

Kunda, Gideon. *Engineering Culture: Control and Commitment in a High-Tech Corporation.* Philadelphia: Temple University Press, 1992.

Langlois, Richard N., and Paul L. Robertson. *Firms, Markets, and Economic Change.* New York: Routledge, 1995.

Lawrence, Paul, and Jay Lorsch. *Organization and Environment: Managing Differentiation and Integration.* Cambridge, MA: Harvard University Press, 1967.

Lazonick, William. *Business Organization and the Myth of the Market Economy.* Cambridge University Press, 1991.

Lerner, Abba. "The Economics of Consumer Sovereignty." *American Economic Review* 62(2):258–66, 1972.

Leslie, Stuart. *Boss Kettering: Wizard of General Motors.* New York: Columbia University Press, 1983.

Lind, E. Allan, and Tom R. Tyler. *The Social Psychology of Procedural Justice.* New York: Plenum, 1988.

Lorange, Peter. *Corporate Planning: An Executive Viewpoint.* Englewood Cliffs, NJ: Prentice-Hall, 1980.

– and Richard F. Vancil. *Strategic Planning Systems.* Englewood Cliffs, NJ: Prentice-Hall, 1977.

Lorsch, Jay, and Paul Lawrence (eds.). *Studies in Organization Design.* Homewood, IL: Richard D. Irwin, 1970.

Ludvigsen, Karl. "The Truth about Chevy's Cashiered Cadet." *Special-Interest Autos* January–February 1974, pp. 16–19.

Luhmann, Niklas. *Legitimation durch Verfahren*, 2nd ed. Darmstadt: Luchterhand, 1975.

McKenna, Christopher D. "'The American Challenge': McKinsey & Company's Role in the Transfer of Decentralization to Europe, 1957–1975." Unpublished manuscript, Department of History, Johns Hopkins University, 1998.

Macneil, Ian R. "Contracts: Adjustments of Long-Term Economic Relations Under Classical, Neoclassical, and Relational Contract Law." *Northwestern University Law Review* 47:854–906, 1978.

Manne, Henry. "Mergers and the Market for Corporate Control." *Journal of Political Economy* 73:110–20, 1965.

March, James. "An Introduction to the Theory and Management of Influence." *American Political Science Review* 59:431–51, 1955.

– "The Firm as a Political Coalition." *Journal of Politics* 24:662–78, 1962.

– and Herbert Simon. *Organizations*. Oxford: Basil Blackwell, 1993.

Marris, Robin. *The Economic Theory of Managerial Capitalism*. New York: Free Press, 1964.

Marx, Karl. *Capital, Volume I*. Middlesex: Penguin, 1976.

Merton, Robert. "Bureaucratic Structure and Personality." In: *Social Theory and Social Structure*, pp. 249–60. New York: Free Press, 1968.

Meyer, John W., and Brian Rowan. "Institutionalized Organizations: Formal Structure as Myth and Ceremony." *American Journal of Sociology* 83:340–63, 1977.

– and W. Richard Scott (eds.). *Organizational Environments: Ritual and Rationality*. Beverly Hills, CA: Sage, 1983.

Meyer, Marshall. "Size and Structure of Organizations: A Causal Analysis." *American Sociological Review* 37:434–40, 1972.

– "Measuring Performance in Economic Organizations." In: Richard Swedberg and Neil Smelser (eds.), *The Handbook of Economic Sociology*, pp. 556–78. Princeton, NJ: Princeton University Press, 1994.

Miles, Raymond, and Charles Snow. *Organization Strategy, Structure, and Process*. New York: McGraw-Hill, 1978.

Miller, Gary J. *Managerial Dilemmas: The Political Economy of Hierarchy*. Cambridge University Press, 1992.

Mintz, Beth, and Michael Schwartz. *The Power Structure of American Business*. University of Chicago Press, 1985.

Mizruchi, Mark. *The American Corporate Network, 1904–1974*. Beverly Hills, CA: Sage, 1982.

– "Who Controls Whom? An Examination of the Relation between Management and Boards of Directors in Large American Corporations." *Academy of Management Review* 8:426–35, 1983.

Mooney, James D. "Selling the Automobile Overseas: How General Motors' Export Business Is Handled." *Management and Administration* 8:27–32, 1924.

Motor Coach Age. "Yellow Coach and GM Buses: 1. Origins; General and Corporate History." *Motor Coach Age* 41(7–8):4–41, 1989.

Nader, Ralph. *Unsafe at Any Speed: The Designed-In Dangers of the American Automobile.* New York: Grossman, 1972.
New York Times. "Waste of Assets of G.M. is Found." *New York Times,* p. A-1, April 12, 1942.
Odagiri, Hiroyuki. *Growth Through Competition, Competition Through Growth. Strategic Management and the Economy in Japan.* Oxford: Clarendon Press, 1994.
Organisation for European Economic Co-operation. *Some Aspects of the Motor Vehicle Industry in the U.S.A.* Technical assistance mission #92. Paris: Organisation for European Economic Co-operation, 1953.
Ouchi, William G. "Markets, Bureaucracies, and Clans." *Administrative Science Quarterly* 25(March):129–41, 1980.
Palmer, Donald, Roger Friedland, P. Devereaux Jennings, and Melanie Powers. "The Economics and Politics of Structure: The Multidivisional Form and the Large U.S. Corporation." *Administrative Science Quarterly* 32:25–48, 1987.
Parsons, Talcott. Introduction to *The Theory of Social and Economic Organization,* pp. 3–86, by Max Weber. Glencoe, IL: Free Press, 1947.
– *Structure and Process in Modern Societies.* New York: Free Press, 1960.
– *The Structure of Social Action.* New York: Free Press, 1968.
– "On the Concept of Political Power." In: Talcott Parsons, *Politics and Social Structure,* pp. 352–404. New York: Free Press, 1969.
– and Neil J. Smelser. *Economy and Society: A Study in the Integration of Economic and Social Theory.* Glencoe, IL: Free Press, 1956.
Perrow, Charles. "The Analysis of Goals in Complex Organizations." *American Sociological Review* 26:854–66, 1961.
– "Markets, Hierarchies, and Hegemony." In: Andrew H. Van de Ven and William F. Joyce (eds.), *Perspectives on Organization Design and Behavior,* pp. 371–86. New York: Wiley, 1981.
– *Complex Organizations: A Critical Essay,* 3rd ed. New York: Random House, 1986.
Pfeffer, Jeffrey. *Power in Organizations.* New York: Harper, 1980.
– and Gerald Salancik. *The External Control of Organizations: A Resource Dependence Perspective.* New York: Harper & Row, 1978.
Polanyi, Michael. *Personal Knowledge: Towards a Post-Critical Philosophy.* New York: Harper & Row, 1962.
Pound, Arthur. *The Turning Wheel: The Story of General Motors through Twenty Five Years, 1908–1933.* Garden City, NY: Doubleday, Doran, 1934.
Powell, Walter W., and Paul J. DiMaggio (eds.). *The New Institutionalism in Organizational Analysis.* University of Chicago Press, 1991.
Przeworski, Adam. *Capitalism and Social Democracy.* Cambridge University Press, 1985.
Putterman, Louis (ed.). *The Economic Nature of the Firm: A Reader.* Cambridge University Press, 1986.
Raskob, John J. "Management the Major Factor in All Industry." *Magazine of Business* 34:23–6, 1928.

Reck, F. M. *On Time: The History of the Electro-Motive Division of General Motors Corporation*. New York: General Motors Corporation, 1948.

Roe, Mark. *Strong Managers, Weak Owners: The Political Roots of American Corporate Finance*. Princeton, NJ: Princeton University Press, 1994.

Roethlisberger, F. J., and William J. Dickson. *Management and the Worker*. Cambridge, MA: Harvard University Press, 1939.

Rothschild, Emma. *Paradise Lost: The Decline of the Auto-Industrial Age*. New York: Random House, 1973.

Roy, Donald. *Socializing Capital: The Rise of the Large Industrial Corporation in America*. Princeton, NJ: Princeton University Press, 1997.

Salancik, Gerald. "Commitment and Control of Organizational Behavior and Belief." In: Barry Staw and Gerald Salancik (eds.), *New Directions in Organizational Behavior*, pp. 1–54. Chicago: St. Clair, 1977a.

– "Commitment Is Too Easy." *Organizational Dynamics* 6(1):62–80, 1977b.

– Jeffrey Pfeffer, and J. Patrick Kelly. "A Contingency Model of Influence in Organizational Decision-Making." *Pacific Sociological Review* 21:239–56, 1978.

Schneiberg, Marc, and J. Rogers Hollingsworth. "Can Transaction Cost Economics Explain Trade Associations?" Draft manuscript prepared for delivery at the Swedish Collegium for Advanced Study of the Social Sciences conference on "The Firm as a Nexus of Treaties," Uppsala, Sweden, June 6–8, 1988. Reprinted in abridged form in Masahiko Aoki, Bo Gustaffson, and Oliver Williamson (eds.), *The Firm as a Nexus of Treaties*, pp. 320–46. New York: Sage, 1990.

Schumpeter, Joseph. *Capitalism, Socialism, and Democracy*. New York: Harper & Row, 1962.

Scott, W. Richard. *Organizations: Rational, Natural and Open Systems*, 3rd ed. Englewood Cliffs, NJ: Prentice-Hall, 1998.

– John W. Meyer, and associates. *Institutional Environments and Organizations: Structural Complexity and Individualism*. Thousand Oaks, CA: Sage, 1994.

Seltzer, Lawrence. *A Financial History of the American Automobile Industry: A Study of the Ways in Which the Leading American Producers of Automobiles Have Met Their Capital Requirements*. New York: Houghton Mifflin, 1928.

Selznick, Philip. "Foundations of the Theory of Organizations." *American Sociological Review* 13(1):25–35, 1948.

– *TVA and the Grass Roots: A Study in the Sociology of Formal Organizations*. Berkeley: University of California Press, 1949.

– with Phillipe Nonet and Howard M. Vollmer. *Law, Society, and Industrial Justice*. New York: Russell Sage Foundation, 1969.

Shanley, Mark. "Straw Men and M-Form Myths: Comment on Freeland." *American Journal of Sociology* 102(2):527–36, 1996.

Sheehan, Robert. "GM's Remodeled Management." In: Martin Carter, Charles Ray, and Walter Weintraub (eds.), *Management: Challenge and Response*, pp. 46–58. New York: Holt, Rinehart and Winston, 1965.

Simmel, Georg. *The Sociology of Georg Simmel*, ed. Kurt Wolff. New York: Free Press, 1950.

References 351

Simon, Herbert. *Administrative Behavior: A Study of Decision-Making Processes in Administrative Organization*, 3rd ed. New York: Free Press, 1976.
- "Organizations and Markets." *Journal of Economic Perspectives* 5:25–44, 1991.

Sloan, Alfred P., Jr. "The Most Important Thing I Ever Learned about Management." *System: The Magazine of Business* 46:140–1, 194, 1924.
- "Make Smaller Profits Pay." *Factory* 37:993–7ff., 1926.
- "'Getting the Facts' Is Keystone of General Motors' Success." *Automotive Industries* 57:550–1, 1927a.
- *The Principles and Policies behind General Motors*. New York: General Motors Corporation, 1927b.
- "Sloan of General Motors Predicts a Revolution in Distribution." *Printers' Ink* 146:88ff., 1929.
- "The Broadened Responsibilities of Industries' Executives." In: J. G. Frederick (ed.), *For Top Executives Only*, pp. 351–71. New York: Business Bourse, 1936.
- in collaboration with Boyden Sparks. *Adventures of a White Collar Man*. New York: Doubleday, 1941.
- "Fact-finding for Management." In: L. Greendlinger (ed.), *Modern Business Lectures*, pp. 5–18. New York: Alexander Hamilton Institute, 1954. (Originally published 1930.)
- *My Years with General Motors*. New York: Doubleday, 1964.
- "Spotlight on Alfred Sloan: The GM Chairman Discusses the Modern Business Corporation." Audiotape interview with Alfred Sloan from "The Business Scene" series, Edward Stanley, interviewer (date of interview unknown). Tucson, AZ: Learning Plans, Inc., 1969.
- "The General Motors Story." Unpublished manuscript version of *My Years with General Motors*, undated (circa 1962).

Staw, Barry. "Knee-Deep in the Big Muddy: A Study of Escalating Commitment to a Chosen Course of Action." *Organizational Behavior and Human Performance* 16:27–44, 1976.

Stiglitz, Joseph. "The Causes and Consequences of the Dependence of Quality on Price." *Journal of Economic Literature* 25:1–48, 1987.

Stinchcombe, Arthur. *Information and Organizations*. Berkeley, CA: University of California Press, 1990.

Stout, Richard H. "When General Motors Was Great." *Automotive Industries* February 1992, pp. 98–103.

Swayne, Alfred H. "Mobilization of Cash Reserves." *Management and Administration* 7:21–3, 1924.

Thompson, G. V. "Intercompany Technical Standardization in the Early American Automobile Industry." *Journal of Economic History* 14:1–20, 1954.

Thompson, James D. *Organizations in Action: Social Science Bases of Administration*. New York: McGraw-Hill, 1967.

United States Congress. *Corporate Profits*. Hearings before the Joint Committee on the Economic Report, Congress of the United States, 80th Congress, 2nd session, December 1948. Washington, DC: U.S. Government Printing Office, 1949.

- *A Study of the Antitrust Laws*. Hearings before the Subcommittee on Antitrust and Monopoly of the Committee of the Judiciary, United States Senate, 84th Congress, 1st and 2nd sessions. Washington, DC: U.S. Government Printing Office, 1956.
- *Administered Prices, Part 6: Automobiles*. Hearings before the Subcommittee on Antitrust and Monopoly, Committee on the Judiciary, United States Senate, 85th Congress, 2nd session. Washington, DC: U.S. Government Printing Office, 1958.

United States Federal Trade Commission. *Report on the Motor Vehicle Industry.* Washington, DC: U.S. Government Printing Office, 1939.

United States of America v. E. I. du Pont de Nemours, General Motors, et al. 126 F. Supp. 235, U.S. District Court for the Northern District of Illinois, Eastern Division, Civil Action 49C-1071, 1954.

United States of America v. E. I. du Pont de Nemours, General Motors, et al. 353 U.S. 586, U.S. Supreme Court Records, Briefs, 1956.

United States of America v. General Motors Corporation. Seventh U.S. Circuit Court, Civil Action 7146, 1940.

Van de Ven, Andrew H., and William F. Joyce (eds.). *Perspectives on Organization Design and Behavior.* New York: Wiley, 1981.

Weber, Max. *The Protestant Ethic and the Spirit of Capitalism*, trans. Talcott Parsons. New York: Scribner, 1958.
- *The Theory of Social and Economic Organization.* New York: Free Press, 1964.
- "Bureaucracy." In: Hans H. Gerth and C. Wright Mills (trans.), *From Max Weber: Essays in Sociology*, pp. 196–244. Oxford University Press, 1978.

Weisberger, Bernard. *The Dream-Maker: William C. Durant, Founder of General Motors.* Boston: Little, Brown, 1979.

White, Lawrence J. *The Automobile Industry Since 1945.* Cambridge, MA: Harvard University Press, 1971.

Williamson, Oliver. *Markets and Hierarchies: Analysis and Antitrust Implications.* New York: Free Press, 1975.
- "The Economics of Organization: The Transaction Cost Approach." *American Journal of Sociology* 87:548–77, 1981.
- "Organization Form, Residual Claimants, and Corporate Control." *Journal of Law and Economics* 26:351–66, 1983.
- *The Economic Institutions of Capitalism: Firms, Markets, Relational Contracting.* New York: Free Press, 1985.
- *Economic Organization: Firms, Markets, and Policy Control.* New York University Press, 1986.
- "Comparative Economic Organization: The Analysis of Discrete Structural Alternatives." *Administrative Science Quarterly* 36:269–96, 1991a.
- "Strategizing, Economizing, and Economic Organization." *Strategic Management Journal* 12:75–94, 1991b.
- "Transaction Cost Economics and Organization Theory." In: Neil J. Smelser and Richard Swedberg (eds.), *The Handbook of Economic Sociology*, pp. 77–107. Princeton, NJ: Princeton University Press/Russell Sage Foundation, 1994.

- *Organization Theory: From Chester Barnard to the Present and Beyond*, expanded edition. Oxford University Press, 1995.
- *The Mechanisms of Governance*. Oxford University Press, 1996.
- and William Ouchi. "The Markets and Hierarchies Program of Research: Origins, Implications, and Prospects." In: Andrew H. Van de Ven and William F. Joyce (eds.), *Perspectives on Organization Design and Behavior*, pp. 347–70. New York: Wiley, 1981.
- and Sidney G. Winter (eds.). *The Nature of the Firm: Origins, Evolution, and Development*. Oxford University Press, 1991.

Winkelman et al. v. General Motors Corporation et al. 44 F. Supp. 960, S.D. New York, 1942.

Wolf, Ronald H. "General Motors: A Study of the Firm's Growth, Its External Relationships, and Internal Organization." Unpublished Ph.D. dissertation in economics, Vanderbilt University, June 1962.

Wolff, Harold. "The Great GM Mystery." *Harvard Business Review.* September–October 1964, pp. 164–202.

Woodward, Joan. *Industrial Organization: Theory and Practice*. Oxford University Press, 1980.

Wright, J. Patrick. *On a Clear Day You Can See General Motors: John Z. De Lorean's Look Inside the Automotive Giant*. Grosse Point, MI: Wright Enterprises, 1979.

Yates, Brock. *The Decline and Fall of the American Automobile Industry*. New York: Empire Books, 1983.

Zald, Mayer (ed.). *Power in Organizations*. Nashville: Vanderbilt University Press, 1970.

Zeitlin, Maurice. "Corporate Ownership and Control: The Large Corporation and the Capitalist Class." *American Journal of Sociology* 79:1073–119, 1974.

- *The Large Corporation and Contemporary Classes*. Cambridge, MA: Polity, 1989.

Index

accounting system: standard volume concept, 228
Administration Committee: formation, composition, and function (1937), 100–2, 104–7, 115–25; role during defense production years, 132–42
Administration Committee (postwar): composition and duties of, 199–200; membership, fiat, and function of, 165–71, 242; participation of division managers in, 280; under 1958 reorganization, 264; role under Curtice, 241–3
agency theory, 15n42
antitrust issues: GM/GMAC restraint of trade, 161–2; owners' initial victory in Du Pont suit (1954), 241; related to Du Pont ownership of GM (1948), 38, 224–5, 232–3, 299; resignations of Du Pont executives from GM, 38, 271; suit against GM (1956), 252; Supreme Court reverses Du Pont decision, 254
authority: conditions for acceptance of, 25; effect of division of labor on, 24; in M-form, 307–14; transformation under Sloan (1923–1933), 64–8
automobile industry: postwar labor union strikes, 175; postwar reconversion, 175
automobile market: competition (1930s), 308–9; dealer dissatisfaction, 248–50; demand (1948–1955), 223; effect of oil price shocks (1973, 1979), 289–91; GM's domination (1930s), 82; GM's push to expand share of, 248–50; GM's share (1952–1954; 1956–1957), 246, 253–4; during and after Korean War, 236, 248–50, 255–6; post-depression, 83–6, 96–100; post–World War II, 175–83. *See also* small-car program

Barnard, Chester I., 25n76, 28
Bassett, Harry, 54
Bendix Aviation, 217–19
Bergland, E. A., 55
Berle, Adolph, 14–15
board of directors: appoints Sloan committee (1957), 254–8; delegation of authority to Administration Committee, 166–9; Sloan's plan to reduce size of (1937), 101, 103–4
bounded rationality: of economic actors, 10; identifying and controlling, 10–11; problems of, 11–12
Bradley, Albert, 94n32, 109–12, 129–30, 225–6, 254
Brown, Donaldson: before and during World War II, 54–7, 74, 88, 106, 110, 113–14, 117, 136, 138, 167–8
Brown, Donaldson (postwar role): concerns related to finances, 228; conflict with Wilson, 183–5; criticism of Sloan's plan, 188, 191–2; criticisms of Wilson, 213–15
Burke, Francis, 231

356 Index

capital: effect of slack capital on owners' actions, 297–8; expansion of fixed and working (1917–1920), 47; GM's postwar shortage of, 177–8; incentives related to slack capital, 38–9, 96–8, 225, 237–9; post-1920 owner control, 56–7; returns on (1937–1941; 1942–1945), 140–1; sources of additional (1946), 202–3

capital market: GM executives' lack of concern with, 112; GM's debenture notes (1954), 244; M-form organization serves as internal, 17–18

capital turnover: components of (1937–1941; 1942–1945), 139–40; conditions for decreased, 139; under wartime conditions, 138–9

Carpenter, Walter S., Jr.: postwar role, 181–2, 193, 203–4, 233; before and during World War II, 88–9, 107, 110, 115, 120–2, 125, 138, 148–9, 164, 167–70

centralization, administrative: under Curtice, 248–56; during defense contracting and wartime production, 127, 129–34; under Donner regime, 271–85; with formation of WEC, 142; as identified by TCE, 16; increases (1930s), 94–100, 107, 308–9; 1950s and 1960s, 309–10; Sloan's view, 308; stages of, 126; trend in GM, 81–3

Chandler, Alfred D., Jr., 14n40, 54n37

Chevrolet division: Cadet, 178–81, 208; Caprice, 292; Chevette, 290, 292; Corvair, 3

coalitions, General Motors: between Curtice and operating side, 248–53; of owners and finance staff, 207–15; realignment of postwar, 177, 183–7

coercion: replaces consent under Curtice, 256; shift toward use of, 94

Cole, Edward, 282, 285–7

Collins, Richard, 54

committee structure: General Motors (pre-1920), 45–50; role in value creation and loss prevention, 13–14. *See also* specific committees by name

competition: in auto market (1930s), 308; inter- and intra-jurisdictional, 54; in post-1955 car market, 273–7; post-depression, 84; postwar automobile market, 157; 175–83; process of evolutionary, 46–7; in small-car and subcompact field (1960s–1970s), 286–9; strategies (1920s), 59–60

Congress: hearings on dealers' grievances, 249–50

consent: absence in new M-form of mechanisms for, 271–3, 279–81; under administrative centralization, 82, 271–3, 279–81, 284; conditions requiring, 127–8; defined, 26; disruption of divisional (mid–late 1950s), 253; effect of policy group system on, 94; factors disrupting, 7; formal and informal mechanisms for, 306; GM's operation in absence of, 285–92; importance and function of, 24–5; norms underlying, 27; in organizational behavior, 25–33, 239–47; and owners' constraints on top management, 295–6; produced at GM, 303–5; produced in Du Pont M-form organization, 303–5; relation to reciprocity, 26; under 1946 reorganization, 223–4; replaced by coercion under Curtice, 256; Sloan's ability to create, 44–5, 64–79, 307–8, 310; strategic use by Curtice, 240. *See also* cooperation

contingency theory, 321

control: of bounded rationality, 10–11; by Financial Policy Committee (FPC), 206–7, 228–9, 234; by GM under Policy Committee, 165; mechanisms in TCE, 20–1; in M-form, 15, 19–22; of production, 136; related

Index

to division of labor, 20. *See also* financial control; owner control
cooperation: in efficiency theory, 17; informal norms, 27; in M-form, 307–14; in modern corporation, 306; with participative decentralization, 310; problems of, 307–8. *See also* consent
Copeland, Lammont Du Pont, 233
corporation, modern: cooperation in, 306; corporate governance in, 285–92; division of labor in, 41; efficiency in, 1; owner control, 295–300; ownership in, 305–6; stages of growth, 8. *See also* governance, corporate
Coyle, Marvin, 151, 178, 180, 182
Curtice, Harlow, 151, 239–52

decentralization, administrative: conditions for development of, 305; in GM organizational structure, 35–8; Sloan's version of, 44–58, 64, 308, 310
decentralization, participative: under Curtice as president and CEO, 240–3; as identified by TCE, 16; new form, 152–60; in 1946 organization, 199; postwar, 163–73, 176; strategies for and against, 68–79; under WAC, 151; with wartime conditions, 142–3; during World War II, 127–8, 132–4. *See also* divisions
decision-making: financial issues (1937), 109–15; by New York office, 154–6, 163–8; under renewed M-form organization, 271
defense contracts: allocation guidelines, 136; allocation within GM, 134–42; importance to GM, 130–1; during Korean War, 235–6; legal issues related to, 160–1; predictable demand, 139
Defense Materials Relationships Committee (DMRC), 129, 131–4
defense production: organizational changes with, 128–34; role of DMRC, 128–42. *See also* War Emergency Committee (WEC)

division of labor: informal norms and expectations, 28; information and resources controlled by each, 20; interdependence with, 19–21; in M-form organization, 4, 19–21, 24; order in modern corporation with, 41; between WAC and policy groups, 154
divisions: attempts at product differentiation (1965–1969), 279; autonomy during wartime, 143–4; autonomy under Durant (pre-1920), 45–6, 49; car divisions lack of input for product planning, 291; with centralization (1934), 94; contract allocation role during World War II, 127–8, 132–4; Du Pont ideas related to, 52; effect in organizations of, 12; lacking representation under renewed M-form, 271–3; management under M-form, 4; managerial hierarchy with, 12; measurement of performance, 17–18; New Departure division, 237; opposition to air-cooled engine, 60; participation under Curtice, 240–1; under participative decentralization, 311; in post-depression centralization, 83–9; rebellion against Donner regime policies, 277; representation on Administration Committee, 167; representation on committees, 311; representation under WAC, 152; response to increasing centralization, 279–92; response to resurrected M-form, 271–2; role during defense production years, 128–52; role in policy groups, 94; role under wartime participative decentralization, 152–60; Sloan's creation of consent in, 44–5; Sloan's ideas related to autonomy of, 49–52; specialization in, 307–8
DMRC (Defense Materials Relationships Committee), 129, 131–4
Donner, Frederic: postwar role, 203–4, 282, 284; before and

358 Index

during World War II, 110, 113–14, 135, 254, 264
Drucker, Peter, 156n91
du Pont, Lammot: postwar role, 188; before and during World War II, 73–9, 88, 91, 98, 100, 103–4, 106, 110, 149, 151, 167–9, 173
du Pont, Pierre, 44, 48, 52–5, 58–63, 71, 73–4
E. I. du Pont de Nemours: concerns related to antitrust issues, 298–9; concerns related to ownership role in GM, 33–42, 91; divests GM stock, 254; legal opinion related to, 194–5; lobbying FPC members, 201; major shareholder in GM, 33–42, 45, 48; operating divisions during World War II, 304n17; ownership in GM, 4–5, 33–42; proposal about GM reorganization (1937), 103–4; success of M-form at, 36, 302–3; view of decentralization, 48–53. *See also* names of specific individuals; owners
E. I. du Pont de Nemours (postwar era): antitrust suit against, 224–5; independent financial report (1946), 205–6
Durant, William C., 45–51

Echols, Angus, 216, 233
economic theory of the firm. *See* firm
efficiency: of M-form organization, 2, 7–9, 14, 307–14; in modern corporation, 1; in organization theory, 315–23; trade-offs between order and, 27; of transaction cost economics, 320–1
efficiency theory: governance, 33; logic of, 17–23
Executive Committee: with centralization (1934), 83, 91; composition and function (1933), 102; departure of Du Pont representatives from, 91; establishment (1918), 46–7, 49–50; Gerstenberg regime, 290–1; post-1920 owner-dominated, 52–3; Roche regime, 285–7; Sloan's appointments to (1924), 71–2
Executive Committee, Donner regime: composition, 285; in 1958 reorganization, 263–5; small-car program, 274–5; standardized parts and components program, 277–8
executives, General Motors: decisions related to labor negotiations, 183–7; focus of financial and operating concerns, 112; Sloan's plan for additional authority for, 183–7; view of decentralization, 36–7

fiat: effect of reliance on, 309, 311, 315; failure in air-cooled car debate, 60–3; at General Motors (1921–1933), 44–58; in M-form, 21–4; post-1920 governance at GM by, 58–63; resistance to, 316–18; Sloan's placing of limits on, 64–7, 311; TCE develops order as, 312; TCE perception of resistance to, 317–18. *See also* coercion; governance by fiat; sanctions
Finance Committee: composition and function (1933), 102; owner-dominated, 35; post-1918 owner-controlled, 46–7, 49–58, 82; in 1958 reorganization, 263–5; during Roche administration, 285. *See also* Financial Policy Committee (FPC)
financial control: with administrative centralization (1930s), 308–9; decline with slack capital condition, 225–33; efforts of owners and GM executives for, 96–100; under M-form, 14–15; M-form organization mechanisms, 15–18; and oversight in resurrected M-form, 258–67, 271; by owners (1918–1933), 44–58; owners achieve, 215–21; by owners after World War II, 177–83; owners' financial veto under 1946 reorganization, 201–7; problems, 224–5; redefinition

(1937), 109–15; by War Emergency Committee, 136. *See also* capital; investment

financial issues: decision-making at GM after 1937 reorganization, 109–15; factors weakening oversight (1948-1950), 233; GM's postwar capital shortage, 177; owners' postwar unwillingness to delegate, 176; wartime policy, 159

Financial Policy Committee (FPC): authority of, 198–200; borrowing decisions (1946), 204; control over pricing policy, 228–9; financial control mechanisms (1946), 206–7; financial veto power (1947-1949), 217–21; loss of control over operations (1948-1950), 234; renamed (1958), 263; role after 1946 reorganization, 225–6; scarcity of information after 1946 reorganization, 227; unintended consequences of, 200–1

firm: efficiency theory of, 17–23, 317; efficiency views of, 7–17; order in economic theory of the firm, 316; rational-choice theory in economic theory of, 315–16; transactions within, 11. *See also* governance, corporate

Fisher, Edward, 151
Fisher, Lawrence, 75, 78
Fisher, William, 78
FPC. *See* Financial Policy Committee (FPC)
Freeland, Robert F., 19n57

General Motors (GM): air-cooled engine program, 58–63; antitrust suit against (1948), 224–5, 232–3; aviation industry interests, 217–19; Curtice's expansion plan (1953-1954), 243–6; decline in performance (1956-1958), 253–4; under Durant, 45–8; expansion program (1950-1953), 224, 234–6; factors shaping organizational form, 39–40; financial crisis (1920), 46–8; financial performance (1921-1987), 324–39; financing expansion of Korean War period, 236–9; issue of new shares (1955), 245–6; military production before and during World War II, 127–8, 134; multidivisional structure, 34–5; Opel subsidiary, 219–21; plan for small car, 178–81; policy making during World War II, 129; post–Korean War expansion, 239–40; postwar expansion plans (World War II), 176–82; postwar planning, 156–8; post–World War I expansion program, 46–7; profits (1948–1950), 234; return to M-form (1958), 224; sit-down strike (1937), 99; success of, 2; trend toward administrative centralization, 81; water-cooled engine, 61–2

General Motors (GM) (postwar era): effect of success, 223–4; financial condition (1946), 201–2; organizational structure (1946), 195–201; postwar reconversion, 175–6; production (1946), 201–2

General Motors Acceptance Corporation (GMAC), 114–15, 161–2

General Motors Assembly Division (GMAD), 277, 280

Gerstenberg, Richard, 286, 289–90
GMAC, 114–15, 161–2
GMAD, 277, 280
Goad, Lewis, 264–5
Godfrey, Edward, 231
Gordon, John F., 264–5
Gottesman et al. v. General Motors (1967), 91

governance, corporate: consent in M-form, 23–33; debate related to GM's postwar structure, 163–73, 176–201; with division of labor, 19–21; by fiat, 24, 58, 64–7, 311; fiat and sanctions in, 21–4; M-form as structure for, 296; in modern corporation, 285–92; postwar structure, 177–83; Sloan's conception, 308; Sloan's recommendations for wartime,

144–5; as social and political process, 6; in transaction cost economics, 9–10; under WAC, 151. *See also* centralization, administrative; coercion; consent; decentralization, participative; fiat; Sloan committee
governance by fiat: failure of, 58; Sloan's reluctance to use, 64–7, 311
Grant, Richard, 94n32
Great Depression: centralization at GM during and after, 77–96; influence on GM innovation, 40–1

Hannum, George, 60
Hardy, A. B. C., 54
Haskell, J. A., 53
Hunt, Ormond, 94n32, 129, 219

inefficiency, sources of, 27–8
inflation: after World War I, 48; after World War II, 177, 228–9
information: divisional control of, 22–3; lacking after 1946 reorganization, 227; mechanism to transmit intrafirm, 13
information asymmetry: in M-form organization, 20–3; in 1937 M-form reorganization, 119–20
investment: GM's return on (1948–1955), 223, 234–5; GM's return on (1950s), 253; post-1950 returns on, 236–9, 253; return on (1948–1956), 246–7; return on (1964–1969), 278

Johnson, E. F., 55

Kettering, Charles, 59, 60
Knudsen, Semon, 282
Knudsen, William, 61, 75, 78, 85, 104–6, 109, 117, 128
Korean War: GM strategy during, 235; outbreak, 234–5
Kornai, János, 297n2
Kuhn, Arthur, 65–6

labor unions: postwar auto industry strikes, 175; sit-down strike (1937), 99; wartime policy toward, 158–9
legal issues: related to bonus plan, 161–2, 166; related to defense contracts, 160–1. *See also* antitrust issues
loss prevention, as task of headquarters, 12–13

Macneil, Ian, 26
management: Curtice's style of, 241; decentralization (1921–1933), 44–58; by divisions under M-form, 4; owners' constraints on, 295–6; Wilson's style, 215. *See also* divisions; executives, General Motors; New York office, General Motors
managerial-discretion hypothesis, 15nn41, 42
managers: division representation on WAC, 152–4, 159; postwar disagreements about corporate governance, 176
Means, Gardiner, 14–15
M-form organization: control mechanisms and problems, 19–22; corporate headquarters feature, 9–10; corruptions leading to inefficiency, 16; divisional spheres of expertise, 308; division of labor within, 9–10, 19–21; Du Pont owners at GM (post-1920), 52–63; effect of, 12; effect on GM (1958–1980), 271; at GM, 35, 41; internal controls of, 15; in managerial revolution, 1; operating divisions under, 4; original justification for, 295; owner–manager relationship, 21; ownership and control under, 15; owners' justification for, 295–6; perfected at GM, 44–5; reintroduction at GM, 6, 258–66; reorganization (1937), 100–8, 123; success at E. I. du Pont de Nemours, 302–3; success of, 2, 11
Miller, Gary J., 20n63
Mooney, James, 94n32, 129–31, 133, 135

Index

J. P. Morgan, ownership in GM, 5n17, 35

Nader, Ralph, 281nn42,43, 282
New York office, General Motors: control during Cole regime, 286; chief operating executive located in, 304; defense contract decisions, 131; Detroit's battle against, 223; finance staff, 112–13; financial control under 1946 reorganization, 223–4; legal staff, 183–4; wartime financial decisions, 159
North American Aviation (NAA), 217–18

oil price shocks: effect on car market (1973), 289–90; effect (1979), 291
OPC. *See* Operations Policy Committee (OPC)
Operations Committee: owners' changes in membership of, 74–5; revival and role of (1920s), 72–3
Operations Policy Committee (OPC): composition of, 199; Curtice's use of, 241–3; inactivity under Curtice, 255–6; as legal subcommittee of the board, 198–200; membership (1955), 242; renamed (1958), 263; Wilson appoints GM managers to (1948), 231
opportunism: of economic actors, 10; identifying and controlling, 10–11; problems of, 12
order: created by consent, 24; created by fiat and sanctions, 24, 320; with division of labor, 41; in economic theory of the firm, 316; efficiency theory, 17; explained by concept of legitimacy, 25–6; in M-form, 307–14; in organization theory, 315–23; realization of, 319; trade-offs between efficiency and, 27; viewed by TCE, 311–14
organization: factors shaping informal, 28; failure of U-form, 11–12; success of M-form, 11; TCE view of, 11
owner control: decline, 233; during defense production years, 128–34; M-form to ensure, 295–6; in modern corporation, 295–300; post-1920 centralization of, 52–63; postwar financial control, 177–83; variation in organizational form, 37–9
owners: attempts to limit GM's postwar expansion, 177–83; authority and power of, 35; beliefs about financial issues, 109–15; concerns related to Curtice, 241, 248–50; confidence and trust in Sloan, 299; disagreement about postwar organization, 163–5; efforts to influence Detroit (1948), 230; efforts to thwart Sloan's decentralization strategy, 68–79; insistence on M-form, 35–9; left out of information loop (1948), 231–2; limits on GM top management, 295–6; opposition to participative decentralization, 38–9; opposition to proposed wartime administrative changes, 145–9; postwar disagreements about corporate governance, 176; response to potential legal issues, 160–3; role after 1937 reorganization, 100–15; version of M-form at GM, 44–58; view of decentralization, 36, 38
owners (postwar): criticism of GM's plan to incur debt, 204–5; influence over GM's financial affairs, 195–201; opposition to Sloan's reorganization plans, 185–8, 191; opposition to small-car project, 178, 180–2; representation on Financial Policy Committee, 198
ownership: J. P. Morgan, 5n17; in M-form organization, 15; in modern corporation, 305–6
ownership control: after GM 1937 reorganization, 109; centralization to loosen, 96–7

performance, consummate: in organizational behavior, 25;

requirements for, 41; Sloan's belief in divisional participation for, 69–79; sources of, 27–8
Perrow, Charles, 19n57
persuasion, in Sloan's transformation of authority, 65
planning: effect of divisions' resistance on, 283–5; factors in transformation of strategic (1934), 90–1; postwar (1943), 157–8; under 1958 reorganization, 271–2
Policy Committee: formation, composition, and function (1937), 82, 100–2, 104–8, 115–25; role during defense production years, 128–42
Policy Committee (postwar era): corporate control, 165; small-car program, 181–2, 201. See also Financial Policy Committee (FPC); Operations Policy Committee (OPC)
policy groups: composition and function of, 93–5, 117–18, 154–5; as governance mechanism, 96–100; policy formulation role, 92–6; Price Procedure Policy Group, 94–5; under wartime production, 154
policy process: policy and product groups during wartime, 154; Sloan's distinction between formulation and approval, 92–6. See also policy groups; pricing policy; pricing pyramid; production; product policy; small-car program
Pratt, John, 54–5, 88
pricing policy: postwar problems, 229; related to standard volume concept, 228–9; shift of responsibility from FPC to OPC, 230
pricing pyramid: under Curtice, 273–4; under Donner, 274–5; modification under renewed M-form, 280; plan, 59–60, 84, 88; price classes of car divisions (1920s), 59–60, 84; revision (1932), 73

production: controls during prewar period, 136; government wartime regulation, 136; product groups under wartime production, 154; wartime statistical and financial controls, 136; wartime use of government-owned facilities, 139–40
product policy: centralization with (1934), 90, 94; divisional competition introduced (1933–1934), 85–8, 91; effect in post-depression market, 97; owner and financial executive opposition to, 88–91
property rights: exercise of, 301–2; of GM owners, 301

Raskob, John, 53, 55, 58, 73–4
rationality: bounded, 10–11; in organization theory, 315–23
recession, U.S.: Great Depression, 40–1, 77–96; and inflation (1920), 47–8
regulation: mandatory side-door crash beams, 288; of wartime production, 136; wartime restrictions on GM's profit margin, 138. See also antitrust issues; legal issues
Reuter, Irving, 78
Roche, James, 285–8
Russell, George, 285

sanctions: in M-form, 21–4; related to air-cooled car debate, 60–3; reliance on, 309
selling concept, in transformation of corporate authority, 64–8
shareholders: Du Pont and J. P. Morgan, 4–5; factors weakening control, 297–9; role under resurrected M-form organization, 271; Sloan as, 5n17
Sloan, Alfred P., Jr., 38, 44–5; on Administration Committee (1945), 5; as chairman and CEO, 225; as chairman of WAC, 151; on divisional participation during wartime, 143–4, 149–50; efforts to loosen ownership control,

96–108; history of GM, 265–6; intervention in corporate affairs (mid–late 1950s), 253; new decentralization plan (1923), 64; opposition to air-cooled engine, 59–63; on performance of Allison engines, 160; plan for M-form reorganization (1937), 100–8; position on postwar diesel locomotive market, 158; pricing pyramid plan, 59–60, 84–5, 88; reluctance to use fiat, 311; retires as chairman of the board (1956), 254; role at GM during World War II, 129–30; role in postwar organizational decisions, 163–8; role in wartime decision-making, 154–6; strategic planning changes, 90–6; transformation of GM's corporate authority, 64–8; view of decentralization, 48–53; on WAC, 151–2

Sloan, Alfred P., Jr. (postwar role): commitment to participative decentralization, 187–95; position on participative decentralization, 176; on prices of GM cars, 229; after 1946 reorganization, 226; reorganization plans, 183–6; on small-car project, 178–9

Sloan committee: appointment (1957), 254–5; findings, 255–7; personnel decisions (1958), 264; recommendations, 257–8, 263; resurrection of M-form, 258–67

small-car program: Chevrolet Cadet, 178–81, 208; Chevrolet Chevette subcompact, 290; Chevrolet Corvair, 281–3; Chevrolet XP-887 subcompact (the Vega), 286–9; front-engine compacts, 282–3; front-wheel-drive compacts (X-cars), 290–2; J-cars, 292; recommended subcompact, 283

Smith, John Thomas, 160–2, 193–4, 216

specialization: creates normative expectations, 29; effect on expertise and authority, 28–30; expectations related to, 308; interdependence created by, 307–8; as source of information asymmetry, 20

standardization: effect of, 278–9; GMAD program, 281–4; of parts and components (1959), 277–80

transaction cost economics (TCE): assumptions of, 10; conception of order under, 311–14; control mechanisms, 20–1; corruptions of M-form, 16; efficiency view of corporation's organization, 9–10; explanation of participative decentralization, 312–13; in theories of the firm, 311–12; understanding limits of hierarchy, 317

transactions: between independent firms, 11; inside the firm, 26

Turner, Frank, 55

turnover: real estate and plant, GM and Chrysler (1934–1941), 123–5; real estate and plant (1942–1945; 1950–1953), 237–8; real estate and plant (1948–1956), 246–7; total net, GM and Chrysler (1934–1941), 123–5; total net (1942–1945; 1950–1953), 237–8; total net (1948–1956), 246–7; working capital, GM and Chrysler (1934–1941), 123–5; working capital (1942–1945; 1950–1953), 237–9; working capital (1948–1956), 246–7

United States of America v. General Motors Corporation (1940), 161–2

U.S. v. Du Pont, 98n41

value creation: decisions related to, 13; as task of headquarters, 12–13

vehicle assembly: Buick-Olds-Pontiac Assembly Division, 277–8; General Motors Assembly Division (GMAD), 277–8

Ver Linden, Edward, 54

veto power: of large GM shareholders, 35; owners' financial veto, 201–7, 217–21

Index

Wagner Act (National Labor Relations Board Act), 100
War Administration Committee (WAC): composition and fiat of, 146–7, 150–1, 170; policy decisions, 152; renaming (1944), 165; role in postwar planning, 157–8
War Emergency Committee (WEC): composition, function, and powers of, 135–6; disbanded (1942), 150; incentives to improve turnover, 141–2; Load Distribution Plan, 136–7, 142; strategy for maximizing returns, 137–41
Warner, Fred, 54
Weber, Max, 25, 28–9
WEC. *See* War Emergency Committee (WEC)

Whitney, George, 107, 217, 227
Wilson, Charles E., 94n32, 109, 128–30, 133–4, 169; FPC issuing orders to (1948–1958), 225; management style, 215
Wilson, Charles E. (postwar role): announces small-car project, 180; Brown's criticisms of, 213–15; conflict with Donaldson Brown, 183–5; as president and CEO, 176, 178, 225; after 1946 reorganization, 226; on scale-back decision (1946), 206
Winkelman et al. v. General Motors Corporation (1942), 161

Zimmerschied, Karl, 60
zone of indifference, 29